AREA HANDBOOK
for
TRINIDAD AND TOBAGO

Coauthors

Jan Knippers Black

Howard I. Blutstein
Kathryn Therese Johnston
David S. McMorris

Research completed August 1975

First Edition

Published 1976

DA Pam 550–178

Black, Jan Knippers, 1940-

Area handbook for Trinidad and Tobago.

"DA Pam 550-178."

"One of a series of handbooks prepared by Foreign Area Studies (FAS) of the American University."

Bibliography: pp. 261-289.
Includes index.
1. Trinidad and Tobago.   I. American University, Washington, D.C. Foreign Area Studies.   II. Title.

F2119.B55   972.9'8304   76–8513

First edition, first printing—April 1976

For sale by the Superintendent of Documents, U.S. Government Printing Office
Washington, D.C. 20402 - Price $5.70

FOREWORD

This volume is one of a series of handbooks prepared by Foreign Area Studies (FAS) of The American University, designed to be useful to military and other personnel who need a convenient compilation of basic facts about the social, economic, political, and military institutions and practices of various countries. The emphasis is on objective description of the nation's present society and the kinds of possible or probable changes that might be expected in the future. The handbook seeks to present as full and as balanced an integrated exposition as limitations on space and research time permit. It was compiled from information available in openly published material. An extensive bibliography is provided to permit recourse to other published sources for more detailed information. There has been no attempt to express any specific point of view or to make policy recommendations. The contents of the handbook represent the work of the authors and FAS and do not represent the official view of the United States government.

An effort has been made to make the handbook as comprehensive as possible. It can be expected, however, that the material, interpretations, and conclusions are subject to modification in the light of new information and developments. Such corrections, additions, and suggestions for factual, interpretive, or other change as readers may have will be welcomed for use in future revisions. Comments may be addressed to:

The Director
Foreign Area Studies
The American University
5010 Wisconsin Avenue, N.W.
Washington, D.C. 20016

PREFACE

Trinidad and Tobago, having achieved independence in 1962, was in the mid-1970s confronting demands for constitutional reform, for a more equitable distribution of goods and services, and for increased national control of resources. Governmental regulation of the economy was extensive, but the petroleum industry, the source of most exports and government revenues, was dominated by companies based in the United States. Per capita income was relatively high, but unemployment was a severe problem, and the ethnic diversity that had given rise to a rich national culture posed obstacles to political consensus.

In late 1975 and early 1976 after the chapter drafts for this book had been completed, some realignment took place among those groups opposing Prime Minister Eric Williams and the dominant party, the People's National Movement. The Democratic Labour Party had split, and its majority faction had been joined by four minor parties to form the United Democratic Labour Party. Representatives of this party had replaced those of the Tapia House Group in parliament. The Democratic Action Congress continued to oppose the government, and the new United Labour Front, bringing together black oil industry workers and East Indian canecutters, was viewed as a potential contender for power.

This book attempts to provide a compact and objective exposition and analysis of the dominant social, political, and economic characteristics of Trinidadian society. The study is based chiefly on published materials, although consultants with firsthand knowledge of the country have provided data not available in print. Differences among scholars on historical and contemporary matters are noted where appropriate.

This study results from the combined efforts of a Foreign Area Studies multidisciplinary team of researchers assisted by the organizational research support staff. Irving Kaplan provided editorial and research assistance in the early stages of the book's preparation. The team was chaired by Jan Knippers Black, who wrote chapter 1 and contributed to chapters 3 and 6. David S. McMorris wrote chapters 2 and 5 and contributed to chapter 6. Kathryn Therese Johnston wrote chapter 4 and contributed to chapter 6. Surjit Mansingh wrote chapter 3, Howard I. Blutstein wrote chapter 8, Paul Bodenman wrote chapter 9, and Basil Buchanan wrote chapter 7. FAS desires to acknowledge the assistance of David Johnson, who provided valuable anthropological data.

English spelling follows *Webster's Seventh New Collegiate Dictionary*. Unless otherwise stated, production and commodity figures are given in metric tons. A glossary of Trinidadian and other terms is provided for the convenience of the reader.

COUNTRY SUMMARY

1. COUNTRY: Trinidad and Tobago, independent in 1962.

2. SIZE, TOPOGRAPHY, AND CLIMATE: Located close to Venezuela on South American continental shelf, two-island state of Trinidad and Tobago has area of about 2,000 square miles, including numerous satellite islets. Trinidad (1,865 square miles) consists of rolling plains and flatlands, broken by the Northern Range covering northern portion with maximum elevations exceeding 3,000 feet; lower range extends laterally across center of island, and third range extends along southern coast. Tobago (116 square miles), twenty miles to northeast of Trinidad, has generally rugged terrain with elevations up to 1,800 feet; only extensive lowland is coral platform at southwestern end. Many rivers and streams on both islands, but none large or navigable. Tropical heat modified by maritime influences and trade winds. Moderate to heavy rainfall varies regionally and yearly. Heaviest on portions of Northern Range exposed to rain-bearing northeast trade winds. Well-defined wet and dry seasons in most of country, and seasonal droughts common in parts of Trinidad lying in rain shadow of Northern Range.

3. POPULATION: In mid-1970s a little more than 1 million. Low and declining mortality rate. Previously high birthrate declined sharply in 1960s in response to active family planning program. Population growth rate during 1960s among lowest in Americas, in part as consequence of massive emigration to North America, but emigration slackened in early 1970s and further slackening expected. Young population in which less than half over age of twenty and less than 4 percent over age sixty-five. Heavy and sustained urban migration during years since World War II; in mid-1970s over half of population urban, concentrated in or near Port-of-Spain and San Fernando in western Trinidad lowlands. Rural settlement pattern one of small towns and farm villages rather than isolated farms.

4. SOCIAL CATEGORIES AND LANGUAGE: According to the 1970 census, Negroes constituted almost 43 percent of the total population, whites about 2 percent and persons of what was termed mixed origin about 14 percent, these groups together forming the so-called Creole segment of the society. The non-Creole segment was made up principally of East Indians, who constituted 40 percent of the total population; the remaining 2 percent included Chinese, Portuguese, Middle Easterners, and others. All speak variations of English, which range from the close approximation to British English spoken by the upper and middle classes

to a Creole language, Trinidad English. Some Trinidadians speak Spanish or French Creole, and these two languages have also affected Trinidad English. Some Indic languages, including a conglomerate called Hindustani, are also spoken, although these are on the wane.

5. RELIGION: Majority are Christians or members of Afro-Christian sects. Lower class Creoles frequently profess membership in both formal denominations and sects such as Shouter or Shango. Majority of Christians are Roman Catholic (about 34 percent of the total) or Anglican (about 18 percent). Non-Christians are Hindus (about 25 percent of the total) and Muslims (about 6 percent). Although most Creoles are Christians and most non-Creoles are non-Christians, some East Indians and practically all the Chinese, Middle Easterners, and Portuguese are Christian.

6. EDUCATION: During early 1970s some 30 percent of population enrolled in schools. More than 80 percent of student body in primary schools and additional 16 percent in general secondary units. Male and female enrollments approximately equal. Higher education available only at Trinidadian campus of University of the West Indies (other campuses in Jamaica and Barbados), a multinational university maintained by Commonwealth Caribbean members. Vocational and technical education program limited and schools poorly equipped. Educational reform initiated in late 1960s, however, aims at expanding and improving vocational and technical schooling and introducing new kind of lower secondary school to give three years' additional schooling to many students. Growing recognition that traditional emphasis on academic secondary schools aimed at university matriculation not responsive to country's acute need for skilled manpower.

7. HEALTH: Generally good conditions of health and sanitation reflected in low and declining incidence of disease and rate of infant mortality. Per capita calorie and protein content of diet meets or almost meets minimum nutrition standards, but diets of low-income families high in starches, low in garden vegetables, deficient in animal protein. Principal causes of mortality: circulatory diseases, respiratory diseases, cancer. General success in campaigns against malaria, yellow fever, and other endemic diseases. Nurses trained in country, but no medical or dental school. Shortage of doctors and dentists results from this and from heavy emigration of medical personnel of all kinds. Shortage in part offset by well-distributed system of public hospitals and health centers for outpatient care.

8. GOVERNMENT AND POLITICS: Formally a constitutional monarchy, queen represented by governor general. Parliamentary government: prime minister and cabinet chosen from majority party in Parliament and responsible to it, but executive is strongest element. A two-party system (occasional third parties and opposition groups small and ephemeral) since well before full independence: the People's National

Movement (PNM) and the Democratic Labour Party (DLP). The PNM has always predominated.

9. ADMINISTRATIVE DIVISIONS: The island of Trinidad is divided into eight counties, which in turn are subdivided into twenty-nine wards. The island of Tobago constitutes the country's thirtieth ward; it is subdivided into nine parishes.

10. JUSTICE: Based on English common law and practice. Consists of Supreme Court of Judicature, High Court, and Court of Appeal. Inferior courts include courts of summary jurisdiction and petty civil courts. Decisions of the Court of Appeal in cases of great importance may be appealed to the judicial committee of the Privy Council in the United Kingdom.

11. INTERNATIONAL MEMBERSHIPS AND ECONOMIC AGREEMENTS: The United Nations and affiliated organizations, the Commonwealth of Nations, the more informal group referred to as the Commonwealth Caribbean, the Organization of American States, the Caribbean Community (CARICOM) and its component organizations including the Caribbean Common Market and the Caribbean Development Bank, the International Bank for Reconstruction and Development, and the Inter-American Development Bank.

12. ROADS, RAILROADS, AND INLAND WATERWAYS: No railroads except sugar plantation short lines. About 4,500 miles of roads, 2,500 paved. No navigable internal waterways.

13. CIVIL AVIATION: Two airports—one on each island. Government airline, British West Indies Airways, provides international service.

14. PORTS: Nine seaports; eight on Trinidad and one on Tobago. Port-of-Spain is principal seaport.

15. COMMUNICATIONS: Domestic telephone and telex service (telegraph exchange service—for subscribers) provided by the government-owned Trinidad and Tobago Telephone Company (TELCO). International services, including maritime communications, and domestic telegraph service provided by Trinidad and Tobago External Telecommunications Company (TEXTEL), owned jointly by the government and Cable and Wireless. Direct dialing to anywhere in the country possible on most of the 66,000 telephones in operation in 1974.

16. ECONOMY: Petroleum production and refining and natural gas production lead the economy, although largest percentage of work force is in agriculture. Sugar, cocoa, coffee, and citrus are leading agricultural products. Moderate degree of industrialization.

17. FINANCE AND CURRENCY: The Trinidad and Tobago dollar (TT$) is the unit of currency and is pegged to the British pound. A wide range of financial institutions, some government owned, provide sufficient credit to the economy.

18. FOREIGN TRADE AND AID: Petroleum and its products are the

leading export category accounting for 80 to 83 percent of total exports. Imports are more varied—crude petroleum, agricultural products, machinery, iron and steel, paper products. Country both receives and gives foreign aid. International institutions are leading source of assistance.

19. ARMED FORCES AND POLICE: Security forces consist of the Defense Force and Police Service. The Defense Force is composed of an army battalion, called the Regiment, having an authorized strength of 750 and the coast guard having an authorized strength of 350. The police having a strength of about 3,800 has primary responsibility for internal security.

TRINIDAD AND TOBAGO

TABLE OF CONTENTS

LIST OF ILLUSTRATIONS

LIST OF TABLES

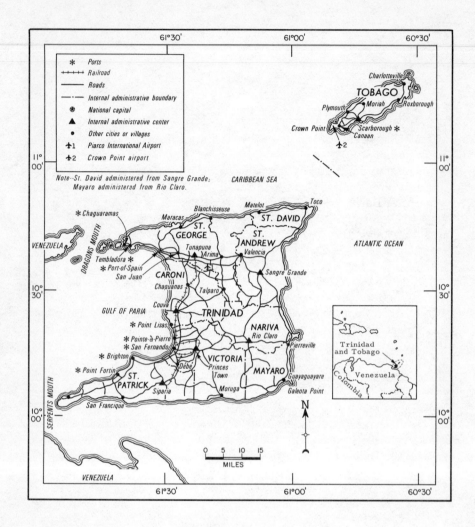

Figure 1. Trinidad and Tobago

CHAPTER 1

GENERAL CHARACTER OF THE SOCIETY

Trinidad and Tobago, an independent state within the Commonwealth of Nations since 1962, comprises two major islands and several satellite islets situated northeast of Venezuela on the continental shelf of South America. With a population of a little more than 1 million in the mid-1970s it was, after Barbados, the most densely populated of the countries in the Western Hemisphere. Urban migration had accelerated in the 1960s, and more than half of the population had become concentrated in and around two cities: Port-of-Spain, the capital, and San Fernando. Both cities are on the Gulf of Paria on Trinidad, the larger island.

Sighted by Columbus on his third voyage to the New World in 1498, Trinidad experienced three centuries of Spanish rule before becoming a British crown colony in 1797. Tobago, of greater strategic importance as a naval port, had a more turbulent history; it passed through the hands of Great Britain, France, Holland, and Courland (a former principality of Latvia) in the seventeenth century and served as a base for pirates from the beginning of the eighteenth century until the British again took possession in 1762. Tobago was recaptured twice thereafter by the French, but it remained under British control after 1803, and in 1889 it was administratively linked to Trinidad. From crown colony status Trinidad and Tobago moved to membership in the short-lived Federation of the West Indies (1958–62) before becoming an independent state.

As Trinidad offered no apparent mineral wealth and the enslavement of the indigenous people led only to a rapid decline in their numbers, the island was neglected and relatively undeveloped throughout most of the period of Spanish rule. Some Africans had been imported as slaves to work the failing tobacco and cacao plantations early in the eighteenth century, but it was the immigration of French planters and their slaves from other Caribbean islands and the transplantation of their sugarcane cultivation that brought prosperity in the two decades before the British took control in 1797.

The emancipation of the slaves in 1834 and the consequent shortage of labor for the plantations led to the introduction of the islands' third major ethnic group—indentured laborers imported from India between 1845 and 1917. Additional settlers from Europe, China, the Middle East, and other Caribbean islands contributed to the cultural complexity of the population over which the British attempted to impose their language, laws, and customs.

1

Each element of the social mosaic has left its imprint on the country's culture; but while the Europeans and later the East Indians sought to preserve their transplanted cultures intact, the Negro slaves and their freed descendants assimilated, synthesized, and created, thereby providing both the aesthetic form and the collective sense of history that gave rise to a distinct national culture. It was also this long-repressed majority that became the motive force in the drive for responsible self-government. Its leaders, drawn from the literary elite as well as from the incipient labor movement in the 1930s and 1940s, pushed first to influence those in power, then to share that power, and ultimately to wield it alone.

The economic system of the two islands has never been a free enterprise one, except in a limited sense. The Spanish colonial rulers, and later the British, assumed responsibility for matters of capital, manpower, and trading relationships, and the colonial powers were at least the ultimate arbiters in matters of production and distribution. Since 1962 the national government has attempted to bring about a structural transformation in order to make the economy responsive to the much broader interests and the quite different demands of an independent state.

The economy of Trinidad and Tobago has been subject to a greater degree of government control than has that of any other Caribbean country except Cuba. The Ministry of Planning and Development, established in 1968, sets overall development policy and general goals. In the mid-1960s the government directly owned about thirty companies and was the major investor in the sugar industry. The petroleum industry, however, which was the source of most exports and government revenues, was dominated by companies in the United States.

Impressive annual gains in gross domestic product (GDP) in the first half of the 1970s had not appreciably mitigated the atmosphere of economic malaise. Inflation, fueled mainly by increased prices of imported goods, had climbed to 25 percent in 1974, and the expansion of the capital-intensive oil industry created few new jobs. The services sector, including civil servants, was the largest and fastest growing sector of the economy, but unemployment, estimated at 14 percent, remained a severe problem.

Employment problems had been exacerbated by the inadequacy of vocational and technical training programs. The country's literacy rate and level of primary school enrollment were among the world's highest, and enrollment at higher levels compared favorably with other Latin American and Caribbean countries; but the availability of professional services was low because the professionally trained and highly skilled had emigrated in large numbers in the late 1960s and early 1970s.

A persistent housing shortage had also posed problems for the increasingly urban population. The clustered settlement pattern, however, had its advantages. Most of the population had easy access to medical facilities, and the rate of incidence of most diseases had been decreasing. There was broad and increasing participation in the market economy. Despite heavy reliance on starches, the average diet was adequate or nearly adequate in numbers of calories and proteins.

The numerical gap between the two major ethnic groups has narrowed within the last decade. The 1970 census indicated that 42.8 percent of the population was Negro, 40.1 percent East Indian, and 14.2 percent mixed—Chinese and Caucasian were the largest of the remaining groups. Some have charged that the figures published by the government are inaccurate and that the East Indian population now outnumbers that of the Negro.

The country's social structure still bears many of the markings of colonial society, including the economic dominance of the white minority, but class conflict has been attenuated by the crosscutting cleavage between the Negro and East Indian subcultures. The per capita income of whites has been several times that of Negroes, and Negro per capita income in turn has been considerably higher than that of the East Indians.

When the cacao export market collapsed in the 1920s, the displaced members of the labor force, mostly Negroes, were able to turn to three sectors of the economy that were experiencing rapid growth: the oil industry, manufacturing, and the service industries. Although East Indians have been well represented among the professions and at the lower end of the commercial sector and have moved into industrial and clerical occupations in substantial numbers since the 1960s, the majority have remained in the agricultural labor market, where they dominate the sugar industry.

Just beneath the wealthiest of the predominantly white business elite in the socioeconomic pyramid is the newly emergent Negro political elite, a relatively insecure group since their status and income derive from office holding. Next is an expanding stratum of local managerial and technocratic personnel, also largely Negro. Merchants and manufacturers—generally Caucasian, Chinese, Middle Eastern, or East Indian—are engaged for the most part in small-scale operations. The organized working classes, Negro and East Indian, have experienced at least a generation of industrial disputes and fare rather well. The least affluent and least powerful members of the society are generally the peasants and the unorganized or unemployed members of the urban work force.

The degree of assimilation that has been achieved between the Negro and East Indian ethnic blocs might enable one to view the whole as a society. That is, there is considerable interaction, interdependence, and tolerance. Tolerance, however, does not imply approval. Each bloc tends to look upon the other with negative indifference, and a sense of community is achieved only within an ambience of ethnic homogeneity.

Trinidadian nationalists of African or mixed African-European descent deplore the alienation of a large proportion of the East Indian population

3

from the majority culture. Many East Indians, however, look askance upon what they consider an invitation to absorption. East Indian spokesmen charge that their people have been victims of discrimination in the civil service and other areas of economic and political life, and the older members of the community have tended to regard Negro values as sensualistic and depraved. Among the younger Trinidadians, however, the recent upsurge of racial and ethnic pride appears to be accompanied by an accelerated breakdown of cultural exclusiveness.

The country's ethnic pluralism, so enriching for its culture, has been troublesome for its politics. Competition and mutual suspicion between Negro and East Indian political movements have made it possible for foreign-oriented elites to play off one group against the other, thereby preventing the emergence of political parties based on common socioeconomic interests.

Although ethnic considerations were significant in the elections that took place between the introduction of universal adult suffrage in 1946 and independence in 1962, the lack of real local power available for redistribution and the common goal of liberation from foreign dominance mitigated ethnic competition. Since independence, however, ethnic cleavage along political lines has deepened. The Negro middle-class leadership of the People's National Movement (PNM), while asserting that the party has achieved a nationalist synthesis, has seen its own position threatened by the demands of the East Indians for a larger share of the fruits of self-government. And many among the upper and middle classes who had earlier been shaken by the radical rhetoric of the PNM had come to see it as a shield against still more radical power contenders.

Meanwhile, the inferior power position of the East Indians has been reinforced by the Hindu-Muslim cleavage within the larger ethnic bloc. The opposition Democratic Labour Party, under Hindu leadership, has drawn most of its following from the sugar belt, while many Muslims of the urban commercial class have gravitated toward the PNM.

The principal objective and major achievement of the founding generation of the PNM was political reform—namely, responsible self-government and national independence. Political reform remained an issue in the mid-1970s, as the Parliament considered proposals for far-reaching constitutional revision. The issues, however, that had given shape to the most serious political confrontations over the past decade had been social and economic reform.

In the late 1960s, under the banner of "black power," a movement actually aimed at increasing the power of the dispossessed of all races was launched. Initiated largely by students and intellectuals advocating economic emancipation and greater national control of resources, the movement spread to the Hindu workers in the sugar belt, aroused the urban lower classes, and climaxed in the so-called disturbance of 1970, in which marches of tens of thousands and a mutiny within the army were put down by troops and police loyal to the government of Prime Minister

4

Eric Williams. Since that time the government has adopted numerous measures, which opposition groups have denounced as unconstitutional, to preclude a resurgence of the movement. Of the new groups that had adhered to the movement only the Tapia House Group and the Democratic Action Congress appeared to be serving as significant focuses of opposition in mid 1975.

Until independence responsibility for the conduct of external relations resided in the British Colonial Office, such relations were largely bilateral and limited to economic and strategic arrangements with the most highly industrialized Western states. Since 1962 the new state has become a member of more than thirty regional, Commonwealth, and global organizations, including the United Nations, the Organization of American States, and the Caribbean Common Market. Through such organizations the country has expressed opposition to racism and colonialism and has sought to promote regional economic integration. It has established relations with several communist-ruled states and has increasingly aligned itself with the third world. It has also expanded bilateral economic ties in order to diversify its trade relationships and sources of investment.

CHAPTER 2

GEOGRAPHY AND POPULATION

The two islands that make up the state of Trinidad and Tobago are situated on the continental shelf of South America and are geographically but not geologically part of the West Indies. Trinidad, much the larger of the two, is at some points within sight of the Venezuelan coast and was once a part of the mainland. Tobago, a few miles northeast of Trinidad, is part of a sunken mountain chain related to the continent. The larger island has one moderately high and two low mountain chains but consists for the most part of flatlands and rolling plains; the smaller island is generally mountainous.

Because it was once a part of South America Trinidad has an assortment of tropical vegetation and wildlife considerably more varied than that of most West Indian islands. Tobago has a generally similar but somewhat less varied assortment. Both islands lie deep in the tropics but are cooled by the marine environment and by the prevailing northeast trade winds. Rainfall is moderate to heavy but subject to considerable regional and year-to-year variations. Tobago has no known exploitable minerals other than building materials, but Trinidad is rich in petroleum and natural gas.

The population of a little over 1 million, made up principally of Negroes and East Indians, is heavily concentrated in and around two major cities on the Gulf of Paria in the western portion of Trinidad. Elsewhere in Trinidad and on Tobago the prevailing settlement pattern is one of small towns and villages. Under the influence of a high birthrate and a sharply declining death rate the population increased rapidly during the years immediately after World War II. In the early 1960s, however, the rate of birth commenced to decline in response to an increasingly effective family planning program; at the same time a heavy outflow of emigrants commenced. During the late 1960s and early 1970s, as a consequence, the rate of population growth was among the lowest in the Americas.

Urban migration was in progress during the 1960s and early 1970s and, with it, agricultural employment was declining. In the mid-1970s agriculture was by far the smallest of the major employment sectors, and much of it was on sugar plantations. Industrial employment was substantial, particularly in the construction industry. The oil fields and refineries, vital to the economy, were capital-intensive operations that provided only a limited number of jobs. The pay and other conditions of employment in the petroleum industry, however, exerted powerful

7

upward pressure on employment conditions elsewhere in the economy. The services sector, the largest and fastest growing, gave employment to most of the country's increasingly large group of civil servants.

The two most serious labor problems to beset the country during the mid-1970s were a critical shortage of skills and an extremely high level of unemployment. The school system had yet to produce the skills needed by the developing economy, and many of the professionally trained and skilled young people had been among the emigrants of the late 1960s and early 1970s. High unemployment had become chronic and showed little sign of abating. It was highest among women and, in particular, among younger workers. The unemployment of young adults had become a socially accepted phenomenon, although during the mid-1970s the government was engaged in various undertakings to combat it.

POLITICAL SUBDIVISIONS

The island of Trinidad is divided into eight counties, which in turn are subdivided into twenty-nine wards. The country's thirtieth ward is the island of Tobago, an independent political entity not attached to any of the counties; it is subdivided into nine parishes. The sparsely populated counties of Mayaro and Nariva are administered as a single unit, as are the more heavily populated counties of St. David and St. Andrew (see fig. 1).

The three incorporated urban centers—Port-of-Spain, San Fernando, and Arima—are not parts of the counties. They maintain their own governments and are considered coequal political subdivisions. In statistical issuances, however, they sometimes are included as parts of the counties in which they are physically located.

The counties vary in size from St. George in the northwest, with an area of 354 square miles and six wards, to St. David in the northeast—an area of 79 square miles and one ward. In 1970 St. George contained 34 percent of the country's population, and St. David contained 0.7 percent. Watersheds of the Northern Range and portions of the Caroni, Ortoire, and a few other rivers serve as natural county borders. Borders consisting of straight surveyed lines predominate, however, and counties do not to any significant extent correspond to geographic regions or concentrations of population by ethnic grouping.

NATURAL FEATURES

Physical Geography

Trinidad and Tobago is composed of two major islands and numerous satellite islets located close to South America on the continental shelf. The islands are not geologically part of the Antillean arc, and some writers group Trinidad and Tobago with Curaçao and the other Dutch islands, the offshore islands of Venezuela, and Barbados as the Continental Island group of the West Indies.

8

Trinidad, second largest of the Commonwealth Caribbean (see Glossary) islands, is roughly rectangular in shape with lateral peninsular extensions at the northeast, northwest, and southwest corners. One imaginative observer described it as resembling the boot of a conquistador. It has an area of 1,865 square miles, an east to west extension varying from about thirty-five to sixty miles, and a north to south extension averaging about sixty miles. The road network is fairly extensive, and on small and compact Trinidad no part of the island is more than a few hours away from any other part. Piarco International Airport, serving coastal Port-of-Spain, is the only major aircraft landing facility on the island currently in regular use; it lies almost one-third of the distance from west to east across the island. Smaller Tobago lies to the northeast of Trinidad and is separated from its sister island by a channel about twenty miles in width. It is cigar shaped and has an area of 116 square miles. Its dimensions average about twenty-five by seven miles.

Trinidad is geologically a detached part of the South American continent, separated from it by the Gulf of Paria, an oval-shaped body of water with narrow straits on the north and south bearing respectively the picturesque names of the Dragons Mouth and the Serpents Mouth. The names were reputedly bestowed by Columbus, and an ancient British whimsy is recalled by the fact that they are bordered by Trinidadian counties named for Saint George who slew the dragon and for Saint Patrick who drove the snakes out of Ireland.

Place names reflect the diversity of the country's ethnic background. Scarborough is English in origin, Fyzabad is East Indian, Rio Claro is Spanish, Grande Rivière is French, Arima is Carib, and Rampanalgas is pre-Carib. The Courland River on Tobago recalls the day when the dukes of Courland, a former principality of Latvia, held suzerainty over that island.

On the island of Trinidad the principal mountain system is the Northern Range, a rugged chain that covers the entire northern portion of the island and includes the highest point in the country, the Cerro del Aripo, with an elevation of 3,085 feet. The Northern Range is geologically an outlier of the Venezuelan portions of the great Andes Mountains. Extending on a slant from northeast to southwest across the middle of the island, the Central Range has average elevations of from 200 to 500 feet and a maximum elevation of 1,009 feet. Along the southern coast the low and discontinuous Southern Range reaches a maximum elevation of a little less than 1,000 feet in the Trinity Hills of the southeast. It was a trinity of adjacent hilltops in the area that allegedly caused Columbus on his third voyage to give the island its name (see fig. 2).

The mountains rise steeply in cliffs on the coastal flank of the Northern Range, but on the southern flank they are deeply indented by river valleys as they slope gently to the broad Caroni Plain, the most extensive of the country's lowlands. The Central Range marks the southern limit of the Caroni Plain, and to the south of the Central Range the Naparima

9

Plain on the west and the Nariva Plain on the east are the island's other major lowland areas. Throughout the lowlands the terrain ranges from flat to gently undulating. Because the bulk of the island's population is concentrated in a western lowland belt extending north to south along the Gulf of Paria and the eastern half of the island is sparsely peopled, it is customary to refer to north and south Trinidad but seldom to east or west.

Rivers on the island of Trinidad are numerous but short. The longest are the Ortoire, which extends thirty-one miles eastward to the Atlantic Ocean in the south, and the twenty-five-mile Caroni, which runs westward to the Gulf of Paria in the north. Neither is useful for navigation. Although countless rivers and streams provide generally good drainage, heavy seasonal rains often cause flooding.

There are no natural lakes, but extensive swamps occur along the eastern, southern, and western coasts. Some are mangrove swamps separated from the sea by wide sandbars. The most extensive of the swamplands are the Caroni Swamp and the Oropuche Lagoon on the Gulf of Paria and the Nariva Swamp on the Atlantic coast to the east. The waters of most rivers and streams drain ultimately through these swamplands.

The generally fertile soils of the northern and central portions of Trinidad are made up of sedimentary rock often re-sorted as alluvium with a considerable mixture of tropical clays. In the south the soils are sandy, unstable, and considerably less fertile than elsewhere. The island includes numerous small mud volcanoes, gas vents, and natural pitch lakes. Earth tremors are common, and the branch of the University of the West Indies at St. Augustine maintains an important seismic laboratory.

Trinidad has relatively few good harbors. On the north coast the shoreline is heavily indented, but the bays are rockbound, and there is no coastal plain between tidewater and the steep mountain cliffs. On the south the water is shallow, and the bays are too narrow for shipping. The east coast is almost unapproachable by sea because of treacherous Atlantic Ocean currents. On the west, however, the land slopes gently from the Gulf of Paria to an interior of fertile hills and plains. Natural harbors are good, although international traffic exclusive of petroleum has become almost entirely concentrated in the harbor of Port-of-Spain. Chacachacare and Monos islands and most of the remainder of the numerous small islands close to the Trinidad shoreline are located in or near the Dragons Mouth. The country claims a territorial limit of twelve nautical miles except in the Gulf of Paria, where seabed limits have been determined by agreement with Venezuela, but surface and fishing limits are not clearly resolved.

The island of Tobago has an uneven terrain dominated by the Main Ridge, a series of mountains near the northeast coast about eighteen miles long with elevations reaching a maximum of about 1,800 feet. South of the Main Ridge are lower hills in which rivers have cut numerous deep

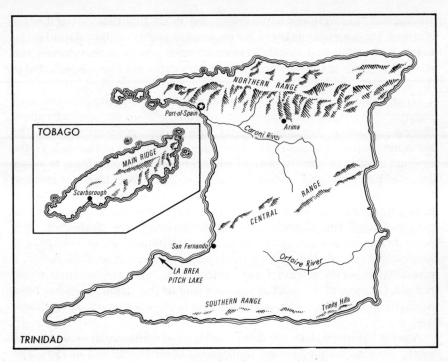

Figure 2. Trinidad and Tobago, Topography

and fertile valleys, and the southwestern part of the island consists of an extensive and fairly level coral platform. Most of the limited amount of level land occurs in the southwest, although narrow patches of coastal plain are found elsewhere, most notably around the mouth of the Courland River, which runs westward into the Caribbean Sea between the coral platform and the Main Ridge. Small rivers and streams are numerous, but flooding and erosion are less serious on Tobago than on Trinidad because the upper slopes of the mountains retain much of their original forest cover.

The town of Scarborough is the only important port, but there are several small harbors, and the coastline is indented by numerous inlets and sheltered beaches. In the southwest the coral gardens of Buccoo Reef are major tourist attractions. Tobago has several small satellite islands; the largest are Little Tobago Island, site of a bird sanctuary, and St. Giles, or Melville, Island.

Vegetation and Wildlife

Because the island of Trinidad was once a part of the South American continent and remains within sight of the Venezuelan shoreline across the narrow mouths of the Gulf of Paria, its vegetation and wildlife resemble those of South America and are considerably more varied than those of other West Indian islands. Plant and animal life on Tobago is generally

11

similar but less extensive in variety and more like that of the Lesser Antilles. On both islands there is a pronounced altitudinal variation in the natural plantlife, and the collections of such plants as mangroves and reeds that occur in the swamplands are very different from those found in drier areas.

Nearly one-half of the country is forested, most of the forested area remaining in government hands and one-third of it set aside as permanent reserves. Lower montane tropical rain forest predominates in the remaining wooded areas of the Northern Range, but in the valleys the original cover has largely been displaced by cacao plantations. In other mountain and lowland regions the characteristic vegetation is tropical forest with some savanna, and along the coast a littoral woodland adapted to salt spray is found. Bamboo stands are extensive near villages, and the mangroves of the Caroni and Nariva swamps are protected from overcutting for use in producing charcoal. Virtually all of Tobago was originally forested, but only on the higher reaches of the Main Ridge, a protected reserve of rain forest since 1763, does the original cover remain. On most of the territory of both islands the virgin forest has been replaced by second growth, or the land has been converted to agricultural use.

Among the more than 100 forest varieties of commercial value are the mora, carapa, mahoe, cedar, mahogany, blackheart, and olivier. The bark of the cupre or princewood is used for making bitters. Teak, cedar, and mahogany are plantation crop trees, and pitch pine is planted commercially on sandy soils.

The beauty of the countryside is enhanced by a striking variety of flowering trees, shrubs, and vines. The immortelle, a forest giant, flaunts scarlet- and salmon-colored flowers and different varieties of the *poui* bear yellow and pink blossoms. The *chaconia*, also called the wild poinsettia or the Pride of Trinidad and Tobago, is the national flower. Forest orchids grow in great variety and profusion, and flamboyant (royal poinciana), bougainvillea, hibiscus, oleander, lady-of-the-night, and various kinds of croton are common. Picturesque palm groves line the beaches of Tobago and are numerous on the eastern and southern coasts of Trinidad.

Legislation limits the hunting of game on crown lands, forest reserves, and ten game preserves and forbids the killing of certain species. Game animals esteemed for the table include the *quenck* or wild hog, the rabbitlike *lappe*, a tropical rodent called the agouti, the *manicou* or opossum, the peccary, the armadillo, and a kind small deer. Squirrels and raccoons can be found, and mongooses were introduced in an effort to control canefield rats. Monkeys and ocelots, not found elsewhere in the West Indies, are occasionally seen in the forests of Trinidad.

There are two national birds—the scarlet ibis, which inhabits the Caroni Bird Sanctuary, and the cocorico, or rufous-tailed guan, which is native to Tobago but not found on Trinidad. The hummingbird, however, is more characteristic of the country. There are about twenty varieties; and Iere, or "land of the hummingbird," was the name that the Carib Indians gave to Trinidad.

The country is a paradise for bird lovers. Common varieties include the mountain-dwelling anvil bird, the chowchow, the keskidee, the cowbird, the Caribbean peewee, and various parrots. Birds seen in swamplands include the snowy egret, the little blue heron, the roseate spoonbill, and the flycatcher. The island of Little Tobago is a sanctuary for the rare greater bird of paradise introduced from New Guinea early in the twentieth century. Listed as edible wildfowl are wild duck, wild pigeons, quail, and a kind of wild turkey called the *paui*. The rare *paui* is found only in the Northern Range of Trinidad and is listed among the world's endangered species.

There are a few poisonous snakes, and anacondas and boa constrictors occasionally find their way into populated places after heavy rains. The alligator, or caiman, inhabits the larger rivers, and in the mid-1970s excessive hunting of the increasingly rare leatherback turtle aroused conservationists to form civilian patrols for its protection during the egg-laying season. Legislation had been presented to protect this species of marine turtle, which weights as much as 500 pounds.

The most productive fishing grounds are in the Gulf of Paria and off the northern coast of Trinidad. Numerous species are found, but the fishing industry is poorly developed. The commercial catch consists principally of kingfish, carite, herring, cavalla, redfish, snapper, and grouper. Other species caught commercially include skipjack, wahoo, spanish mackerel, bonito, yellowfin tuna, dolphin, and tarpon. The *cascadura* is a popular freshwater fish. Shrimps are found in abundance in the Gulf of Paria, and common seafoods include large crayfish known locally as lobsters, tiny mangrove oysters, and a small clamlike mollusk called *chip-chip*.

Mineral Resources

Located on the northern flank of the great Venezuelan petroleum zone, Trinidad and Tobago has the only important known oil and gas deposits in the West Indies. Aside from petroleum, however, the country's mineral resources are limited. Unexploited iron deposits said to be in commercial quantities occur in the Northern Range, and there are some small Trinidadian deposits of coal. Quarrying is important on both islands. Locally used building materials include limestone, diorite, porcellanite, gypsum, and various clays, gravels, and sands.

Petroleum is the country's lifeblood. Its discovery is attributed to Sir Walter Raleigh, who in the sixteenth century is said to have caulked his ships with pitch taken from the great pitch lake at La Brea near the coast of the Gulf of Paria. The remarkable La Brea deposit—the term is Spanish for tar or pitch—is the largest of several on the island of Trinidad. It consists of more than 100 acres of pure asphalt with reserves estimated at 45 million tons. The viscous material is solid enough to be walked upon, but cavities formed by excavation quickly fill as the lake replenishes itself from subterranean seepages. The lake surface is subsiding about six inches a year as a consequence of exploitation of the material, but according to one estimate the reserves at the current rate of utilization will last for nearly 600 years. The asphalt requires no processing and is in common use both for the surfacing of Trinidadian roads and as an export commodity.

Trinidad's discovery oil well was drilled in 1902 in southeastern Mayaro County, where the Lagoon Bouff, a small pitch lake, is located. Production continues in this vicinity, but beginning in 1911 a series of richer petroleum and gas fields were discovered in the southwest in the general vicinity of La Brea. The pitch lakes led directly to the petroleum discoveries, and asphalt was once used for the distillation of lamp oil. In rural localities the kerosine used for home lighting is still known locally as pitch oil.

The first offshore petroleum, the Soldado field in the Gulf of Paria, discovered in 1955, was followed by the North Marine field a little to the north in 1959. Production from the known oil fields had commenced to decline, however, when the first of several extensive oil and gas fields were discovered in 1971 in the Atlantic Ocean off the southeastern coast near Galeota Point. In 1975 the new Atlantic oil fields were estimated to have reserves sufficient for more than twenty years of exploitation at current production rates; there were also gasfields with extensive proven reserves. Further exploration was in progress or leases had been granted for exploratory operations off the northern and eastern coasts and in new locations in the Gulf of Paria.

Climate

Although Trinidad and Tobago's location at about 10° north latitude places it deep within the tropics, the country's marine environment plus the prevailing northeasterly trade winds have a modifying effect on the tropical heat, and visitors from the temperate zone acclimatize readily. Days are warm, but temperatures decline considerably in the evening. The seasonal variation does not exceed 5°F, but from year to year there is some variation in temperature.

The mean year-round average temperature for the country during the years from 1962 to 1972 ranged at 8:00 A.M. from 76.7°F to 77.9°F. The lowest and highest 2:00 P.M. averages were 84.5°F and 86.6°F. A mean maximum of 88.6°F was recorded in 1968. Humidity, somewhat higher than the West Indian average because of proximity to the South American continent, ranged from 85 to 87 percent at 8:00 A.M. and from 64 to 67 percent at 2:00 P.M. Temperature levels on Tobago are generally similar to those on Trinidad, but the island's smaller size and greater marine exposure have somewhat greater moderating effects.

A dry season, more clearly defined than on most West Indian islands, occurs from January through mid-May, and a short interruption of the rainy season usually occurs in September. In most of the country no month is entirely dry, but during the rainy period the monthly precipitation exceeds that in the dry period by a margin of three or four to one. In spite of the small size of the country, however, there is considerable regional variation in the pattern of rainfall, and there is a sharp variation from year to year. On Trinidad rain is carried in by the northeast trade winds, and the crests of the Northern Range receive as much as 150 inches a year in an annual cycle that does not include a dry season; but in portions of the western lowlands almost totally dry months are recorded, and droughts are frequent. Between 1962 and 1972 in the eastern belt of Trinidad rainfall ranged from an annual total of 71.7 inches to 115.0 inches. In the much drier western belt the range was between 59.3 and 77.0 inches. On Tobago rainfall reaches 150 inches on crests of the Main Ridge but decreases rapidly southwestward to less than 45 inches on the coastal platform, where serious drought sometimes occurs during the dry season. The irregularity of the rainfall pattern of Trinidad and Tobago was underlined in 1973 and 1974 when droughts and floods, both of economically damaging proportions, were sustained.

Cumulus clouds form early in the day over the eastern coastal belt of Trinidad, even in the dry season, and deposit rain in short downpours as they drift westward across the island. The rain usually ceases quickly, however, and even in the rainier and cloudier eastern belt there are few days without periods of brilliant sunshine. In the country as a whole, the period of sunshine averages a little more than seven hours daily with little variation from year to year.

Cold air masses blowing down out of North America spend themselves before reaching Trinidad and Tobago. Trade winds and local breezes are usually light and continuous, and the country lies slightly below the hurricane track. Violent local storms sometimes occur, however, and in 1962 hurricane Flora diverted from the customary track, bringing devastation to Tobago. Flora was totally unexpected but not entirely unprecedented; an earlier hurricane had raked the island in 1847. Moreover, tropical storm Alma slashed across it in 1974 before acquiring full hurricane strength.

SETTLEMENT PATTERNS

The first capital of the island of Trinidad was at San José (now St. Joseph) on the southern slopes of the Northern Range and thus away from the then mosquito-infested coastal lowland. In 1774 it was moved to the site of the present Port-of-Spain because of the excellence of its natural environment. The shelter from the prevailing northeast winds provided by the mountains of the Northern Range combined with deepwater anchorage and a firm landing place made up ideal port conditions. The fertile earth of the immediate hinterland was the first to be farmed, and immediately to the south stretched the extensive Caroni Plain, which was to become the center of the island's economically dominant sugarcane culture. The early pattern of settlement in which the population was concentrated on the western lowlands of the island was not destined to change. In 1970 almost 90 percent of the island's population lived in four counties facing westward on the Gulf of Paria, and most of these lived within a few miles of the shoreline.

The plains facing the Gulf of Paria south of the Central Range also became an important sugar and farming area at an early date, and the development of the petroleum industry during the twentieth century served further to consolidate the western lowlands as the area of greatest population density. The southern coastal town of San Fernando had developed early as a port and a market center for the sugar and cacao growers of the interior, but the town was in the heart of the oil fields region, and with the influence of the nearby wells and refineries it became a major industrial center and the country's second urban center in size. At the same time, other settlements on the southern coast of the Gulf of Paria, such as Point Fortin and Brighton, grew into towns largely because of the growth of the petroleum industry.

In part the continued concentration of the population in the west resulted from the fact that it was the first region to be settled. It was expedient to develop lands near the Gulf of Paria before venturing further afield, and the small size and compactness of the island made it unnecessary to delegate to settlements in the interior administrative authority that might have encouraged the growth of their populations. As time passed and roads and the transportation system improved, Port-of-Spain and, to a lesser extent, San Fernando and Arima came increasingly to provide market and service facilities for the entire island and as a consequence to discourage the growth of other market towns.

The continued dominance of the western lowlands was also a matter of geography. Soils and climatic conditions as well as the closeness of established settlements encouraged intensive agricultural development of the west. In addition the best harbors were on the Gulf of Paria. The north coast had no accessible hinterlands; the waters of the south coast were shallow; and the waters of the east coast were too turbulent. Early settlers were discouraged from landing, and with the passage of time it became increasingly easy to transport produce overland to Port-of-Spain. By the mid-1970s even San Fernando had lost most of its importance as a shipping center to Port-of-Spain, which was located only about twenty-five miles to the north (see Natural Features, this ch.).

Local government in Trinidad and Tobago is carried on for the most part at the county level through county councils. Only the three urban municipalities have their own governments and are definable urban areas. There is no Trinidadian definition of an urban locality for statistical purposes, and regular issuances of the Central Statistical Office (CSO) do not include data on the urban and rural populations. Statistical issuances of international organizations sometimes give the combined populations of the municipalities as the urban total, but a large portion of the

16

Table 1. Trinidad and Tobago, Population by Political Subdivision,
1960 and 1970

Political Subdivision	1960		1970		Intercensal Change	
	Number	Percent	Number	Percent	Number	Percent
Municipalities:						
Port-of-Spain	93,954	11.3	67,867	7.2	−26,087	−27.8
San Fernando	39,830	4.8	37,313	3.9	−2,517	−6.3
Arima	10,982	1.3	11,792	1.2	810	7.4
Counties:						
Caroni	90,513	10.9	115,035	12.2	24,522	27.1
Mayaro	6,080	0.7	7,900	0.8	1,820	29.9
Nariva	17,226	2.1	20,917	2.2	3,691	21.4
St. Andrew	32,590	3.9	39,167	4.1	6,577	20.2
St. David	6,032	0.7	6,144	0.7	112	1.9
St. George	256,478	31.0	319,188	33.8	62,710	24.5
St. Patrick	108,218	13.1	117,124	12.4	8,906	8.2
Tobago (ward)	33,333	4.0	39,280	4.2	5,947	17.8
Victoria	132,721	16.0	163,483	17.3	30,762	23.2
TOTAL	827,957	100.0*	945,210	100.0	117,253	14.2

* Figures do not add to 100.0 because of rounding.

Source: Based on information from Organización de los Estados Americanos, *América en Cifras 1974, Situación Demográfica: Estado y Movimiento de la Población*, Washington, 1974, p. 14.

country's people live under urban conditions in extensive metropolitan areas surrounding the corporate limits of Port-of-Spain and San Fernando. There is general agreement that urbanization increased rapidly during the 1960s and that by 1970 the urban population had reached or exceeded 50 percent of the total. According to an Inter-American Development Bank report it increased between 1960 and 1974 from 39.2 to 54.1 percent. The indicated annual urban growth rate of 4.4 percent during the period would have meant a null or slightly negative growth rate for the rural population, a trend consistent with the sharp decline in agricultural employment recorded during the 1960s and early 1970s (see Labor Force, this ch.).

Census returns for 1960 and 1970 show sparsely populated Mayaro to have been the fastest growing county, but the densely populated counties of Caroni, St. George, and Victoria were next in order (see table 1). The municipalities of Port-of-Spain and San Fernando both sustained actual population declines, but the losses reflected not depopulation of these centers but the replacement of dwellings by commercial and industrial establishments within their corporate limits and the movement of people into the surrounding metropolitan areas.

A 1972 commercial publication asserted that 56.7 percent of the population of the country lived in Port-of-Spain and San Fernando, a proportion that must have included some rural areas. Since this proportion approached the 1970 combined total for the two municipalites plus the surrounding counties of St. George and Victoria (62.2 percent), a substantial urban spillover into Caroni County from Port-of-Spain and into St. Patrick County from San Fernando was implied. In Port-of-Spain, residential suburbs during the mid-1970s had spread along the valleys of Diego Martin and Maraval and the valleys of the St. Anns and Cascade rivers, westward toward the peninsula of Chaguaramas, and eastward as far as the town of Tunapuna. Trinidad City, an entire new urban complex, was growing up on the site of a cornfield near the Piarco International Airport, and the thrust of Port-of-Spain was being felt at Arima, half the distance across the island.

The increasing density of settlement, particularly in western Trinidad, has clouded the distinction between an urban environment and a rural one. In the two big metropolitan areas patches of urban settlement were jumbled together with farmlands. In addition some workers living in areas that could be considered urban rode buses to work on nearby farm plots, and others resided on farms and rode to work in nearby urban shops and factories. Further still, workers might busy themselves during one season of the year as rural farmhands and during another season as urban commercial or industrial personnel.

During the late 1960s and early 1970s the government had become concerned over economic and social problems created or worsened by the pace of urbanization. Heavy demands were being placed on the housing, schools, health facilities, and public services of the metropolitan centers, and the already high level of unemployment was being pushed upward. A substantial portion of the national territory remained in the public domain, and the need to locate rural people on family-sized farms profitable enough to keep them in the countryside was increasingly urgent. Most of the public land was forested or otherwise poorly suited to farming, but the Crown Lands Development Project was initiated in 1967 and by 1972 had settle about 1,000 families on new farms. In addition, after the occurrence of civil disturbances in 1970 small farmers were granted tax exemptions in the hope of dissuading them from leaving the land for the imagined opportunities of the city.

Consideration was given also to the dispersion of industry in order to relieve the specific pressures of Port-of-Spain and San Fernando. In the mid-1970s a proposal for the development of a secondary industrial center in St. Patrick County, the county's slowest growing area between 1960 and 1970, was being studied. The project was to be centered in Point Fortin, where light manufacturing industries would be established. Agro-industry would be developed in the area, and such facilities as roads, housing, and public utility services would be installed. There was hope, too, that the development of the new offshore petroleum and gas fields off the east coast would attract migrants to the sparsely populated southeastern part of the island.

18

Although Trinidad and Tobago in the mid-1970s was the most densely populated country in the Americas after Barbados, there were few small towns or large villages and no really big urban centers other than Port-of-Spain and San Fernando. Under the heading "major towns" an official 1973 publication listed in addition to these two centers only Arima, with a population of less than 12,000, and the Tobago town of Scarborough, with a population of about 3,000. The prevailing pattern of rural settlement was one of numerous village settlements with populations of 300 or more and fewer than twenty larger settlements with populations of more than 1,000.

About half of the country's small towns and large villages are located on the coasts and serve as fishing centers or secondary ports. The remainder, including all of the county-level administrative centers except Scarborough, are located inland and are situated on roads or at crossroads. The numerous small rivers are not suitable for navigation and have not played an important part in determining the pattern of settlement.

Some of the rural population lives dispersed on individual farms, but the common pattern is that of nucleated villages or line villages that lie strung out along the roads. The larger village usually contains a church, a police station, and almost certainly a primary school. It may also contain one or more stores, but the country store is much less frequently encountered than in most developing countries. A large majority of the rural people of Trinidad live within a relatively short distance of Port-of-Spain or San Fernando. Bus or collective taxi transportation is inexpensive, and the relative ease of a shopping visit to one of these centers discourages the development of commercial establishments in the countryside.

The pattern of settlement on Tobago is comparable to that on Trinidad. Scarborough is the only real town, and most of the island's population is concentrated nearby on the southwestern coral platform. The town of Plymouth on the northwest serves the farmers of the Courland Valley, and most of the remaining population is strung out in settlements on or near the southern coastline. Tobago has suffered from chronically depressed economic conditions, and in the early 1970s it was estimated that more people born in Tobago resided on Trinidad than on their native island. It has registered some economic progress through development of the tourist industry and other means, however, and despite the havoc accomplished by hurricane Flora in 1962, during the 1960s it experienced a rate of population growth somewhat higher than that of the country as a whole.

POPULATION STRUCTURE AND DYNAMICS

In the mid-1970s Trinidad and Tobago had a population somewhat in excess of 1 million, but the exact number was uncertain. The 1970 census had shown the population to be 945,210, with the notation that the total might be subject to upward revision for omission. This figure has been used in most subsequent statistical issuances of international organizations, but a charge that the census had been manipulated caused the CSO in 1975 to announce, in refuting the charge, that the first preliminary census count had totaled a little over 931,000 and that later calculations had indicated an underenumeration of 9 percent. An adjusted figure of some 1,025,000 would be the result. This total is extremely close to the 1,026,750 for 1970 announced by the CSO in its annual population estimate, which appeared before release of the census figure and which continued to be used by some sources after the census release. According to a CSO estimate published in mid-1975, however, the December 1974 population was 1,061,850.

As reported in the 1960 census the population was about 834,000 (revised upward from 828,000), and the annual rate of population growth was 1.4 percent on the basis of the 1970 census report or a substantially higher 2.1 percent on the basis of the official 1970 estimate. The lower rate has been the more frequently quoted, but even the higher rate was far below the nearly 3 percent reported for Latin America and the Caribbean area as a whole during the period.

Fragmentary data and estimates during the early 1970s indicate a leveling off of the growth rate, which a commercial Trinidadian publication reported to be 1.3 percent for 1972. In 1975 a CSO official announced to the press that the population trend of the last several years had been somewhat lower than expected and that the most recent CSO projections would probably be revised downward. Revised projected populations of 1,080,000 for 1975 and 1,150,000 for 1980 were suggested.

The rate of population increase has responded to a sharp decline in the birthrate only partially offset by a correspondingly sharp decline in the rate of mortality that has resulted from improved conditions of health and sanitation. The birthrate rose steadily during the 1940s and reached 38.6 per 1,000 of the population for the 1951–55 period and 39.1 in 1960 before commencing an almost unbroken annual decline to 24.5 per 1,000 in 1970. It then turned upward slightly to 25.0 in 1972 and 26.5 per 1,000 in 1973; in 1975 a CSO spokesman reported 27.0 per 1,000 of the population as the current birthrate. Public authorities attribute the generally downward trend in fertility to success of the country's active family planning program and point also to a decline of 32 percent in the proportion of illegitimate births between the 1940–45 period and 1970.

The actual number of registered births dropped from 32,880 in 1962 to 26,116 in 1971, and a downward movement was reported in each county and municipality of the country. No comparative statistics on birthrates by ethnic group are available, but Hindu and Muslim women marry somewhat earlier than Negroes and tend to have somewhat larger families. The first report from the 1970 census, showing almost 43 percent of the population to be Negro and over 40 percent to be East

Indian, reflects a substantial relative East Indian population gain since 1960 and suggests a relatively higher East Indian birthrate (see ch. 4).

Crude death rates plunged from 12.1 per 1,000 of the population in 1950 to 7.9 in 1960. The rate continued downward during the 1960s and held steady at 6.8 from 1970 through 1972. Infant mortality dropped from 80.3 per 1,000 live births in 1950 to 39.8 in 1969 and 28.3 in 1972. The sharp decline in mortality was reflected in a life expectancy that between 1946 and 1970 increased from 53.0 to 64.1 years for men and from 56.0 to 68.1 years for women.

During nearly all of its history Trinidad and Tobago's natural increase of population (excess of births over deaths) had been supplemented by a population gain resulting from immigration. During the years 1960 through 1963 immigrants slightly exceeded emigrants in number, but in 1964 the balance turned negative, and a net loss of 2,120 in population resulted from external migration. The annual net loss increased progressively during the late 1960s and reached an all-time high of 17,370 during 1970, a year in which net emigration so nearly equaled the natural increase of births minus deaths that the net population growth was a mere 820, or a rate of 0.08 percent. Net emigration declined to a little more than 7,000 in 1971 and again in 1972 before rising to 9,620 in 1973.

During the 1950s and early 1960s the flow of migrants out of Trinidad and Tobago had been far lower than that from most other Caribbean islands, and the country had received relatively more immigrants. Most of those emigrating had gone to the United Kingdom, but a British restriction on immigration from Commonwealth of Nations countries was imposed in 1962, and the flow shifted toward North America. The sharp decline in net outflow registered after 1970, however, resulted from more stringent immigration controls imposed both in the United States and in Canada, and in the early 1970s Trinidadian demographers reported that at least a short-run rise in the country's population growth rate could be anticipated as a consequence. A lively interest in emigrating to North America continued, however, and 1975 issues of the *Trinidad Guardian* carried advertisements offering assistance to skilled visa applicants in need of job offers in the United States.

Until late in the 1960s the government did not show much concern over the implications of the increasingly massive outflow of people; on the contrary, in 1966 it had initiated a policy of encouraging the emigration of domestics to North America as a means of alleviating unemployment. Moreover, a large proportion of the people leaving the country were young women, and the loss of so many females of childbearing age provided a particularly welcome brake on the rate of population growth.

Nonetheless, the emigration has been costly for the country because a substantial proportion of the emigrants were educated and skilled young adults, many of them trained at government expense. In the peak emigration year of 1970 about half of the emigrants to the United States and Canada were dependents or other nonworkers. Among the economically active, however, 15.1 percent were professional or technical workers, 2.7 percent were administrative or executive personnel, 22.4 percent were clerical or sales workers, 34.5 percent were production process workers or craftsmen, and only 25.3 percent were miscellaneous or unskilled workers. Among the professionals emigrating during the 1960s and early 1970s, doctors, nurses, and engineers were the most numerous, and it is estimated that between 1965 and 1971 the professional and technical workers leaving the country equaled one-fifth of the labor force in these categories during 1970.

Between 1953 and 1967 about 20 percent of the young Trinidadians who had studied at the University of the West Indies emigrated, and between 1962 and 1969 an estimated 30 to 40 percent of those engaged in studies abroad did not return to the country. The failure of the average level of educational attainment of employed males in Trinidad and Tobago to rise more than 0.6 percent annually between the years 1965 and 1970 despite a phenomenal growth of school enrollments is attributed to the heavy flow of emigration by the best educated young people.

Emigration during the 1950s was more than counterbalanced by immigration, mainly from the Windward Islands and Barbados. As a result of the formation of the short-lived Federation of the West Indies and the designation of Port-of-Spain as its capital, immigration rules were liberalized, and between 1957 and 1959 about 12,000 West Indian immigrants entered the country. Largely unskilled, they became a burden on the economy, and since 1959 various stringent restrictions on the employment of aliens have been in force. The number of immigrants from all countries rose from 1,853 in 1961 to 1,916 in 1962 but thereafter declined irregularly to 290 in 1971, 269 in 1972, and 190 in 1973. The lure of high Trinidadian wages proved irresistible to some workers in neighboring islands, however. In the early and mid-1970s the remaining trickle of legal immigration was supplemented by frequent illegal entries, and the Port-of-Spain press from time to time reported approvingly the expulsion of illegal immigrant workers who were depriving Trinidadians of jobs.

The Trinidadian coefficient of masculinity (number of males per 100 females) declined from 100.5 in 1946 to 98.8 in 1960. The 1970 census shows the coefficient to have further declined to 97.8 in a population consisting of 477,910 females and 467,300 males. A progressively lower proportion of males is characteristic in developing countries where improving health conditions bring about a decline in maternal mortality and permit the naturally greater longevity of women to assert itself. The 1970 census report, however, was sharply at variance with the official 1970 population estimates, in which the earlier decline in the coefficient of masculinity was reversed and a gain to a figure of 102 was indicated.

Population statistics by age and sex for 1970, available only from the official estimates for that year, showed males to be in a majority at birth and to remain in a majority in subsequent age-groups up to the age of sixty-four. At ages older than sixty-four the number of women exceeded the number of men by progressively larger margins.

The population in 1970 was a young one in which 41.2 percent were under the age of fifteen, and 52.1 percent were under the age of twenty. Some 22.1 percent of the population were forty years of age or older, and 3.7 percent had reached the age of sixty-five. Only 3.1 percent of the male population had reached sixty-five, the age at which men became eligible for benefits under the country's new social security program. The urban migration of the 1950s and 1960s was reflected in an age pattern in which city dwellers were somewhat older than people in the countryside. Some 24.2 percent of the inhabitants of Port-of-Spain as compared with 17.8 percent of the population as a whole were forty-five years of age or older.

FAMILY PLANNING

The history of family planning in Trinidad and Tobago dates from the opening in 1956 of a clinic in San Fernando under auspices of the privately operated Family Planning Association (FPA). A second clinic opened in Port-of-Spain in 1959, and several additional units were established in the early 1960s. The early efforts of FPA, however, were handicapped by lack of community and government support, church and some political opposition, and funding and administrative problems.

It was largely through the perseverance of a group of medical professionals that the movement remained in existence through its early years. In 1961 it became affiliated with the International Planned Parenthood Federation (IPPF), and the draft of the government's Second Five-Year Plan (1964–68) gave cautious approval to the concept of family planning by advocating "a better balance between birth rates and death rates." By 1965 some three urban and two rural planning clinics were in operation, and polls of local community leaders showed a favorable response to the concept of family planning.

Encouraged by these polls, the officeholding People's National Movement (PNM) named a committee to determine the party's policy toward family planning. The committee's report was favorable, and in 1967 the PNM requested the government to initiate a national program. In response the Population Council was appointed by the cabinet and instructed to advise the minister of health on the organization of a program to coordinate all family planning activities in the country; with assistance from the IPPF and the Pan American Health Organization measures were developed and placed in operation.

The new Population Council was headed by a cabinet-appointed chairman who presided over a membership that included government members, community members, and representatives of the FPA and the Catholic Marriage Advisory Council (CMAC). The CMAC had been founded in 1964 to advise couples on family planning methods compatible with their moral beliefs and had undertaken instruction in the temperature-rhythm method of birth control.

Once committed to the support of family planning, the government at once set about establishing its own network of clinics. In 1971 the government program received substantial assistance in the form of a US$4 million credit from the International Bank for Reconstruction and Development (IBRD, also known as the World Bank) for construction of medical facilities to be used extensively in connection with family planning. The new facilities were to include a 100-bed maternity hospital in Port-of-Spain and seven new health centers in which family planning sessions were to be held. A nurses training school and a family planning institute, in which training of personnel and family planning research would be conducted, were also to be established in Port-of-Spain. The IBRD program was to include the installation of a family planning clinic at the San Fernando Hospital.

From its inception in 1956 the planning program progressed slowly in the number of new acceptors registered and reached 450 in 1960. A sharp increase in 1964 and 1965 was recorded as the FPA clinics introduced oral and intrauterine contraceptive methods, and in 1965 there were nearly 8,000 new acceptors. The number then dropped to fewer than 3,000 in 1967, but with the initiation of the government clinics it soared to about 16,000 in 1969; slightly over half of the new acceptors attended government facilities. A slight decline in 1970 was attributed to social unrest in the country during that year, adverse press notices concerning oral contraceptives, and the reaching of a point close to saturation in the extent of contraceptive use. In 1970, however, old and new acceptors made up about one-fourth of the female production between the ages of fifteen and forty-four, and thirty-six clinics were in operation in all but the most inaccessible and sparsely populated parts of the country. By 1971 the number of clinics had increased to forty-six, including thirty-six operated by the government, eight operated by the FPA, and two operated by the CMAC. The announced goal of the program was ninety clinics and 20,000 new acceptors a year by 1980. The larger clinics were open daily or two or three times weekly, and the remainder were open when needed or as frequently as staffing limitations permitted.

The progress of family planning during the early 1970s was uneven. In particular the program came under attack in 1973 when the FPA announced that because of the high rate of teenage abortions it would issue free contraceptives to girls over the age of fifteen. The announcement was met by protests from Roman Catholic, Hindu, and Muslim spokesmen, leaders of some political parties, and a few community leaders. In the mid-1970s, however, Trinidad and Tobago was one of only about a half-dozen Latin American and Caribbean countries in which the government was actively sponsoring family planning and in which the birthrate since 1960 had registered a decline. In addition, construction of the new maternity hospital was proceeding ahead of schedule, and progress was being made on all of the training and research facilities being built with the IBRD credit.

LABOR FORCE

In Trinidad and Tobago the labor force in many respects has characteristics typical of an advanced rather than of a developing country. Wages, standards of living, and the proportion of the adult population in the labor force are relatively high. General educational achievement, urbanization, and monetization of the economy are all well advanced, and in much of the economy capital-intensive rather than labor-intensive production is emphasized. The technologies of production in use, however, are suited to mature economies where technical skills and capital are readily available and labor is in short supply, but the opposite obtains in Trinidad and Tobago.

Structure

The labor force edged upward in number from 358,000 in mid-1965 to 376,000 in mid-1973 (see table 2). These figures were assembled from twice-yearly government labor surveys; data from the 1970 census showed an absolute decline in employment of 31,000 from 1960. Such a trend seems highly unlikely in light of the expansion in economic activity that occurred during the period, and the census data are therefore seldom used. The participation rate (percentage of total population in the labor force) as indicated by the 1965 and 1973 surveys declined from about 40 percent to less than 36 percent during the period. The indicated average annual increase of about 2,100 workers was only a fraction of 1 percent of the labor force total, a surprisingly low proportion since people reaching working age during the period were born during a time of rapid population growth. It was also a period of heavy emigration, however, and in the peak emigration year of 1970 as many as 9,000 economically active people left the country (see Population Structure and Dynamics, this ch.).

In mid-1973 some 76.7 percent of the members of the labor force were wage earners, 13.8 percent were self-employed, 6.9 percent were employers, and 2.6 percent were unpaid family workers. The proportion made up of wage earners was one of the highest in the Americas and had risen substantially since 1969. The proportions in all other categories had declined, and the proportion of unpaid family workers had declined sharply.

The lines between the sectors of economic employment cannot be clearly drawn, and statistics concerning numbers employed in each sector are not necessarily exact. Many farmers and fishermen, in particular, work seasonally in other occupations, and the largely unskilled urban labor force works in any sector in which employment is available. Moreover, on compact and densely populated Trinidad the distances are short, and it is not too difficult for a rural resident to work in a nearby urban center.

Between 1965 and 1973 the most pronounced shift in employment involved a decline in the primary sector of agriculture and related activities. A relative drop in primary employment had been in progress since the end of World War II, but in 1965 the primary sector remained the largest employer. By 1973, however, it had dropped behind most of the other major sectors. The decline involved such factors as the mechanization of sugar harvesting but resulted principally from the urban migration of farm people motivated by the hope for better jobs and better living conditions. It was so pronounced that during the late 1960s and early 1970s seasonal shortages of farm manpower appeared despite a critically high countryside level of unemployment.

In mid-1973 about 31 percent of the primary sector was made up of farm operators, fishermen, and foresters who were employers or self-employed, and the remaining 69 percent were paid or unpaid workers. According to one estimate, in the late 1960s there were about 3,000 full-time and 2,200 part-time fishermen.

The sugar industry was by far the largest agricultural employer; in the early 1970s it was estimated to have given employment to 10 percent of the country's working force—although this percentage included industrial personnel engaged in sugar processing as well as agricultural workers engaged in sugar culture. The industry was dominated by the great Caroni Sugar Company, which employed about half of all workers in the sugar fields and mills and was 55 percent government owned.

Harvesting by hand, the traditional form of canecutting, is an arduous and dangerous occupation that is generally regarded as degrading. Despite the unpopularity of the work, the powerful sugar unions initially fought mechanized harvesting but agreed to its introduction after securing agreements that corresponding cutbacks in harvesting personnel would be made only by attrition. Limited mechanical harvesting commenced in the early 1960s and was expanded on a phased basis. In 1975 the Caroni company announced that still more mechanical harvesters would be introduced and noted that manual workers had become difficult to replace—the younger generation was no longer interested in employment of this sort.

The petroleum industry, both a mining and a manufacturing activity, is essential to the economy. Because it employs advanced technology and is highly capital intensive, however, it is of limited importance as a direct employer of manpower. Nonetheless, it stimulates employment elsewhere, and its influence is felt throughout the labor force. In particular, the high wages and generally desirable conditions of employment that the well-organized petroleum union has exacted and that the companies can afford to pay have exerted upward pressure on wages and

Table 2. Trinidad and Tobago, Labor Force by Occupation and Sex, June 1965 and June 1973

Occupation	June 1965				June 1973			
	Males	Females	Total*	Percent of Total	Males	Females	Total*	Percent of Total
Agriculture, hunting, fishing	58,500	25,000	83,400	23.2	45,100	12,700	57,800	15.4
Manufacturing, mining, quarrying	49,800	15,300	65,200	18.2	55,100	15,400	70,400	18.7
Construction, public utilities	40,900	2,700	43,600	12.2	55,800	5,100	60,900	16.2
Commerce	32,500	21,600	54,200	15.2	35,300	27,400	62,700	16.7
Transport and communications	24,300	2,400	26,600	7.4	24,800	3,000	27,800	7.4
Services	32,000	42,800	74,800	20.8	44,000	38,300	82,300	21.9
Seeking work for first time	4,200	6,700	11,000	3.1	3,900	6,300	10,200	2.7
Not adequately described	....	....	....	....	3,500	300	3,800	1.0
TOTAL*	242,300	116,500	358,800	100.0	267,400	108,500	376,000	100.0

* Figures may not add to total because of rounding.

Source: Based on information from Trinidad and Tobago, Central Statistical Office, *Labour Force by Sex, Age, Industry, Occupation, Type of Worker,* LF 1-4, (Continuous Sample Survey of Population, Publication No. 5.), Port-of-Spain, May 1966, Table 2; and Trinidad and Tobago, Central Statistical Office, *Labour Force by Sex, Age, Industry, Occupation, Type of Worker,* LF 1-12, (Continuous Sample Survey of Population, Publication No. 24.), Port-of-Spain, October 1974, Table 2.

employment conditions in other employment sectors. The discovery and development of the new oil and gas fields off the eastern coast of Trinidad in the early 1970s promised some new jobs, but there was little hope for substantial additional employment in petroleum and petroleum-related undertakings. It was estimated that the creation of a new job in a planned petrochemical complex would cost seventy-eight times as much as the creation of a job in the labor-intensive garment industry.

After a dramatic growth during immediately preceding years, employment in manufacturing during the late 1960s commenced a period of stagnation. The possibility of establishing new import substitution industries was nearing exhaustion. There was a sharp rise in wage rates, and among nonunion employers a fear of union intervention acted as a disincentive to taking on new workers. Factory production tended to be capital intensive, but impressive employment gains were registered in the generally labor-intensive garment industry, where employment increased from 225 workers in nine factories in 1962 to 6,000 workers in twenty-five factories in 1971.

The manufacturing industry in 1975 appeared more likely than other sectors to generate new employment during the coming years. In particular most of the factories worked only a single shift and, although unions tended to oppose introduction of the multiple shift system, it remained a potential source of many new jobs. In the early 1970s about 2,000 longshoremen handled cargo on the busy Port-of-Spain docks, some working as many as seventy-seven hours weekly; it was estimated that a double shift would have added at least 500 new jobs.

Official statistics conceal the level of employment in the construction industry by reporting it collectively with employment in the services sector areas of electricity, gas, and water. According to one report, however, during the 1970s there were about 36,000 workers engaged directly in construction and an additional 13,000 engaged in associated activities, such as the production of building materials. A construction boom occurred during the late 1960s and early 1970s, and employment rose sharply. Much of the work, however, was in government projects designed primarily to ease unemployment.

During the late 1960s and early 1970s the largest and fastest growing sector of employment was the tertiary or services sector, which included utilities, commerce, transport and communications, and personal services. In this sector the largest and most dynamic element was the public one. In November 1971 there were about 57,600 government employees, including 43,600 in the central government, 11,000 in local governments, 100 in diplomatic missions abroad, and 2,900 in such statutory boards as the National Housing Authority and the Tourist Board. By May 1974 the total had risen to 61,200, not including the statutory boards. In addition a large number of business enterprises were government owned, particularly in the fields of transportation and communications, and in the early 1970s it was estimated that one-third or more of the country's jobholders were employed by the government. Moreover, the public sector dominated the market for educated people by employing some two-thirds of all professional and technical workers and two-fifths of all clerical personnel.

There are relatively few legally admitted alien workers in the country, although an undetermined number have entered illegally. Work permits are not easy to obtain, and foreigners cannot be employed unless it can be shown that no Trinidadian capable of filling the position is available. Foreign-owned businesses, however, remain important employers. According to a 1975 report appearing in the *Trinidad Guardian*, about 180 companies with full or majority foreign ownership employed some 25,000 Trinidadians.

Most of the labor force is concentrated in the heavily populated areas of western Trinidad. In mid-1973 about 68 percent were located in the counties of St. George, Caroni, and Victoria plus the municipalities of Port-of-Spain, San Fernando, and Arima. Most of the agricultural labor is performed by East Indians on the island of Trinidad and by Negroes on predominantly rural Tobago. Negroes and persons of mixed blood predominate in industry and commerce and fill most of the civil service positions. White Europeans and North Americans engage largely in professional, managerial, and technical occupations; and Chinese, Syrians, and Lebanese usually are urban dwellers engaged in small business operations.

Age and Sex Distribution

The labor force participation rate of persons fifteen years of age and older (percent of the population engaged in economic activity) declined from 64.2 percent in mid-1965 to 59.9 percent in mid-1973. The decline, which was somewhat sharper for female than for male workers, is in part explained by an expansion of education that kept an increasing number of young people out of the labor force for a greater length of time and by a decline in employment of people over the age of sixty as a result of improved retirement programs. A decline in the participation rate, however, was also registered by workers in most of the middle age groupings (see table 3).

Trinidadian labor force surveys count only persons over the age of fifteen, and child labor is almost nonexistent; the 1960 census showed only about 1,000 workers aged ten to fourteen, and persons under the age of eighteen cannot be employed in undertakings involving the lifting of weights likely to be injurious to them. In general girls under the age of sixteen cannot be employed in industrial night work.

Overall the number of female workers dropped by about 8,000 between mid-1965 and mid-1973, but this decline was more than totally absorbed in the agricultural sector, where the number of female workers fell from 25,400 to 12,700. A substantial number of women had formerly been employed in the canefields where mechanical harvesting was being introduced. In addition women are believed to have constituted somewhat over half of the flow of migration from county to town during the 1960s; and in mid-1973 they made up nearly 35 percent of the labor force in Port-of-Spain and San Fernando as compared with less than 29 percent for the country as a whole.

Unemployment is consistently higher among women than among men, and in mid-1973 women made up only 27.1 percent of the labor force holding jobs. Among the employed they made up 49.7 percent of the unpaid family workers, 31.2 percent of the self-employed, 24.8 percent of the wage and salary earners, and 11.6 percent of the employers. Well over half of the unpaid female workers were in the agricultural sector, but the number had dropped by nearly 50 percent since 1965. The relatively large number of self-employed women included small shop-keepers and vendors and persons engaged in artisan work such as dressmaking.

In mid-1972 women held about 26 percent of the positions in government employment, principally in the fields of education and health, where they were in majorities. In public employment women held 38 percent of the administrative, professional, and technical positions and 10 percent of the positions involving manual labor.

Skills

The economy during the mid-1970s suffered from an acutely deficient supply of skilled labor. The shortage did not result from a lack of formal education, for the general level of schooling attained by labor force members was relatively high by the standards of developing countries. In mid-1973 only 3 percent had never attended school, and only 2 percent had left school after attending preprimary classes. Some 23 percent had attended only primary school, and 40 percent had attended the senior primary classes that were the regular channel of entry into the labor force. Some 23 percent had incomplete secondary educations, and 6 percent were the holders of secondary school certificates. About 2 percent had university educations. Information was lacking concerning the remaining 1 percent.

The trouble lay not in the amount but in the kind of education provided. The regular schools were highly academic in character, and the enrollments in the few and poorly organized vocational schools were low. In the mid-1970s, however, the country was engaged in an educational reform program aimed primarily at the correction of this defect (see ch. 6).

The skill shortage was worsened by the lack of coordinated apprenticeship and on-the-job training programs, but a more serious consideration during the 1960s and early 1970s was the emigration of many of the most highly skilled and educated workers. During this period a large proportion of the emigrants were professionals, managers, and skilled workers (see Population Structure and Dynamics, this ch.).

In the mid-1970s the supply of professional skills was nowhere in seriously short supply and was sufficient in some employment sectors.

Table 3. Trinidad and Tobago, Labor Force Participation Rates by Age and Sex,
June 1965 and June 1973
(in percent)

Age-Group	June 1965			June 1973		
	Male	Female	Total	Male	Female	Total
15–19	63.8	29.1	46.4	57.9	23.8	41.1
20–24	96.0	46.7	70.8	94.0	47.6	70.4
25–34	98.0	43.4	70.2	96.8	40.1	70.0
35–44	98.5	48.0	72.9	97.9	41.3	70.2
45–54	97.7	51.8	75.6	94.7	41.1	69.2
55–59	92.6	44.8	69.7	94.4	40.7	70.9
60–64	71.0	33.6	52.9	76.4	23.6	49.6
65 and over	55.3	18.5	33.9	39.2	13.7	25.6
15 and Over	87.9	41.1	64.2	83.6	35.3	59.9

Source: Based on information from Trinidad and Tobago, Central Statistical Office, *Labour Force by Sex, Age, Industry, Occupation, Type of Worker,* LF 1–4, (Continuous Sample Survey of Population, Publication No. 5.), Port-of-Spain, May 1966, Table 1; and Trinidad and Tobago, Central Statistical Office, *Labour Force by Sex, Age, Industry, Occupation, Type of Worker,* LF 1–12, (Continuous Sample Survey of Population, Publication No. 24.), October 1974, Table 2.

Planners of major construction programs, for example, reportedly found the local supply of architects adequate. Critical shortages, however, occurred in managerial and technical skills and, to a slightly lesser extent, in skilled manual occupations. In these areas of employment the shortages operated as a severe constraint on job creation. Work on construction projects was in several instances reported to be running well behind schedule because of a shortage of skilled manpower and, despite the high general unemployment level, skilled workmen experienced little difficulty in finding jobs.

In the face of the existing shortage of skills, demand for them is expected to increase rapidly. In 1970 a Ford Foundation study led to the conclusion that between 1970 and 1985 the demand for professionals would rise 90 percent, the demand for technicians would be up 108 percent, and the demand for skilled workers would rise 68 percent. The small industrial boom that was in progress during the mid-1970s as a consequence of the inflow of oil dollars might be expected to accelerate growth in the demand for skills. It has been calculated that a planned aluminum smelter will require 2,200 skilled construction workers out of a total of 3,100, and both it and a proposed iron and steel complex will require a large majority of skilled workers for permanent operation.

Unemployment

Unemployment during the early 1970s was an increasingly serious problem. As reported by the International Labor Organization, the level declined irregularly from about 15 percent during the years 1955 to 1956 to 12.5 percent in 1970. During the 1960s it averaged between 13 and 14 percent, but after 1970 it turned irregularly upward and reached 17.5 percent during the second half of 1973. At the beginning of 1975 an unofficial estimate located it at about 18 percent, but later in the same year an official estimate of 17 percent became available.

The periodic government labor force surveys for the most part show somewhat lower unemployment levels but give insight into the kind of worker most frequently unemployed. According to the December 1973 survey, some 17 percent of the labor force was unemployed, and 63 percent of these workers had actively sought work during the week preceding the survey. The remainder were able and willing to work but had not sought employment for longer periods of time or had not actively engaged in job hunting. Unemployment figures in Trinidad and Tobago are inflated by the practice of counting as members of the labor force all persons able and willing to perform work whether or not they are actively seeking it and whether or not they have been employed at any previous time.

The overall unemployment rate for women was 24 percent as compared to 14 percent for men, and the proportion of women actively seeking work was much lower. During the late 1960s and early 1970s the female unemployment rate tended to be relatively highest in periods of highest overall unemployment and to show a much sharper up-and-down movement than the male rate.

Unemployment is highest among young people. At the end of 1973 the rate stood at about 39 percent for workers between the ages of fifteen and nineteen years and 26 percent among those between the ages of twenty and twenty-four. For those between the ages of twenty-five and fifty-four it reached a low of 7.6 percent before rising to more than 10 percent between fifty-five and fifty-nine and declining once more to 6.5 percent among those sixty years of age and older. The proportion of unemployed persons actively seeking work was highest in the middle years. Nearly 40 percent of those aged fifteen to nineteen and 64 percent of those aged sixty-five and over had not sought work during the week preceding the survey.

Unemployment reveals a distinct pattern in relation to education in that it was lowest among those with no schooling or a great deal of schooling and highest among those with an intermediate number of years in school. At the end of 1973 the rate stood at 7 percent for those with no schooling, 9 percent for those with one or two years of primary school, 15 percent for those with the full five years of junior primary schooling, and 19 percent for those who had completed the senior primary school that customarily lead to vocational training (see ch. 6). It reached a high of 25 percent for those with incomplete secondary schooling but declined to 4 percent among those who had received a secondary certificate and to 2 percent for those with university educations. In addition to having the lowest unemployment rate, the uneducated and the highly educated had the lowest proportion of the unemployed actively seeking work.

Low unemployment among the totally uneducated is a consequence of extreme poverty and a willingness to accept any job including one that may be a form of underemployment or disguised unemployment. The low rate among the highly educated is a consequence of the demand for skills of all kinds and is reflected in an extremely low unemployment rate among white-collar groups. The very high rate among those with completed primary and incomplete secondary schooling results at once from the highly academic nature of the education received, its failure to teach practical skills, and the high levels of aspiration encouraged by it. The existence of a pattern in which unemployment among those with no formal education was at a rate less than one-third of that among those with incomplete secondary schooling highlights the voluntary nature of much of the country's unemployment. Young people who have progressed part of the way through the secondary school's highly academic curriculum think of the wages and other conditions of employment offered in the petroleum industry and in some big manufacturing concerns or of civil service assignments and are reluctant to accept such jobs as those in the canefields.

The relatively large size of the wage-earning sector in the labor force has tended to raise the level of overt unemployment but to hold underemployment to a level probably well below the average for Latin America and the Caribbean area. Although underemployment is not susceptible to exact statistical measurement, persons working fewer than thirty-three hours per week are generally considered underemployed; at the end of 1973 some 17 percent of the country's jobholders actually engaged in work during the survey week were employed fewer than thirty-three hours; 6.4 percent were employed fewer than seventeen hours. Of female personnel 25.7 percent worked fewer than thirty-three hours, and 12 percent worked fewer than seventeen hours. Underemployment as measured in number of hours worked was lowest among wage earners and employers and highest among the self-employed and the unpaid family workers. Some 50 percent of the latter worked fewer than thirty-three hours, and 26 percent worked fewer than seventeen hours of the survey week.

The disproportionately high unemployment rate among younger workers is considered one of the country's most serious socioeconomic problems, but it has become a chronic condition that meets with social acceptance and is encountered in pronounced degree in Jamaica and elsewhere in the West Indies as well as in Trinidad and Tobago. Per capita income is among the highest in the Americas, family ties tend to be strong, and it is often possible for youths to continue to live with relatives rather than accept unattractive work at low pay. The disturbances of early 1970, however, were in large part fomented and sustained by groups of unemployed young people and gave an increased sense of urgency to the unemployment issue. In addition the sharp decline after 1970 in the flow of emigration that had consisted largely of young working adults gave warning of a still greater need for additional jobs in the immediate future.

In response the government has engaged in a variety of efforts to meet the unemployment problem, with particular reference to the case of younger workers. First among these have been the educational development plan and youth training programs designed to keep young people in school and out of the labor force for a longer period of time as well as to give them skills making them more readily employable. In addition the government has endeavored to promote employment through farm settlement and farm credit, youth organization activity, housing, urbanization, and a special works program that provided jobs in construction and maintenance, particularly in rural areas. It has also acquired purchased equity in financially troubled firms in order to retain workers in their jobs and has offered tax incentives to firms creating new job opportunities. Some public employment has been entirely or primarily for the purpose of alleviating unemployment. The Special Works Programme, for example, includes a limitation—often evaded—under which a worker is not to be employed for more than ten days in any fourteen-day period on a single project, in order that after ten days the employment may be temporarily terminated and another person may be given a chance to work. In his budget speech of 1975, however, the minister of finance estimated that during the year TT$39 million (for value of the Trinidad and Tobago dollar—see Glossary) would be spent on tax incentives and other measures to create permanent jobs.

CHAPTER 3

HISTORICAL SETTING

The islands that constitute Trinidad and Tobago, since first sighted by Christopher Columbus in 1498, have been conquered and abandoned, pillaged, settled, and developed by peoples from all parts of the globe. The complex multiethnic culture of the new state reflects several centuries of European exploration, colonial power struggles, and the importation from Africa and Asia of slaves and indentured laborers to work on the plantations.

The indigenous inhabitants of the islands—the warlike Caribs, who flourished in Tobago, and the more peaceful Arawaks, who outnumbered the Caribs, in Trinidad—were ultimately subdued and enslaved by the Spanish conquerers and settlers and by the end of the eighteenth century were nearing extinction. Throughout most of that period, however, Spain's interest was centered on the mineral-rich areas of the American continents. Except for the exploits of an occasional adventurer in search of the legendary El Dorado, Trinidad was virtually ignored, while strategically situated Tobago was plundered and claimed by a succession of European navies and pirates.

Some Africans were brought to Trinidad as slaves in 1702 to boost the production of cacao, but it was not until the Spanish crown opened up the island to immigration in the last quarter of the century that settlement and agricultural productivity showed dramatic increases. French planters and their slaves came by the thousands from other Caribbean islands, bringing their knowledge of the cultivation of sugarcane; and liberalized trade rules, along with a bustling illicit traffic, converted the island into an entrepôt.

Trinidad came under British control after a minor skirmish between the British navy and the Spanish garrison at Port-of-Spain in 1797 and was formally ceded to Great Britain by the Spanish crown in 1802. Meanwhile the British had taken possession of Tobago in 1762 and, except for periods of French control from 1781 to 1793 and 1802 to 1803, it remained in British hands and was formally ceded to Great Britain in 1814. It was not until 1889, however, that Trinidad and Tobago were administratively linked; thereafter Tobago was administered from Port-of-Spain as a ward or political subdivision of the larger entity.

The assumption of de facto control by the British proceeded gradually in Trinidad. Initially Spanish law and local political organization remained formally in effect, being replaced in piecemeal fashion by British forms and customs. Moreover, the preponderant European element in the population during the nineteenth century was neither Spanish nor English but French. Beneath the musical chairs of competing European powers and cultures, however, the foundation for a unique national culture was being laid by the assimilative and creative forces at work among the African slaves and their freed descendants.

An 1803 census listed 20,464 slaves out of the population of 28,000. Slavery was abolished by law throughout the West Indies in 1834. The slaves were obliged to serve an additional six years on the plantations as "apprentices," but the apprenticeship plan proved unenforceable, and it was abolished in 1838. Once freed, the former slaves abandoned the large estates and in many cases established their own small farms. The consequent shortage of agricultural labor induced the British government to subsidize immigration under an indenture system. Efforts to attract North American Negroes and Europeans were not very successful, and in 1844 the British government gave permission for the West Indian colonies to import labor from India.

The indenture system, always controversial for economic as well as humanitarian reasons, was abolished in 1917 as a concession to the rising tide of nationalism in India, but by 1921 the so-called East Indians accounted for almost one-third of Trinidad's population. Culturally exclusive and slower than the Negroes to assert themselves politically, they tended to occupy the bottom rung of the social ladder.

Problems in marketing, as well as in production, led to a decline in the sugar industry during the nineteenth century; by the end of that century exports of cacao had overtaken those of sugar in value. Agricultural products were overtaken as producers of revenue in the early twentieth century by the rapidly developing oil industry. As early as 1938 oil accounted for 70 percent of Trinidad's total exports; by 1965 it accounted for 80 percent. This capital-intensive industry provided little employment, however.

Until after World War II Great Britain found the diversity and competition among the islands' ethnic groups ample excuse to withhold political concessions. Mass labor movements generated by the economic crises of the 1930s, however, evolved into political movements, and in 1956 the British succumbed to their pressures to grant the islands self-government. The newly-elected government opted for membership in the Federation of the West Indies, which came into being in 1958, but Jamaica's withdrawal in 1961 precipitated the federation's collapse. In 1962 Trinidad and Tobago became a united state and an independent member of the Commonwealth of Nations.

EARLY HISTORY: INDIANS AND SPANIARDS

The recorded history of Trinidad and Tobago dates from the arrival of Columbus in 1498. He was on his third transatlantic voyage when on July 31 he sighted three points of an island, which he named Trinidad in honor of the Holy Trinity and claimed for the Spanish crown. Landing for water, provisions, and relaxation in the south at present-day Erin Point, Columbus also observed much of the coastline and waters of the island, naming for posterity such prominent features as Serpents Mouth and Dragons Mouth (see ch. 2). He also made a short expedition into the fresh waters of the mouth of the Orinoco River and along the Venezuelan coast without, however, realizing that he had touched an immense continent. Columbus sighted Tobago and Grenada but sailed on for Margarita and concluded his voyage at the previously discovered island of Santo Domingo.

Columbus and his men had but slight contact with the indigenous inhabitants of Trinidad but were impressed by their graceful appearance and peaceable behavior. Subsequent Spanish contacts with the island's inhabitants were mostly violent because of the inhabitants' strong resistance to Spanish efforts to enslave them for agricultural or mining work in other Spanish possessions. Consistent and effective efforts to subjugate and develop Trinidad were not made by the Europeans until the latter part of the eighteenth century, so that the indigenous population escaped immediate obliteration by war, slavery, and disease, which afflicted such populations on some other Caribbean islands. At the end of the sixteenth century the indigenous population was estimated at 3,500; in the mid-eighteenth century it was over 2,000, or two-thirds of the total; and by 1831 its members numbered only 762.

At the beginning of the sixteenth century the Spanish priest Bartolomé de las Casas pleaded for humane treatment of the peaceful Amerindians (indigenous peoples of the Americas), and the Spanish monarchs, Queen Isabella and King Ferdinand II, restricted enslavement to the warlike Caribs. Perhaps to justify capture the European settlers of Trinidad and Tobago long mistakenly described the indigenous peoples as Caribs. Archaeological work in the twentieth century, especially by J. A. Bullbrook, helped to correct that view. Trinidad was apparently peopled by Ienian Arawaks, an agricultural and fishing people like the closely related Tainan Arawaks elsewhere in the Caribbean. A more warlike cannibalistic people known as Caribs had been migrating northeastward from the South American mainland and had replaced the Arawaks in some places; but differences in burial patterns suggest that the Caribs flourished on Tobago, having bypassed Trinidad except perhaps for small settlements in the north and east.

The Ienian Arawaks of Trinidad wove cotton and made pottery; their other artifacts were made of bone or shell, and polished pebbles were used for ornaments and trade. They lived in clearings in the forest on high ground and close to water in settlements of about fifteen huts. Their refuse dumps (middens) reveal that fish, shellfish, and cassava were their main articles of diet. The position of headman, or cacique, was probably inherited matrilineally. Music, dancing, and ball games were known. Crimes of violence or adultery and harsh punishments were apparently rare.

Many efforts were made by the Spanish, especially by the Capuchin monks, to convert the indigenous people to Roman Catholicism. The Dutch and English made efforts to spread Protestantism on Tobago. In neither case were the results impressive. As the history of other parts of the Spanish empire illustrates, there was a basic contradiction between the twin impulses of colonial expansion—the spread of Christianity and the exploitation of labor for gold. The writings of de las Casas and Francisco de Vitoria and the pious proclamations from the throne represent one side; on the other are the frankly rapacious statements and actions of the conquistadores. Ultimately both Awaraks and Caribs succumbed to near extinction, leaving little more than a few place names (such as Naparima, Arima, Tacarigua, Couva, Tunapuna, Piarco, and Siparia) to commemorate their presence. Only a few hundred persons who identify themselves as Amerindians survive in the mid-1970s (see ch. 4).

Spanish Rule

Most histories of Trinidad skim over the three centuries of Spanish rule except for the two decades preceding capitulation to the British in 1797. There are, indeed, few events worthy of record in comparison with those in other parts of Spanish America. The character of modern Trinidad is to some extent a consequence of its relatively late exploitation by the Europeans, however, so that features of the earlier period allowing Trinidad to be almost ignored acquire significance.

Within forty years of the initial voyages of discovery, Spain had expanded its dominion over the mainland and islands of much of the Western Hemisphere. Exploration, religious conversion, and the acquisition of territory and precious metals were simultaneously pursued. Sugarcane, citrus fruits, and cacao plants were introduced early—not always with success—and the indigenous cassava, cotton, maize, and tobacco were cultivated for consumption and export. In this enormous Spanish effort Trinidad's importance was negligible. It had no mines of gold or silver, its mangrove oysters did not produce pearls; its inhabitants were not easily enslaved, and it lay south of the main routes of ships sailing through the Greater and Lesser Antilles. On the mainland Spain's attention focused on rich Mexico and Peru, for which the main port of supply was Cartagena (in what is now Colombia). Very few explorers initially recognized the strategic value of an island commanding the mouth of the Orinoco. Thus Spanish chronicles of the sixteenth century contain few references to Trinidad.

Trinidad and Tobago were included in the fief of Diego Columbus, but no effort was made to settle the islands; Spanish ships restricted themselves to capturing slaves. From 1530 onward several governors attempted to subjugate Trinidad and engaged in constant warfare with the local people but with little success.

Toward the end of the sixteenth century Trinidad became a part of the legend of El Dorado through the exploits of men—the Spanish governor, Don Antonio de Berrio, and the English adventurer Sir Walter Raleigh. The legend of El Dorado, the golden land or the golden one, was part mythology, part memory of a discontinued indigenous ritual, and part hint of Inca civilization, but it spurred the European quest in South America. De Berrio was infected with the drive to discover El Dorado and to head a rich third marquisate in the Spanish empire. He envisioned Trinidad as a flourishing entrepôt attracting trade and settlers and valued it for its excellent harbor, Pitch Lake, virgin forests, and most of all its strategic position from which to continue his search for El Dorado. He made three journeys along the Orinoco without success, and his tenure as governor of Trinidad was crippled by dissension with his colleagues, illness ending in insanity, and threats from English expeditions.

In March 1595 Sir Walter Raleigh arrived off Trinidad with three ships, which he caulked with pitch from the lake at La Brea. He was also in pursuit of El Dorado and tried, with some success, to establish friendly relations with the local people and to use them against the Spanish garrison and as guides up the Orinoco. Raleigh captured de Berrio and took him along, but the trip provided no more than hazardous adventures, which Raleigh's pen has left to posterity. In 1617, one year before his execution in London, Raleigh returned for another unsuccessful quest for El Dorado. Meanwhile young Fernando de Berrio, governor of Trinidad, had abandoned the search for gold mines and was prospering in trading tobacco with Dutch and English merchants, a practice forbidden by Spanish law. Trinidad in the seventeenth and eighteenth centuries was a victim of the dwindling fortunes of the Spanish empire.

Spanish monopoly of trade and settlement in the Americas was challenged by other Europeans beginning in the latter half of the sixteenth century. Motives of private greed, religious conflict, and national assertion were mixed when French, Dutch, and English ships, acting with or without the approval of their governments, attacked the rich Spanish convoys of merchant and war ships and ports. Coastal towns frequently changed rule and suffered raids from pirates, especially if their position was vulnerable; hence Tobago rather than Trinidad appears more prominently in the chronicles of the time. But all the Spanish Indies were affected by the difficulties that their formal and stratified defenses had in withstanding the attacks of fleet and mobile predators.

Generally speaking, the highly centralized administrative structure of the Spanish empire, combined with its religious and commercial rigidity, proved a weakness rather than a strength. In 1511 the Royal Audiencia was established with jurisdiction over the islands and mainland; it acted as a court of appeal and a restraining authority on governors. It served, however, to inhibit initiative and to aggravate personal rivalries among the Spanish officials. Similarly in matters of trade the Casa de la

Contracción was opened in Seville in 1501 to control all trade and later to fulfill other administrative functions with respect to the colonies. But because Spain could not meet the needs of its overseas empire for goods or slaves and because legal monopoly was not officially abandoned, the whole commercial-administrative apparatus was open to corruption and disloyalty. Spanish colonial laws were influenced by the church and contained many humanitarian provisions with respect to the Amerindian and the African slaves, but they were seldom enforced with sincerity. Although the Spanish Inquisition in the New World was mild by the standards of the old and had jurisdiction only over Europeans, the church made little headway. Of the missions established by the Capuchins in Trinidad in the 1680s several had to be abandoned after attacks by the Arawaks.

The Spanish empire upheld the principles of mercantilism, which formed the conventional economic wisdom of Europe until late in the eighteenth century. According to mercantilist theory, a nation's wealth was equal to its reserves of gold and silver, colonies were valuable assets existing solely for the benefit of the metropolitan country, imperial trade and industry were protected by prohibiting or restricting the use of foreign goods or foreign ships by colonials, and the system was backed by armed force. Only with difficulty could the aggressive actions of individuals be distinguished from national policies. The fact that French, Dutch, and English corsairs and colonial companies deliberately undermined the mercantile empire of Spain did not prevent those nations from putting into effect the same principles with respect to the possessions they acquired. Caribbean territories were valuable for their products, for the legal or illegal trade they provided, and also as pawns for exchange in the dynastic and national power struggles waged in Europe until the Napoleonic wars.

It quickly became obvious to Spain that the riches of the New World could not be realized without regular and reliable supplies of cheap labor. But neither the enslavement of the indigenous peoples nor the flow of indentured European convicts in the sixteenth century provided labor sufficient to meet the growing demand of the colonies' sugar plantations. Partly in response to de las Casas' appeals against overworking the Amerindians, the Spanish monarch in 1510 gave authority for Negro slaves—already used in Spain and Portugal—to be taken to Hispaniola (modern Santo Domingo and Haiti). In 1517 he gave permission for 4,000 slaves a year to be transported from Africa to the Americas. In 1538 the *asiento*, or exclusive right to supply African slaves, was sold to a group of German merchants by Spain. The legal limits placed on numbers and on traders were far exceeded by the illicit trade in slaves that sprang up, usually with the tacit connivance of Spanish colonial officials.

After England acquired West Indian colonies of its own in the seventeenth century, and especially after it took over Jamaica in 1655 and developed the sugar industry there, English trading in slaves assumed great importance. By the Treaty of Utrecht in 1713 Great Britain gained the legal right to sell African slaves to Spanish territories—after the ships paused in Jamaica. The triangular trade between Africa, Great Britain, and the Americas, of which slaves were the most important and profitable commodity, stimulated the burgeoning industry and shipbuilding in such towns as Bristol, Liverpool, and London. Before the 1780s there were few voices protesting the trading and exploitation of Africans; the British monarchy, Parliament, Anglican Church, and commercial sector all supported it.

Trinidad's few settlers and small Spanish garrison could not compete for slave labor, overall in short supply, so that it was left virtually undeveloped. The introduction of some slaves in 1702 enabled increased production of cacao, but experiments with sugarcane failed, and cacao was also discontinued between 1725 and 1756; such trade as existed in slaves or other goods was carried on mainly with British traders.

Trinidad suffered neglect partly because it had been under the administrative jurisdiction of the presidency of distant Bogotá since Don Antonio de Berrio's days. The Spanish regarded the Trinidad-Guiana region as on the periphery of the empire, of some strategic value but of no economic importance. The province of Venezuela, producer of cacao and tobacco, attracted settlers with their cattle. The establishment of Dutch settlements in Curaçao, Surinam, and northern Brazil inspired enough fear among the Spanish to stimulate the Capuchin missions to undertake agricultural and settlement work; but in 1707 a royal decree limited them to religious work, largely because they protested the excessive workload and ill treatment of their charges. Despite the shortage of labor, Trinidad's production of cacao was impressive until the failure of the crop between 1725 and 1728 bankrupted the growers. In 1731, when administrative changes were introduced, Trinidad was once again dependent on Bogotá, whereas Guiana was detached. More important, the province of Venezuela was created a captaincy general and its commercial importance clearly recognized. Only in 1777 was an effort made to integrate the two territories.

From 1731 to 1777 Trinidad added one more strand to its special character. This was the emergence of the cabildo, or town council, as a vocal and vital institution representing the colonial community. The financial and administrative powers of the cabildo were limited unless the governor was absent, and there was an inherent conflict involving substance and prestige—as over the question of whether the cabildo should attend the governor at his residence. The strain between the cabildo and the governor flared into open conflict in the 1740s when the governor attempted to put an end to contraband trade. There was a revolt of the cabildo which was put down, and some prominent citizens left the island for Havana or elsewhere, so that Trinidad lagged further behind other West Indian islands in development. The cabildo remained an important body for the expression of public opinion and advice to the governor and cooperated closely with the last and probably greatest Spanish governor, José María Chacon. It continued to function under British rule until 1840, when it was converted into a purely municipal body for Port-of-Spain.

The fall of Havana to the British in 1762 brought a belated recognition in Spain of the need for colonial reforms, which were projected for the region as a whole and for Trinidad in particular toward the end of 1776 when the American war of independence began. The reforms were motivated by the desire to achieve economic development on Trinidad through liberalizing trade and commercial activity and by encouraging a cosmopolitan population to settle the land. They were not, however, coordinated with the administrative reforms simultaneously taking place in the new captaincy general of Venezuela with which Trinidad was now linked. Twenty years later the prospering and cosmopolitan colony was left virtually undefended because of the administrative divisions of responsibility within the Spanish empire.

French Settlement

The reforms of 1777 were introduced by Governor Manuel Falquez, who was instructed to attract as many French settlers as he could, especially from those islands that had recently passed under British rule, by promising them grants of land. He was permitted to admit other immigrants as well, provided they were Catholic, but told to keep out citizens of Great Britain, Holland, and Denmark who were Protestant and considered hostile to Spain. Falquez was given instructions to encourage trade by giving licenses to new settlers, but he was also asked to root out contraband traffic and corruption. The governor entertained two influential Frenchmen—G. M. Nol and P. R. Roume St. Laurent—who are believed to have greatly spurred the influx of French settlers into Trinidad. Spain's representative in Caracas was also a strong advocate of economic development and intensified contact with the French. The war among European states after the declaration of American independence further strengthened the Spanish-French alliance against Great Britain. This then was the background to the famous royal cedula of 1783.

The cedula of 1783 put into effect ideas about economic development that had already been evolving. It was amended in an even more liberal direction in 1786. Broadly speaking, the cedula contained provisions on immigration and commerce intended to attract foreign talent and capital to Trinidad.

With respect to immigration, the cedula stipulated that incoming foreigners must be Roman Catholic, subjects of nations friendly to Spain, and prepared to take an oath of allegiance to Spain and to abide by Spanish law. Every such immigrant, if white, would receive approximately thirty acres of land for every member of his family and half again as much for every slave he introduced. No head tax or personal tribute would be levied on the settlers, and after five years—during which they were free to emigrate—they and their children would have rights and privileges of naturalization, including eligibility for public office.

The cedula was not racially restrictive and foresaw a future class of settled and property-owning colored (see Glossary) and Negroes. Colored immigrants, however, were entitled to only half the land allotment given whites and a proportional amount for accompanying slaves. Since slave labor was at least as important to the colony as landowners, the cedula suspended duties on imports of Negro slaves at first for ten years and then in perpetuity. Settlers were licensed to obtain slaves from other islands, provided Spanish ships were used. In addition contracts were placed with an English firm estimating an annual demand for 4,000 slaves.

Many of the controls over commerce were liberalized by the 1783 cedula and further by the new governor, Chacon. Exports to Spain in Spanish ships were exempted from duty. Trade with France and French colonies was encouraged by lowering duties; trade with the mainland captaincy, from which supplies of cattle, horses, mules, and flour were expected was also encouraged. Spain undertook to supply the agricultural implements needed by the new settlers and also opened a sugar refinery for Trinidad's sugar exports. The settlers were permitted to establish more refineries as needed. Foreigners were urged to register their merchant ships in Trinidad, but restrictions were placed on wood cutting and shipbuilding by nonsettlers, especially the British and Dutch. Efforts were made to remove impediments to the cultivation of land through lenient occupancy and cultivation laws and distribution of crown lands.

Under Chacon's governorship Trinidad fast developed into an entrepôt supplying European goods to the mainland—both legally and illegally. Because of Spain's inability to supply the needs of non-Spanish settlers, an illicit trade sprang up. British merchants were especially active in this and were relied on to supply slaves, provide credit, and transport sugar exports, all to such an extent that among Trinidad's predominatly French settlers the word *foreigner* became synonymous with the British.

Chacon was given enhanced powers to simplify and improve the administration of the island. He made Port-of-Spain the formal capital and tried to improve its facilities. He reorganized the administration of the colony into three divisions with a commissioner of population in charge of each. The commissioners were charged with providing census reports, supervising agriculture, planning roads, policing the island, and ensuring adherence to the slave code of 1789. This law was considerably more humane than those in the English or French colonies, partly because of the influence of the Roman Catholic Church on Hispanic law, partly because northern and southern Europeans differed in their views on maintaining social distance along color lines, and partly because slaves were more highly valued in the labor-short economy. Chacon's reforms also aimed at efficiency but had the full support of the leaders of the population as represented in the cabildo and judicial elective offices. Inevitably the reforms led away from dependence on the captaincy general of Venezuela to which Trinidad was legally attached; this had serious consequences for subsequent defense of the island.

The effects of metropolitan liberalism and improved government in Trinidad were soon apparent. In 1765 the total population of the island numbered 2,503, of whom over half were native. Falquez' initiatives and Roume St. Laurent's efforts had brought in 523 freemen, white and colored, and 973 slaves. With the passing of the 1783 cedula the population grew to 11,533 by 1787 and to 17,643 by 1797. Of these last, 2,086 were white, 4,466 free colored, 10,009 Negro slaves, and only 1,082 Amerindians. (Figures vary slightly from source to source because of unreliable census reports of the times.)

The preponderant element in Trinidad's population was French, not Spanish, and French Creole (see Glossary) culture remained a dominant ingredient in nineteenth-century Trinidad. The French influx was natural not only because Spain was no longer able to fulfill its imperial mission but also because the French in the West Indies most easily fulfilled the qualifications for immigration under the 1783 law. Indeed, there had been a conscious effort to marry Trinidad's need for settlers with the discomfort of the French, white and colored, under British rule. Moreover, the French Revolution of 1789 stirred royalist or revolutionary fervor among all French-speaking people, and an increasing number fled the exigencies of the revolutionary wars that had carried over into the Caribbean by settling in Trinidad. Although the French element later clashed with the British, their contribution to Trinidad's development must not be underestimated.

In 1787 the first sugar plantation in Trinidad went into production; ten years later there were 159, of which three had water mills and one a windmill. By 1797 there were 130 coffee estates, sixty cacao estates, and 103 cotton estates, all producing for export.

Chacon was aware of Trinidad's weakness in the face of envy from other powers and its lack of defenses. Spain had never maintained more than a tiny garrison on the island but, now that new interest was being taken in its development, Great Britain became covetous of possession. A confrontation between a French and a British ship in Port-of-Spain harbor in 1796 did not flare into a serious incident but brought home the danger inherent in the overall situation. The outbreak of war in Europe, Great Britain against Spain and France, was immediately transposed to the Caribbean. Chacon drew up plans for defense and called urgently for increased land and naval forces. He was sent some reinforcements in September 1796, and in January 1797 Admiral Apodoca arrived with four ships and one frigate. But the land forces were undermined by yellow fever, inadequate training, lack of administrative support from the mainland, and generally low morale. Further, the sentiments of the population, especially the free colored, were in doubt, and the egalitarian ideals of the French Revolution and the revolt in Grenada in 1796 were believed to have led to unrest among the slaves. Thus the island was ill prepared for the inevitable British attack.

In February 1797 a British fleet of seventeen ships commanded by Admiral Harvey appeared off Trinidad carrying a land force of nearly 8,000 men under Sir Ralph Abercromby. Feeling himself hopelessly outgunned and outnumbered, Apodoca preferred to set fire to his ships and sink them rather than suffer defeat. The fortifications of the island were not yet complete, and much of the garrison deserted Port-of-Spain. After a minor engagement British forces entered the capital, and Chacon submitted to an honorable capitulation. The Spanish crown ordered an inquiry into his and Apodoca's behavior for failing to fulfill their responsibilities. Chacon pleaded superiority of British forces, lack of fortifications and funds, low morale and disease among the militia, and doubts about the population. Though deprived of position, Chacon subsequently vindicated his reputation.

BRITISH RULE: THE EARLY YEARS

The passing of Trinidad into British hands did not immediately make much difference to the life of the island. Abercromby left Lieutenant Colonel Thomas Picton as governor with instructions to ensure British possession but to continue the operation of existing laws. A policy of conciliation toward the inhabitants was adopted; all subordinate civil and judicial officers were confirmed in their posts, although an Irish immigrant, John Nihell, was appointed chief justice, a new office. The reason for this initial delay was the uncertainty of the final disposition of Trinidad at the conclusion of the war. On the one hand Picton and others appreciated the strategic position and natural resources of Trinidad and coveted it as a British possession; on the other the rising tide of opinion against the slave trade in England and the opposition of the powerful West Indian interest in the British Parliament to the acquisition of a competing sugar-producing colony made it possible for Great Britain to use Trinidad as a bargaining point in the peace negotiations and to refuse sovereignty.

Trinidad formally passed under British sovereignty by the Peace of Amiens in 1802. It was placed under the sole control of a governor as a colony of experimentation. Great Britain was unwilling to extend governmental procedures operating elsewhere in its colonies to the unusually cosmopolitan population of Trinidad, which contained such a high proportion of colored. As the correspondence between Picton and the colonial secretary in London showed, the introduction of elective principles would bring to the front the explosive question of whether to give the vote to free and property-owning colored people. Whatever the decision, they concluded, important elements of the population would be seriously disaffected. Therefore no elective offices were introduced into Trinidad. When the governor was given an advisory legislative council in 1831, it consisted entirely of nominated (appointed) members, mostly from the plantocracy.

Picton's governorship became a highly controversial one. His energy, initiative, and absolute powers introduced administrative efficiency, internal security, and economic prosperity. The police force was reorganized, its strength increased, and its range of duties broadened; the powers of the cabildo and the audiencia, which had often acted to frustrate Spanish governors, were virtually superseded; trade with the mainland was actively pursued, and production increased.

Spanish legal and administrative practices were rapidly eliminated, however, without being systematically replaced by English law. Property disputes and other civil cases could properly be decided only according to Spanish law, but every new officer appointed was invariably an Englishman, and the precedents of the older English colonies were also used. In 1813 English was used for meetings of the cabildo, and it was introduced as the language of the law courts in 1814. Only in 1832, however, was that mainstay of English civil liberties, the concept of habeus corpus, applied to Trinidad; thereafter other English laws were introduced.

One example of the confusion was the slave law. Picton's code of 1801 was described as generous and humane, as it reflected the church-influenced standards of the Spanish slave code allowing manumission, encouraging marriage between slaves, and permitting time for religious instruction. But it was also geared to the ideas of efficiency prevalent in the British sugar colonies and was therefore harsher than the Spanish law (in letter if not in practice). What became the best known example of confusion in legal practices was a minor case of theft in which a young woman, Louisa Calderon, provided testimony under torture. The issue of admissibility of torture under Spanish law and the legitimacy of Picton's ordering torture perfunctorily became a cause célèbre on which long written discussions were carried out in Trinidad and Great Britain.

The Calderon controversy is notable as one incident in a more deep-seated conflict on the island. This derived mainly from the influx of new British immigrants who formed an "English party" and demanded legal and constitutional rights similar to those prevalent in such other West Indian colonies as Jamaica and Barbados. They were joined by other members of the urban population who resented Picton's authoritarianism and found a sympathetic ear in the liberal and aristocratic Colonel William Fullarton. There was also a latent conflict, however, between the English party and the French, who still dominated the agriculture of the island and resented the beginnings of anglicization. The competition between English and French—both white and colored—was to continue far into the nineteenth century. Picton promised to protect the Spanish, French, and colored elements of society from the exploitation inherent in rule by a planter-dominated assembly, but he personally doubted the loyalty of the non-English elements. Picton chose to solve his administrative problems by adopting a strong and efficient paternalism.

The British government was unable to decide the issue one way or the other—even as it seemed momentarily unable to decide whether Trinidad should be run as a colony with or without slaves. Instead of assembly rule or governor's rule, the British Parliament decided that Trinidad should be governed by a three-member commission. It appointed Fullarton, formerly of the East India Company, first commissioner and Samuel Hood naval commissioner and retained the services of Picton.

Picton and Fullarton clashed at their first official encounter, and their differences of approach and opinion were soon sensed and exploited by the local elites. Fullarton's several criticisms against Picton's stewardship led to his bringing criminal charges on the issue of Louisa Calderon's torture. The case, which excited considerable controversy, was tried before the Privy Council. Picton was initially found guilty but subsequently was vindicated. Fullarton died before a second trial could be held. Trinidadians sent Picton British pounds (£) 4,000 to help defray his costs—he returned it for the rebuilding of Port-of-Spain after the disastrous fire in 1808.

Trinidad's incorporation into the British Empire took place at a time of obvious transition in the character of the empire. Its boundaries and ethnic composition had been drastically altered by the successful revolt of the thirteen North American colonies and by new conquests in India and the West Indies, inhabited by nonwhite, non-English-speaking peoples. The principles of mercantilism had been theoretically challenged by Adam Smith, and the advocates of free trade were gradually winning practical application of their tenets. Great Britain's older West Indian colonies, relying on a monopoly market and dominated by a planter class, were in financial decline and were losing some of their influence with the British government. The institution of slavery, on which they depended, was under attack as inhumane and immoral by a group of brilliant evangelicals and propagandists, including William Wilberforce, Thomas Clarkson, and James Stephen and his son. There were no clear guidelines for new acquisitions of territory as were evolved later.

By reserving Trinidad as a colony of experimentation Great Britain admitted its uncertainty about how to govern this unusually cosmopolitan island, but it found no new dynamic ideas to replace plantocracy other than the old standby of royal prerogative and imperial control. During the nineteenth century Trinidad and Tobago evolved along lines strikingly similar to the other British Caribbean territories.

Perhaps the most influential reasons for Great Britain's missing an opportunity to create a new society and political system in Trinidad were subconscious and psychological. Despite some contemporary evidence to the contrary, the British ruling class was convinced that tropical colonial development depended on large plantations worked by cheap labor and that there was an innate hierarchy among ethnic groups with the English at the top, other Europeans below, and non-Europeans considerably lower. Further, although Whitehall retained real power, its governors in Trinidad often allowed themselves to be influenced by local powers. Thus crown colony government in Trinidad posed as a trustee for the entire population but actually became an agent for the large planters, usually resident in Great Britain. Nineteenth-century Trinidad was dominated by the questions of how to obtain and keep a regular supply of plantation labor and how to meet the religious and educational needs of a multiethnic population.

Trinidad was much affected by policies enunciated in London on the basis of imperial concerns over which Trinidad had little influence. One example was the abolition of the slave trade and then of slavery within the British Empire. The controversy over this issue was debated for decades on the floor of the British Parliament. The final victory of the abolitionists is remembered chiefly as a vindication of humanitarianism, and the image of the antiabolitionists is tarnished by accusations of cruelty, but commercial considerations were important motivations on both sides. The sugar trade and the share of the older British West Indies in it against competition from Santo Domingo and Cuba was a vital issue at the end of the eighteenth century. Cutting off supplies of slave labor was expected to help the British West Indies, already saturated with labor, and the British government under William Pitt attempted to secure international agreement on abolition of the slave trade. The French, Spanish, and Dutch governments refused to comply. Great Britain's sugar market was affected by the Napoleonic wars and labor supplies from India, and a coalition of interests in Parliament led to the unilateral abolition of the slave trade within the British Empire in 1807, accompanied by a prohibition of insurance on slave ships.

In Trinidad, meanwhile, Great Britain continued the cosmopolitan policies of Spain's last governors to attract European settlers. Many came from other Caribbean islands; those who brought with them large households and numbers of slaves were entitled to large shares of land. The practice of kidnapping slaves continued, and a substantial intercolonial slave trade developed after 1807. In the guise of domestic servants, slaves were transferred from the less profitable older colonies to the virgin soils of Trinidad and British Guiana (acquired from the Dutch at the same time). Between 1813 and 1821 Trinidad received 4,000 such slaves, largely from Grenada and Dominica.

The many strands in Trinidad's population at the start of British rule were reflected in a breakdown of the 1803 figures. Of a total 28,000, the English-speaking numbered 663 whites and 599 free colored; the Spanish 505 and 1,751; and the French 1,093 and 2,925; slaves totaled 20,464, the majority being French speaking.

The fluctuations brought about by the Napoleonic wars drove large numbers of French and Spanish subjects, mainly colored, from other islands to Trinidad. In addition peons who were a mixture of several racial strands arrived from the mainland and took to farming cacao in the northern foothills. English settlers also came looking, but for opportunity rather than refuge, and like the French set up sugar plantations. By 1838 a total population of 36,655 comprised nearly 4,000 whites, 12,000 colored, and about 20,000 apprentices, that is, slaves. In this startling increase of population the one group that practically ceased to exist was the indigenous people. Numbered at about 2,000 at the turn of the century, they were reduced to 520 by 1838, living in small settlements at Arima, Savanna Grande, Toco, and Cumano; they had been killed by disease or rum or had fled from fear.

British merchant houses soon found a footing in the new colony. Such firms as William Eccles and Company and Edward Gibbs and Company were linked with steamship companies, the marketing of sugar, and the whole network of British capital and parliamentary lobbies. Such companies rapidly became the most important sectional interest on the island. As early as 1838 one-third of the estates in Trinidad were owned by nonresidents, and the proportion was to increase with the years. Resentment of expatriate dominance of the economy was to become a major tension in the twentieth century, but it was implanted early in British rule.

The cosmopolitan, almost Levantine character of Trinidad was reflected in the character of its capital, Port-of-Spain, which had an atmosphere more akin to that of Alexandria, Egypt, than to Bridgetown, Barbados or Kingston, Jamaica. But its dominant white minority was split into factions by religion and language. In the 1830s four-fifths of the island was Roman Catholic; and in 1834 thirteen of the eighteen churches were Roman Catholic, and there was a bishopric in Port-of-Spain. In 1835 the Church of England was given a grant for building schools and churches, and in 1837 the Presbyterians commenced the building of Greyfriars Church.

The large free colored community of Trinidad was also divided by religion and language. In addition they were at the most sensitive point in race relations and found the British rulers and settlers totally unsympathetic to their rights. They were subjected to curfews and head taxes and forbidden public assembly like slaves rather than free men. Many discriminatory regulations were abolished in 1826, but social discrimination remained. As a class they were feared for their alleged revolutionary potential and probably suffered most from the hardening of the race barriers in the nineteenth century. After 1826 they were no longer eligible for commissions in the militia and police, and their position as property holders did not bring them respect as in Spanish times.

Their changing position in society was reflected in their participation in Carnival, which had been introduced by the French as an urban festival. Initially Carnival was celebrated among the upper class Creoles in a rigidly segregated fashion. After the emancipation of slaves, Carnival became a means for the masses to break out of their normal routine and also to express ridicule or indirect attack on their social superiors and on the government. The whites began to shun street demonstrations and feared for their safety in the annual commemoration of Canboulay (see Glossary), celebrating emancipation. The participation of the coloreds was uneasy, indicative of their ambivalent self-identification with the white property owners on the one hand the black masses on the other. During the 1840s and 1850s Carnival was often subject to governmental restrictions and official strictures. Gradually during the late nineteenth century, Carnival progressed toward its twentieth-century position as a truly national festival, absorbing contributions from various ethnic groups in Trinidad and permitting the participation of all (see ch. 4; ch. 5).

Emancipation of Slaves

Abolition of the slave trade was only the first victory of those in Great Britain who for various reasons opposed slavery. Their next target was to improve treatment of existing slaves. Therefore much of the contemporary literature on the subject is concerned with arguments for and against such things as the flogging of female slaves or procedures for manumission. Because of the firm opposition of West Indian planters to any interference in labor relations, the British government in 1823 chose to introduce, by orders in council, model slave codes in the crown colonies of Trinidad and British Guiana; they thereby hoped that the example would be followed in the self-governing colonies. This code was an elaboration of Picton's ordinances of 1801, which followed Spanish law.

The 1823 reforms included: abolition of the whip as an inducement to labor, though it was retained for chastisement; abolition of the Sunday market so as to give the slaves another day off and time for religious instruction; procedures for purchase of manumission by field and domestic slaves; prohibition of flogging of female slaves and freedom of females born after 1823; admissibility of evidence given by slaves against masters in courts of law; the appointment of the protector of slaves, who would keep official records on number and punishments of slaves; and encouragement of savings, marriage, and family life among slaves. Considered generous for the times, the reforms were opposed by other West Indian planters who feared further concessions. Trinidad already prided itself on treating slaves well in the amount of food and rest provided them, and the reforms made little practical difference. On the contrary, manumissions fell off because the fees were appraised upwards to about £ twenty-five a head, and only 611 manumissions took place between 1824 and 1826. The position of the protector was difficult.

In 1823 emancipation became the avowed objective of the Anti-Slavery League, which had formerly argued only for a gradual decay of the institution. In Great Britain the abolitionists in Parliament were joined by representatives of the India company interests who aimed for an equalization of sugar duties from the East and West Indies (accomplished in 1846.) Meanwhile slaves all over the West Indies had become "infected" by the teachings of the missionaries and by the talk of imminent emancipation. There was a rash of slave revolts in Jamaica and Barbados and restiveness in Trinidad. While the argument between property interests and humanitarianism continued, emancipation by revolt became a real possibility because of the spread of revolutionary ideas exported again by France in 1830.

The Emancipation Bill skillfully combined humanitarian principles with concessions to the planters. It was passed on August 29, 1833, and came into effect on August 1, 1834. Although slavery was legally abolished throughout the British West Indies, the slaves were to be released only gradually, after serving a further six years as apprentices, and their owners were to be compensated to the total amount of £ 20 million, of which £ 1,033,992 was allocated to Trinidad and £ 233,875 to Tobago. The amounts of compensation were calculated on the basis of number and value of slaves and showed the high average value of slaves in Trinidad— £56 per head—as compared with Tobago and Barbados— £ 25 per head—or Jamaica— £ 23 per head.

Not surprisingly, the law of emancipation was bitterly criticized by the planters and ecstatically received by the slaves, who did not appreciate its subtleties. Trinidad's governor, Sir George F. Hill, prepared for August 1, 1834, by appointing a large number of special justices and alerting the militia for special duty. On the day itself hundreds of the newly freed marched into Port-of-Spain and resolved not to continue work on the plantations. Neither reading the Riot Act, nor arrests and punishment, nor advances by the army affected the crowd. But despite the alarm in Port-of-Spain, emancipation was accomplished in Trinidad without real disturbance. The apprenticeship system proved a failure: the large acreages of land available for squatting and cultivation made it impossible for the planters to keep these half-free tied to the plantations as they were able to do in Barbados. In June 1838 the governor proclaimed the end of apprenticeship.

The British Parliament was unambiguously in favor of large plantations, for which labor had to be obtained at low cost. Fears of what might happen to plantations without apprenticeship led the colonial secretary to instruct the governors of the West Indies colonies not to release crown lands easily but to keep the price beyond the reach of persons without capital and to disallow occupancy except to those with legal title. This was a reversal of earlier government practices in Trinidad where cheap crown lands were used to induce settling. In 1838 Hill made squatting a punishable offense and doubled the price of crown lands. These measures were not effective as there was little survey of lands and less administrative personnel; moreover, clearing and cultivating forestland for more than a year traditionally brought ownership rights.

The 1840s saw a great increase all over the island in the number of small farms cultivated by former slaves and the mushrooming of produce markets along the roads. On the large estates crop production and profits fell steadily between 1835 and 1840, no new expansion took place, and about a dozen estates were abandoned. Only 4,000 former slaves remained on the plantations. The planters resorted to inducing Creole labor to work their estates by offering regular hours and relatively high wages in addition to housing, food, and rum allowances. But they continued to demand a docile labor force and low turnover in order to compete in the British sugar market.

Immigration and Indian Indentured Labor

The West Indian planters pressed for liberal immigration policies to solve their labor problems. The West India Committee in London was not without friends and influence in Parliament and, although Trinidad lacked an official colonial agent, Charles Marryat unofficially represented the planter interests there. The arguments used were, briefly, that immigrants would create competition for jobs among the "indolent" Creole workers who lacked the "good character" to work willingly on plantations; that wages could thereby be reduced to more economic levels; and that in order to compete with European beet sugar and slave-produced Brazilian and Cuban sugar the British West Indies must reduce their labor costs. The British government leaning toward free trade was not against mobility of labor in principle, and the Colonial Office through commissioners was given the charge of superintending emigration movements.

In Trinidad a resolution of the Legislative Council in 1838 called for recruiting agents to produce immigrants for whom they would be paid bounties. First preferences were for West Africans and Europeans, as earlier experience with American and West Indian Negroes had not satisfied the planters. Soon after the end of the Napoleonic wars, attempts had been made to settle in Trinidad British Negro troops and American Negroes taken prisoner or freed from slavery. The east coast was selected as a suitable site for the disbanded West India Regiment, recruited largely in West Africa, and groups of American Negroes were settled in Manzanilla in the north. It was hoped to open unpopulated areas, construct an island-wide network of roads, and keep the free Negroes separated from contact with slave labor on plantations around Port-of-Spain. During the 1820s the settlements appeared to be prospering, and clergy were requested to open schools and churches. The settlements were, however, endangered by the heavy preponderance of males, difficulties in marketing crops, tendencies toward casual labor, and most of all by government economies in roadbuilding, land allocations, and pensions. The settlements were closed in 1843, and surviving pensioners were permitted to commute cash pensions due to them.

Between 1806 and 1833 limited efforts were also made to import

Chinese from Hong Kong, Singapore, and Calcutta to settle as peasant farmers and also to replace Negro domestic slaves. The small numbers of Chinese who came to Trinidad at that time were almost all men without families and unused to agricultural work. After the middle of the nineteenth century a larger number came to the West Indies as contract labor, but they tended to drift into the towns, where they acted as brokers and distributors of food and as small shopkeepers. They came mainly from Canton and settled in Trinidad in scattered towns, endeavoring to retain marriage ties with other Chinese. In the late nineteenth and early twentieth centuries the Chinese acquired a higher status; they tended to ignore island politics and organized themselves into various semisecret societies.

After emancipation the efforts to attract West Africans and American Negroes continued, and by 1850 about 3,000 and 1,000 respectively had been settled in Trinidad. But neither group took kindly to plantation work. The same was true of the Europeans who immigrated to Trinidad in the 1840s. A small number of English and Scots of the poorer classes obtained posts on plantations but found the life too hard. A larger number were employed as clerks and managers in the expatriate-owned plantations. There were French and German immigrants too, but Trinidad offered few opportunities for them in contrast with the wide open lands of North and South America. The Portuguese of Madeira proved a more durable group. Forced from their island by the decline of vineyards and by religious intolerance, they were drawn to the cacao estates in Trinidad and into the retail trade. Cacao from Trinidad was exported mainly to Spain until technical improvements in the British manufacture of chocolate at the end of the century raised British demand and Trinidad supply of what was known for a time as brown gold.

In July 1844 the British government gave permission for West Indian colonies to import labor from India at their own expense but with some imperial assistance. Calcutta and Madras were designated as ports of embarkation in India. Recruiting agents were paid bounties and were active in the cities and the depressed areas of the Ganges valley. From the start the indenture system was a purely economic undertaking, and no attention was paid to the possible implications of introducing one more ethnic component into the West Indies. Initially Trinidad was allotted 1,000 people and British Guiana and Jamaica 2,000 each; over time Jamaica discontinued importation, and British Guiana consistently exceeded Trinidad. After the first shipload of 226 Indians arrived on the *Fateh Razak* from Calcutta in 1846, more than 5,000 arrived by 1848. After a three-year suspension because of the post-1846 collapse of the economy, between 1851 and 1870 a further 43,519 Indians were imported, of whom fewer than 4,000 returned to India. By 1921 Indians in Trinidad numbered 122,117 out of a total population of 365,913, but of these only 37,341 had been born in India.

The transfer of labor from India to Trinidad was made under

complicated ordinances intended to protect the Indians as well as the plantation economy and to provide government supervision. As they were amended and applied in practice, however, the rules for indentured labor became the framework for what has been aptly called a new system of slavery. The protector of immigrants was seldom sensitive to the laborers' needs or capable of communicating with them.

Generally Indians were indentured for five years, after which they were guaranteed free passage home. But in 1847 this was amended to five years of work free of absences computed by the employers, who were not at all anxious to lose their experienced workers and tended to prolong the period indefinitely. Although the British and Indian governments did not permit Trinidad actually to rescind the provision of a free passage home, the provision was made increasingly difficult—by extending the indenture period to ten years, by demanding taxes and payment to defray costs of passage, and by failing to provide ships.

According to the rules, Indians were to be allotted to estates in parties of twenty-five or fifty under a headman, or sirdar. Medical care, housing, provision gardens, monthly food rations, and yearly allotments of clothing of Indian style were to be provided by the employers. The medical and housing provisions were notoriously inadequate, and later inquiries revealed the poor health of the Indians to be a direct result of unsanitary housing, inadequate food, and almost nonexistent medical relief. Rigorous hours of work were stipulated in the rules, which failed to mention the custom of payment by task then prevalent in Trinidad. During the off season hours were fixed from 6:00 A.M. to 4:00 P.M. with a one-hour meal break; there were no limits on working hours during the crop season. The wages of twenty-five cents a day for an able-bodied male were lower than the prevailing Creole rates. As an inquiry in 1937 revealed, wages on sugar plantations rose only ten cents in almost 100 years.

Because some of the incoming Indians were unsuited for heavy agricultural work or recoiled against the harsh treatment they received on some plantations, they tried to leave their places of work and look for better conditions. Therefore the regulations were tightened so that no Indian might leave a plantation without a leave ticket or a certificate of discharge from his employer, which he had to carry on his person at all times. This unique obligation partly accounted for the scorn in which he was held by the rest of society.

Indian indentured labor became the mainstay of the sugar plantations, other estates being unable to afford large groups of laborers. The Indians were left the arduous work of hoeing and weeding against which the freed slaves had rebelled. Their contribution is revealed in the increase of Trinidad's sugar exports from 10,334 tons in 1833 to 53,847 tons in 1896. By virtue of the work they did the Indians were derisively called coolies (from the Hindu *kuli*, an unskilled worker), an epithet that has persisted to the present. But an unforeseen result of the new system of slavery was an increase in peasant agriculture, as Indians were encouraged to surrender their rights of free passage in return for buying crown lands and as planters allowed them to cultivate rice for themselves to keep their wages low. The movement of Indians in the late nineteenth century into swampy rice-producing regions around sugar estates increased food production on the island and raised the price of land; Indians also became small-scale sugar cane farmers.

Trindad was able to pay for its indentured labor by an initial loan from London, paid back by 1870. The question of how to pay for what came to be seen as a necessity was decided in 1853 by levying a tax on planters requesting indentured labor—later all planters were taxed even if, like cacao estate owners, they employed no indentured labor—and by imposing excise duties on rum and import duties on wine and spirits. This placed an unfair burden on the small producers and was therefore benefical to the large absentee-owned sugar estates, as Norman Lamont and other opponents of the indenture system argued before the Royal Commission on Sugar in 1896. The other argument against the system, that it depressed Creole wages, was harder to demonstrate since Creole workers found that increased sugar production and the opening of central refining factories also increased the number of better paying jobs for them. But despite controversy in Trinidad over the indenture system—seldom couched in humanitarian terms—it was ultimately abolished only as a result of a rising tide of nationalism in India that put pressure on the British government in India to undertake in 1912 and 1913 a comprehensive inquiry of all colonies to which Indians had been exported as indentured labor. In 1917 when other concessions were being made to Indian public opinion, the British government of India abolished the indenture system.

Between 1850 and 1870 the Indians, or East Indians as they were called, became an integral part of life in Trinidad. It was during those years that stereotyped images developed that were hard to break down even after independence. The image was generally derogatory but contained several contradictions. For example, Indians were despised for doing menial work but also noted for their obvious self-respect; they were criticized for appearing in poor and ragged clothes and barefoot and resented because as a group they were more thrifty than the Creoles. This was indicated by their acquisitions of land and ornaments. The docility and unassertiveness of Indians were noticed; yet they were believed to be violent because fights among themselves usually involved the handy cutlass and because their ignorance of the English language and indenture laws made them always the largest single group in the island jails. Indians were resented as birds of passage who would return rich to India; yet much was done to compel them to stay on the plantations. Few returned to India with significant assets, and the fact that most of the community put down roots in Trinidad was not recognized.

Other possible reasons for the antipathy between Creole Negro and Indian were, first, that the white minority above despised both and deliberately educated both to despise themselves and each other; second, that the Creole Negro, long at the bottom of the social ladder, welcomed cause to look down on a group still lower; and third, that the Indians came with an old culture as exclusive and complex as the European and made no secret of their repugnance for Negroes , especially in sexual relations. Because of the nature of their employment, lack of education in English, religion, and traditional disinclination to mingle, Indians clustered in their own communities. While making substantial concessions to their new environment, especially the relaxation of caste rules, they displayed a high degree of cultural peristence. Unaccustomed and perhaps unwilling to assert themselves politically, they remained outside the early movements for self-goverment in Trinidad. Only a few sugar plantation workers were awakened to agitational tactics in the 1930s, and the post-1946 mass politics found most Indians unprepared (see ch. 4; ch. 7).

Religious Controversy and Accommodation

According to the terms of the 1797 Capitulation, inhabitants of Trinidad were assured free exercise of their religion. Most of them were French- or Spanish-speaking Roman Catholics, and their priests came mainly from France or the French Antilles. The British governor became the patron of the Roman Catholic Church in Trinidad, which for administrative purposes was transferred in 1820 from the See of Venezuela to the newly created See of the British West Indies. The Anglican Church, however, gained influence in Trinidad as a consequence of the economic and political rise of the English party; soon the most important planters and merchants belonged to the still small Church of England. In 1841 Trinidad was made an archbishopric in the Anglican administrative organization of the West Indies.

Tensions between the French and English in Trinidad were exacerbated not only by the worldwide rivalries of the two countries but also by religious resentments created by government actions in Trinidad. During the 1840s the two groups disputed the place of the Church of England in Roman Catholic Trinidad. The colonial government actively assisted the extension of the Anglican church by paying stipends to its clergy. In addition an 1844 ordinance imposed the ecclesiastical laws of England on the island. Protests and counterprotests following these moves were aggravated by deteriorating personal relations between the leading members of the community; non-English members complained of English arrogance and complacency. During the 1850s the religious dispute concerned the right of the Roman Catholic Church to appoint a bishop of its own choosing in a British colony regardless of the wishes of the colonial government. Once again, personal antipathy between

Governor Charles Elliot and the Italian bishop, Vincent Spaccapietra, and between English and non-English priests was evident, and government preferences were expressed in financial terms. The conflict was eventually resolved by the Colonial Office in 1857.

These religious-administrative controversies had not actually interfered with freedom of worship by Catholics or Protestants. But in 1863 a marriage ordinance was introduced to tighten the application of English marriage laws in Trinidad and to penalize clergy and individuals who flouted them—which many Catholics did for economic or social reasons. The ensuing uproar of protest from all classes of Roman Catholics had less to do with the detailed clauses of the ordinance than with their resentment over attempted anglicization. In 1865 the offending marriage ordinance was amended, and in 1870 the Ecclesiastical Ordinance of 1844 was repealed.

Through this memorable defeat of the English party, Roman Catholics and Anglicans were once again placed on an ostensibly equal legal footing, though government financial assistance was disproportionately higher for the Church of England. During the 1870s the Colonial Office ordered equalization of stipends and officially declared a policy of nondiscrimination among denominations. Thus nonconformist churches, such as Moravian, which like the Presbyterian and Baptist were active in missionary and educational work in Trinidad, also became entitled to government assistance. Government insensitivity to the sentiments of the Roman Catholic majority did not entirely disappear, however, as the sharp and bitter controversy over the Divorce Bill in the 1930s was to demonstrate.

During the mid-nineteenth century the policy of anglicization was closely associated with the career of Charles Warner, attorney general from 1844 to 1870. Warner belonged to a family that had established itself in the West Indies in the seventeenth century and owned the large Woodford Dale estate on Trinidad. Warner was an Eton-educated gifted and ambitious lawyer who was inflexibly determined that Trinidad become English in feeling, language, and institutions. No transient governors could afford to ignore his power as head of the English party on the island, though they often clashed with him. The end of Warner's public career came during the governorship of Arthur Gordon, who was openly sympathetic to the Roman Catholic Creoles and in favor of opening up crown lands to peasant proprietorship; he was naturally opposed by Warner. In fact Warner's forced resignation was a consequence of irregularities in his private legal practice rather than public policy matters; the Colonial Office took an active role in the prosecution. Warner lived until 1887, long enough to see the gradual but real rapprochement between the English and Creole elements on the island and the recognition of the contribution of Creole families through their appointment to the Legislative Council; in 1840 only one Creole had been among the nonofficial members of the council (see ch. 7). The leading figure in the legislative councils of the 1920s was Captain Andrew Arthur Cipriani, of Corsican descent.

Education

Vacillation by the colonial government was obvious in matters of education. During the first five decades of British rule no general plan of public education was formulated, mainly because the Colonial Office believed that differences of language, religion, and race would make any single system impossible to apply in Trinidad. Education was in the hands of the churches; the government provided some funds but exercised no control or surveillance. The churches competed with each other but seldom attempted to appreciate the real needs of neighborhoods. Governor Lord Harris (1846–54) found that fifty-four day schools in the colony were attended by little more than 1,000 children. The 1851 census revealed that only about 9,000 of a population of 68,609 were literate. Most of the literate were in the towns; the countryside was neglected educationally.

Lord Harris, once a schoolteacher himself, resolved to alter this unsatisfactory state of affairs and caused a comprehensive new scheme to be drawn up. Briefly, it was intended to introduce free, general, and secular education throughout the island through a network of ward or government schools managed by a board of education and financed through a new system of local taxes levied on landowners. It was hoped that landowners would become active citizens in their neighborhoods. Textbooks were ordered from England, and the superintendent of the normal or training school set up in Port-of-Spain came from England. Government assistance to denominational schools was to be phased out as the new ward schools became established.

About thirty ward schools were established under Lord Harris' scheme, as well as the Queen's Collegiate School for secondary education in Port-of-Spain. But they did not keep pace with the population, and they were opposed by the churches, which stood to lose the funding for their own schools. Furthermore, many of the administrating wardens opposed the concept of free primary education altogether. Because of the transfer of Harris, the death of the superintendent, and the lack of clear direction from the board of education, the scheme languished. A report of 1869 gave a devastating account of the primitive physical facilities, the inappropriate Irish textbooks, poor attendance, and inadequate knowledge of English in the ward schools. (Notwithstanding the accuracy of the report, the ward schools managed to produce the brilliant, creative J. J. Thomas, author of the first Creole grammar and also of *Froudacity*, a biting and witty rejoinder to James Anthony Froude's notorious and libelous *The English in the West Indies*.)

During the 1870s a dual system of government and denominational schools was followed, the latter enjoying considerable autonomy. Open admissions were imposed on all schools, but in fact enrollments were mainly by denomination. By 1898 there were fifty-seven government schools and 147 religious schools with a total enrollment of almost 25,000. The rivalry and controversy between the two systems were never fully resolved. In 1889 another commission advocated the abolition of government schools, concluding that it was not the duty of the state but of the parents to educate their children at their own expense and that primary education should be restricted to the bare minimum: the three Rs. The colonial government passed on its responsibility to the churches, largely for economic reasons but also because it did not believe that uniformity in education was possible or desirable. The principle of free and compulsory education was not accepted in late nineteenth-century Trinidad. More public monies were spent on the importation of indentured labor than on education, on prisons than on schools. As Eric Williams was later to put it, crown colony government did not need citizens, only laborers and clerks.

Although the principle of secular state-run schools was accepted when no other alternative was possible, the rural population was left largely uneducated. The most obvious victims were the children of Indian plantation workers, even though the Colonial Office ruled that they should be provided free education. This was largely a result of leaving primary education in the hands of the churches. Indians generally withheld their children from school partly because with their limited wages children's work on plantations was an economic asset, partly because they feared proselytization by Christians, and partly because of the paucity of ward schools. Neither plantation owners nor wardens considered education necessary for agricultural labor.

The education of Indians from the late nineteenth century was mainly the work of the Canadian missions led by John Morton and missionaries from the Canadian maritime provinces who were moved by the sad plight of the Indians. They were also inspired by the desire to convert the "heathen" Hindus and Muslims to Presbyterianism. By the late 1870s Morton had established twelve primary schools in southern Trinidad, of which one was government assisted and nine were supported by the planters of the area. Many Indians later to become prominent were educated in these schools and testified to the strong pressures for religious conversion. The work of the Canadian missions was probably crucial in the gradual emergence of Indians into the mainstream of a Trinidadian society functioning along Western, Christian norms. The schools also provided one route of mobility from the plantations to urban life. Nevertheless, the prejudices of the missionaries tended to reinforce existing racial stereotypes and divisions in society between Negro and Indian and further introduced a distinction among Indians between Christian and non-Christian, which inhibited their group identity and public participation. The educational handicap persisted and was commented upon by the Educational Commission of 1931, when only six of

366 students at Queen's Royal College were Indians. The commission recommended the establishment of government-aided Indian schools, and Indian organizations began to found their own schools to redress the balance (see ch. 6).

Secondary education was provided by the government-run Queen's Collegiate School and the Roman Catholic Saint Mary's College, both in Port-of-Spain, and Naparima College in San Fernando. At no time during the colonial period was secondary education mass oriented, and there was considerable rivalry between the two Port-of-Spain institutions catering to the English and Creole elites respectively. By the end of the nineteenth century, however, a system of scholarships opened a few places a year to the gifted sons of poor parents. The secondary school certificate became a prerequisite for junior positions in the colonial civil service and for those who sought upward mobility through university education and the professions. The education imparted was very good, especially in contrast to that of primary schools.

Through scholarships and a complementary system of pupil-teachers a new class of colored professionals arose to play an increasingly important role in island affairs. In addition there were three annual scholarships for university study in the United Kingdom for which competition was extremely keen. Trinidadian scholars thus absorbed and enriched the liberal and radical intellectual-political movements of prewar Great Britain (see ch. 6). University education in Canada and the United States also created links between the educated classes of Trinidad and North America.

THE UNION OF TRINIDAD AND TOBAGO: EARLIER HISTORY OF TOBAGO

In January 1889 Tobago became a ward of Trinidad on the initiative of the British government. The two colonies were united into one with common laws and tariffs. Tobago retained separate internal administration, was permitted to send one unofficial member to the Legislative Council (a privilege unrealized in fact for two decades because of inadequate transportation), and had its name included in that of the new colonial entity. Amalgamation was not desired by the citizens of either colony. The move was suggested and implemented by the British government as an economy measure, because it was not prepared to bear the expenses of administering a small island that had lost its earlier strategic and commercial importance and because it could not compel the elected legislative assembly of Barbados to accept the responsiblity for Tobago.

The history of Tobago can be summarized as one of sudden rise from obscure Carib settlement to prominence in European rivalries; a shuttlecock existence for two centuries between several competing sovereigns and colonists; a period of prosperity, settlement, and self-government based on a slave-sugar economy; and the steady decline of that system until collapse into the partial obscurity of union with Trinidad.

Tobago is situated in the direct path of the trade winds and has many safe anchorages and watering places. These were invaluable assets in the days of sailing ships and account for Togabo's prominence in the chronicles of the time compared to Trinidad, which had neither. Although Columbus probably sighted Tobago in 1448 and English sailors claimed to have visited the island in 1580, Tobago did not enter the politics of European westward expansion until early in the seventeenth century. Inhabited by Caribs likely to attack would-be colonists and visited mainly by pirates who found there a refuge from authority or woodcutters from Barbados who needed its timber, Tobago remained for some time the sylvan retreat later described by Daniel Defoe in *Robinson Crusoe.* But its isolation did not last long. Between 1626 and 1802 the little island changed hands twenty-two times; European states, trading companies, and even individuals all vying for possession. Their claims were usually drawn up in the form of royal decrees, but possession rested only on force, and many skirmishes were fought on and off the shores of the narrow, fish-shaped island.

The earliest successful settlements by Europeans were made by the Dutch, who built the first fort and kept returning after every defeat. Other early arrivals were the Courlanders (from a principality of Latvia), authorized to come by Charles I of England on condition that only Courlanders and English be allowed to settle there. In 1655 the Courlanders shipped Tobago's first exports of the indigenous tobacco (from the Carib smoking receptacle from which Tobago got its name), sugar, pepper, and ginger. The Duchy of Courland was soon absorbed by Sweden, however, and the Spanish in the Caribbean were jealous of any trade and settlement outside their control. The Dutch, French, Spanish, and English—the Caribs playing an active role as well—continued to compete through diplomacy, surprise attack, general war, and occasional efforts to attract settlers with slaves into sugar cultivation. Tobago, lacking formal government and for some time in a state of unarmed neutrality, became a sort of pirates' republic, colorful but brutal men of every nationality using its havens to raid the valuable transatlantic trade.

The development of Tobago's plantation economy and assembly government was postponed until the late eighteenth century. The Treaty of Paris (1763) awarded it to Great Britain. It was closely associated with Barbados to the east. In 1781 the French captured Tobago and followed a systematic policy of development and settlement copied from other French islands and similar to the Spanish policy being pursued in Trinidad at the time. In addition the Tobago settlers were given the right of self-government through an elected assembly. By 1771 the population of the island was only 5,084, of whom 243 were white and 4,716 were

African slaves. By 1791 the population was 15,102, of whom 541 were white and 14,170 were slaves. The production of sugar was doubled but at the expense of spices, cotton, and indigo. Although there were slave uprisings in 1770 and 1798, the French code was relatively mild and contained many provisions designed to encourage the breeding of slave children and the preservation of good health on an island where disease—probably yellow fever—was endemic and the slave mortality rate considerably higher than the birthrate.

In 1802 Great Britain again acquired Tobago, and its possession was subsequently ratified by treaty. Tobago retained its self-governing status, but there were many clashes between the narrowly elected assembly (extension of the franchise in 1860 increased the number of voters from 102 to 215) and the British-appointed governor, especially over the issue of slavery. Nineteenth-century Tobago followed the path of steady economic decline similar to that of Barbados and other British West Indian islands brought about through inefficient methods of sugar production, emancipation of slaves and their preference for small-scale land proprietorship over plantation work, and changes in British sugar import policy. Some laborers were imported from Europe, West Africa, and Barbados, but the most interesting development in the nineteenth century was the métayer system of cultivation, a crop-sharing payment instead of cash wages.

Tobago's economic decline was paralleled by its loss of political importance in the British Empire and in the West Indies. Great Britain made efforts in the 1870s to amalgamate the smaller islands of the eastern Caribbean under a single administration but was frustrated by the opposition of the planter-dominated assemblies in Barbados. In 1884 the collapse of the firm of Gillespie Brothers in London ruined most of the sugar estates in Tobago, for which the firm acted as creditor. A British inquiry commission once again recommended federation of the island colonies as a solution to their economic problems; Tobago resisted. The Sugar Commission of 1886 and the British government appeared to find West Indian problems almost insolvable, and the British government's goal became economy in government. In 1886 the crown colonies of Trinidad and Tobago were joined for tariff purposes, and suggestions were made for improving communications across eighteen miles of water. Two years later Tobago became a ward of Trinidad.

For a time Trinidad sought economic relief by selling to the United States market, but there was a general movement of resident planters from sugarcane to cacao growing. The Royal Commission of Inquiry 1897 recommended greater diversity of agriculture through peasant proprietorship and fruit cultivation and also the establishment of the Imperial Department of Agriculture in Trinidad to assist in this process. Fruit cultivation did not succeed as much as cacao, which enjoyed a booming market until the late 1920s. By 1899 exports of cacao were valued slightly more than those of sugar.

THE ECONOMY AT THE BEGINNING
OF THE TWENTIETH CENTURY

The end of the nineteenth century saw a near collapse of the sugar industry in Trinidad and Tobago as in the West Indies generally. The older methods of sugar refining were less efficient than those used in central factories and, although the first central factory for processing cane had been established in Trinidad in 1872, the general use of these factories was postponed until the twentieth century. The increase in the size of sugar estates and in the frequency of absentee proprietorship also may have contributed to inefficiency. There were forty-two estates in Trinidad in 1866 and only fifty-two in 1896. Further, West Indian cane sugar could not compete in prices or production with cane sugar produced in Cuba, Brazil, or Java (Indonesia). More important, however, for the sugar market was the spectacular increase in the production of European beet sugar during the course of the nineteenth century. By 1895 the total beet sugar production amounted to half the total sugar production in the world. The increase of sugar consumption in Great Britain and the government's desire to provide cheap sugar for British consumers led to increased buying in world markets and a decline in the proportion of imports from the West Indies.

The most important development in the economy was the discovery of oil in southwest Trinidad. The existence of the world's largest pitch lake at La Brea had stimulated explorations for oil, and there had been some use of small quantities since the mid-nineteenth century. But not until 1904 did Great Britain show consistent interest in oil exploration in Trinidad. In 1910 the British government made the historic decision to convert the fueling of ships of the Royal Navy from coal to oil; it became imperative to find oil within the British Empire, which at the time produced only 500,000 tons out of a world production of 28 million tons. The period between 1910 and 1920 saw the largest spurt of registration of oil companies in Trinidad. By 1912 production stood at 486,000 barrels each year and by 1917 at 1.6 million barrels. The first exports of oil were made in 1911 to New York and in 1914 to the British Admiralty. Thereafter oil was a permanent bolster to the revenues of the colony, amounting to 70 percent of the total exports in 1938 and 80 percent in 1965.

The main areas of oil production were Fyzabad, Point Fortin, and Pointe-à-Pierre. In 1913 refineries were established at the two latter ports by United British Oilfields of Trinidad (a Shell subsidiary) and Trinidad Leaseholds (sold to Texaco in 1957). Their refining capacity soon outstripped local production, and there were three other refineries operating as well. Thus almost from the start of its entry into the oil market Trinidad imported crude oil for reexport. Trinidad's share of world oil production was small, but its proportion in British Empire production was very high.

Oil production and the relatively higher wages paid by the industry did have an elevating effect on the economy, but the expatriate ownership of the industry, the leakage of profits out of the colony, and the low royalty payments reinforced the problems of the agrarian sector. The island as a whole benefited but little from the oil industry in the preindependence period. Moreover, the oil industry was capital intensive and mechanized, so that its value as an employer was low. In 1919, for example, only 2,400 people were employed by the oil industry and in 1939 only 13,000. The highest number—20,000—was reached in 1959, after which there was another decline. Agriculture continued to be the major employer in Trinidad. An interesting sidelight into colonial politics is provided by the struggle of the colonial government to retain rights of oil exploration for British-based companies against the gradual and ultimately complete requisition of those rights by United States companies.

CONSTITUTIONAL CHANGES IN THE TWENTIETH CENTURY

The decision to rule Trinidad through crown colony government without elective institutions was made by Great Britain in the context of controversy over the abolition of slavery and the enfranchisement of the non-English and colored majority on Trinidad. By the end of the nineteenth century Trinidad had made the transition through emancipation, and the diverse ethnic elements were adjusting to one another as permanent parts of a small island society (see ch. 4). Many members of this society, especially the white and colored Creoles, concerned about their lack of control over government and taxation and about the failure of the British government to alleviate their economic problems, began to press for reforms of the crown colony system. Until responsible self-government was finally achieved in 1956, there was intermittent pressure on Great Britain from different groups in Trinidad to widen the basis of political participation. Failure of the petitionary methods led to the formation of organizations and then to political parties. Economic crises intensified discontent, and mass labor movements were born in the 1930s.

The British government did not relinquish the absolute power it enjoyed until post-World War II developments spurred it to divest itself of responsibility for dependencies. Governors and commissions of inquiry found the diversity and competition of Trinidad's ethnic groups ample excuse to withhold political concessions or to weight them by giving the governor additional powers to act as balancer. The fact that the Colonial Office was confronted with similar problems and demands in all the small eastern Caribbean islands led it to look for solutions: amalgamation of administration and revenues through some kind of association or federation to include relatively wealthy Trinidad. But through it all the colonial government remained opposed to any real transformation in the established socioeconomic system. Inadequate leadership postponed the emergence of a discernible mass national movement in Trinidad until Eric

Williams seemed to generate one in the mid-1950s. Thus notwithstanding the achievements of men like Cipriani, Uriah Butler, or Albert Gomes, constitutional reforms in Trinidad and the abortive experiment in federation seemed to serve more as instruments for the pursuit of personal ambition and group rivalry than as means for national development. Many of the tensions of the mid-1970s in Trinidad, to say nothing of those of the 1940s and 1950s, were the consequences of attempts by various groups to achieve influence within the restrictions of a crown colony.

The earliest organized movement to amend the crown colony system in Trinidad was that of the Legislative Reform Committee, active during the 1880s and 1890s. It drew its membership from property owners and professionals—Creole, English, and colored. They pleaded for the inclusion of elected members on the Legislative Council but suggested a franchise restricted to property owners of mature age, financial substance, and fluency in English. At the time the Legislative Council consisted of twenty-one members—ten official and bound to support the governor and eleven unofficial but more or less obliged to support the governor to sustain their nomination; the governor himself had an original as well as a casting vote. Despite the limited nature of their demands, proposals of the reform committee were turned down by the Royal Commission of Inquiry of 1897 and the Colonial Office.

A more lively controversy took place at the turn of the century between the government and the Port-of-Spain city council over matters of financial grants and the raising of water rates. The conflict was referred to the British colonial secretary, who suggested that an elected municipal council with an official mayor and an annnually approved budget might be an efficient solution to the problem. The conflict between city and government continued and was at least as responsible for the water riots of 1903 as the admitted eccentricities of the water supply system and the decision to meter water usage. A pioneering if limited role in these developments was also played by the Trinidad Workingmen's Association (TWA), founded in 1897. It campaigned for elective institutions and an end to Indian indenture, which depressed local wages, and it made the first successful effort to organize Negro workers.

World War I, although it elicited a spurt of patriotism and financial donations to the British Empire, assisted the movement toward self-government and self-consciousness. The West India Regiment's wartime duty consisted for the most part of noncombat labor functions in the Middle East. One officer of the regiment, Captain Cipriani, found in himself a talent for organization, born of his sympathy for the discrimination his Negro soldiers often experienced. He never lost that sympathy or talent. The end of the war was marked by a rise in prices, the disgruntlement of ex-servicemen, and a rash of labor strikes and riots all over the British Caribbean, along with increased agitation for representative government. The TWA was revitalized in Trinidad under the leadership of Cipriani, and between 1919 and 1934 it became the new mass-based force in politics.

The Colonial Office responded to the postwar disturbances by sending the parliamentary under secretary for the colonies, Major E. F. L. Wood (later Lord Halifax), on a tour of inquiry in the West Indies. The Wood Report of 1921 was an epoch-making document, although cautious in its recommendations. Wood favored a modicum of political reform so as to elicit public opinion and reinforce confidence in the stability of the government. At the same time he saw no reason for an immediate grant of self-government in a colony with a heterogeneous population and no disinterested representative leisured class (except the British officials). Accordingly Wood recommended an increase in the membership of the Legislative Council to include seven unofficial members elected on a restricted franchise, six nominated unofficial members free to form a majority with the elected unofficial members on issues not of great substance, and twelve elected official members who with the governor would guarantee the government's power to function. The council was so constituted between 1929 and 1941. Wood rejected the demands made by the East Indian National Congress in Trinidad to base representation on communal electorates, because he saw communal electorates as a disintegrative force in an emerging society.

Elections were held in 1925 on the basis of the Wood reforms. They were exciting only in Port-of-Spain: there Cipriani competed for votes against a wealthy businessman and won about 57 percent of those cast. Of an island registration of 21,794 voters, only 6,832 actually cast their votes. Government continued in its usual way of undynamic, benevolent autocracy. The main events of the 1920s were the opening of the Imperial College of Tropical Agriculture in 1924, which drew students and government agricultural officers from all over the West Indies and West Africa, and the signing of reciprocal trade agreements between Canada and the West Indian colonies collectively in 1920 and 1925. The overall economy of Trinidad benefited from both measures and from increased production of cacao and petroleum. In official records of the time frequent reference was made to Trinidad's relative prosperity and obligation to assist poorer West Indian colonies. The worldwide economic depression beginning in 1929 affected Trinidad disastrously, but the British governmen had no palliatives to offer.

The growth of national consciousness in Trinidad between the two wars was mainly the achievement of Cipriani. Eight times mayor of Port-of-Spain, an indefatigable speaker in the Legislative Council, and outspoken in his criticisms of the government, Cipriani claimed to represent the "unwashed and unsoaped barefooted men." His constantly reiterated slogan was "agitate, educate, confederate" because he saw clearly that without unity, education, and consistent pressure the West Indian masses were doomed to be ignored. He became a hero of the masses at a time when his European descent was an asset not shared by his contemporary mass leader in Jamaica, Marcus Garvey. Cipriani's achievements were many. He built up the TWA into an organization with forty-two affiliated sections in Trinidad and thirteen in Tobago, claiming a total membership of 130,000 in 1934. It was thus a major instrument of unionization and politicization of workers.

Cipriani's failures were partly the consequence of the age in which he grew up. His outstanding characteristic—and failing—was his belief in the British Empire and in the honor of the English gentleman and the British Labour Party. Many of Cipriani's speeches contained long quotations from the writings and speeches of J. Ramsay MacDonald, Labour Party leader and prime minister of Great Britain from 1929 to 1935. Cipriani modeled his TWA and Trinidad Labour Party on British prototypes and pressed for legislative reform of labor laws and trade unions in conformity with those in force in Great Britain. He claimed the right of self-government because West Indians were not "primitive Africans" but the equals of Englishmen, and he could never understand why the British labor governments did not fulfill their anti-imperialist platforms formulated while they were in opposition.

Cipriani was able to make the racial leap of identifying with and mobilizing the Negro, but he could not do so with the Indian. For the most part he relied on his Young India Party followers to reach the plantation Indians for him, apparently without his making a personal appeal. The membership of the TWA and early trade unions included few Indians. The fault lay not only in Cipriani's personality but in the character of the Indian community at the time. Still isolated on the plantations or preoccupied with narrow communal and familial concerns and problems of acquiring wealth and property, the Indians remained indifferent to Cipriani's campaign for self-government and federation. There were, of course, isolated exceptions, among them one of the ablest men of his generation, Adrian Cola Rienzi, who unionized the plantation workers in the mid-1930s and played a crucial role in the postriot negotiations of 1937. But Cipriani mistrusted his able lieutenant because he found his ideas too radical.

Therein lay the final shortcoming of Cipriani's movement: its radical verbalizations extended only to the political realm and left untouched the economic base of the colonial system. Cipriani was a leader and a patriot but not a political thinker who could organize a mass movement into a revolutionary one. By 1935 the TWA was in the process of disintegration, hastened by the economic troubles of the time and Cipriani's apparent capitulation to the established forces on the matter of minimum wages. He was too old to seize the opportunities offered by the mass upheaval of the 1936–37 period but died in 1945 a universally respected man.

Cipriani also made the Legislative Council something more than a rubber stamp. It was on the council that he led the campaign for compulsory education, championed the local teachers, opposed all forms of racial discrimination—as in admissions to the Imperial College of

Tropical Agriculture—and argued for increased employment of locals over foreigners. As mayor of Port-of-Spain he followed this by purchasing the foreign-owned electric company and by pressing for payment of higher royalties from foreign oil companies. In the Legislative Council, as in the mayor's office, Cipriani faced the full opposition of the colonial system, which meant officialdom in alliance with the vested property interests and the chambers of commerce. Sometimes accused of being a Bolshevik, Cipriani was warned not to misuse his privilege of free speech in council and was probably fortunate not to have been put under restraint.

Cipriani used every vehicle to carry out his campaign for raising national consciousness. One of them was the *Socialist,* a paper of the Trinidad Labour Party, into which the TWA was converted in 1934. Another was the West Indian Conference of 1932, which was in Dominica and attracted an eager band of nationalists from the eastern Caribbean islands. They, like Cipriani, called for self-government as the right of an educated, civilized, and united West Indian nation. The movement, like Cipriani's base of support, was eroded by developments of the 1930s favoring a more radical approach.

THE DISTURBANCES OF 1936: CAUSES AND CONSEQUENCES

Many elements of strain in Trinidad reached a breaking point in the mid-1930s. The sugar crisis, the cocoa crisis, and the worldwide depression exposed the fragile base on the island's economy. The subsequent disturbances and social unrest, however, took place when Great Britain and its colonies were climbing out of the depression, because at that time the injustice of the economic system was most obvious. As subsequent inquiries revealed, Tate and Lyle Company, which owned four of the five large sugar estates operating in Trinidad, was able to pay shareholder dividends ranging from 5.5 to 7.5 percent by dint of rigid economies at the expense of wages and the stabilization of prices through allocation of production quotas made by the International Sugar Conference of 1937. Similarly, from 1935 to 1936 oil profits jumped, and dividends were paid in London amounting to 30 percent of those profits although the workers in the oil fields were offered a two-cents-an-hour increase in wages with no fringe benefits when they demanded a living wage. Even the governor, Murchisson Fletcher, expressed indignation at the behavior of commercial companies and their lack of contribution to the island economy—for which frankness he was soon transferred.

Economic injustice was aggravated by the race factor. The 1930s saw an increase in the number of expatriate officials and commercial employees chosen in preference to locally born candidates. West Indian nationalism was fed by the resentment of educated coloreds who were passed over for whites. Many of these foreigners had worked in South

Africa, where they had acquired habits of dealing with Negroes that the West Indians were not accustomed to and would not tolerate; this was particularly true in the oil fields and refineries, where the introduction of segregated facilities aroused ire. The slow but distinct movement of Indians into urban industry and oil proved another source of racial tension. The invasion of Ethiopia by Italy and Great Britain's ineffective diplomacy during the crisis had a tremendous emotional impact in the West Indies, whose inhabitants were beginning to be proud of their African heritage. The racial undertones to the Trinidad disturbances were brushed over lightly by the Forster Commission's report of inquiry in 1937 but were not underestimated by the more broadly based and more eminent Moyne Commission in 1938 and 1939. Strikes were widespread, and many incidents that took place during the strikes were expressions of racial aggressiveness normally suppressed or channeled into the subtle hostilities so tellingly described by the Trinidadian author C. L. R. James in his novel *Minty Alley*.

The oil workers' strike was led by Uriah Butler, whom the Forster Commission depicted as a "a fanatical negro." He was born in Grenada about 1891 and became a follower of Cipriani during World War I. Attracted to Trinidad by employment in the oil fields, Butler quickly became involved in politics and displayed the attributes of a born political agitator. He was of the masses and could speak in their idiom and communicate his sense of divine mission. He applied a kind of evangelical zeal to the emancipation of the workers, and he soon cut loose from Cipriani, whose "white liberalism" he found ineffective.

Between 1935 and 1937 Butler rallied the oil workers to his banner and founded the British Empire Workers and Citizens Home Rule Party in 1936. Butler fulfilled a historical purpose in being the one man who could articulate the wishes of the workers and offer them alternatives for action while keeping their trust. He had often been accused of using racial issues to displace Cipriani as a national leader, but in fact Cipriani at the time was not a spokesman for the workers' demands. Since the employers refused to make acceptable concessions to the workers and the governor and acting colonial secretary thought negotiation was morally and politically imperative, Butler and his associate Rienzi became the channels of communication between the government and the workers after the strike had degenerated into riots.

Another cause for the disturbances was the lack of mechanisms for collective bargaining or labor-management dialogue, so that grievances accumulated until an explosion point was reached. Without unions workers were isolated and afraid to voice complaints. The Colonial Office had granted permission to establish an industrial court in 1920, but this was never appointed. Similarly, although the imperial government, as a consequence of its membership in the International Labor Organization, circulated model legislation for minimum wages and employer-employee relations and suggested the formation of labor departments, the Trinidad government did not act on the recommendations. Relations between management and labor were worst in the oil and sugar industries, coffee and cacao being somewhat insulated from the events of 1937. Unionization of labor was made more difficult by virtue of the fact that until 1943 no laws protected the right of peaceful picketing or gave unions immunity from tort action.

The man mainly responsible for the formation of the two most powerful unions on the island was Rienzi. With Governor Fletcher's blessings Rienzi launched the Oilfield Workers Trade Union, joined by 7,000 out of 9,000 workers, and then the All Trinidad Sugar Estates and Factory Workers Trade Union. But only 2,000 out of approximately 34,000 workers in the sugar industry, mostly Indian, joined the union, demonstrating once again the difficulties of mobilizing the Indian plantation workers or forming a united front on a class and economic issue, even under Indian leadership. (The incongruity of Rienzi's Brahman caste and his left-wing ideas may have made him suspect to more orthodox Indians.)

Absence of worker-management communications was one symptom of the general lack of representative institutions in the colony. Members of the Legislative Council themselves recognized their ineffective role as a crown colony government. Governors and officials fulfilled both ceremonial and executive functions but, although supposed to act as trustees for the whole colony—according to the post-World War I doctrines common around the British Empire—usually were mindful of the needs only of the chambers of commerce and the imperial government. Fletcher took his function as trustee more seriously and publicly chided the employers for their consistent insensitivity that led to the "purge" of those held responsible for the disturbances. Although Fletcher was speedily removed from Trinidad, a powerful commission also recommended a more social service-oriented welfare policy.

The disturbances in the West Indies shook the British government to the extent that in 1938 a commission of inquiry chaired by Lord Moyne and containing three vocal members of the British Labour Party was sent out. Despite efforts to couch its comments in language that would not adversely affect Great Britain's war support efforts in the colonies, the Moyne Commission's report was one of the most cogent criticisms of the colonial system in the West Indies. It was supplemented by other nonofficial warnings. The report itself was not made public until after the war, but some of its recommendations were put into effect in 1940, mainly through the office of the comptroller of development and welfare set up for the British Caribbean and associated with the Anglo-American Caribbean Commission during and after the war. As the name implies, these recommendations were of an economic and social nature.

The Moyne Commission was cautious in suggesting constitutional change for Trinidad. It was unwilling to concede the applicability of self-government, but it proposed making the system more representative by permitting an increased number of elected members in the Legislative Council and the inclusion of some of them on official committees and the governor's executive council. The commission also recommended the introduction of adult suffrage in the undefined future. Ambiguity also surrounded the Moyne Commission's suggestions about federating the British West Indies; they found the idea attractive and desirable but doubted its immediate practicability.

Neither conservatives nor radicals in Trinidad were satisfied with the recommendations; their implementation became the occasion for heated debate. In April 1941 constitutional change was effected by increasing the number of unofficial elected members on the Legislative Council from seven to nine and reducing the official membership from twelve to four and the governor's vote to one. Six nominated unofficial members remained on the council. On the executive council as well there was a majority of unofficial members, though the governor retained ultimate authority and veto power.

The issue of adult franchise raised much controversy, as seen in the debates of a franchise committee between 1941 and 1944. Some wanted income or literacy qualifications. The question of a literacy test divided even those who advocated adult franchise, and the Indians saw a language requirement for English directed purely against themselves. But the Indians were not united on the franchise issue either; such young radicals as Rienzi supported the idea of universal suffrage, whereas others vigorously opposed it for fear of being outvoted by a Negro majority on the island. The matter was referred to the Colonial Office, which recommended a wide basis of suffrage. The 1946 elections were held under universal adult suffrage.

The outbreak of World War II and, more important, the Anglo-American Lend Lease Agreement of 1940 brought tremendous changes to Trinidad. The lease of the deepwater harbor at Chaguaramas Bay brought many American and Canadian military personnel and their traditions of racial interaction. It also led to a spate of construction works, which employed thousands of workers at higher wages than in the past and left such lasting contributions as the north coast road to Maracas. American money and technical knowledge flowed into the colony, but so did ample opportunities for organized vice. The well-known calypso "Rum and Coca Cola," referring to mother and daughter both working for "the Yankee dollar," immortalized these facts. Oil exports expanded as the Trinidad refineries imported increased amounts of foreign crude for reexport. Something of a boom atmosphere prevailed on the island for the duration of the war. In 1945 the steel band was born and, like Carnival and the Muslim festival Hosein, it soon became incorporated into the national culture (see ch. 5; ch. 6).

POSTWAR CHANGES

The main issues before Trinidad between 1946 and 1956 were the advance toward responsible self-government and incorporation in a West Indies federation. The decisions on both issues were made by the British government with only some references to attitudes within Trinidad. Internal politics were characterized by a high degree of public participation, an absence of organized political parties—hence a fluidity of leadership—and a coalescence of the Indians into a self-aware group with its own leadership. Under the conditions of adult suffrage, candidates with radical programs gained success.

With the wider consciousness brought by the war and the Caribbean Labour Congress-sponsored movement for a self-governing federation, a feeling for the West Indies as a community grew concurrently with nationalism. Thus the party with the most radical platform fielding candidates in the 1946 election was the West Indian National Party (WINP), founded in 1943 by David Pittin of San Fernando. The WINP called for redistribution of land, nationalization of oil and other extractive industries, general diversification of the economy, and free education and medical care. The WINP did not suggest how its welfare program would be financed. For the elections of 1946 it joined the United Front, led by Jack Kelshall, which capitalized on the name of Cipriani. Contrary to expectations, all trade unions did not join the United Front. Butler spurned efforts to attract him to the party and led his own party.

The 1946 elections were fought by individuals rather than parties. Labels were accepted for expediency, but race and the efficacy of campaign managers persuaded more voters than issues did. The United Front seated only three candidates, but one of them, Gomes, won a seat in Port-of-Spain against Butler, whose party had more overall success.

Albert Gomes came into politics in the 1930s, was active in the trade union movement, and represented himself as a logical successor to Cipriani, whose seat he won in 1946. Of Portuguese descent, Gomes had the advantage of belonging to what the sociologist Ivar Oxaal calls the "middle minorities," between Negro and Indian and therefore acceptable to all (see ch. 4). His political tactics, too, straddled the conservative and radical configurations that soon developed. After the constitutional changes in 1950, Gomes was chief minister in all but name. He tried to function as a mediator between capital and labor, forcing both to make concessions before issues came to a head. He tried to retain imperial protection for the staple exports of Trinidad and to diversify the economy by giving generous tax exemptions to prospective investors. Although criticized for these allegedly colonialist leanings, the semiautonomous government of Trinidad had little choice; it lacked the power to transform the economic base of the colony, especially as long as real power was retained by London and federation was in preparation. Subsequent governments have not acted very differently.

Gomes' irrepressible personality, oratorical skills, and enormous girth made him a well-known figure throughout the West Indies. But he was also associated with the chaotic, selfish, capricious politics of the 1950s, in

72

which "bossism" and corruption were widespread and integrity, zeal, and unity little in evidence. Campaigns were conducted along personal, almost magical lines as described by V. S. Naipaul in *The Mystic Masseur*. Gomes lost the election of 1956 and was eventually forced to leave the country and live in comparative obscurity in London after Williams came to power.

Constitutional reform in Trinidad was debated at various times after 1946. Tutelary democracy and semiresponsible form of ministerial government were introduced after 1950, but the grant of full self-government was retarded because of the absence of at least one or two strong national political parties—considered a prerequisite for the functioning of a cabinet system. Political personalities took sides in the debate along some predictable lines: conservatives asking for gradual changes as in the recommendations of the majority report of the Constitutional Reform Committee of 1946 and radicals demanding more genuinely representative and democratic institutions.

In addition Indians formed associations and became another recognizable group with a separate point of view on reform, that of an ethnic minority constituting 36 percent of the population but fearing for their cultural and political survival in a mass democracy. The new political activism of Indians was slightly influenced by the successful independence struggle in India but more directly reflective of their altered economic position in Trinidad. Since the 1930s Indians had been moving up into business and professional status by acquiring property and education. The Indian drive for property and trade has been a subject of speculation in Trinidad and has been brilliantly portrayed in Naipaul's *A House for Mr. Biswas*. The political effect of this socioeconomic movement was to give influential Indians attitudes similar to those of the commercial classes. At the same time the formation of the East Indian National Congress and the activities of such socioreligious associations as the Santan Dharma Maha Sabha, which tried to import teachers and visitors from India, tended to strengthen the cultural links of the community with the Indian subcontinent.

During the early 1950s this vitalization of the Indians was given an organizational character through the leadership of Bhadse S. Maraj, whose wealth went largely into such philanthropic endeavors as the founding of schools for Indians. In this period for the first time Indians won the right to have their religious marriages—Hindu and Muslim—recognized as legal and to have their dead cremated according to Hindu rites. In the past, censuses had reported a high rate of illegitimacy among Indians simply because no unregistered marriage was considered legal for inheritance purposes. Maraj's influence soon converted the sugar belt into an ethnic voting block. Within the Legislative Council Ranjit Kumar, born in India, was allied with the radicals on economic issues and sought to protect the future of Indians as a minority community by arguing against literacy qualifications in English and suggesting communal representation. Indians were commonly believed to oppose the idea of federation because their ethnic proportion would be reduced. Actually their views were more complex and not uniform, hinging on economic policies and on unlimited immigration as well as the constitutional and ethnic factors of federation.

Because of the multiplicity of political parties and imminence of federation, constitutional reform was postponed in 1955. At that time the Indians were the best organized group on the island, and non-Indians disliked the idea of the coming to power of the largely East Indian People's Democratic Party (PDP). Elections were scheduled for 1956.

THE RISE TO POWER OF ERIC WILLIAMS

The years 1955 and 1956 form a watershed in Trinidad. They saw the rise of a new kind of political leader and a new kind of political party that made national education and unity their goal. The new leader was Eric Williams, who had an impressive academic record and direct experience with the Caribbean Commission. The new party was the People's National Movement (PNM), which grew out of the Political Education Group and the Teachers Economic and Cultural Association. Thus the core of the new movement was the educated and professional colored class.

Williams gives in his autobiography *Inward Hunger* an account of what went into the making of a prime minister. Besides his ambition, determination, and capacity for long and concentrated work, perhaps the most pertinent aspect of his personal development was the recurrent feeling of being slighted for racial or ideological reasons. This probably contributed to his intense achievement orientation and desire for recognition, first through scholarship and then through politics. Williams' career at Oxford, at Howard University, and in the Caribbean Commission has been well documented. In 1955 he resigned his research position with the commission. It had brought him valuable knowledge of the area, but he was convinced that the organization was an imperialist agency. He returned to Trinidad and, through the sponsorship of the Political Education Group, launched a series of lectures designed to educate the public on Negro history in the Caribbean and on other political and economic issues. Using public libraries and the public square in Port-of-Spain as his platform, Williams created what came to be called the university of Woodford Square.

His disclosures on slavery, capitalism, and colonialism had a profound influence on his mass audience. Although his constitutional and economic ideas were moderate, his rhetoric was revolutionary. His manner was dry and pedagogic, but his organization was skillful, and he soon became a mass hero. Williams revealed the hardships of Indian indenture, and he sympathized with the Indians' urge to become educated and to participate; he also stood for multiethnic nationalism internally and third world solidarity externally, but he attacked the PDP at every opportunity, accusing it of being the mouthpiece of communal Hindu interests.

During the elections of 1956 the major issues were given an airing: education through denominational or government schools, the role of the press, family planning, morality in public life, and the position of ethnic groups in society. The PNM claimed that there was nothing inherently lacking in Trinidad that would preclude the creation of a national movement, and it stood for the multiethnic ideal. It tried to adhere to this ideal in its choice of candidates and to a certain extent succeeded in attracting some white Creoles and non-Hindu Indian members to its core of colored and Negro professionals. Yet racial violence underlay the election campaign. At the same time all the established interests of business, the press, and the Roman Catholic Church combined in opposition to the PNM and thereby enhanced its mass appeal and national character.

In the election of September 1956 Trinidad and Tobago placed a political party—the PNM—in the Legislative Council with a majority of elected seats (thirteen out of twenty-four). The party won 39 percent of the vote, with an especially good showing in the urban areas. The PDP won only five seats and the Trinidad Labour Party two. The governor, on instructions from London, followed this victory by the innovative step of filling the nominated seats from those acceptable to the majority party rather than from representatives of special interests, thus increasing the working majority of the elected element. Between 1956 and 1962 the PNM consolidated its hold, and the opposition rallied behind the Democratic Labour Party (DLP), which contained several groups, including the PDP. Although this crystallization of independent politics into a two-party system seemed desirable, their cleavage along ethnic lines augured ill for the future (see ch. 7).

Great Britain had advocated a federation of the British West Indies after the war, and in 1947 a conference was held at Montego Bay, Jamaica, to enable representatives of the various colonies to discuss the subject. Trinidad's representative, Gomes, stood for a self-governing federation. The committee set up to draft a detailed plan of federation presented its report in 1949, and it was debated in the colonial legislatures for another two years. Many of the negative responses to the draft plans for federation arose from the very limited nature of its constitutional proposals, violating the major motivation for federation among West Indians: independence. With some reservations, the Trinidad legislature voted in favor of joining the federation. Thereafter a series of committee reports, conferences, and draft plans attempted to accommodate the various views prevailing among the colonies and the imperial government on the subject of federation in practice.

Trinidad and Tobago was especially affected by some of the federal proposals made during the planning stage. One was freedom of movement among the territories, which Trinidad opposed because it had consistently faced an influx from other West Indian islands since the development of the oil industry. The other was the choice of a capital; the relevant committee first disqualified Trinidad because of the alleged corruption in its public life and the "disturbing element" of the Indian population and then suggested Chaguaramas Bay. Since that was an American base and negotiations for its release were protracted and acrimonious, Port-of-Spain became the temporary and only capital of the federation. The third issue arose after the federation had been formed and concerned whether it should be a highly centralized agency for regional economic change or a decentralized administrative entity. Views on this subject were polarized between Williams' advocacy of the former, put forth in his *Economics of Nationhood,* and Jamaica's preference for the latter.

Differences of opinion among West Indian leaders were not softened by ease of personal communication. On the contrary, their mutual regard was eroded by their inability to deal with each other as equals and colleagues and their necessary dependence on London. Moreover, each one was preoccupied with building his own political base and resolving problems of internal administration. In Trinidad the first federal elections of 1958 were a defeat for Williams and a victory for the DLP. The DLP, however, had too many fissiparous tendencies to cope successfully with the PNM within Trinidad. In 1961 it chose a new leader, Rudranath Capildeo, in the hope of projecting a wider appeal, but neither his personality nor his program was equal to the task. Williams and the PNM continued to consolidate their hold through programs of economic development, changes in constituencies, and exploitation of the emotionally charged issue of winning back Chaguaramas from the Americans.

Relations between Trinidad and the other federal governments continued to deteriorate. When Jamaica opted out of the federation in 1961, a last-minute effort was made to persuade Trinidad to save the federation, if necessary by creating a united state with the smaller eastern Caribbean islands. Williams declared that "ten minus one is nothing" and guaranteed the breakup of the West Indies federation. In August 1962 Trinidad and Tobago was granted independence.

CHAPTER 4

SOCIAL SYSTEM

Despite party slogans, national mottoes, and middle- and upper-class ideology proclaiming the contrary, Trinidadians are neither racially nor culturally a unified people. Their ancestors came from several continents and represented many ethnic backgrounds whose institutions, values, and stratification systems were disparate, if not genuinely conflicting, and whose impact had not been erased by 1975. Moreover, the colonial experience, as well as that of slavery and indentureship, left deep marks on the society and its value systems; as a consequence, white—particularly British—values and traditions are elevated, and Negro and East Indian modes are deprecated.

Nevertheless some observers felt that by 1975 distinct trends toward greater and more equal interaction between distinct groups could be discerned. This was perceived as a transitional phase between the minimal interaction of the past and truly interethnic society heralded by many prominent Trinidadians. Regardless of the kind of interaction, the perceptible change over previous patterns, and the rate of this change, it was apparent that the society was not static but dynamic and one in which the potential for change was present.

Three groups have had the largest impact on the society and have generally shaped its character: Negroes—descendants of African slaves, whites—descendants of European colonials, and East Indians—descendants of indentured servants from the Indian subcontinent. Negroes and whites, whose arrival predated that of the East Indians, together formed what in Trinidad and Tobago was termed a Creole society, in which Negroes constituted a numerical majority but whites dominated politically, economically, and socially. The children of their union—called colored (see Glossary) or mixed (see Glossary)—fell in the middle and were left to adapt to the white-dominated society as best they could. The later arriving East Indians and smaller numbers of Chinese, Portuguese, and Middle Easterners were never accepted into this Creole society, a reflection both of the mistrust and opposition of the established population and of their own desire to preserve a sense of cultural distinctiveness.

In 1970 about one-half of the population was Creole, that is, fell within the census racial categories of white, Negro, or mixed; and the other half was non-Creole, the overwhelming majority being East Indian. The differences between Creoles and non-Creoles are so great that many observers say they indicate distinct societies with unique cultural institutions. Moreover, the numerous groups within the Creole and non-Creole frameworks are categorized according to their perceived "race"—in Trinidad both a biological and a social concept. The criteria that designate race are based on notions of skin color, ethnicity (country or continent of origin), religious belief, and wealth.

In general, interethnic relations have been characterized by want of knowledge and lack of communication. Even though Trinidadians of all ethnic backgrounds may live near each other and occasionally attend each other's festivals, such physical proximity has not engendered intermarriage or even interaction to any great degree. Stereotyping, diversity among cultural backgrounds, occupational segregation according to the ethnic group, and racial and religious endogamy have helped to preserve social distance and prejudice.

For Creoles, color plays a very important part in determining racial categorization and social status. Nevertheless, physical aspects are only a part—if the most vital part—of the criteria. Nonphysical attributes such as education, wealth, job, ancestry, and adherence to contemporary European norms and patterns of "correct" English speech may enhance or temper the relative importance of one's color. Generally the interplay of these criteria has determined the historical patterns of power and privilege, although since independence dark-skinned Trinidadians have generally taken over the political sphere from lighter skinned European expatriates and Creoles. The shift of political power has primarily benefited the Negro middle class with respect to jobs and material possessions. Light-skinned Creoles, however, continue to dominate the business community and the economic system of the country and, in the social realm, values, norms, and institutions remained essentially unchanged.

Patterns of ethnic concentration persist. Settlement patterns reveal some mixing of Creole and non-Creole groups, but many residential areas are predominantly Negro, white, or East Indian. Negroes are concentrated in industrial urban areas in and around Port-of-Spain, San Fernando, Arima, and Pitch Lake and the oil fields in the southwest. East Indians provide the bulk of the rural agricultural labor, especially in the sugar belt in the west. Other non-Creole groups are generally urban. Whites and colored are concentrated in urban areas; groups of French descent live in the north. In Tobago the bulk of the population is Negro.

The greatest intercultural differences are perceived and preserved in the institutions of family, religious life, and language. The family acts as the key agent of socialization. Creoles, on the one hand, stress monogamy, legal marriage, and the nuclear family as the ideal approaching contemporary Europe, but only a small percentage—those in the middle and upper classes—ever approximate this ideal. Lower class Negro Creoles generally follow the legacy of slavery: casual mating patterns that may or may not end in formal matrimony, high rates of illegitimacy, and a mother-centered family. East Indians, on the other hand, retain the ideal of the patrilineal extended family. Although it has been altered and eroded by the increasing independence of children and women, it retains its essential flavor and characterizes most social intercourse.

Religious life also differs between Creoles and non-Creoles, as well as within these groups. The basic breakdown is Christian and non-Christian, Roman Catholicism and Anglicanism predominating in the former category and Hinduism and Islam (to a lesser extent) in the latter. Upper and middle-class Trinidadians adhere strictly to European-influenced Christianity, the middle class preserving a more devout and fundamentalist attitude. The lower class usually belongs to either the Roman Catholic or the Shouter church—an evangelical, emotional version of the Baptist Church, with some African elements. Members of the lower class may adhere simultaneously to one of the sects of African origin: Nigerian-influenced Shango or Dahomean-influenced Rada. Shango has a much larger following. Both incorporate a pantheon of African deities, many of whom are identified with Christian saints, and both place great importance on possession and emotional and musical participation in services. Obeah is a form of black magic practiced among the lower class of all beliefs and races.

Even for the several thousand East Indian Christians and a small Muslim community, Hinduism is the crux of Indian identity. It represents a heritage, a way of life, and a feeling of cultural superiority. Nevertheless, it is a much more standardized and simpler faith in Trinidad than in India and lacks some of its important societal correlates, such as the caste system. Moreover, in order to compete with Christian missionaries, Hindu holy men gradually changed their format, serving the sick and having weekend services. Thus although Hinduism has retained some symbolic differences, it has come to resemble Christiantity in a number of functional aspects.

Trinidadian use of English ranges from the Creole of the lower class to the standardized Trinidad English of the middle and upper classes. Colloquial Trinidad English evinces many elements of the other colonial languages, French and Spanish, as well as some Africanisms. In addition French or Spanish Creole is also spoken in some isolated areas. Some East Indians still speak an Indic language, but its usage is decreasing in favor of English. The language most commonly spoken by older East Indians is Hindustani.

CULTURE, CLASS, AND COLOR

By the middle of the nineteenth century the bases of Creole society had been formed. Successive waves of European colonization by Spanish, French, and English assured light-skinned people the elite status accompanying centuries of economic and political domination and the social and cultural prestige of the plantation owner. The lowest rungs on the social ladder were reserved for African slaves and their freed descendants. Thus color, class, and culture converged to elevate whites, debase Negroes, and make upward mobility possible only for those of mixed ancestry willing to forget their African heritage and adopt European manners and education.

Indentured labor—mostly East Indian but some Chinese—arrived after the bases of the Creole society had been established. Different values, languages, religious beliefs and practices, and family patterns were held by Creoles and non-Creoles, making communication and intermarriage difficult and assimilation almost impossible. This was heightened by the fact that the East Indians and Chinese resisted assimilation into the Creole complex, which they considered inferior to their own cultural heritages. In the late nineteenth and early twentieth centuries Middle Easterners and Portuguese also came in and were assimilated into the Creole complex to varying degrees.

By the mid-1970s Trinidad had become a microcosm of the world's races. Social scientists trying to grapple with this enormously complex yet tiny society found it difficult to interpret the position and cohesiveness of the various groups within the society and to divide and delineate the numerous groups present (see fig. 3).

The position of various groups vis-à-vis the society as a whole and the degree to which the society itself can be considered to be integrated are still matters of considerable debate. One school, including such scholars as the Trinidadian sociologist Lloyd Braithwaite, adheres to a consensualist approach, holding that the internal cultural differences are fairly superficial and the national institutions pervasive. It sees the society as heterogeneous but not necessarily plural, that is, composed of essentially separate sections.

The other school adheres to a pluralist approach, that the concept of the society is essentially that of separate cultural systems existing under one government. The level of integration is low. Pluralists emphasize institutional and organizational differences, intergroup conflict, coercion from above, and class rivalries. The chief proponent of this school of thought has been a Jamaican, Michael G. Smith, who defines cultural pluralism as a "condition in which two or more different cultural traditions characterize the population of a given society."

According to this theory the Trinidadian government and the economic system alone serve to keep the social order intact. The political system defines and delimits interaction between the various groups and regulates the chances for conflict and integration. The economic system does roughly the same thing. It encompasses the entire society, dividing labor and meeting out rewards according to ethnic background and cultural affiliation.

In Smith's view cultural pluralism exists not only between Creoles and non-Creoles but within the Creole complex as well, dividing those who follow European-based institutions from those following patterns estab-

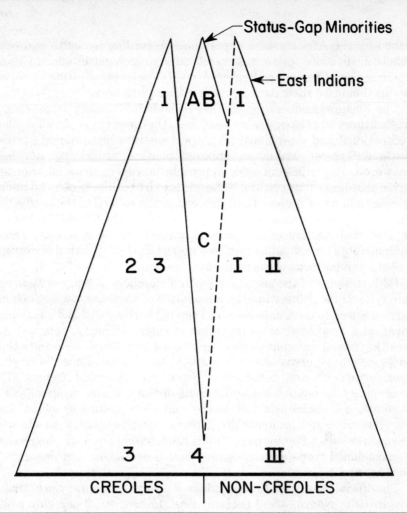

Status-Gap Minorities

East Indians

CREOLES | NON-CREOLES

MAJOR DISTINCTIONS		
CREOLES	NON-CREOLES	
	East Indians	Status-Gap Minorities
1 Whites	I Christian converts	A Chinese
2 Colored (mixed)	II Muslims	B Portuguese
3 Negroes	III Hindus	C Middle Easterners
	4 Douglas	

Note--Position of numbers in the pyramid should not be taken as exclusive relative position of each group in the society but as a general indication of stratification trends.

Source: Based on information from Ivar Oxaal, *Black Intellectuals Come to Power*, Cambridge, Massachusetts, 1968.

Figure 3. Trinidad and Tobago, Trinidadian Social and Ethnic Structure in the Mid-1970s

lished by the African slave experience. According to Smith and other scholars, divisions follow a hierarchical arrangement in which Creoles dominate non-Creoles and lighter skinned Creoles manifesting European norms dominate their darker, more African brothers.

The disagreement as to whether Trinidadian society is consensual (institutions are basically similar but the society is divided along occupational and class lines) or plural (separate institutional systems jostle for power within an imposed political order) has not been answered. Regardless of basic approach, however, all social scientists agree that important cultural differences exist both between and among Creoles and non-Creoles. There is a consensus as well to the notion that the social system works to the advantage of the light-skinned Creole and to the disadvantage of his darker skinned Creole and East Indian compatriots through education, job opportunities, wealth distribution, values, and patterns of social interaction.

Both students of the social system and members of it agree upon certain criteria for delineating the boundaries of various groups. Such criteria are used to designate race, in Trinidad both a social and a biological term, and are based on perceptions of color, ethnicity, religion, and wealth. Official designation has been based largely on color and ethnic background, whereas social scientists and Trinidadians themselves consider wealth and social class important additional factors. This discrepancy accounts for the different definitions and groupings. For example, one social scientist in the mid-1960s distinguished at least thirteen ethnic groups: five white (foreign whites or *békés*, local whites or "French creoles," Portuguese, Middle Easterners, and Spanish-speaking Venezuelans); three each of colored and East Indian; and one each of Chinese and Negro.

The official census has condensed these groupings from seven in 1960 to five in 1970: Negro, 42.83 percent; East Indian, 40.12 percent; white, about 2.0 percent; Chinese, 0.86 percent; and mixed, 14.17 percent. Another category, other races, includes the few Carib Indians on the island. These, along with the Chinese, East Indians, Portuguese, Middle Easterners, Jews, and Spanish-speaking Latin Americans, fall into the non-Creole society, although to differing degrees. Some Portuguese, for example, may be considered Creoles if they are married to Creoles or possess a number of other Creole traits. Whites, Negroes, and colored (those of mixed white and Negro ancestry) are considered Creoles. Those groups of East Indian or Chinese and Negro mix may be classified as either Creoles or non-Creoles, depending upon family or reference group.

Between Creoles and non-Creoles ethnicity and religious differences are acutely acknowledged; Creoles, regardless of their relative whiteness, feel superior to non-Creoles. If economic and educational factors are held in equilibrium, the dark-skinned Creole will generally rank higher than his lighter skinned East Indian compatriot. Moreover,

Christian East Indians find easier acceptance and gain higher social standing among Creoles than do Hindu and Muslim East Indians.

Creoles

Among Creoles pigment is a major diagnostic feature of color, and color is among the most important criteria for distinguishing status. Light skin, especially in combination with European features and straight hair, is the most favored physical appearance, whereas very dark skin, African features, and kinky hair are deprecated. Such feelings influence one's choice of associates and marriage partner. They also shape one's self-perception and continue to overshadow national mottoes and models of racial egalitarianism. Moreover, color consciousness is pervasive throughout Creole society, among both upper and lower classes and especially for those in the middle.

Nevertheless the various aspects of physiognomy reflect only one part of how Creoles perceive and define color. Ancestry, wealth, life-style, and education—all components of class and culture—also play a role in color ascription. The popular Caribbean phrase "A rich Negro is colored, but a poor colored is Negro" reflects the importance of these other factors. Whatever their appearance, those in the upper class tend to be regarded as white or colored, whereas those Creoles in the lower class tend to be regarded as black or Negro. In speaking of his fellow countrymen, sociologist Braithwaite states that some Trinidadians "bear fairly marked negro characteristics, but are by definition white. The term Trinidad white . . . indicates that the person is not really white but passes for white in Trinidad society."

The desire to appear light skinned has moved many women to extreme measures. At one time rural women powdered themselves so heavily they appeared ghostlike. In the 1970s women still preferred the European to the "natural" or Afro look and worked to lighten their skin through cosmetics and straighten their hair with hot combs. Such African-influenced styles as the Afro hairstyle were not popular because of the persistent and pejorative notions of kinky hair as "bad." Nevertheless some dark-complected Trinidadians who are secure in their high status and are well traveled and well educated have felt increasing alignment with international currents of "black pride." Moreover they have seen the East Indians consistently maintain their ethnic identity through material culture such as dress and are encouraging their Negro compatriots to dig into their African past for similar symbols of solidarity.

For the most part, however, attempts to set up an African-based counterculture to rival European culture have not had much success at the upper reaches of the society. Despite efforts by the government and others to upgrade the concept of blackness, pervasive values concerning the superiority of the British legacy die hard. Thus those at the top of the social ladder and those who are actively engaged in ascending that ladder must adopt the manners, values, language, education, and occupations that are the legacy of the British. The prominence of cricket as the national sport is only a small indication of the degree to which Trinidadians think of themselves as British.

Awareness of color varies with class. White Creoles of British or French descent have taken both their elite status and their white skin for granted, believing the two to be inextricably linked. Despite the changing composition of the upper class and the greater percentage of Negroes and colored at upper levels of government and business, the upper class remains culturally, if not physically, white. Skin color has also been a marginal issue for those at the very bottom of the hierarchy, whose self-image has been traditionally—if negatively—rooted in the legacy of African slavery. For the poor Negroes at the bottom and the wealthy whites at the top there is little use, or need, for fighting the prevailing system.

It is among those Creoles who aspire to higher status that color becomes a critical issue and tempers the character of most relationships. These aspirants to the middle and upper classes are the most sensitive toward issues involving physical appearance, associates, ancestry, correct speech, and other outward manifestations of whiteness. In an effort to move upward, Negro men may marry white women of lesser social standing or education in order to "improve the color." They also shun association with people darker than they to exhibit their acceptance in a lighter group.

Creoles feel that certain values and personality traits are also a function of race. Such genetic determinism leads them to connect blackness with laziness, promiscuous behavior, and poverty and to connect whiteness with the reverse of those traits. Stereotyping also occurs to a great degree between Creoles and non-Creoles and is generally a result of colonialism. It perpetuates feelings of both racial and national inferiority, especially among those in greatest contact with the white, Westernized industrial world. Political leaders and intellectuals alike join in condemning this self-contempt as the most damaging result of colonialism and the Trinidadian internalization of white values. It is reflected at every level from interpersonal interaction, to selective hiring practices, to sensitivity over census classification and beauty contests.

Non-Creoles

Several ethnic groups are present in the Trinidadian social structure that are not fully assimilated into the Creole complex: East Indians, Chinese, Middle Easterners, and Portuguese. There are also very small concentrations of Jews, Spanish-speaking Venezuelans, and "Spanish" local-born people (those of Spanish colonial extraction), and Amerindians. This last group, which Trinidadians term *Caribs* (actually encompassing both Caribs and Arawaks), numbered only 2,000 in the 1960 census and actually contained little unmixed Amerindian blood; perhaps none were pure Amerindian.

Except for the Caribs, the original inhabitants of the islands, all other groups arrived on the scene after the basic Creole society had been formed. Most of them came on a temporary basis with the intention of returning home. Although some did return a great many stayed, losing ties with their original homeland and coming to regard themselves as Trinidadian, if not Creole. Their ethnic seclusion varies and has been maintained through self-imposed isolation and resistance to assimilation, reinforced through Creole exclusion. Those groups most easily assimilated into the Creole complex have been those who, for ethnic and religious reasons, bear the closest resemblance to the strived-for European ideal and those whose numbers have been fairly small. Thus, the Portuguese and Christian Middle Easterners have been able to be assimilated more easily than the Chinese and East Indians.

East Indians are by far the largest non-Creole group—representing two-fifths of the entire population in 1970—and their impact upon Trinidadian society is the most profound. Their numbers have increased rapidly, from an estimated 130,000 in 1922 to over 373,000 in 1970. Their percentage of the total population has also increased, growing by nearly 5 percent between 1969 and 1970 while the percentage of the Negro population actually decreased. It is conjectured that by 1980 the number of East Indians will actually surpass the number of Negroes because of their higher birthrate and slower assimilation into the mixed category.

Because of the size and cohesiveness of their community, East Indians in Trinidad manifest a distinctive and flourishing culture. They have a religious tradition, family structure, material culture, and value system that distinguish them from the Creoles. According to David Lowenthal, a prominent West Indian scholar, East Indians are marked by other separatist features such as group endogamy, a stereotyped and reciprocated animosity toward and avoidance of the Negroes, and a cohesiveness and pride in their Indian heritage. Although they have not been a particularly vocal segment of the society, their potential strength in political and business circles is considerable. Increasingly they compete with Creoles for national power and status, representing a strong and unified subculture in Trinidadian society.

A total of about 143,000 indentured laborers—referred to as "Coolies"—were brought from India between 1845 and 1917, mainly from Northern India (see ch. 3). Because they embarked from Calcutta they were known as "Kalkatiyas" to distinguish them from those who emigrated from the port of Madras in the south and who were referred to as "Madrasis." One out of every six or seven immigrants was Muslim, the remainder being Hindu. In the second half of the twentieth century these proportions had changed considerably: the ratio of Hindus to Muslims had decreased from four to one, whereas one in five of those regarded as racially East Indian identified himself as Christian. There is much to suggest that the majority of East Indian Christians have been converts from Hinduism.

There is disagreement among scholars as to the degree of Indian culture retained and the degree of Creole culture adopted. There is less survival of traditional traits than among most other Indian communities abroad, and some traditions that have persisted in Trinidad have been gradually changed in India itself. The degree of adoption of Creole culture varies with nearness to it. Thus wealthy, highly urbanized Christian East Indians are more likely to neglect traditional Indian ways in favor of the more Westernized Creole norm than are their isolated, rural fellows. Moreover East Indians may not be aware of their adoption of certain Creole forms. V. S. Naipaul, a Trinidadian author of East Indian descent, has stated, "We were steadily adopting the food styles of others, but everything we adopted became our own; the outside was still to be dreaded."

Four institutions have helped preserve East Indian cultural autonomy: caste, religion, family, and material culture. Most social scientists agree that of these institutions caste has suffered the greatest alteration and material culture the least. The caste system has dissolved as a functional form for the most part, surviving mainly to reflect prejudice, personality, and life-style. The *jati*, the unit of local organization or subcaste so important in India because it defines status and occupation as well as determines marriage, no longer functions as a vital element among Trinidadian East Indians. Only half the marriages take place within a caste or within a *jati*. To some degree the four varnas, the traditional Hindu divisions, have remained, substituting for *jati* corporate identity and corresponding with social class, although they lack the proscriptive and prescriptive powers once incorporated by the *jati*.

It was difficult to preserve caste lines and the traditional concepts of pollution and purity for many reasons. Estate conditions and plantation life in general were incompatible with caste lines. Enforced residence in barracks, field and factory work, and labor requirements violated caste distance in rituals of food preparation and occupational role. Moreover Creole planters frequently ignored or reversed caste hierarchy in establishing authority. Maintaining a functional distribution of caste skills on a given plantation was next to impossible because certain of these traditional skills were simply not represented. Finally, the low number of women—the man to woman ratio was four to one—made the possibility of *jati* marriage difficult from the start.

In the mid-1970s caste survived as a mark of status and an element of cohesion, but it had acquired a certain flexibility found in Creole institutions. Concepts of purity and pollution have become less rigid, and residential segregation is no longer strictly observed. Brahman— traditionally the highest of the four varnas—has become a term of general respect not restricted to those of Brahman ancestry. In the same

86

way such low-caste names as Chamar—the traditional leather-working *jati*—are used for insult. Such terminology is not contingent upon a person's caste or status and in fact may be used in referring to a Creole.

In contrast to the weakened institution of caste, religion remains the principal focus in the expression of ethnic cohesion and the dissemination of traditional Indian culture. It is also the principal organizer of activities and beliefs, taking over in part some of the traditional functions of the caste system. Hindu-Muslim differences have remained steadfast and in the 1970s preoccupied East Indians far more than did caste differences. The dominance of Creole culture, however, has tended to minimize and encapsulate these religious differences. Consequently Muslims and Hindus live together, follow the same social patterns, and regard themselves and are regarded by Creoles as one people (see Religious Life, this ch.).

The institution of the family has also been successfully transplanted from India, and it is from the family that East Indian children learn the values inherited from their culture. The strength and unity of the family act as pillars holding up the East Indian community at large. The patrilineal extended family and parental influence in the selection of mates help to preserve its strength and secure its position as the focus of love and loyalty for all East Indians. This is especially true of those living in self-sufficient isolated villages (see Family Life, this ch.).

Indian material culture has proved to be one of the most durable elements of East Indian life-style. Language, clothing, and food experienced similar patterns of retention, gradual disappearance, and reappearance under the scepter of ethnic separatism after Indian independence in 1947. Food is probably the most ubiquitous and influential cultural survival. Indians adhere to certain traditional dietary norms and have adopted minimal food habits from the Creoles. Moreover such foods as rice now belong as much to the Creoles as to the East Indians.

Other non-Creole groups present in the society constitute only a small fraction of the total. Chinese, the second largest group—and the only other non-Creole ethnic group distinguished by the census—numbered under 8,000 in 1970. Lowenthal has chosen to call such groups status-gap minorities because they fill the gaps in the social and economic structure left vacant by or taken over from the Creoles. Like the East Indians, status-gap minorities—which include Portuguese and Middle Easterners in addition to the Chinese—retain separate ethnic identities and a degree of communal autonomy. Unlike the East Indians, however, they have gained a status that is comparable and in some cases superior to that of the Creole middle class.

The Portuguese, for example, were largely brought from Madeira as indentured laborers. They quickly moved off the plantations and into urban retailing, however, and with the capital they acquired they began to emulate the values of the British elite. In the 1860s their prominence in trade gave way to Chinese competition, and since that time they have moved into the professions and the civil service. Despite their wealth, education, light skin, and other accoutrements of Creole elite status, the survival of exclusively Portuguese social clubs attests to the survival of Portuguese identity and incomplete integration of this enclave, which numbers less than 4,000.

The Chinese also enjoy a high, if separate, position in Trinidadian society. The economic significance of this group far outweighs their numbers of political power. Their achievement is a result of the social structure they encountered upon their arrival in the Caribbean during the nineteenth century. The Chinese were able to fill an important position by developing the market for commercial goods. In this way they acted as brokers in the distribution of dry goods, manufactured items, and food. Their impact in the commercial sector is so great that "Chinee shop" has become synonymous for little store. Moreover, some Chinese have become quite wealthy through trade and the acquisition of urban real estate.

The Chinese are mostly urban; more than one-third reside in Port-of-Spain alone. Nevertheless, they are not localized, and their settlement pattern is scattered. There is no Chinatown in either of the two major cities. Reasons for this dispersal vary, but the locations of the best markets and the notion that distance between Chinee shops lessens competition for everyone have been important determinants.

Chinese Trinidadians have become oriented to Creole cultural patterning in many respects and share Creole views and values to an increasing degree. They are among the best educated members of the society and hold occupations of prestige and power. Before the 1949 revolution in China, children were sent to the mainland for a university education, but since then they have been sent to North America or Europe. Although marriage is preferably endogamous, parents do not resist liaisons with educated white European expatriates, indicating that they have adopted Creole color values. Various organizations have the purpose of keeping alive Chinese organizations and customs, but even these are increasingly infiltrated by those of mixed Chinese-Negro or Chinese-East Indian ancestry.

Several remaining groups of people have been generated by miscegenation between Creoles and non-Creoles or between such groups as Chinese and East Indian. The largest group of this nature are the *douglas*, of East Indian and Negro extraction. *Douglas* (from the Hindi word meaning "bastard") may be grouped with either non-Creoles or Creoles but are usually grouped with the latter because of their skin color and Christian religion. A few of the women are Hindu and may be found in East Indian communities, usually at the bottom of the social scale. Studies indicate that liaisons—either legal or clandestine—between East Indians and Negroes are infrequent, even in areas of relatively high interaction, and tend to occur more often between Creole women and

East Indian men who are Christians. Children of these liaisons suffer no particular stigma, although they usually find greater acceptance among Creoles than among East Indians.

Interethnic Relations

There is considerable disagreement over the nature of interethnic relationships among Trinidadians: their frequency, intimacy or lack of it, and how or if these relationships fit into a general societal pattern of discrimination. A cursory survey of interactions in the public domain—residential patterns, for example—seems to indicate that differences are negligible, lending weight to the notion that Trinidad is a racially egalitarian society. Some authors and many Creole politicians, as well as many members of the middle and upper classes subscribe to this view. They point to the existence of a positive form of "cultural pluralism"—one in which there is minimal conflict in the daily interaction of varying groups and acceptance and respect for cultural differences.

In a similar vein one anthropologist in the early 1950s suggested that Trinidad was such a conglomeration of ethnic mixtures that each group had internalized—or at least come to appreciate—the life-styles of the other groups. Moreover the large number of Creoles, the pervasiveness of their culture, and the longer period of their cultural dominance have caused other groups to become at least partially acculturated by Creolization (see Glossary). This viewpoint, which emphasizes Creolization, cultural mixing, and the evolution of a cosmopolitan syncretism of various groups, is called plural acculturation and is also a major ingredient in Creole middle-class ideology. It implies a flexibility of cultural norms that function like interchangeable parts, so that a member of one subculture never feels totally out of place in another. The classic example of plural acculturation is the Hindu who became a Presbyterian to enter a mission normal school, then switched to Roman Catholicism to become a teacher in a Roman Catholic school, and finally ended up a Muslim to qualify as a teacher in a Muslim school.

Such kaleidoscopic changing over is the exception rather than the rule, however. Many authors and some politicians in the 1960s and 1970s took a more realistic, although less flattering, approach to interethnic relationships. They began to view such protestations of solidarity as superficial, even untrue. They stressed that statements of faith in national integration and assertions that ethnic differences were negligible and unimportant are common to public discourse and political rallies but are not the case in the real world. C.L.R. James, Trinidad's most famous political writer, states, "Everybody in public life pretends that ethnic differences do not exist . . . they talk about them only to one another and in whispers." Rarely can any group—social, political, or economic—transcend the boundaries of ethnic loyalty and social distance. Such groups are either ephemeral—existing for a certain purpose and then dissolving when that goal is reached—or they tend to reinforce the mutual ignorance and stereotyping that already exist between the groups.

Over the years certain key features have emerged that explain the continuing and pervasive lack of mutual knowledge and communication: early and persistent stereotyping, the genuine diversity of the cultural backgrounds, the tendency for certain kinds of occupations to become linked to certain ethnic groups, and the highly endogamous marriage and mating patterns. Rather than adopt or adapt, Trinidadians have learned to tolerate existing differences and have developed an attitude that one social scientist characterized as "negative indifference." Negative indifference is tolerance without positive acceptance of the intrinsic validity of the beliefs and life-style of the other group.

Stereotyping began early and largely followed British lines. It has fostered isolation and ignorance and has engendered negative and inclusive group stereotypes. Many Creole stereotypes derive from the nineteenth century, when there was a general lack of understanding of or interest in the customs of the indentured newcomers. Of course by this time stereotypes surrounding the Creole genetic mix had already been formed, elevating the whites as capable, intelligent, and morally superior and debasing the Negroes as stupid and morally backward.

In the mid-1970s these stereotypes continued to play an important although quiet role in the expression of interethnic relations. Although such stereotypes could not be considered a scientific description of ethnic traits, they did suggest ways in which Trinidadians of differing origins perceived each other. Traits that figured in the stereotypes were held to be genetically determined. Thus Creoles, regardless of color, viewed East Indians as frugal, and East Indians for their part followed white Creoles in casting aspersions on lower class Negro sexual mores. Chinese and Middle Easterners, enjoying evident economic success, were characterized as acquisitive but were admired as effective and reliable businessmen. In fact Chinese are often called in to mediate disputes between East Indians and Creoles.

Regardless of the pervasiveness of Creolization, the endurance of genuine cultural and psychological differences fosters continuing social distance. Not all Creoles are urban, and not all East Indians are rural, but that is substantially the pattern. Moreover Creole family structure is looser, encouraging its progeny to function as individuals and gain status through schooling in European language, culture, and manners, as well as through conspicuous consumption. East Indian families are much tighter units, encouraging dependency, conformity, self-control, and thrift. Consequently East Indians function as part of a nuclear family unit that in turn functions within the larger unit of the village. East Indians have resisted sending their children to school, fearing they would be converted to Christianity and therefore lost to the family and community units. Once East Indian children reach the secondary school level, however, they tend to become much more competitive than Creoles.

Social distance is further fostered by the fact that certain occupations have become linked to certain ethnic groups, based on historical position or inferred racial characteristics. Such criteria have tended to keep East Indians in occupations of lowest status. They have become linked to agricultural work, particularly labor-intensive activities. If they enter business it is usually with the help of family savings, rarely with the support of the Creole business community. Even though the commercial, technical, professional, and white-collar occupational strata are increasingly multiracial, they remain culturally homogeneous, reflecting upper class Creole norms. Moreover, Creoles still tend to reserve a good share of these jobs for themselves, darker Creoles entering the polity and lighter skinned and white Creoles pursuing business. Creoles of all color shades are found in the professions, although the standard is invariably European.

Business follows the professions and government service in the local occupational hierarchy and is strongly influenced by the model of the British system. Within the business sector itself the descending hierarchy has been: traditional firms, foreign-owned firms, and "newer" local firms. Traditional firms frequently contained whites, Negroes, Chinese, and colored, giving the appearance of being well integrated. One study indicated, however, that even the interethnic interaction experienced in these traditional firms did not necessarily foster better communication or understanding between the groups. There appeared to be several reasons for this: the unquestioning acceptance of traditional, racially biased, business ways; the lack of adequate minority representation among organizational planning groups, the lack of initiative within the white group (invariably the managers) in improving interethnic relationships; and the maintenance of several separate levels of organization for each group.

As a consequence of these factors, whites retain control of the large businesses. Chinese are considered the most effective business administrators. East Indians have started their own companies and have thereby minimized their contact with outsiders. Negroes make no united racial effort as do other ethnic groups, they tend to compete with each other. In the mixed category there is shade discrimination, those with "whiter" features gaining greater acceptance in business groups.

Trinidadians have strong convictions as to what occupations a member of a given ethnic group may or may not pursue. In one short story by Naipaul, a Negro man apprenticed himself to a Chinese family to learn to make bread, only to discover he could not succeed on his own as a baker. One of his friends replied, "It don't *look* nice" (to have "Negro people meddling with food in public places"). Everyone had trouble accepting a Negro as a baker, just as they would have accepting an East Indian as a carpenter or a Chinese as a farmer. The would-be baker finally concluded "every race have to do special things." He solved his problem by fixing up his bakery to look Chinese and never showing his face in the front of the shop again.

Endogamy—both racial and religious—is one of the strongest factors encouraging social distance between groups. East Indians generally disapprove of ethnic intermarriage, as do other non-Creoles. Moreover, although East Indians frequently claim that Creoles are trying to assimilate them through intermarriage, there is little evidence to support this. Even within the Creole group, which is uniformly Christian, there is considerable sensitivity over the choosing of a marriage partner.

One study of the town of San Fernando and its outlying areas revealed that the more rural and isolated the community, the more likely it was conservative and endogamous. Within the town itself, both racial and religious endogamy were preferred among both Creoles and non-Creoles. Creoles who did form unions with non-Creoles did so with East Indian Christians. Moreover there was a greater occurrence of Creole wives and Hindu or Muslim husbands than vice versa—probably because of the greater isolation and smaller numbers of East Indian women. Compared with a small community of East Indians, those in San Fernando showed greater exogamy among East Indians in general and Hindus in particular. Intermarriage between Muslims and Creoles was virtually nonexistent.

Although distance is maintained through these four vehicles—stereotyping, cultural difference, occupational segregation, and endogamy—these are not necessarily the areas of greatest stress. Moreover the intensity of stress varies with locale. In general protest occurs more frequently in urban areas and in national politics than in local affairs. It centers on educational, occupational, and political inequalities; on East Indian resistance to assimilation and demands that Creole culture recognize specifically East Indian features; and on Creole fears of East Indian political dominance.

East Indian complaints focus on the civil service, the police force, and the schools; and statistics show their complaints to be justified. In the early and mid-1960s, for example, East Indians constituted 40 percent of the population but only 11 percent of the civil service and less than 3 percent of the police force. Schools are also dominated by Creole teachers, exacerbating East Indian fears of absorption. East Indian complaints of educational discrimination occur in three areas: inadequate rewards to Indian students, predominance of Negro teachers, and European- and Christian-biased values that are taught. Moreover East Indians feel that the Trinidadian school system and the society in general have long denied legitimacy to East Indian culture. Indian music is only played for two hours daily on the local radio stations. Among other things East Indians accuse newspapers and the Ministry of Education, Culture, and Community Development of encouraging Creole cultural activities and festivals at the expense of those of East Indian origin.

Despite the continuing social distance, discrimination, and even friction that are occasionally generated between the groups, there are indications that these problems could lessen with time. First, as East Indians grow in political and economic strength they are more likely to gain a greater say in cultural matters as well. Increasing urbanization has meant a decrease in residential segregation—at least for rural East Indians. Many more now live and work in close proximity to Creoles and still maintain their unique ethnic identity. Finally, those who are a racial mix, like the *douglas,* and those East Indians who have become Christianized are the first signs of genuine homogenization. These two groups act as cultural brokers for the Creoles and the non-Creoles, although their roles as yet are weak and their power minimal.

SOCIAL STRATIFICATION

Social stratification can be seen in terms of three classes: upper, middle, and lower. Individual status within this system is defined by a complex of educational, income, occupational, and color factors—with color playing a key role. Although nearly every ethnic group is represented in every stratum, there is a three-part rule of thumb that generally applies in matters of stratification: Creole over East Indian, light skin over dark skin, and Christian over non-Christian. Thus keeping educational, occupational, and income factors stable, a Creole would have higher status than an East Indian, a Christian than a non-Christian, and so forth. Nevertheless the achieved status derived from education, job, and wealth can readily change an individual's standing within the social hierarchy.

In the mid-1970s the range and rigidity found within these classes were based on both achieved status and the ascribed status that had helped to dictate colonial stratification. There has been some change in class criteria, class composition, and mobility patterns, giving the impression of greater fluidity. But the old color-based criteria have not been completely eroded throughout the system and are still selectively applied in such areas as business. Genuine change in stratification would call for complete abandonment of traditionally ascriptive and white-oriented values in favor of those that could be achieved on the basis of personal merit alone.

Social mobility—both upward and downward—is available within the system. Upward social mobility has put the upper class, and especially the middle class, in a state of constant flux, with new applicants constantly vying for entrance. Independence, accumulated wealth, and political power have created ethnic-based groups that compete for status. East Indians particularly have begun to move out of the lowly agricultural work to which they had been traditionally consigned and into industrial and clerical work. The capital they initially acquired through landownership is being converted into industrial and mercantile channels, and increasingly they are being found as members of the middle and even upper classes.

Although social mobility is not uniformly possible for all regardless of class or color, it does occur in certain circumstances. Trinidadians intuitively know in which areas they may move ahead given their ethnic background. For example, Negro Trinidadians know they have a better chance of moving up within the civil service than in the business community. Those of East Indian descent have greater access to family-based businesses than to civil service posts. White Trinidadians rarely attempt to gain a political following, opting for business instead.

Education remains one of the primary avenues by which lower class individuals may improve their social position. Nevertheless there are also many constraints that restrict education as a means of social mobility. The nature of the educational institution can either hamper or facilitate success, as can parental attitude. If family resources are limited, if the school is poorly equipped, or if parents fear education as a tool of Creole assimilation, then the student is apt to receive a minimal education and a poor one at that.

One study indicated that these restrictions have been quite effective in maintaining the traditional stratification system. It was shown that the quality of the school—its socioeconomic context—was a prime socializing agent and also one of the bastions of the existing stratification system.

Another avenue of social mobility is association. Trinidadians believe that whom you know is more important than what you know, and they act accordingly. People at lower levels try to maintain beneficial relationships with overseers and foremen in order to receive favors and better their position. Those at higher levels accumulate influential friends and academic honors, knowing they will benefit them more than administrative or technical experience. Nepotism is commonplace and widely accepted in the society. It is a well accepted tenet that promotions and appointments will go to members of the family or ethnic group.

Several studies of the business community have clearly indicated the importance of family and associates for advancement. Since many of the private businesses were family-centered operations, the question of nepotism frequently arose. One study showed that the greatest proportion of business elites to gain their position through inheritance were non-Creoles: Syrians, Lebanese, Portuguese, East Indians, and Chinese. The greatest proportion of business elites to gain their position through promotion or being hired at the top were white. In fact it was shown that whites with little work experience and little education tended to be hired over others with more education and technical training, thus allowing universalistic criteria in the form of educational qualifications to give way to particularistic criteria applied through the informal mechanisms of "contact."

Given the constraints upon upward mobility it is understandable that hope for movement upward far exceeds its incidence. Nepotism, impediments to a good education, disparities in living conditions, and the continuance of archaic institutions and values are obstacles to some of the most promising aspirants to higher status. Furthermore differential treatment by such institutions as law and education separate the middle and upper classes from those in the lower class and distinguish between Creoles and East Indians. In such a situation communication between groups and classes is impaired, and consensus—whether it be social, economic, or political—is difficult to reach.

Upper Class

Despite a variety of ethnic origins, the upper class follows a variation of twentieth-century British values and institutions. Except for a few still residing on plantations, all are urban dwellers. They are well educated, well traveled, cosmopolitan, interested in literature and the arts, and schooled in a form of English that closely approximates the mother tongue. During colonial times they dominated the political, economic, and social spheres, but since the 1950s and the rise of the People's National Movement (PNM), their power in the political arena has been reduced. In the 1970s many upper class members were found in the traditional professions, such as law and medicine. Others were found engaged in profitable entrepreneurial activities: banking, export-import, and natural resource exploitation.

The upper class is composed of individuals of all colors and ethnic backgrounds yet holds to a single standard. The free colored of the nineteenth century—free before emancipation—had already become acculturated to the values of the white French Creole elite and rose to important positions under the British as supreme court justices, planters, civil servants, and professionals. They, along with the wealthier and educated non-Creoles and foreign whites, developed a society that was small in number but that led the larger national society to view success and beauty in terms of approximation to upper class European life-styles and Caucasian physical appearance.

For the most part these are the same kinds of individuals found in the upper class in 1975. Foreign whites (called békés), important as social arbiters, have been reduced in number. The local whites, often called French Creoles regardless of national origin, dominated in business and as landowners but have also decreased in number. Increasing numbers of powerful East Indians, Portuguese, Chinese, and Middle Easterners have found their way into the upper class. Many are professionals or wealthy businessmen, engaged in banking, rum distilling, and commerce. A few have entered politics or attained high-level cabinet posts. Such non-Creole elites frequently serve as intermediaries or brokers between Creoles and East Indians.

Within the upper class, nuclear family and household coincide, and ethnic endogamy predominates, helping to preserve family power and wealth. The authority structure is bilateral, and the kinship structure is small and tightly knit, giving the family the functions of status placement and socialization. Among upper class Creoles, European norms regarding marriage and child-rearing are practiced, fostering more divorces than illegitimate births. Children are encouraged to become independent and well educated and to develop international interests. As a consequence of this and the emphasis placed on British culture, many young Trinidadians develop a great affinity for England. Non-Creole upper class families also practice endogamy and value education but generally place greater emphasis on ethnic identity. For example, even though many upper class East Indians are Christian, they still value Hinduism as the common thread in the Indian identity.

Conditions since independence have led many white upper class Creoles to leave for and many expatriates to return to Europe and North America. With their traditional bases of political power eroded and the growing awareness of both lower class Negroes and East Indians, many white Creoles became increasingly apprehensive. There has always been a tendency to perceive the masses as hostile, accompanied by a disregard for and an ignorance of lower class mores. This has been true for upper class colored as well, who do not readily identify with the Creole folk culture. Antiwhite rhetoric among lower class militants has been kept to a minimum, even during peak periods of racial strife. Furthermore it has usually been directed at powerful foreign nations and tourists rather than Trinidadians themselves. Moreover it does not represent the sentiments of a large percentage of the lower class who, for good or ill, still evince feelings of respect for and emulation of the upper class.

Middle Class

Middle-class Trinidadians exceed even the upper class in their varied ethnic representation. Moreover there is less consensus as to values and institutions. In the upper class, Creole values clearly dominate; and although they may not be adhered to by the entire upper class, they dictate correct public behavior and form the parameters of social interaction. But in the middle class there is a distinct clash of values, with East Indians and Creoles in clear conflict under the canopy of middle-class criteria. Middle-class people interact with each other and compete for the same social, economic, and political positions, which is why distinctions are more important than in the lower class, where levels of interaction and competition may be muted or even nonexistent.

The aims, aspirations, and alliances of this class have been emulative of the upper class, although political movements such as the PNM have tried to give the middle sector a sense of class-based identity. Such attempts, however, have only united middle-class members of similar ethnic backgrounds and aggravated ethnic differences. Class resentments toward Creoles have been exacerbated by the ethnic and potential political solidarity of the East Indians. The East Indians resent the fact that most middle-class jobs have gone to Creoles and that unequal standards of education and cultural bias are slowing down the entrance of East Indians into the middle class.

Nevertheless such competition denotes expansion, and this expansion could never have occurred without independence. In terms of jobs, greater opportunities, and material benefits emanating from independence, the middle class has cornered the market. They are the main recipients of government-sponsored education and housing programs as well. For racial and historical reasons they were excluded from decisionmaking circles and thus had little experience in management until the mid-1950s. But since then their expertise in these areas has increased. They have tended to want to rely on foreign capital rather than to generate it at home, a bone of contention for many of the leading politicians. Their growing political acumen, however, indicates that such problems may resolve themselves in the future.

For the most part the middle class is confused and ambivalent about its role in the wider community. Because of this insecurity and lack of empathy with lower segments of the population, the middle class is often even more fearful than the upper class of the majority it represents. It has been said of the middle class that no group has been louder in denouncing racism, yet no group is as sensitive to color or as fearful of a popular revolution that would strip them of their newly acquired privileges. Because of underlying hypocrisy, most lower class Trinidadians envy and emulate the middle class while mistrusting their protestations of concern. Militant black power advocates and East Indian radicals have accused the middle class of complacency—even compliance—toward the forces that keep the masses of Trinidadians uninformed and poor.

Most middle-class East Indians are fairly recent arrivals to that status. The most outstanding feature of East Indian public life is the extent to which its growing contingent of the middle class stays in the shadows. It is not a homogeneous group; divisions occur between Hindu and Muslim and between them and Christians. Although most publicly profess Christianity, many continue to regard Hinduism and other elements of Indian culture with quiet reverence. This class of East Indians usually possesses secondary or higher education and consists of doctors, lawyers, teachers, students, small businessmen, and clerical workers. Politically it cannot identify with the predominantly Negro Creole-based PNM and has gradually gravitated toward the Democratic Labour Party (DLP).

The middle class likes to emulate the upper class as much as possible and frequently adopts elite norms and values. Families tend to be patriarchal, with marriage being a slightly relaxed version of its Victorian ancestor, especially among Creoles. To distinguish themselves from lower class Negroes, whom they consider promiscuous, middle-class Creoles sharply differentiate between legitimate and illegitimate children. Furthermore they are more acutely aware of color than any other class and seek to marry lighter skinned people whenever possible to carry them even farther away from the Negro masses. The middle-class Creole is more traditionally Christian than the African-influenced lower class and more fervently Christian than the upper class. Middle-class members of all ethnic groups may convert to Christianity in order to better their social position.

Sometimes the middle class is found in rural villages, although for the most part its orientation is avowedly urban. Creoles may represent the government as civil servants, teachers, or local police, but they are usually not considered community members per se. Non-Creoles are frequently found as shopkeepers and moneylenders and are also now regarded as part of the community. The reason for this cosmopolitan orientation rests in the fact that members of the middle class realize opportunities for mobility are generally much greater in the city.

Lower Class Non-Creoles

A few people in the middle or status-gap minorities—Chinese, Portuguese, Middle Easterners—hover at the upper reaches of the lower class as peddlers, shopkeepers, or grocers. In urban areas they are probably regarded as lower class because of their lack of education, lower income, and occupational position. But in the villages they may be locally regarded as middle class, having an education and income superior to the agricultural workers around them. In fact in the villages such people may wield considerable power, having connections with government or police officials and frequently serving as creditors to local farmers. Status-gap minority middlemen are found in both Creole and non-Creole villages as participants but not assimilated members of the community.

The vast majority of the non-Creole lower class is East Indian, however. They have traditionally represented a rural, non-Christian, and isolated enclave that intermingles infrequently with the rest of the society. Since the 1920s there has been a gradual movement away from these rural communities and into the cities, as witnessed by the fact that in 1960 East Indians constituted one-fourth of the population of San Fernando, the second largest city on the island. Although these urban East Indians may be Christian, Muslim, or Hindu, Hindus and Muslims in general occupy the lowest socioeconomic position. Muslims are generally more urban than Hindus, tending to cluster in cities as shopkeepers where they outnumber Hindus, who outnumber them four to one on a national scale.

Urban East Indians have not retained traditional Indian customs to the same degree that their rural neighbors have. Caught by the temptations of upward mobility and surrounded by the Creole materialistic life-style, many eschew the Hinduism and frugality of the past in favor of Christianity and conspicuous consumption. Moreover patterns regarding pollution and food taboos are even harder to maintain in the city than in the country, as are traditional work divisions. Increasingly, urban East Indian children follow their Creole peers in exerting their independence by opting for higher education and the personal selection of a mate.

Rural East Indians constitute Trinidad's silent minority, representing one of the last bastions of Indian culture in the New World. In spite of urbanization and industrialization their position has changed little since 1891, when the percentage of East Indians engaged in agricultural activities was estimated at 78 percent. In recent years, and especially since independence, they have become one of the most talked about, speculated about, and studied groups in the society. Intellectuals and politicians alike have made an effort to understand their culture, but the majority of Trinidadians continue to regard them with ignorance and indifference. Rural East Indians remain where they were originally placed, in the sugar belt on the western third of the island.

Once their indentureship was over, East Indians were induced to stay on the island through offers of money and land. The cultural and ecological situation permitted them to nucleate and build ethnic communities in the plantation areas, working on both plantations and private plots. Rice and sugar cultivation were instrumental in the persistence of Indian culture and Indian residence in the rural areas. These two crops had been well known in India since ancient times—the word *sugar* in fact being a corruption of Sanskrit and Hindi words. Rice had been a staple for centuries and was also considered sacred in many Hindu rituals.

Lower class East Indians have remained attached to the religion, community and family organization, and material culture of India to a greater degree than any other class. They concentrate on growing and milling rice, accumulating capital, and setting up family businesses. As in northern India, children marry young, daughters marrying outside the district, whereas the sons stay close to the parental home. Values remain decidedly family and community oriented, and the wealthy East Indian peasant is expected to do good works rather than hoard his fortune or spend it on consumer goods. Religion has great importance in the lives of these people. Many of the traditions of the Vedas (ancient sacred books) are kept, as well as the special worship of certain gods and goddesses, and festivals such as Diwali (the festival of lights) and Phagawa (the spring festival) continue to be major holidays for lower class Hindus (see Family Life, Religious Life, this ch.).

Lower Class Creoles

There are a few whites at the bottom of the social scale—poor laborers from Barbados and Grenada called "Scotland Johnnies"—and some colored, but the great majority of lower class Creoles are Negroes. A great many are found in urban areas as skilled and unskilled laborers, longshoremen, or in service occupations. They represent the growing numbers of the urban proletariat who are gradually gaining a greater say in the political and economic development of the country. These urban dwellers are often upwardly mobile, unionized, politicized, and cognizant of their class potential. They encourage their children to attend school and seek powerful, wealthy, and light-skinned associates and mates in the hopes of getting white-collar jobs.

Lower class Creoles practice farming but unlike the East Indians alternate estate wage labor on coconut, citrus, cocoa, or sugar plantations with subsistence farming. Scarcity of land is one of the major problems for the Creole peasant. Holdings usually range from a simple house plot to five acres or more. Most landholdings are small and scattered, however, with villagers working as many as three separate plots of land at a time. The net result is that few peasants can rely completely upon their land for a living. The consequence of this is occupational multiplicity—the holding of a variety of jobs. This life-style has led many social scientists to regard them as neither fully peasant nor fully proletarian but a combination of the two.

In addition to their agricultural activities, members of this class fish, hunt, work on road repair or construction, or drive buses and taxis. Estate work varies, as do salaries. Employment is irregular and cannot be depended upon to provide a full living. Some women work on estates as domestics or seamstresses or have small confectionery shops. Many women do not work outside the home at all, or they help their husbands on their private plots. Despite differences in occupation among lower class Creoles there seems to be little difference in total amount of money earned or status bestowed. Moreover color and education, which are important on a national scale, seem to be less important in rural areas where everyone is very dark and poorly educated and where formal education matters little to farm life.

One very important index of status to the rural dweller is the ability to "live independent." This may mean different things in different communities, but independence in general is associated with assured income, self-employment, and certain occupations. In any community the shopkeepers and landed peasants who possess livestock are considered independent. Moreover possession of certain materials goods, a better house and better clothing, and association with important people are also indexes of importance and status.

Of all of the classes, lower class Creoles show the strongest influence of the slave experience and the plantation heritage. Their family system parallels that of both African and slave models in its strong matrifocality. Family authority and responsibility normally fall to the mother, and the composition of the household unit reflects the dominance of her role (see Family Life, this ch.). Religious practice contains a high degree of emotional participation in the service, whether the belief is in fundamentalist Christianity or an Africanized version of Christianity (see Religious Life, this ch.). In contrast to the more politicized urban Creoles, the rural lower class remains largely outside the political and legal framework of the society.

FAMILY LIFE

It is in such institutions as the family that the concept of the plural society is most clearly demonstrated. At the same time, however, European, African, and Indian family patterns have persisted and, although modified by colonialism, the slave experience, and Creolization, they remain clearly distinguishable and associated with certain elements and classes of society. Throughout Trinidad the family, regardless of ethnic background, fulfills certain roles. It is the focus of love and loyalty as well as the key instrument in the process of socialization—into both the nation and the ethnic group. In fact ethnic identity is most strongly preserved at the family level.

Attention to ethnic identity and family makes most Trinidadians careful genealogists, especially those seeking a higher position in the society. Evidence of high-caste ancestors helps in selection of a mate. Conversely, evidence of low-caste ancestry may evoke prejudice from higher caste in-laws. Most East Indians prefer endogamous marriages, but they object less to matches between whites and East Indians than to those between colored or Negroes and East Indians. Other non-Creoles seek to retain ethnic identity through endogamous unions as well. Creoles carefully trace any "white" blood in their backgrounds, preferring to emphasize the Irish great-great-grandfather over darker ancestors. The smallness and insularity of the society make interaction with relatives and a knowledge of one's ancestry difficult to avoid.

Another characteristic common to all Trinidadian families is the sexual segregation of recreational activities. Regular companionship between men and women is rare, married or not. All social interactions are separated by sex, as are clubs and more informal gatherings. Men meet at bars, clubs, front room shops, in each other's homes, or on street corners. Women also meet at home, although separately from the men, at the market, at church, or at the local water hole.

Children are uniformly regarded as a blessing, and emotional ties are usually stronger between parents and children than between spouses. Large families are considered ideal—especially among the lower classes—and children are loved and wanted regardless of the inconvenience their birth may bring about. The mother-son tie is reputedly the strongest of all family ties among both East Indians and Creoles. Men may rely on maternal care into their thirties, and even afterward, in East Indian households where members of three or more generations may live under one roof.

Despite the similarities in function, the structural differences between Negro and East Indian families are marked. Even the common experience of colonial life did not homogenize or modify traditional patterns completely, although the overall effect of the uprooting and transplanting has been noticeable. Plantation life and slavery did far more to alter family patterns among black Africans than indentureship did for East Indians. In fact most scholars attribute lower class Creole family patterns to the plantation heritage. The standards of sexual license and parental irresponsibility were imposed upon the slaves by their white masters, who had little interest in promoting permanent sexual unions between them.

Many more East Indian family traits and values have remained intact, although there have been alterations. The extended family household dominated by the eldest male is still considered the ideal, but it is gradually being supplanted by the household made up of a single, nuclear family consisting of a husband, his wife, and their children.

Plantation life had elevated the status of the East Indian woman. Few were brought to the islands, and the numerical imbalance worked to the woman's advantage, eroding the traditional dominance of husband over wife.

A 1970 study comparing marriage and family practices of lower class Negroes and East Indians concluded that basic differences remained. More East Indian women were legally married and at a younger age than Negro women. The former placed a greater initial emphasis on marriage. Among Negro women the importance of marriage grew with age. East Indians tended to have a more monogamous view of sexual expression than Negroes and less tolerance of illegitimate births. Two out of three Negro mothers in the study had illegitimate children, in comparison to one out of every ten East Indian women.

Sexual mores and family life also differ between those whose ancestors were slaves and those whose were masters. For example, a double standard persists from the time when a man's sexuality was measured by the number of his exploits and offspring. White plantation owners felt free to consort with their female slaves and encouraged the male slaves to do likewise. As a consequence extramarital mating is a common pattern for both high- and low-status Creole males. The strictness of the double standard increases as one ascends the Creole social ladder, upper class women placing more emphasis on Victorian attitudes of correct sexual behavior.

Courtship patterns also vary greatly among ethnic groups. It is still the practice for East Indian fathers to go in search of a husband for their daughters. The choice is subject to the girl's approval, however, which is different from the past. After marriage the girl goes to live with her husband's family under the jurisdiction of her mother-in-law.

Lower class Creole courtship differs radically from this pattern. The man usually seeks out the girl and begins courting her at home. Several terms have evolved to describe this pattern, which typically involves sexual relations. Frequently called "visiting" unions, they vary in degree of stability and commitment. After one or more such relationships— which usually produce children—a couple may enter into a common-law union. All such relationships are easily dissolved, and one may have many such unions in a lifetime. Furthermore, extramarital unions are also common for both men and women, the women exchanging sexual favors for material support. Invariably, however, children reside with the mother, and their primary loyalty is to her. Loyalty to fathers and stepfathers depends upon the paternal treatment the child receives.

RELIGIOUS LIFE

Religion has served a variety of functions in Trinidad. For many, particularly the Hindu East Indians, it has become a symbol of ethnic solidarity and cultural superiority. For lower class Negroes it has served a combination of purposes, both social and religious. Not only does it attempt to explain and regulate supernatural phenomena, but it also provides an avenue for social intercourse and entertainment. For those seeking upward mobility, conversion to one of the established Christian churches may be helpful.

Most of the Chinese have become either Roman Catholic or Anglican. About one in every five East Indians is Christian, usually Presbyterian.

The 1970 census listed about 63 percent of the population as belonging to various Christian denominations, 25 percent Hindu, 6 percent Muslim, and 6 percent other. Among the lower class Christians it was common to profess one of the various Afro-Christian cults, including Shouter, Shango, and Rada, as well as professing membership in one of the Christian denominations. This was not seen as inconsistent behavior and was openly professed by most people.

The Trinidadian Constitution guarantees freedom of religion and, for the most part, does not interfere in the religious life of the people. It does give financial help, however, and in 1971 sixteen religious groups received a total of TT$136,000 (for value of the Trinidad and Tobago dollar—see Glossary) for ecclesiastical expenses. The primary recipients were generally also those with the largest following: Roman Catholic (TT$50,000), Hindu and Anglican (TT$30,000 each), and Muslim (TT$10,000). A total of thirteen other Protestant denominations received between TT$1,000 and TT$10,000 each. Spiritualists or Afro-Christian cults, which have no centralized organization, received nothing.

The official view of the cults reflects the sentiments of the articulate and influential segment of the population, who generally wish to ignore but not necessarily destroy them. Ordinances passed in the 1920s prohibiting the practice of obeah—a form of black magic—have not been seriously enforced, as witnessed by the small number of arrests compared to the actual incidence of magic practices. Ordinances pertaining to drum playing and bongo dancing have not been enforced against religious groups. The law enacted in 1917 that made the Shouter church illegal was repealed in 1951. Even so, although the sect's regular services were conventionally Baptist, spirit possession was practiced on the side, and there was little official attempt to regulate it.

The majority of Christians were either Roman Catholic (33.6 percent) or Anglican (18.1 percent), reflecting the heavy colonial influence of the French and English. The rest were Presbyterian, Baptist, Methodist, Seventh-Day Adventist, Moravian, Church of God, and smaller groups—none representing more than 5 percent of the population. Nearly 5,000 of the 6,500 Moravians were in Tobago, where there were also heavy concentrations of Seventh-Day Adventists and Methodists. Denominational choices reflect church colonialism in the past and the continuing association of Roman Catholicism and Anglicanism with elite status. Since independence the long-standing resentment against the structure of white religious domination has become more apparent, however, with black power demonstrations at the Port-of-Spain Cathedral and editorials condemning the continuing presence of foreign—mostly Irish and Flemish—priests when the number of locally born priests would suffice.

Nevertheless upper class religion, like family life and values, continues to be European oriented. Members attend church more as a sign of social solidarity with their class than as a genuine profession of religious belief. Middle-class Christians are usually more serious in their religious belief. Whereas upper class attitudes are perfunctory, middle-class attitudes are literal and rigid, and they see Christian teaching as a guide to public as well as private moral behavior. Generally, except among Roman Catholics, doctrine is more fundamentalist, church attendance is more regular, and religion is more important to middle-class than to upper class Trinidadians.

The belief systems of lower class Christians and the institutional structures and emotional significance of their services reflect both the fundamental, evangelical, and revival forms of Christianity and the spiritualism of their African ancestors. Their gods are accessible to prayer and persuasion, and spirits play an enormous role. These spirits possess otherworldly powers, which they can bestow upon certain people or use themselves to direct human actions.

There are two kinds of African-influenced belief popular among Trinidadians: Shouter and Shango (the practices of Rada are similar to those of Shango). According to Melville Herskovits, a prominent Afro-Caribbean anthropologist, the Shouters represent "a point of transition between African religion—represented in Trinidad by the Shango Cult, and undiluted European forms of worship."

The Shouters, who prefer to be called Spiritual Baptists, developed during the nineteenth century without the aid of a revivalist movement. Their churches are independent and small but have flourished since the lifting of the ban on their services in 1951. They are a demonstrative and fundamentalist cult whose faith in the supernatural is more orthodoxly Christian than that of the Shangoists. The five points they emphasize as being the basis of their faith are those found among the fundamentalist movements that flourished in the United States among Protestant sects in the early twentieth century. They are: the inerrancy of the Bible, the virgin birth of Jesus Christ, life after death, the physical resurrection of Jesus Christ, and the authenticity of the Gospel miracles. Like the

American Negro charismatic sects, Shouters place great emphasis on participatory worship—hand clapping, dancing, singing, shouting, and trances.

The Shango cult developed during the nineteenth century as persons of African descent—mainly Yorubas of Nigeria—combined traditional beliefs and practices with elements of Roman Catholicism. The pantheon of Shango deities, or orishas, includes not only Shango himself—the god of thunder—but a dozen others. These are generally paired with Roman Catholic saints, although there is no uniform agreement as to pairing, and some saints who play a role are not equated with any African deity. Spirit possession is a vital phenomenon. One of the orishas "mounts a horse"—possesses a follower—and temporarily takes over the bodily functions of that individual. Dreams and visions are also important and may be interpreted by a Shango leader. Among the most important African features are animal sacrifices, *pierres* (thunderstones symbolizing the major powers of the cult), dancing, drums, and supernatural beings who interfere in men's lives. Among the European features are the Bible, Roman Catholic prayers, candles, crosses, incense, and spontaneous praying.

There is considerable mixing of Shango and Shouter belief, and some cult leaders carry on both practices, but separately. People may participate in both. The recognized difference, however, is that Shango is not a faith or a religion per se that can be joined, whereas the Shouter church is. Shango is kept out of deference to African ancestral deities, whereas Shouter pays respects to Christianity. Such objects as crosses, candles, and rosaries are used by both groups, and some ritual acts are the same. Moreover healing practices are virtually identical and include anointing with olive oil, brewing curative teas and prayer.

Hinduism in Trinidad, the largest non-Christian religion, is a synthesis of varying factions and beliefs. Although East Indian immigrants brought with them all the metaphysical, intellectual, and ritualistic traditions of the Indian states from which they came, they pursued their religious beliefs quietly, holding no festivals and building no temples until the 1860s. In the 1970s many elements of Hinduism remained, including traditions traceable to the Vedas and the belief in the triad of gods— Brahma the creator, Vishnu the preserver, and Siva the destroyer— three manifestations of the supreme God.

Nevertheless, with the erosion of the caste system much of Hindu belief has also passed away, and it has become a more homogeneous and simpler faith than that found in India. The ordained duties of the four varnas (or classes) of people, the four stages in life, and the four goals in life (righteousness, vocation, fulfillment of desires, and release from cyclical birth and death), as well as theories of reincarnation and transmigration of the soul, are known to many elderly people but are not as familiar to the younger generation.

In addition to the erosion of Hindu belief over the years other factors have contributed to its change, simplifying and standardizing Hindu ritual. The position of Hinduism as the focus of ethnic solidarity and identity, plus the constant presence of the surrounding Creole culture, have contributed to wider and more universalistic definitions of Hinduism that have ignored the finer internal distinctions of caste, ritual, and belief. Competition from Christians—largely Canadian Presbyterian missionaries—has caused many Brahman priests to adopt similar practices: holding services on weekends, visiting the sick, and counseling.

The Madrasi Indians, who came from southern India, are of different ethnic origin and are looked down upon by those whose ancestors came from the north. Many of them retain very little of their Hindu faith and instead adhere to beliefs and practices similar to those of lower class Negroes.

Another major faith, Islam, claimed 58,000 adherents in 1970, over 6 percent of the population. The majority of these followers traced their origins to the Indian subcontinent; relatively few—if any—were recent converts. Muslims attend several mosques, which are distributed throughout the country, are members of an active Islamic association, which publishes a monthly newspaper, and celebrate the major Islamic festival—Ramadan—as a national holiday. A number of highly visible followers have prominent positions in the society and the government. Nevertheless there was some speculation that many lower class Muslims were being assimilated either into the general Creole structure or into East Indian Hindu enclaves. These Muslims exhibited little ethnic solidarity and were regarded as generally more susceptible to Creolization than Hindus.

Many authors have emphasized the mixing and crossing over of religious belief and magic practice. They point out that Roman Catholics also participate in African-based rituals, that Christian East Indians celebrate the Hindu festivals of Diwali and Phagawa and hold Hindu curing or thanksgiving services secretly at home, and that there is large Hindu attendance on Good Friday at the Benedictine monastery.

A striking example of syncretism is the combination of East Indian and African magic traditions. Priests of one religion may perform services for members of another. For example, Hindu pandits may perform a High Mass for Negro petitioners who have not had their prayers answered in the Christian churches, Shouter temples, or Shango yards. Similarly, an East Indian may employ obeah men in curing a relative, protecting himself, or vexing an enemy. Generally such crossovers and mixing occur among members of the lower class; the higher one climbs in the social pyramid the more clearly delineated each faith is. Moreover such mixing is not an indication of the weakening of one particular religious practice or another but is indicative of the gradual synthesis of all religious beliefs in Trinidad.

LANGUAGE

Although the official language is English, three Creole languages and some Indian languages continue to be spoken in Trinidad and Tobago. The three Creole languages—English, French, and Spanish—have a European lexical base and significant syntactic input from African languages. Trinidad English is the Creole form spoken and understood by all classes and differs from the standard English spoken in Great Britain. Whether Trinidad English differs so greatly from standard English as to be considered a separate language is a topic of scholarly debate, although it more closely approximates standard English than the Creole dialects spoken in other Caribbean islands. It is certainly not as different from British English as, for example, Haitian Creole is from French. The fact that no sharp break exists between Trinidad English and standard English—that it is more nearly a continuum—reinforces the notion of one language with several degrees of variation.

Trinidad English is accorded a lower status than standard English by the majority of the population, although it is the sole form of communication of the lower classes. Innovations in the language come from these strata, who usually also understand English but have difficulty communicating in it. Given the variability of Creole, Trinidadians can adjust their speech to their audience. Thus an upper or middle-class housewife would speak a more Africanized language to her maids and a more anglicized version to her friends. Usage of "proper" English, however, is critical to upward mobility, and high-status Trinidadians are quick to criticize each other for faulty or Creolized speech, especially in public.

The elements of society responsible for the drive to popularize and destigmatize Trinidad English have been the intellectuals, writers, scholars, and calypsonians—those who write calypsos. Authors, poets, and playwrights have been incorporating Creole in their work for several decades. Although the speech represents that of the lower class, there is no attempt to deprecate or mock it. Calypsonians are the chief innovators and disseminators of speech and slang expressions within Creole. Calypsos are so universally popular and well received by all strata of society that these innovations are readily adopted throughout the society.

The persistence of French, as both a local patois and an influence on Trinidad English, is remarkable since the French never governed Trinidad. French so predominated that even after English became the official language, French continued to be more widely spoken than either English or Spanish. French patois is still spoken nearly two hundred years after British ascendancy—in rural areas in the north originally settled by planters and their slaves.

The French patois spoken in the mid-1970s was not necessarily an intelligible language to the average French tourist. It had evolved into what some scholars consider a separate language and others consider a highly distinctive dialect. In any event the French patois was influenced by slave talk and has produced its own idioms as well as retaining archaic forms. The same can be said for the Spanish spoken in isolated enclaves of the mountain valleys of the north.

The evolution of speech patterns and vocabulary of Trinidad English has been heavily influenced by French and Spanish. It is accentuated— unlike the English spoken in Jamaica or Barbados—by the musical intonation of Spanish and French as well as of West African languages. It is spoken so rapidly that many native English speakers have a difficult time keeping up, leading at least one scholar to draw a parallel between it and the rapid tempo of Caribbean Spanish.

Many words have been borrowed from Spanish and French, particularly from the former. Spanish words have been corrupted so that the pronunciation frequently differs, final consonants are dropped, and words change from one part of speech to another. In words of French derivation one apparent characteristic is the simplification of the final vowel. Moreover there appears to be an unusual influence of French spelling on Spanish-derived words, so that *lapa*, a Venezuelan term for a large rodent, becomes *lappe* in Trinidad. In addition many place names, literary forms, and elements of folk culture are French or Spanish. Musical instruments, dances, festivals, and foods are also heavily influenced. Almost all names of flora and fauna on the island are French.

The use of Indic languages—referred to as Hindustani or *Dési Bhása* (native language) by the native speakers—is dying out. The status of English as not only the lingua franca but also the prestige language has eclipsed the usage of Hindustani among East Indians. Most of the younger generation do not speak any Indian languages, and although they may understand one, they will not readily admit to this. Younger East Indians feel that Hindustani is not useful in the complex cultural milieu or in the increasingly competitive economic or political sectors. Even though they may speak Hindustani fluently as children, they turn to the English language as they grow up.

At first glance Hindustani is not identifiable with any specific Indic language, and its speakers readily admit to being embarrassed about not being able to speak "correct" Hindi. It is generally assumed that Trinidad Hindustani is a direct descendant of a form of Hindi spoken in eastern India, called Bhojpuri, although considerable syntactic and morphological changes have occurred. Despite the discrepancies between this language and that spoken in India, Hindustani has frequently been a rallying point for East Indians seeking acknowledged cultural separatism. Some have even suggested that it become a required language in the school system.

CHAPTER 5

LIVING CONDITIONS

The pleasant tropical environment of Trinidad and Tobago is reflected in a generally easy tempo of life, although this same environment had taken a heavy toll from disease until such scourges as cholera, yellow fever, and malaria were brought under control. Socioeconomic conditions in the mid-1970s were profoundly affected by the development of a settlement pattern in which people lived for the most part in population clusters rather than on isolated farms, by the physical separation of the two islands, by the heavy concentration of the population in the western lowlands of Trinidad, and by the small size of that island and its relatively good transportation system, which placed most of the population within a few hours' travel of Port-of-Spain. Of general importance in shaping the way in which people have lived during the years since World War II has been the broad and increasing participation of the population in the market economy, the generally high level of income, the increasing migration from rural to urban localities, and the massive emigration to North America that took place during the 1960s and early 1970s.

To the social attitudes and practices derived by Trinidadians from their African heritage had been added those acquired from the British example and those developed under the system of plantation slavery that had prevailed until the early nineteenth century (see ch. 3). The end of slavery and the importation of large numbers of East Indians as indentured laborers added another set of attitudes and practices, and in the mid-1970s the numerically predominant Negro and East Indian ethnic groups continued to live somewhat apart from one another and under somewhat different conditions. Finally, the years since World War II had been marked by increasingly close ties with North America and an increasing impact from North American influences.

The average diet was adequate or very close to adequate in numbers of calories and proteins, but most of the population relied heavily on starches and consumed relatively small amounts of green vegetables and animal protein. East Indian clothing was frequently seen, but there was no distinctive national dress, and clothing worn reflected the warm climate and the purchasing power of the wearer. There was a fairly serious housing shortage, particularly in urban localities, despite an energetic public housing program. Most of the houses were small, and concrete was the most common building material in contemporary use, although older houses were often of wood and urban shantytowns were constructed largely of scrap materials. In rural as well as in urban localities, most of the housing units had electric wiring and either piped in or easy-access water.

Health conditions were generally good. The mortality rate was low, the incidence of most diseases was declining, and hospitals and outpatient facilities were well distributed around the two islands. Doctors and dentists received their training abroad, but graduate and auxiliary nurses were schooled in local facilities. Medical personnel of all kinds were generally well trained, but during the 1960s many had emigrated, and during the early 1970s there was a severe shortage of doctors and dentists.

A national social security program put into effect in 1972 was designed to cover all of the country's workers and their dependents eventually. Benefits under it were more substantial than those offered in programs of most countries in Latin America and the Caribbean area, and in 1975 the first persons to retire under it commenced to receive benefits. There were also a large number of private pension programs, and until the national program was established there had been a variety of small programs for civil servants, a relief program for persons without funds and unable to work, and a pension program for the destitute elderly. Payments to beneficiaries under these preexisting programs continued after establishment of the national program. A variety of private welfare and welfare-related programs were in existence, and families and communities provided assistance for destitute members. In general the various public welfare mechanisms, the extent to which public educational, health, and other services were available, and the generally high level of family income left relatively few in extreme want.

The British influence on Trinidadian life was nowhere more conspicuous than in the field of sports. Addiction to cricket rivaled or exceeded that in the United Kingdom, and an almost equal enthusiasm for soccer and horseracing was at least in part British derived. The county's twelve national holidays included a Hindu and a Muslim day of observation. The world-renowned Trinidadian Carnival was not an official holiday period, but during it work virtually halted, and it and the other holidays were occasions for community feasting, displays, music, and dancing. Featured in festivals and on occasions of all kinds were the famous calypso songs, often satirizing persons and events of local importance, and the steel bands in which the instruments were finely tuned sections of old oil drums.

The clustered pattern of settlement and the accessibility of Port-of-Spain or other urban centers to most of the population provided a variety of recreational outlets. Each village had its soccer team, most people lived within reach of a motion picture theater, and nearly everyone had friends and neighbors nearby to exchange informal visits with or to invite to a wedding or a baptism. It was a largely pluralistic society, however, in which East Indians and Negroes enjoyed their leisure time in a generally amicable mutual exclusivity. The entire population enjoyed Carnival, but the two dominant ethnic groups did not mix extensively in clubs, on social occasions, or during informal gatherings and visits.

DIET AND NUTRITION

Data concerning the nutritional adequacy of the Trinidadian diet vary substantially, but several sources indicate that in the early 1970s the daily per capita consumption in calories was a satisfactory 2,500 or more, and one source estimated the 1970 per capita daily consumption of protein at 83 grams, far above minimum requirements. According to an Organization of American States report, during the 1964–66 period the per capita daily intake included 2,361 calories, 63.9 grams of protein (including 26.4 grams of animal origin, and 57.7 grams of fats and oils (including 29.0 grams of animal origin). According to one calculation, however, in 1970 the caloric intake was 97.9 percent of minimum recommended requirements, and the consumption of protein was 82.5 percent of the minimum.

In 1972 the Caribbean Foods and Nutrition Institute, a Commonwealth Caribbean (see Glossary) research and study organization in which Trinidad and Tobago participates, reported that nutrition standards among the country's lowest income groups were considerably higher than those of corresponding groups in most other developing countries. Nutrition appears to have improved considerably during the 1960s, however, for a 1961 survey by the World Health Organization (WHO) indicated substantial nutritional deficiencies. The WHO survey is dated but remains important to the extent that it indicates a pattern. It showed the nationwide calorie intake to be 96 percent of recommended minimum requirements, but in three low-income suburbs of Port-of-Spain it was 72 percent, and in San Fernando and Sangre Grande it was below 90 percent. About 40 percent of all women and children suffered to some degree from anemia, as compared with a much smaller 8 percent among adult males; protein deficiency was found principally among children.

Ethnic predispositions, religious dietary restrictions, and diverse levels of family income result in sharp differences in food consumption patterns, although there is very little variation in consumption patterns by geographic region. Negroes consume several times as much bread as do East Indians. The latter eat correspondingly more flour in the form of traditional *roti* pancakes. East Indians consume the largest quantities of dried legumes but the least amount of meat. Hindus eat relatively little flesh other than fish; the religion of Muslims constrains them from eating pork, but they consume almost as much beef as do Negroes and somewhat more fish. Almost half of the caloric intake of the population as a whole is derived from cereals, and lower income groups in particular tend to

111

neglect green and yellow vegetables, fruits, and milk. As a consequence the diet is frequently deficient in certain vitamins and minerals, such as vitamin A, riboflavin, and iron.

The national diet is heavily dependent on imported foodstuffs, which in 1972 accounted for 18 percent of the value of all commodity imports exclusive of crude oil imported for refining (see ch. 8). The principal food imports were rice, flour, condensed milk, meat, fish, and canned and packaged items. In 1970 it was calculated that 49 percent of the calories and 71 percent of the protein consumed were imported.

Traditionally agriculture has been concentrated in the production of lucrative cash export crops, such as sugar, cacao, coffee, and citrus fruits, and relatively little effort has been made to achieve self-sufficiency in food for the domestic table. During the late 1960s and early 1970s, however, meat and vegetable production rose sharply. Rice production, in particular, soared, and in early 1975 self-sufficiency in pork production was predicted by the end of the year.

Apparent annual per capita meat consumption rose from forty-seven pounds in 1962 to fifty-nine in 1970. Beef and pork, consumed in approximately equal quantities, were the most popular kinds of meat, although their consumption was limited by Hindu and Muslim dietary restrictions. Poultry consumption, however, increased sharply from 5.7 pounds per capita annually in 1956 to 22.6 pounds in 1967, and in 1975 the *Trinidad Guardian* reported that Trinidadians had become the second heaviest chicken eaters in the world—an estimated 14 million domestically raised chickens were killed for the table annually. The consumption of milk and eggs was on the increase during the late 1960s and early 1970s but was not substantially above the average for the Caribbean area.

An annual per capita consumption of nearly eighteen pounds of fish and other seafood during the 1964–66 period placed Trinidadians among the heaviest consumers of these products in Latin America and the Caribbean area. It is the East Indians, however, who give the country its ranking position; the remainder of the population eats relatively little seafood. Although the waters around Trinidad and Tobago abound in fish and shellfish, imported salt cod and tinned salmon and sardines are substantial consumption items. An extensive 1971–72 household budgetary survey found that only about 62 percent of the money spent on fish was for fresh or frozen varieties: the remainder was for salted, smoked, or canned products. A preference for salt fish developed during the period when refrigeration was unknown and fresh fish quickly deteriorated. This remembered preference coupled with a popular prejudice against frozen fish limits the potential of refrigeration as a means of increasing seafood consumption.

During the 1964–66 period the consumption of legumes, nuts, and seeds in Trinidad and Tobago was the highest in Latin America and the Caribbean area, a consequence of the heavy East Indian consumption of legumes. Green and yellow vegetable intake, however, was somewhat below the average for the region. The most typically Trinidadian of the garden vegetables is *callaloo*, a green leafy vegetable. Eggplants—known locally as melongenes—onions, pumpkins, and cabbages are also popular. Canned peas and vegetable soup are of sufficient popularity for their prices to be quoted regularly in government statistical issuances.

Cereal consumption is high, wheat flour and rice being the principal items used. Tuber consumption is relatively low, white and sweet potatoes and dasheen—the local name for taro—being the most popular.

The moderate consumption of sweets and fruits is about average for Latin America and the Caribbean area. In 1971 the apparent annual per capita consumption of sugar was a little more than ninety pounds. Among the most frequently eaten fruits are oranges, bananas, grapefruit, mangoes, and pineapples. Fresh and canned oranges and orange juice are the most in demand; bananas are second. Imported apples, pears, peaches, and grapes are Christmas season specialties.

The average Trinidadian family breakfasts on bread, coffee or cocoa, and perhaps eggs. A typical lunch is substantial and may consist of meat, rice, a green vegetable, fruit, and a beverage. Dinner is largely a repetition of lunch. It is not served until 8:00 or 9:00 P.M., however, and prosperous families frequently break the long gap between lunch and dinner with a substantial late afternoon tea that may include cheese and biscuits, hot scones, and perhaps kippers.

Trinidadian cookery, as cosmopolitan as the country, features an immense variety of British, East Indian, Spanish, North American, African, European, Chinese, and Creole dishes. The British influence is seen in the frequency with which beef and kidney pie and black pudding are encountered, and the East Indian influence is reflected in the countless dishes made with rice and curry powder. Numerous soups and stews are of Creole origin, and Port-of-Spain has countless Chinese restaurants.

Among the most typical Trinidadian dishes is *sans coche*, a ragout of pork, salted beef, pig's tail, onions, chives, and other ingredients served with dumplings. *Callaloo* and crab is a thick Creole soup; pork souse is a spicy Creole dish garnished with cucumbers and onions and served either hot or cold; *roti* is an East Indian concoction of curried meat in a pancake wrapping; and *tum-tum* is made by mashing green plantains. *Accra*, a specialty of Tobago, is salt fish pounded with seasonings and yeast, shaped into small cakes and fried, and served with fritters called *floats*.

Among the popular desserts is kisses Angostura, a concoction of egg whites, vanilla, chopped nuts, and angostura bitters. Customarily, however, fruit is served at the end of a meal. Locally produced soft drinks, grapefruit juice, and ginger beer are served in local shops known as parlours. Beer consumption soared from about 7.6 million quarts in 1967 to 15.5 million quarts in 1971. The national alcoholic beverage is locally produced rum, however, and many rum drinks are flavored with the country's own angostura bitters.

CLOTHING

In the absence of a surviving indigenous population, there is no distinctive traditional form of native apparel. Western dress is worn by all elements of the population, but the country's ethnic diversity is reflected in the frequent appearance of colorful saris (frequently spelled sarees) Sikh turbans, Spanish lace mantillas, and Chinese split skirts and trousers. Batik and madras are popular fabrics.

Unusual and striking clothing is frequently seen. Dress uniforms of the police and the Defense Force are eye catching; judges of the Supreme Court of Judicature wear wigs and robes; and the remaining European population still often dresses for dinner. People save up all year to purchase elaborate and flamboyant Carnival costumes, and the words *trendy* and *mod* have come into common usage to describe the attire of some young city dwellers.

Everyday wear is generally informal, although adults seldom appear in shorts, and slacks for women are accepted but not particularly popular. Businessmen wear shirts and ties during the day, although jackets are worn for all evening occasions. Suits in darker colors predominate. There is no particular favored or customary style for women, but suits and skirts and blouses are worn much less frequently than dresses, and the many high-fashion dresses worn include original designs that have been acclaimed abroad.

The lightest of cottons and synthetic fabrics are used in clothing for both sexes. There are many good tailors and dressmakers, but clothing made in the country's numerous factories predominates, and there is little home sewing or weaving. Ready-made clothing is produced for export as well as for domestic wear, but piece goods are imported. Straw hats are worn regularly as protection against the hot sun in the countryside, and light straws are frequently part of the costume of fashionable urban women. Because of the sweltering heat of the daytime hours and the torrential nature of the frequent but brief downpours, umbrellas rather than raincoats are the customary means of protection against the rain.

Business suits are still worn by some segments of the society, most notably bankers, but the Caribbean "jac suit" and "shirt jac" are rapidly becoming the most common forms of business dress. The jac suit is a shirtless suit, usually a semibelted jacket worn either with or without a scarf at the neck. Within the government only the governor general and the prime minister continue to be seen regularly in the conventional suit and tie. Increasingly in the mid-1970s evening attire was informal for men, who wore dressy jac suits and shirt jacs, handwoven Afro shirts imported from West Africa, or bush jackets. Women, however, continued to dress relatively formally in long gowns or skirts, formal pants suits, or occasionally long African robes.

The customary dress of the villager differs from that of the urban dweller only to the extent that the man's open-necked shirt and trousers and the woman's dress are more likely to have seen multiple washings; shoes and new clothes are reserved for special occasions, such as weddings and excursions to town. The wardrobe of both urban and rural working-class families includes some dress clothes, and working garments have frequently seen previous service for leisure time use. Men spend far more on dress shirts and trousers than on work shirts and pants, and women spend far more on party dresses than on work dresses.

HOUSING

Census reports for 1960 and 1970 show the number of housing units to have increased from 180,846 to 210,197. On the basis of population figures from the same censuses, it appears that the increase in number of houses approximately kept pace with the increase in the number of people, the ratio of people to housing units having declined very slightly from 4.6 to 4.5.

Keeping pace with population growth, however, was not enough; an absolute housing shortage of more than 50,000 units had been estimated in 1966. In addition during the 1960s and early 1970s the age-group that was forming new families and requiring housing for the first time had been born in a period of rapid population growth as compared with the slow rate of growth registered during the 1960s (see ch. 2).

Furthermore, the 1960s and early 1970s was a period of heavy migration from country to town, and each family making the move meant that one more housing unit was needed. The heavy flow of emigration that occurred during the late 1960s had been largely of young adults and had done much to relieve the demand for additional housing, but the flow had slackened after 1970 and was expected to slacken still further in the late 1970s, a period during which the already serious housing shortfall could be expected to worsen rapidly unless there were a sharp rise in the rate of residential construction. By 1970 there was already an annual shortage of at least 3,000 in the number of housing units built. About 3,000 housing units were being constructed annually and, according to a Ministry of Housing estimate for that year, 6,000 were needed to accommodate population growth and new families. This demand plus the need for slum clearance and the replacement of obsolete and substandard dwellings would bring overall need for new housing to 10,000 a year.

Most dwellings are small. In 1970 more than 75 percent had one, two, or three rooms, although 10 percent had five or more. In this calculation storage spaces, passageways, and utility rooms, such as kitchens and bathrooms, were not counted. The occupancy rate in 1970 was somewhat higher in country than in town, and there were discernible ethnic distinctions in the occupancy pattern. According to an unofficial source the East Indian population had an urban occupancy rate of 5.2 persons per dwelling and a rural rate of 6.4; the Negro population had urban and rural rates of 4.9 and 5.2 respectively.

Housing styles are varied and sometimes fantastic in the older parts of urban centers, and wooden construction is common. Some gingerbread Victorian and Second Empire dwellings with multiple-peaked roofs and innumerable rooms survive. Most of the urban construction is relatively new, however, and in the fast-growing suburbs the houses are most frequently single-story units of concrete and tile. High-rise apartment blocks are found with increasing frequency, particularly in slum clearance areas.

The most fortunate lower income urban families live in modern concrete single-family or multifamily units built with government assistance. Older housing of lower income families consists typically of wooden structures with corrugated metal roofs and plank floors raised a few inches off the ground to avoid dampness. The dwelling may be a single room fifteen feet square with a screen to mark off the sleeping space and a kitchen located in a separate shed. The poorest dwellings are clustered in squatter shantytowns and are built of tin cans, gunnysacks, crates, and rotten lumber. In the early 1970s there were estimated to be 6,500 of these squatter dwellings in the country, two-thirds of them located in the Port-of-Spain area. Not all were entirely of marginal construction, however; nearly all had windows, and nearly one-third had electric wiring. Moreover, the proportion of housing consisting of urban squatter shanties—about 3 percent—was among the lowest in the Americas.

In the countryside the more prosperous families occupy wood or concrete houses with tile or metal roofing. The solid and spacious East Indian dwellings give an appearance of affluence that is often misleading; many were built painstakingly through the thrift and hard work of more than one generation of inhabitants. The more common rural home has one, two, or at most three rooms, a mud or slab floor, and a thatched or metal roof. Walls are frequently of wattle filled with mud that has been mixed with grass. The surface may be *leepayed*, a process of whitening and smoothing by applying a solution of water and earth in progressively thinner layers. Behind the house there is usually a kitchen and an outhouse or a pit latrine. Where electricity is not available, the family relies on kerosine lighting from what are known as pitch-oil lamps.

Trinidad and Tobago's small size, clustered pattern of settlement, and relatively high standard of living and degree of economic development have combined to produce one of the most extensive networks of public services distribution in Latin America and the Caribbean area. The Water and Sewerage Authority (WASA) of the Ministry of Public Utilities is responsible for both urban and rural water supply. According to 1970 Pan American Health Organization (PAHO) data, 96 percent of the population had access to a piped water supply, and about 59 percent lived in homes with indoor piping; the remainder with water service had easy access to public mains, standpipes, or tanks. The PAHO data showed that 83 percent of the urban and 40 percent of the rural population had indoor piping.

In addition to being available to nearly all of the population, the WASA water is pure and can be drunk without treatment. The supply, however, is irregular. In the dry season service may be curtailed temporarily, and in early 1975 the *Guardian* urged the formation of voluntary civilian patrols to prevent wastage from easy-access water supply installations. In some localities the WASA uses trucks to distribute water seasonally or regularly.

Sewerage, also supplied by the WASA, is much less extensive. The 1970 PAHO data showed only 17 percent of the population, virtually all of it urban, living in dwellings with sewer connections. The proportion served, however, can be expected to increase fairly rapidly; between 1962 and 1971 the proportion of residential construction permits approved in which the units were to be served with water-utilizing sewage facilities rose from 50 to 74 percent.

In the mid-1970s Port-of-Spain, San Fernando, and Arima had municipal sewage disposal systems, and systems were in operation in some suburban localities surrounding these centers and some oil field areas. Septic tanks to accommodate single dwellings had become customary in other more densely populated areas where the water supply was adequate and reliable, but there was a not always reliable septic tank cleaning service. Elsewhere in the country inexpensive privy cesspits were used.

Residential electric power is supplied by the Trinidad and Tobago Electricity Commission through three power stations on Trinidad and a standby plant on Tobago. Nearly all urban housing units receive electrical service, and during the late 1960s and early 1970s the commission was extending service to an increasing number of rural homes through the Assisted Wiring Scheme; it provided low-cost terms for installation attractive to both homeowners and contractors. Under the scheme between 1968 and 1972 electrical service was brought to more than 2,000 additional rural dwellings, including nearly 600 on Tobago, which had not received electricity until 1952. In addition some large agricultural enterprises and some of the more prosperous rural home-owners maintain their own generators.

Residential construction during the 1960s and early 1970s was predominantly urban. The population in the countryside was not increasing, and the greatest need for new houses was in the fast-growing metropolises. New construction was concentrated in the spreading suburbs of Port-of-Spain and San Fernando. The smaller population centers— Arima, Scarborough on the island of Tobago, and the larger county administrative centers such as Sangre Grande—did not experience significant residential construction.

By far the busiest of the residential construction areas were the Port-of-Spain suburbs such as Diamond Vale, a modern housing complex catering to the needs of lower middle income families. Located in the Diego Martin Valley northwest of the city, it was being developed as a mixed capital venture, and a 1974 commercial publication reported that some 1,500 housing units had been constructed. An example of integrated development by private capital to provide both housing and small factories was taking place at Trinidad City, a 1,600-acre site near Piarco International Airport. It was hoped that this center would become a complete community with a population of more than 100,000, schools, shopping centers, and all modern amenities.

Rural Trinidad and Tobago since World War II has been an area of out-migration, and relatively little rural housing construction has taken place. Most of it has been accomplished under the Better Villages Program and a program to provide low-cost housing loans for sugar industry workers. The Better Villages Program, initiated in 1963 as a partnership between large business firms and the government, is designed to slow the pace of urban migration by improving the quality of village life. Among its techniques are the provision of loans at nominal interest and other incentives for home building and home improvement. Most sugar industry workers formerly were housed in company barracks, but a program of low-interest housing loans financed by a levy on sugar exports was initiated in 1951, and by the end of 1973 nearly 10,000 units had been constructed under it in nearly 100 villages, most of them in Caroni and Victoria counties.

Existing public housing institutions were centralized by 1962 legislation in the National Housing Authority, an autonomous agency responsible to the Ministry of Housing. Rather than engaging directly in dwelling construction, the housing authority has made credit available to individuals and institutions and provided incentives to private enterprise to construct houses for lower income families.

High construction costs, shortage of land, and inadequate long-term financing have discouraged private initiative in housing construction, but the number of houses financed through the National Housing Authority increased sharply during the late 1960s. According to an Inter-American Development Bank (IDB) report, the number jumped from 884 units during the 1964–68 period to about 3,000 during the years 1969 and 1970. Public financing, however, appears to have only replaced private funds; between 1962 and 1973 the total number of permits for the construction of residential units ranged narrowly above and below an average of about 3,000 per year.

In 1972 a new source of housing credit was opened through establishment of the National Insurance Board, the country's new national social security agency (see Welfare, this ch.). Early in 1975 it was reported that the agency had collected TT$80 million (for value of the Trinidad and Tobago dollar—see Glossary) in pension funds, that TT$26.5 million of funds had already been placed in private housing and commercial building schemes, and that an additional TT$16 million had been committed to residential mortgages. The insurance board was acting as its own agent in placing its money and in mid-1975 was advertising rates of 9 percent for mortgages of under TT$50,000 and 9.5 percent for mortgages of between TT$50,000 and TT$125,000.

In 1975 a small industrial upsurge resulting from offshore petroleum discoveries during the early 1970s was reported to be giving a substantial boost to the home building industry. Current statistics were not available, but the pent-up demand, the local availability of nearly all of the construction materials required, and the building industry's heavy reliance on the abundance of unskilled labor had combined to create a climate very favorable to a housing boom. It was badly needed, for heads of families unable to afford a house or to secure a mortgage were writing frequently to the Port-of-Spain press with complaints that rents had become impossible for the average family. A modest one-bedroom apartment costs TT$150 monthly, and a house in one of the better suburbs might be TT$2,000 or more.

HEALTH

During the late 1960s and early 1970s conditions of health and sanitation continued an improvement that had been steadily in progress throughout the middle years of the twentieth century. Between 1968 and 1972 central government expenditures on health moved upward from 1.6 percent to 2.2 percent of the gross domestic product (GDP). Most of the population took advantage of public medical services, which were offered either free or at moderate cost. According to an extensive 1971–72 government survey, rural and urban households in all income brackets expended an average of TT$3.57 monthly on doctors and TT$0.65 on dentists as compared with TT$2.97 on medical and pharmaceutical products. Households in the lowest income bracket, less than TT$20 monthly, spent TT$1.69 on doctors and TT$0.24 on dentists; those in the highest bracket, TT$1,500 or more, spent TT$5.45 on doctors and TT$2.80 on dentists.

Health Hazards and Preventive Medicine

Between 1960 and 1971 diseases of the circulatory system remained the most frequent cause of mortality, the number of reported cases having risen from 1,468 to 2,831; about half of the deaths were from hypertensive heart disease. Complications on the respiratory system held second place but rose only slightly in number, from 662 to 684; pneumonia was the most frequent cause, followed by bronchitis and related ailments. Cancer, causing 493 deaths in 1960 and 676 in 1971, held third place.

Diabetes mellitus was responsible for 380 deaths in 1971 and was the fourth serious cause of death during the year. During the 1960s and early 1970s Trinidad and Tobago and some other Caribbean islands suffered the highest rates of mortality in the Americas from this disease. Other significant causes of mortality during the period were gastritis, enteritis, and related diseases; vitamin deficiency diseases and anemias; tuberculosis; and tetanus.

119

The record of reported cases of notifiable infectious and other communicable diseases for the period from 1962 to 1972 showed a generally downward trend that reflected the success of the country's preventive medicine program. Influenza declined from 8,851 to 4,027 cases; dysentery from 1,598 to 230; whooping cough from 632 to 111; hookworm from 847 to 243; chicken pox from 1,370 to 219; and tuberculosis from 398 to 116.

Not all of the communicable diseases were on the decline between 1962 and 1972. In particular, cases of polio were up from twelve to 140. The sharp rise, however, resulted from an outbreak that commenced in 1971 and continued through early 1972; only three cases had been reported in 1970, and fewer than ten cases had been reported each year since 1964. Between 1962 and 1972 the cases of measles increased moderately from 150 to 167, but the trend had been generally downward since 1967. Cases of ophthalmia neonatorum, an eye inflammation of the newly born often leading to blindness, rose from thirty-two to sixty-six, but only eighteen cases had been reported in 1971. Pneumonia cases increased sixty-nine to 208, and cases of enteric fever were up from eighty-four to 130; for both the trend during the period had been generally upward.

The high incidence of yaws was a matter of particular concern. During the 1970–72 period more than one-third of the yaws cases in the Caribbean area reported to the PAHO occurred in Trinidad and Tobago, and the Caribbean area was responsible for more than 90 percent of the cases reported in the Americas.

The incidence of leprosy is higher than in most of the tropical countries of the Americas. In 1968 there were 1,461 cases in the active register; the 65.6 percent of this total suffering from the tuberculoid form of the disease was the highest in the region. A little less than one-half of the active-register cases were under surveillance; about 30 percent of these were hospitalized in the country's one leprosarium, and the remainder were under treatment as ambulatory patients. No new cases were reported in 1969, but eight cases were reported in 1970 and twenty-five in 1971.

During the 1960s and early 1970s certain patterns were visible. Anemia and parasitic and respiratory disease were related to poor nutrition and were most prevalent in lower income groups. Infant mortality was low and declining, but it too was highest among low-income groups and was frequently a consequence of premature delivery induced by malnutrition, hookworm, anemia, or excessive work during pregnancy. A progressive decline in deaths from infectious diseases had been accompanied by a rise in those from cancer and cardiac and vascular diseases. In addition the incidence of major diseases appeared to have different patterns in urban and in rural areas. The incidence of infectious and parasitic complaints in Port-of-Spain was only about one-half that in the rest of the country, but the incidence of cancer and digestive diseases was double.

In the mid-1970s particular concern was expressed over a resurgence of veneral disease. Statistics were available only for cases treated in public clinics, and the true incidence was believed considerably higher than indicated in the reported figures. Reported gonorrhea cases, however, reached a high of 10,451 in 1973 but declined significantly to 7,153 in 1974. Early infectious syphilis cases were up from 523 in 1973 to 631 in 1974. Venereal disease was most serious in certain urban localities and in the nineteen to twenty-four years age-group. The separate V.D. Division in the Ministry of Health, in operation since 1944, maintained free treatment clinics at strategic points around the country. In addition veneral disease screening was conducted in prenatal clinics and in connection with the country's active Family Planning Programme (see ch. 2).

In a statement in 1975 calling attention to reorganization of the V.D. Division and expansion of its control program, the minister of health noted that treatment of venereal disease could not be considered apart from the general context of health care. The principle of integration of health services to reduce the stigma attached to such diseases as tuberculosis and leprosy as well as gonorrhea and syphilis was one of the basic tenets of the 1967–76 National Health Plan.

The incidence of drug addiction is relatively low, but alcoholism is considered an increasingly serious problem. An extensive household budget survey conducted by the government during 1971 and 1972 among families in all income categories found that 3.3 percent of the budget was allocated to the purchase of alcoholic beverages as compared with 0.8 percent for soft drinks. Speaking in 1965 to a convention attended by members of more than sixty Alcoholics Anonymous groups, a Ministry of Health officer stated that the existing Alcoholic Centre in Port-of-Spain was operating well and that at least five additional centers would be developed. Ultimately a treatment center in each county and on Tobago would be in operation.

In connection with the enactment in 1975 of a controversial bill facilitating the detention of persons believed to be suffering from mental illness, the Ministry of Health observed that nearly one-half of all hospital beds were occupied by psychiatric patients and that more than one-half of all persons who sought medical attention did so because of ailments of a psychiatric nature. In mid-1975 the Ministry of Health was engaged in implementing a system of community mental health care aimed at decentralizing the operations of St. Ann's Hospital, the country's psychiatric health care center—upgrading its services and providing psychiatric care and preventive measures to the country's population through local and community health facilities. The key element in the new program was to be the new category of mental health officer, an official who would perform, direct, and coordinate community mental health work in an assigned district.

Colonial administrations were generally effective in providing

Trinidad and Tobago with health and sanitation services, which had the effect of reducing the death rate and the incidence of disease to levels approaching those existing in developed countries. Infant mortality had declined, and such killer diseases as malaria, cholera, and tuberculosis had gradually been brought under control. In the 1970s public health authorities paid special attention to waste disposal, to maintaining pure water supplies, and to the inspections of foodstuffs and slaughterhouses. The general level of community sanitation was relatively high, and Port-of-Spain, in particular, was considered a healthful city.

The most extensive of the country's ongoing preventive medicine programs is malaria control, which was initiated in 1941 with a malaria survey scheme conducted with the assistance of the Rockefeller Foundation. In 1972 some 79 percent of the population lived in areas originally infested but eradication was considered complete, and the program was listed by the PAHO as in the final or control stage. No deaths from malaria had been reported since 1962, and the examination of more than 15,000 slides in 1972 had found only two to be positive. Nevertheless active control procedures, such as the examination of slides, spraying of the houses, examination of mosquito and larval specimens, and cleaning of drains, were continued. The cost of control measures during 1972 was TT$307,563 as compared with TT$209,265 in 1962.

No cases of yellow fever were reported between 1962 and 1972, but in 1972 Trinidad and Tobago was listed by the PAHO as reinfected by the aëdes mosquito, the vector of the disease, and the country had returned to the "attack stage" despite the absence of new cases. Reinfestation had occurred in Port-of-Spain and several other localities, and vigorous surveillance and attack operations were reported to be in progress, including administration of yellow fever serum to school children and to workers in forest areas.

The campaign against tuberculosis, including the administration of vaccinations to primary-school children, was successful in halving the incidence of the disease between 1968 and 1971. There were no tuberculosis deaths in 1971, and the rate was among the lowest in Latin America and the Caribbean area. During the early and mid-1970s a combined serum for immunization against diphtheria, whooping cough, and tetanus was being administered regularly to preschool children; a mid-1975 press announcement that there had been a poor response to the year's series and that it would be repeated was accompanied by a warning that children not inoculated would be refused admittance to school in the coming September. Compulsory immunization of children against certain major communicable diseases as a precondition to school admission was a regular practice.

Medical Personnel and Facilities

According to an Inter-American Development Bank (IDB) report there were 444 medical doctors, sixty-two dentists, and 2,815 graduate and auxiliary nurses in practice in Trinidad and Tobago during 1972. In 1969 the PAHO had reported that there were 441 doctors, sixty-two dentists, and 2,097 nurses (1,440 graduate and 657 auxiliary). The PAHO report further indicated that there were 4.3 doctors, 0.6 dentists, 13.8 graduate nurses, and 6.3 auxiliary nursing personnel per 10,000 of the population. The ratios for doctors, dentists, and auxiliary nurses were somewhat below the average for Middle America and substantially below the average for South America. The ratio for graduate nurses, however, was third highest among the countries of both regions.

In 1971 about three-fifths of the doctors (258), one-third of the dentists (twenty-one), and a substantial majority of the graduate and auxiliary nurses (1,627) were staff members of government institutions. An estimated 90 percent of the doctors in private practice and correspondingly large majorities of other privately employed medical personnel were located in the heavily urbanized western portion of Trinidad.

During the late 1960s and early 1970s the country's medical corps was very substantially decreased by a massive emigration in which professionals and technical personnel of all kinds participated in disproportionately large numbers (see ch. 2). During the 1964–68 period about ten dentists commenced practice in the country, and thirteen emigrated; PAHO statistics indicate that the number in practice actually declined from ninety-three in 1962 to sixty-two in 1969. During the late 1960s the number of graduate and auxiliary nurses emigrating annually was estimated to range between 19 and 34 percent of the number graduating from Trinidadian schools of nursing. The turnover rate was particularly high in the public health field, where between 1964 and 1968 some 847 students nurses were recruited, 667 qualified as public health nurses, and 432 resigned in order to emigrate or for other reasons. During the early 1970s nurses who had been trained at government expense were required to pay a release bond if they failed to serve in government facilities for periods of time based on the length of their training.

The shortage of doctors and dentists in the early 1970s was in large part a consequence of the absence of training facilities. There was a medical school on the Jamaica campus of the University of the West Indies, but few Trinidadians attended it; no medical training facility existed on its St. Augustine campus in Trinidad and Tobago. There was no dental school on any University of the West Indies campus. In mid-1975 the minister of health announced that the government had agreed to the establishment of a medical school at St. Augustine after a request by the University of the West Indies and recommendations by a special committee of the IDB. There were no plans for establishment of a University of the West Indies dental school in Trinidad and Tobago, however, and plans for one in Jamaica remained indefinite.

In addition to lacking a medical school of their own, young Trinidadians who were anxious to prepare during the early 1970s for a career in medicine were severely restricted in their choice of a school abroad. The government was considering relaxation of the terms of the medical registration ordinance in force, but current procedure limited full registration for practice in the country to doctors who had been trained in Commonwealth of Nations medical schools. Most of the physicians currently in practice had been trained in the United Kingdom, but in 1975 it was reported that the country's medical corps included twelve Indian nationals as well as eighteen Trinidadians who had attended Indian medical schools.

Unlike doctors and dentists, nursing personnel are for the most part trained at home. Graduate nurses receive their preparation at the Port-of-Spain Nurses' Training School, and auxiliary personnel receive their training under a program that was initiated with the assistance of the United Nations Children's Fund (UNICEF) in 1967 as a one-year nonprofessional course of study to teach simple nursing skills. It was later expanded to a two-year curriculum. In 1975 work was in progress on expansion of the capacity of the Port-of-Spain school, constructed in 1961, from 200 to 500 students, with the help of a loan from the International Bank for Reconstruction and Development (IBRD, also known as the World Bank). The IBRD credit also included funds for the Community Health Training Center at Arima for training of basic, auxiliary, and graduate nursing students in domiciliary nursing and community health. The Arima facility was to be completed early in 1976.

The relative adequacy of the supply of graduate nurses in Trinidad and Tobago results largely from the fact that in the Caribbean area the status of a trained nurse as a professional and the importance of her role are generally recognized. In Latin America there is not the same recognition; nurses of all kinds are generally in extremely short supply, and heavy reliance is placed on auxiliaries. Still greater emphasis on the graduate nurse was indicated by the temporary suspension of the training program for auxiliary personnel announced in 1975 by the minister of health. He stated that his ministry was reassessing the need for nursing auxiliaries, indicating that, when the training program was resumed, the number of annual recruits would be well below the current number of about 150. At the time, however, graduate nursing personnel were being recruited from the United Kingdom.

The shortage of medical personnel of most kinds is in part counterbalanced by a relatively large number of hospital beds; these are better distributed throughout the countryside than in a majority of the countries of Middle and South America. A 1969 PAHO hospital-bed distribution chart shows that, among sixteen countries of the two regions, Trinidad and Tobago ranked second in the number of beds per person in capitals and largest cities and third in the remainder of the country.

During the early 1970s there were approximately 5,000 beds available in the country; in 1971 there were 4,708 beds in government institutions and an estimated 250 beds in private hospitals. The total was slightly less than the 5,209 reported for 1968 by the PAHO, apparently because of the closing of one government unit and a reduction in the number of beds at St. Ann's Hospital. The PAHO data for 1968 indicate that, of the country's twenty-four hospitals, eighteen were public and six were private but that 95.3 percent of the beds were in the public units. Nineteen were general hospitals, and five were for special purposes. About 43.7 percent of the beds were for general care, 30.3 percent for mental illnesses, 6.5 percent for tuberculosis, and 19.5 percent for other special purposes.

The largest and best equipped of the country's general hospitals in the mid-1970s was located in Port-of-Spain; the second largest, located in San Fernando, was being expanded, and district hospitals were well distributed. There was also a large, modern hospital on Tobago. Supplementing the hospitals were health centers that provided outpatient curative and preventive services free of cost to the public during specified hours. Staffed by public health personnel, they were visited weekly by doctors; nurses were usually in attendance. In 1972 there were nearly 100 of these units in operation, principally in less densely populated areas. Only four were located in Port-of-Spain and one in San Fernando, but there were eleven in predominantly rural St. Andrew and St. David counties and sixteen on the island of Tobago.

A small but significant private supplement to the public medical program is furnished by the St. John Ambulance Brigade. Established soon after the énd of World War II in Port-of-Spain, the organization receives a very small government subsidy (TT$5,900 in 1975) but is primarily a voluntary welfare group. In 1975 it operated four ambulances—two in Port-of-Spain and one each in San Fernando and on Tobago. The brigade wears striking black and white uniforms and in addition to providing ambulance services furnishes training in first aid and auxiliary nursing, administers first aid and nursing care to the injured and sick, and supports a junior cadet corps.

In mid-1975 it was reported that the foundations of the new 100-bed Mount Hope Maternity Hospital in Port-of-Spain had been completed four months ahead of time. The hospital was a part of the population project undertaken with assistance of a 1971 IBRD credit. In addition in late 1974 the government had entered into a loan contract and a technical cooperation agreement with the IDB. The loan contract involved a credit of US$5.3 million, the sum to be devoted to construction of thirty-one additional health centers on both islands and to construction of a new block of buildings adjacent to the San Fernando Hospital. The block was to accommodate a pathology department, a physiotherapy department, prenatal and family planning clinics, and a 170-bed pediatric department. Under the Technical Cooperation Agreement nonreimbursable funds amounting to US$270,000 were to be used to improve the Ministry of

Health administration and upgrade technical and professional personnel in the fields of medical records, nursing training, and maintenance and repair of hospital equipment.

WELFARE

The extremes of poverty characteristic of many developing countries are seldom encountered in Trinidad and Tobago. Among the factors contributing to the absence of extreme need is the high level and relatively even distribution of income which, coupled with the existence of an extended family system, frequently makes it possible for unemployed or otherwise impoverished family members to receive support from within the family group for extended periods of time. In particular, Hindus and Muslims remained on the periphery of society and largely dependent on one another for welfare until after the granting of the adult franchise in the late 1940s; and the tradition of informal assistance within the family or the community has remained strongest among them.

The relatively wide range of public services available includes education, medical and child care, housing, nutritional assistance, and supporting systems of welfare, including relief services and pensions for the elderly. In addition many business enterprises have established pension and other welfare schemes for their workers, and there are various private cooperative welfare programs and voluntary welfare activities.

The country's first nationwide social security program, the National Insurance Scheme, was created by 1971 legislation and commenced operations in 1972 under direction of the eleven-member National Security Board, on which employes, workers, and the government were represented. Before creation of the new system, assistance had been granted by the government out of its general revenues to certain categories of the needy and the aged, and there were various benefit plans for government workers and their families. The two principal forms of direct public welfare were social assistance and old-age pensions. Social assistance, introduced in 1931 and several times restructured, offered small relief payments to needy persons. In 1971 about 27,600 individuals, two-thirds of them children, received some TT$2.4 million in relief payments. Old-age pensions, inaugurated in 1939, provided small stipends to persons aged sixty-five years or more who had resided in the country for a minimum of twenty years and whose income did not exceed a specified maximum (TT$23 monthly in the early 1970s). In 1971 some 27,500 old-age pensioners received a total of about TT$4.2 million. The old-age program included pensions for blind persons aged forty and over.

Social security for public workers was provided under individual ordinances for such categories as firemen, policemen, and teachers, and a separate plan made provision for widows and children of persons in the public employ. There was also a provident fund to which participating public workers contributed 4 percent of their wages and a later established plan for daily paid public workers that offered an option of continuing under the provident fund or transferring to the new plan. Requirements and benefits under these several programs differed widely, but in 1968 about 5,000 public and statutory board pensioners were receiving a monthly pension averaging about TT$180. In contrast, old-age pensioners were receiving a monthly average of about TT$18.

Only a single private pension scheme was in operation before 1939, but by 1971 more than 150 were in existence, eighty-eight of them formed between 1966 and 1971. One of the programs was noncontributory, but a 1969 report by the supervisor of insurance indicated that in all of the private plans reporting workers had contributed 31 percent and employers 69 percent of the funds. Most of the private funds were small ones; the amount donated by employers in the petroleum industry, however, contributed significantly to the total.

The 1971 National Insurance Scheme entered into effect in April 1972. Existing public pension plans were merged with it but continued in effect for persons not protected by the new program, and payments continued to be made under the preexisting plans to persons already receiving benefits. The 1976 budget allocated funds "to provide relief to old-age pensioners, to those receiving social assistance, and to the public service pensioners."

The National Insurance Scheme was ultimately to be mandatory for all employed persons between the ages of sixteen and sixty-five, including agricultural workers, domestics, and apprentices. It was, however, introduced in phases; paid workers were to be first, and employers and self-employed workers were to be included at later dates. Benefits to both men and women were to include an old-age pension upon reaching the age of sixty-five or a reduced pension at the age of sixty after a minimum of 750 weeks of contributions. Widows' pensions were to equal 50 percent of the pension of the insured, and smaller stipends were to be provided for children; the total survivors' pension was not to exceed 100 percent of the pension of the insured. Provision was also made for sickness and maternity benefits of up to 60 percent of earnings, and blindness and funeral allowances were to be provided. Normal old-age pension payments were scheduled to commence at the end of 1974, and in May 1975 the press reported that the first worker on the island of Tobago had qualified for retirement under the new program.

Employers were to pay two-thirds of the insurance cost (averaging 5.4 percent of earnings). Workers were to pay one-third (averaging 2.7 percent of earnings) except that the entire cost for the lowest paid workers (less than TT$16 weekly in 1972) would be borne by the employers.

In mid-1975 the National Insurance Board purchased newspaper space to reassure readers the the highest possible current contribution to its program was TT$7.45 weekly, of which the worker would pay only TT$2.45. For this contribution he would receive a monthly pension of as much as TT$134 for life upon reaching the age of sixty-five. He would derive sickness benefits of as much as TT$216 a month for six months; if after six months he was still unable to resume work, the benefit could be converted into a lifetime disability pension of up to TT$134. The advertisement also reminded readers of the maternity and survivor's benefits contained in the program and concluded that the contribution rates were extremely moderate ones.

The welfare of sugar industry workers is promoted by the Sugar Industry Welfare Committee, a statutory board that administers the Sugar Industry Labour Welfare Fund. The fund derives mainly from a fee levied on each ton of sugar exported and from loans to sugar workers under the Housing Loans Scheme, initiated in 1952. The maximum loan granted during the early 1970s was TT$3,000, repayable in twenty years at an interest rate of 1 percent annually. The loans have enabled a large proportion of the workers in the sugar industry to build their own dwellings and have largely eliminated the barracks in which plantation workers were formerly housed (see Housing, this ch.).

Emphasis on private welfare in the form of mutual help schemes tended to decline in the 1960s. Between 1962 and 1971 the number of friendly societies providing sickness and survivor benefits dropped from 334 to 290, and the membership in them dropped from 94,000 to 30,700. Similarly credit union membership declined from 27,000 in 1962 to 25,800 between 1962 and 1970. In the country's one large building society, however, between 1961 and 1969 the number of share investors rose from 4,658 to 6,074, the number of depositors from 1,026 to 1,735, and the number of borrowers from 1,723 to 1,767. In addition the government was committed to the development of cooperatives and supported cooperative education courses extending down to the school-age population. In 1970 there were nearly 800 small cooperatives in such fields as consumption, fishing, marketing, agriculture, and charcoal production.

Church groups and voluntary organizations, such as the Rotary clubs, are active in welfare undertakings. The privately supported Trinidad and Tobago Blind Association maintains workshops in Port-of-Spain, San Fernando, and the Santa Cruz Valley on the island of Tobago. In 1975 the three workshops had a total of more than 100 members. The organization also maintains on Tobago a school for blind children, which in 1975 had about forty-five students. In addition the private St. John Ambulance Brigade provides welfare-related medical services. (see Health, this ch.).

PATTERNS OF LIVING AND LEISURE

Holidays and Business Hours

The country's twelve nationally observed public holidays are New Year's Day (January 1); Good Friday (variable); Easter Monday (variable); Labour Day (June 19); Whit Monday (variable); Corpus Christi (variable); Discovery Day (first Monday in August); Independence Day (August 31); Eid-ul-Fitr (variable); Diwali (variable); Christmas (December 25): and Boxing Day (December 26). Diwali and Eid-ul-Fitr, days of religious observation for Hindus and Muslims respectively, are movable dates determined by the phases of the moon. Before 1967 all religious holidays were Christian.

Although there is no legal requirement to observe a day of rest, Sundays and holidays are recognized as such, and overtime is paid for labor performed during them. Saturday is designated an early closing day for stores. A bank holiday occurs in August, and work comes to a near halt during Carnival on the Monday and Tuesday immediately preceding Lent.

Port-of-Spain stores and businesses are usually open from 8:00 A.M. to 4:00 P.M. Monday through Thursday. Department stores close during the noon hour on Fridays but remain open to a later hour, and grocery and liquor stores close at noon on Thursdays. Regular banking hours are from 10:00 A.M. to 5:00 P.M. Mondays through Fridays, although many banks close at 1:00 P.M. daily and reopen for an afternoon period one day a week.

Consumption Patterns

By the standards of developing nations, Trinidad and Tobago is a wealthy country, one in which the income is fairly evenly distributed and the entire population participates in the market economy. The unpaid family worker is fast disappearing; the farmer sells rather than barters his crops; and the fishermen returning with his catch to an isolated fishing village is met by brokers waiting to bargain for the kingfish and snapper. The self-sufficient subsistence farmer is virtually unknown, and in the early 1970s less than 2 percent of the average household budget was absorbed by the imputed cost of homegrown food. This proportion was determined in a detailed government household survey of expenditures of 2,800 urban and rural families in all income brackets and in all parts of the country during the period from August 1971 to August 1972. The publication of the Trinidad and Tobago Central Statistical Office, in which the findings of the survey appeared, noted as significant that the country had a sophisticated market economy with a high degree of currency transactions in the rural sector.

During the early 1970s the per capita gross national product (GNP) was the equivalent of about US$1,000—higher than that in any other Commonwealth Caribbean state or dependency with the possible exception of Barbados and among the highest in the third world. According to one source the average monthly income of the wage and salary earners, who made up nearly 80 percent of the labor force, rose from the equivalent of US$132.50 during the first half of 1965 to US$153 during the first half of 1971. Of these paid workers, over 65 percent earned between US$100 and US$500, less than 29 percent earned under US$100, and a little more than 6 percent earned in excess of US$500. The median male wage was nearly US$170 per month, but the female wage was under

US$100. A large proportion of the employed women, however, were dependents whose incomes supplemented those of the heads of household. Among employed persons in the upper income brackets, it could be generalized that the share of total income enjoyed by the wealthy was somewhat smaller and the share enjoyed by those in the upper middle brackets was larger than that in most developing countries.

Income increased substantially during the 1960s; according to one calculation it increased 55 percent in current values and 35 percent in real values between 1962 and 1971. Moreover the average family's standard of living rose in response to the newly independent country's policy of creating employment, redistributing income, and providing subsidies to low-income groups in the form of free or inexpensive public services, health care, education, and housing.

Gains in real income were interrupted during the early 1970s as wages in the nonagricultural sector between mid-1970 and mid-1974 rose only from a base of 100 to 145.6 while consumer prices increased from 100 to 156.4, despite a program of subsidization of the prices of basic food items and petroleum in order to keep a rein on spiraling costs. In the mid-1970s, however, the small industrial boom triggered by new offshore oil and gas discoveries gave hope of further real gains.

In the early 1970s a consumer economy was emerging. Between 1962 and 1971 the amount spent on refrigerators had doubled, and in the early 1970s the per capita consumption of newsprint was the highest in the Caribbean area. A 1972 businessman's publication reported one registered motor vehicle for every eleven persons and one telephone for every seventeen. It also reported, however, that with the exception of Guyana the Trinidadian cost of living was the lowest among the Commonwealth Caribbean states.

The increasing maturity of the economy was shown also in one of the less desirable characteristics of a developed country; Trinidadians were learning to throw things away. A newspaper article in mid-1975 noted that a two-week cleanup campaign in the Port-of-Spain area alone had resulted in the removal of 350 automotive vehicles. The most troublesome of the economic problems was chronically high and apparently worsening unemployment (see ch. 2). Combined unemployment and underemployment was such that an estimated one-third of the population at any given time was failing to participate fully in the country's progress.

According to the 1971–72 household budgetary survey, the lower income families canvassed were spending well in excess of income. Those with monthly incomes of less than TT$20 spent an average of TT$102.50, and those with incomes of between TT$50 and TT$99 spent an average of TT$155.55. Some of the indicated expenditure items were imputed ones, such as the value of homegrown food, of household repairs, or of imputed rent in owner-occupied dwellings. It appears probable, however, that the lower income households were headed by unemployed workers or that one of several workers in the household was unemployed and that the households had some savings or were able to secure loans or otherwise gain access to funds. Considerable inelasticity in household spending habits was apparent.

The survey revealed that the overall proportions of expenditures were similar to those of a developed country in the sense that considerably less than half were devoted to food and other nondurable consumer goods and considerable amounts were expended on such items as wearing apparel and household furniture and furnishings. Some 34.7 percent of the budget went to food and related expenses, 15.8 percent to wearing apparel, 21.6 percent to housing, 4.2 percent to health, and 15.5 percent to transportation; the remaining 8.2 percent was devoted to education, entertainment, and other expenses (see table 4). Households with incomes of less than TT$20 per month spent about 46 percent on food, and those with monthly incomes of TT$1,500 or more spent only 27 percent on food and correspondingly more in other consumption categories; the spread between lowest and highest income households in proportions of income spent on food was substantially less than that found in most developing countries.

Other expenditures varied between the lowest and highest incomes in a generally predictable pattern, but several peculiarities emerged. The relatively large proportion of income spent on transportation reflected a consistently high proportion of income spent by all income categories on purchase and maintenance of motor vehicles, the poorer households spending relatively more. In addition the poor spent more on bus fares and relatively more on taxi service, much of it for collective taxis operating on scheduled routes. More prosperous households spent proportionately more on all kinds of public and private entertainment, but poorer households spent proportionately as much or more than prosperous ones on radios and relatively more on television sets. Domestic help was not engaged by households making less than TT$200 monthly, but those with incomes in excess of TT$1,500 spent an average of over TT$60 monthly on help.

The household budgetary survey did not include information on income set aside as savings, and data concerning life insurance premiums and other special forms of saving were too incomplete to indicate a pattern. In August 1974, however, bank deposits were reported at a record TT$917.4 million as compared with TT$736.1 million a year earlier. The bulk of the deposits were on time deposit, where an attractive annual interest rate of 11 percent was offered. Traditionally ordinary savings deposits had been the largest component in bank liabilities, but the appeal of the new time accounts had caused depositers to switch.

The large number of unemployed or underemployed persons coupled with the volume of goods and services available to people with money to spend suggest a generally low propensity to save. Tradition has it that East Indians are more likely to save money than other elements in the population. Specific data in this connection are lacking, however, and limited studies do not confirm that there is a greater East Indian tendency toward thrift.

Recreation

Cricket has been described as the national mania, and the more illustrious batsmen and bowlers have been immortalized in calypso songs. The cricket season runs from January to June, and the pace of business slows when test matches are being played. Soccer—sometimes but not invariably known as football—is scarcely less popular, and its season, conveniently, lasts from July to December. Cricket stands preeminent in Port-of-Spain, but it requires considerable equipment. Soccer needs only a flat place and a ball, however, and almost every rural village has a soccer team. Both sports are of such interest that the outcome of an important match rates banner front-page headlines in the Port-of-Spain press.

Next in popularity is basketball. There are men's and women's leagues, and in mid-1975 the Trinidad Amateur Basketball Association erupted in protest over the failure of the government to supply funds for sending a Trinidadian representative to the Central American and Caribbean championship games; money had been provided for the transportation of teams for netball and field hockey, two other sports played extensively by both sexes. Netball, similar to basketball, is very popular in the Caribbean area.

Track and field events, commonly known as athletics, also attract large numbers of competitors and spectators. The track meet has limited popularity in Latin America but is immensely popular throughout the West Indies, and Trinidad and Tobago has produced performers of world championship caliber. Trinidadian champions appear often in Madison Square Garden events, and top performers from abroad regularly make their appearance in events held in Port-of-Spain.

A large proportion of the country's tennis courts are at private tennis clubs, but public courts and players are sufficiently numerous to justify a Port-of-Spain public courts championship tournament, and even Tobago has produced public courts players worthy of press notice. Tobago as well as Trinidad has championship caliber private golf courses. Excellent fishing is available the year round, and a hunting season extends from October through March.

A private yacht club is situated a few miles from Port-of-Spain, but the best swimming and surfing beaches of Trinidad are on the sparsely populated eastern flank of the island. Maracas Bay, however, is located about fourteen miles from downtown Port-of-Spain and offers good swimming and surfing. Tobago has countless sandy coves, and Buccoo Reef on the island's southeast coral platform is internationally renowned for snorkeling, spearfishing, and observation of coral gardens. Trinidadians are not notable devotees of water sports, however, and the

Table 4. *Trinidad and Tobago, Household Expenditures
by Category, 1971–72*
(in percent)

Category	Percent of Total
Foods, Beverages, and Tobacco:	
Meat	3.2
Poultry	3.0
Fish	1.8
Dairy products, fats, and oils	6.2
Fruits	1.2
Green and yellow vegetables	2.6
Cereals and starches	6.0
Sugar	1.1
Hot beverages and other foods	4.0
Soft drinks	0.8
Alcoholic beverages	3.3
Tobacco	1.5
Total	34.7
Wearing Apparel:	
Men's and boys' clothing	5.0
Women's and girls' clothing	3.5
Infants' clothing and accessories	1.1
Clothing materials	2.2
Tailoring and dressmaking charges	1.0
Footwear	3.0
Total	15.8
Housing:	
Accommodation	8.5
Fuel and light	3.0
Furniture	1.7
Floor coverings	0.1
Soft furnishings	1.0
Household equipment and appliances	3.5
Household operating costs	3.8
Total	21.6
Health:	
Medical services	1.2
Medicines	0.9
Other health expenses	0.4
Personal hygiene and care	1.7
Total	4.2
Transportation:	
Own vehicles	7.1
Travel and maintenance	3.2
Hired transport	5.2
Total	15.5
Other:	
Education	2.0
Entertainment	1.5
Personal and financial services	0.5
Miscellaneous	4.2
Total	8.2
TOTAL	100.0

Source: Based on information from Trinidad and Tobago, Central Statistical Office, *Household Budgetary Survey 1971–1972*, (Continuous Sample Survey of Population, Publication No. 22.), Port-of-Spain, July 1974, Table 15.

country's considerable assets in surf and sand are important primarily as tourist attractions.

Many other sports and games are popular. Billiards clubs hold regular competitions, and match results are reported prominently in the press. There is a table tennis club, and Trinidadian players engage in international as well as local competitions. In table tennis, as well as in lawn tennis, East Indians are particularly active. Among the nonathletic games, bridge and chess have large followings, and the opening of the 1975 draughts (checkers) championships received extensive press coverage. Among the sports and hobbies clubs are a national fencing association, a light aeroplane club, a kennel club, a philatelic society, a caged bird association, and a rifle association.

The national sports program is conducted under the direction of the appointed National Sports Council, which reports to the Ministry of Education, Culture, and Community Development. Competition is usually amateur, although professional boxing is popular; a majority of the competitors are from the Caribbean area, but boxers from elsewhere are sometimes seen. Horseracing is also conducted on a professional basis, and meetings are held in Port-of-Spain's Queen's Park, San Fernando, Arima, and on Tobago. On Tobago, goat races are a unique feature of Easter week. Legal betting shops throughout the country handle domestic racetrack results and pay track odds on cabled results of British horse and greyhound races.

Gamblers may also participate in the fortnightly national lottery in which prizes range from TT$60,000 for a winning ticket to TT$30 in consolation money to holders of tickets bearing the last two digits of the top prize numbers. There is also a popular although illegal numbers game; each number is associated with a particular animal, and dreaming of an animal is a sure sign that the associated number will win in the next drawing. Cockfights are held illegally, but betting on them is substantial. There is a Trinidad and Tobago Cockfighters' Association, and in mid-1975 a move to legalize the sport was arousing considerable controversy.

For all their devotion to sports and games, Trinidadians reserve their fullest enthusiasm for Carnival, held on the Monday and Tuesday before the beginning of Lent. Only the Carnival in Rio de Janeiro rivals it in world reputation and, although Carnival is observed only in Port-of-Spain and to a lesser extent in San Fernando, people from all over the country come to the capital for the event, which marks a peak in the tourist season. The élan of Carnival is predominantly Negro, but it is an annual period of madness for all Trinidad and Tobago; even the somewhat clannish East Indian population has come to participate extensively.

The festivities commence at 5:00 AM. on Monday with what is called the *jour ouvert* (pronounced, and sometimes spelled, Ju-vay). People flood the streets to "jump up"—a kind of shuffle in time to the music. In Port-of-Spain opening activities center in Independence Square, where the king of Ju-Vay is crowned, and prizes for the best costumes are distributed. The crowd disperses at about 8:00 A.M. but returns in early afternoon as the full carnival commences. Leaders of various costumed groups have decided in secret on the design of their elaborate dress. Carnival songs have been written, and great honor is bestowed on the composer and the band of the song selected by popular vote as the "road march" of the year's Carnival. There are parades with up to 2,000 marchers participating, and there is much dancing and music. Floats are specifically excluded from most competitions, but there are large-scale individual costumes, which despite their size must be a part of the costume and movable by the wearer alone. The shango, rada, bongo, and bele are all dances that, except in some isolated rural localities, are seen rarely except at Carnival.

The two most important elements of Carnival, uniquely Trinidadian and indispensable to Trinidadians during Carnival or any other time, are calypso singers and steel bands. The first calypso songs were improvised. Most contemporary ones are formally composed, although improvised ballads can still be heard. The usually irreverent and satirical subject matter ranges widely and includes social customs, public figures, sex, love, and topical matters. Leading singers have splendid names, such as Mighty Sparrow and Blind King Iere. Calypso vocalists perform throughout the year at public and private events and in clubs and hotels. Their proper setting, however, is the calypso tent, which in actuality is never a tent but may be anything from a public hall to a structure improvised from palm fronds or corrugated metal. The tents open in January and continue to offer calypso performances through the Carnival season.

The second of the indispensable elements of Carnival, the steel band, is of surprisingly recent origin. It appears to have made its debut suddenly and spontaneously in the course of celebrations marking the end of World War II, and the first steel drums are variously reported to have been pie plates and lids of garbage cans. Sections of forty-two gallon oil drums discarded by the wartime United States Naval Base at Chaguaramas, however, were soon found to make ideal drums; the tops could be so finely tuned that the players could play a wide variety of musical genres. Steel band players, known as panmen, formed groups with such names as Sun Jets and North Stars.

There was a natural affinity between calypso singers and steel bands, and a happy union between the two promptly took place. In the mid-1970s both could be heard throughout the world, and their popularity at home remained undiminished. A typical article appearing in a 1975 edition of the *Guardian* announced that a fund-raising party for a Port-of-Spain school would feature refreshments, bingo, calypso singers, and two steel bands.

The twelve national holidays are occasion for a variety of festivities. In particular All Souls' Day is marked by the lighting of candles, and one feature of the Christmas season is the *parang*—a kind of house-to-house

Christmas caroling to the accompaniment of guitars—imported from Venezuela. The Muslim feast of Eid-ul-Fitr and Diwali—the Hindu Festival of Lights—are both national holidays. In addition the annual Muslim festival of Hosein draws thousands of worshipers and spectators. It commemorates the martyrdom of two Islamic princes, features enormous *tageahs* representing their tombs, and is accompanied by much drumbeating and stick fighting. Hindus also celebrate Ramilla, a nine-day enactment of the story of Ram—a major deity of the Hindu pantheon—done in a kind of theater-in-the-round. The East Indian festivals draw thousands of spectators but remain essentially by and for Hindus and Muslims.

During the years since independence there have been spectacular developments in folk music, dancing, and singing, and on alternate years a folk festival and a music and arts festival take place. Motion picture attendance has remained among the highest in the Americas. Per capital attendance declined from 9.1 times yearly in 1962 to 8.4 in 1969 as a consequence of competition from television and other forms of entertainment, but the government's 1971–72 household budgetary survey found that motion picture admissions absorbed slightly over half of all funds expended on public entertainment. United States films make up most of the motion picture fare, but a substantial number of East Indian films are also imported

The survey's analysis of money devoted to the purchase of recreational equipment underlined the Trinidadian's fondness for children—by far the largest expenditures were for toys and play accessories. Photographic equipment placed second, and sporting equipment was a distant third.

The social interaction of the East Indian community with other elements of the Trinidadian population has tended to lag behind its political and economic integration, although this exclusivity is less pronounced among younger Hindus and Muslims. East Indians seldom join mixed clubs, and those among their elites who are club members belong to the West India Club or the Himalaya Club, both of them exclusive. Mixed voluntary and commercial clubs such as the Rotary are dominated by whites and persons of mixed race, and such occasions as religious festivals and weddings seldom bring the ethnic groups together. In general the East Indian and Negro elements who make up the bulk of the population maintain separate cliques, fraternal societies, and religious organizations and rarely meet in the visits between friends and neighbors that remain an important informal recreational outlet for both.

CHAPTER 6

EDUCATION, CULTURE, AND MASS COMMUNICATION

In the mid-1970s nearly all children of primary school age were enrolled in schools, and the smaller enrollments in secondary schools were rising rapidly. Higher education was available only at the Trinidad campus of the University of the West Indies, a multinational entity administered jointly by members of the Commonwealth Caribbean (see Glossary) states and dependencies; many Trinidadian students, however, were enrolled at universities abroad. The country's literacy rate and level of primary school enrollment were among the world's highest, and enrollments at higher levels, as well as attendance and retention rates, compared very favorably with those in other countries of Latin America and the Caribbean.

The Draft Plan for Educational Development (1968–83) called for the introduction of a new kind of lower secondary shcool to be attended by all students continuing their education beyond the primary level. This school was designed to provide further general education for students who under the previously existing system would have either dropped out of classes on completion of the primary level or enrolled in one of the few and inadequate vocational schools.

The development plan also called for sharply increased emphasis on teacher, vocational, and technical education and on reform of the curriculum to include more practical subjects and more material relevant to the country's particular socioeconomic needs. By 1975 considerable progress had been made in establishing new lower secondary schools, but other phases of the plan were proceeding slowly.

The traditional system still in force with some modifications in 1975 had been subjected to increasing criticism; its emphasis on academic studies was designed to prepare students for university matriculation that would be possible for only a few and produced an excessive number of secondary-level graduates whose academic schooling left them poorly prepared to find jobs. The shortage of vocational and technical schools and the mediocre training in those that were available had resulted in a critical shortage of skilled manpower, which the educational development plan sought to relieve.

At both primary and secondary levels most schools in the public sector were tuition-free institutions funded by the government but operated by religious denominations and known as assisted schools. Unlike the government-operated schools, most denominational ones were segregated by sex. There were few private primary schools, but the increasing demand for secondary education had led to a sharp increase in private secondary school enrollment during the 1960s. In the mid-1970s the only current information on numbers and kinds of schools and the distribution of enrollments in them was based on fragmentary estimates and preliminary statements; the most recent complete official report on educational statistics, issued at the end of 1974, was for the school year ending in 1971.

In postindependence Trinidad and Tobago no school denied admission to any student because of his race or religion. In general, however, the best education was offered in assisted schools operated by Christian denominations, and most colored (that is, of mixed ancestry—see Glossary) parents, who made up the bulk of the growing middle class, enrolled their children in these institutions. Black (locally Negro) students made up most of enrollment in government schools, and a large proportion of East Indian students attended their own Hindu and Muslim schools. Substantial numbers of Negroes and East Indians, however, were enrolled in Christian denominational institutions, which had proved to be fairly effective instruments of national integration and upward social and economic mobility. Hindu and Muslim denominational schools had been established only after World War II and had come into being largely as a means of preserving the East Indian cultural heritage. They had developed curricula similar to those of the government and Christian denominational units, however, and they too had proved effective as instruments of upward mobility (see ch. 4).

Through centuries of European colonization, African enslavement, and East Indian indentureship, Trinidad has evolved into one of the most complex cultures in the Western Hemisphere. Given the confluence of ethnic heritages, many experts feel that a unified culture is still in the nascent stage. Although Trinidad possesses numerous cultural elements, however, the most outstanding element and common denominator has been the Creole. Creole culture is a polyglot of African slave cultures overlaid with successive waves of Spanish, French and, lastly and most permanently, English colonial culture. In the 1970s Creole constituted one of two distinct folk traditions. The other was East Indian—transplanted in the middle of the nineteenth century by indentured workers from the subcontinent of India who entered the islands after the bases of Creole society were established. East Indian and Creole folk cultures are most commonly manifest in music, dance, and oral tradition, and after a century of interaction—however superficial—some common elements have emerged. In more formal cultural activities, such as writing, painting, and scholarship, both of these folk cultures have been superseded by English tradition. Authors, artists, and scholars have followed European painting styles and literary techniques although their themes have been largely Caribbean.

Before 1930 there was little cultural activity other than local folkloric expression. As in other West Indian islands, however, political, social, and cultural factors coalesced in the 1930s to produce a literary revolution. Writers became the vanguard of political and social movements to portray the masses—both black and East Indian—sympathetically and to cope with the polyglot ethnic background of the islands. Literary magazines arose that encouraged contributions from all over the British West Indies, and Creole dialect—previously a speech pattern identified exclusively, and negatively, with the lower class—became a popular and acceptable form of literary expression (see ch. 4).

The average Trinidadian, however, was not ready for this call to action, and authors found an alternately hostile or unresponsive audience at home. The upper and rising middle classes resented the attempt to upset the status quo, whereas the lower classes of urban workers and peasant groups were ill prepared to be an audience for or to follow up the potential implications of this work. As a consequence of these frustrations and the lure of larger and more appreciative audiences abroad, many authors emigrated, most to England but some to the United States. This pattern of emigration remained unbroken into the 1970s.

Public awareness, however, began to catch up to these literary forerunners, and the surge in writing and representative painting since 1950 is directly related to the growth of national feeling. Self-discovery on a personal, ethnic, and national level has underscored much of the writing and art since then.

Movements in scholarship, the graphic arts, and the theater are still largely in the nascent stages. A lack of British scholarly interest and a Trinidadian anti-intellectualism combined to inhibit the growth of scholarly tradition until the mid-1950s. Since then, however, there has been a steady growth of scholarly work, particularly in history and the social sciences, some of it by men, such as Prime Minister Eric Williams, who are also deeply involved in politics.

Artists have yet to receive much popular acceptance in Trinidad and Tobago. There has been little formal training available to them and little or no social or economic incentive to pursue art as a profession rather than an avocation. Growth of the theater has been plagued by similar technical handicaps—a dearth of trained actors and directors as well as a lack of financial backing and a limited audience.

In contrast to the sluggish development of the other arts, music and dance have a rich and ancient tradition. Folk music has become the source and impetus for original music and dance forms, although often based on African patterns. Spanish, French, and English influences on musical instruments and forms are also present, preserved intact, or combined with African influence. Popular ballads differ from folk music in that they are attributed to specific composers and are used as modern dance music. The calypso, which evolved from the folk culture, is considered a popular ballad.

Since 1962 the government has attempted to gain tighter control over the mass media in order to prevent their libelous use and to encourage national development and the building of a national identity. To some extent the government has succeeded, largely through efforts to implement the Third Five-Year Plan (1969–73). By the mid-1970s the government owned the only television station and one of the two radio stations. Roy Thomson, a prominent foreign investor, had been largely divested of his monopolistic holdings, including controlling interest in the local newspaper. The public had become more aware of the potential of the media, and local productions were on the rise.

EDUCATION IN THE SOCIETY

The pattern of education and its place in society have changed profoundly since the slave era and substantially since the achievement of independence. The changes have occurred slowly, however, and many remnants from the past could still be observed in the mid-1970s.

During the days of slavery the wealthier planters sent their children to England for schooling, and literacy was considered undesirable for slaves or beyond their comprehension. Missionaries and private groups maintained the few schools that provided the rudiments of education for poor whites and free coloreds.

The school system that developed after emancipation consisted largely of classrooms maintained by denominational groups. A few government schools were opened, and a teachers college was established in 1852, but public participation in the educational process was principally in the form of financial help to private institutions. Private secondary schools appeared, and an 1870 ordinance established the basis on which secondary units were to be entitled to grants-in-aid from government funds.

There was a sharp break between primary schooling and schooling at the secondary level. Secondary schools were designed to cater to the children of the elite, and their highly academic curriculum was designed as preparation for admission to British universities; vocational schooling was virtually nonexistent. These academic secondary schools, however, served as a means of access to white-collar vocations; and as early as the 1880s it was possible for a Negro peasant by patient industriousness to give his children educations enabling them to enter the teaching profession, the constabulary, or the lower rungs of the civil service. East Indians, entering the country in large numbers after the emancipation of the slaves, occupied the lowest run of the social ladder and had minimal access to schools (see ch. 3).

Until well after the beginning of the twentieth century, educational facilities—particularly those at the secondary level—were concentrated in and near the population centers of Trinidad's west coast. The first secondary school on Tobago was not opened until 1925. A denominational school supported by funds raised by popular subscription without government help, it gave young Tobagonians their first real opportunity to seek nonagricultural careers, and its graduates have included many leaders in government and business.

During the late colonial period education advanced slowly and in the face of some opposition. A legislative proposal in 1926 that sought to restrict the hours of employment of school-age children during school periods was opposed on the grounds that education of the entire agricultural population would be ruinous to the area's economy.

The social system of the late nineteenth century was pluralistic. Whites and other members of the elite remained apart from the small, predominantly colored middle class, and both groups were sharply differentiated from a divided rural working class made up largely of Negroes and East Indians.

As a consequence of complex economic and political developments after the start of the twentieth century, education gradually became an avenue into the middle class for educated coloreds and a few Negroes in urban localities. The subordinate rural population received little education and showed relatively little interest in such schooling as was available, an attitude that has been attributed to the absence of supporting economic and social institutions without which formal schooling had no readily apparent value.

In urban localities, where the supporting institutions were present, the rate of growth in school attendance and of upward social and economic movement increased as the twentieth century advanced. Negro children whose parents had migrated from the countryside attended urban schools and were assimilated into the advancement patterns of whites and middle-class coloreds. Later increasing numbers of East Indian children became involved in the same process, and the large number of Hindus and Muslims in Trinidad and Tobago gave the development of education during the twentieth century a pattern different from that occurring elsewhere in the British West Indies.

At the beginning of the twentieth century few East Indians were literate. As recently as 1931 no more than 27 percent were able to read and write in English, and most of these were Christians. A new era in the education of the East Indian population, however, commenced with the granting of the adult franchise in 1946 when, as a consequence of political expediency, the opening of East Indian schools became possible. The first Muslim unit was established in 1949, two Hindu schools opened in 1952, and by 1971 the sixty-six East Indian primary and intermediate institutions in operation had nearly 13 percent of the total enrollment at those levels. There were also a substantial number of students in East Indian secondary schools. Corresponding data for secondary school enrollment are not available, but in the late 1960s at least four of the approximately twenty denominational secondary schools were Hindu or Muslim.

By no means all East Indian students in the 1960s and early 1970s attended their own denominational institutions. Before the first sectarian schools were established, increasing numbers of young Hindus and Muslims had attended government and Christian denominational schools. They had met with some discrimination but, in general, fitted in so well that some East Indian leaders had become alarmed over the potential erosion of the traditional culture. East Indian schools were established in large part to offset this apparent trend.

With the creation of a distinctive East Indian system, unprecedented numbers of Hindu and Muslim children sought educations. In increasing numbers the best students among them took the secondary school examinations leading to university entrance and competed for the better paid and more prestigious jobs. As East Indian students became more numerous, they showed themselves to have a particular advantage over their Negro and, to a lesser extent, over their colored schoolmates. A survey in the late 1960s showed that their established cultural tradition and strong family support gave them a strong sense of identity and an exceptional confidence in their ability to attain their educational goals and to move upward, even when placed in a hostile school environment. Colored students shared this quality to a less pronounced degree, but black students tended to feel confidence in their ability to realize their educational ambitions only when in a predominantly Negro school environment.

Creole leaders feared and East Indian leaders hoped that the schools would perpetuate cultural identity, but contrary to expectations the new institutions furthered rather than hindered integration. Schools had some traditional East Indian trappings, but the curriculum was modeled on the prevailing British pattern. This important concession was necessary in order to provide students with the means of entering higher status occupations in the face of some continued discrimination. Thus the sectarian system soon proved itself effective in a role very different from the one originally intended.

The educational program that independent Trinidad and Tobago inherited from the colonial administration was patterned on the British model and possessed a structure and content very similar to those of other Commonwealth Caribbean members. Most Trinidadians interested in education were anxious to remodel this externally imposed system into a national one responsive to the country's particular needs, but during the years that followed independence the desire to change continued to be offset by a reluctance to stray far from the British model. In 1975 students completing secondary school were readying themselves for General Certificate of Education examinations still prepared and graded in the United Kingdom.

At the beginning of the postindependence period the best schools at both primary and secondary levels were the assisted Christian denominational institutions. Although overtly discriminatory admission policies were not practiced, these schools were attended by children of the predominantly colored middle class. Negro students were most numerous in the government schools, and East Indian children attended their own denominational institutions, although there was some racial mixing in schools of all kinds.

Tuition was free at both primary and secondary levels, but highly competitive examinations and the limited number of places available severely limited the number of students who could be admitted to secondary schools. Thus at the age of eleven or twelve many found it necessary either to leave school altogether or to engage in two years of postprimary schooling and to enter one of the few vocational schools. Similarly only a few of those accepted in the highly academic secondary schools went on to universities, and the majority were left without having acquired skills useful in commerce and industry. The failure of the educational system to produce a sufficient number of skilled workmen and technicians was the most serious criticism leveled against it during the 1960s.

Success in school tended to be measured by achievement in academic studies and the status and prestige attached to paper qualifications to be exaggerated. Survivors of the school system were naturally attracted to professional and administrative employment. Business held relatively little attraction for the best educated, but among the less successful academically a strong preference for white-collar work tended to create a situation conducive to high unemployment among young adults and artificial labor shortages for some kinds of manual work.

The bulk of the changes in the educational program during the 1960s involved administrative centralization and increases in the number of school places, although the ground work for increased emphasis on practical studies was laid. Over strenuous Roman Catholic objections, the government and assisted schools were placed under more stringent government control in 1965. History texts were revised to teach the area's past, Caribbean history was made a compulsory part of the curriculum, and the new mathematics was introduced at both primary and secondary levels. Little was done about introducing the study of East Indian or African subjects, however, and in the early 1970s the restructuring of textbooks to relate to instructional needs was still in the formative stage.

In the mid-1970s many people, parents in particular, still seemed to prefer a continuation of the traditional emphasis on academic education leading to professional and white-collar jobs to a shift in emphasis to the practical schooling needed by the economy. In mid-1975 an educational crisis arose over the delay in progress of the educational development plan (see The School System, this ch.). Complaints by teachers associations, parent groups, and individuals received extensive press coverage and editorial support. The amount and intensity of the complaints underlined the general interest in education and the recognized importance of its place in society: the value popularly attached to possession of a good education was rivaled only by the possession of wealth.

EDUCATIONAL ADMINISTRATION AND FINANCE

The Ministry of Education, Culture, and Community Development administers the overall planning and development of the public school system, staffing, programs of study, and school supervision. The Ministry of Tobago Affairs is largely responsible for school administration on Tobago, however, and the Ministry of Agriculture, Lands, and Fisheries is largely responsible for agricultural schooling below the university level. The Office of the Prime Minister is responsible for liaison with the University of the West Indies, an autonomous multinational institution that maintains campuses in Trinidad and Tobago, Jamaica, and Barbados. The university is operated and financed jointly by member states and dependencies of the Commonwealth Caribbean.

A growing minority of the public primary and secondary schools are operated directly by the government and are known as government schools. The majority, known as assisted schools, are owned and operated by voluntary agencies—usually Christian, Hindu, and Muslim denominational groups—but are financed by government grants (see table 5). Official documents customarily report enrollment and other data for the two kinds of institutions together under the heading "government and assisted schools." The few vocational, technical, and agricultural schools are government operated, and there are numerous privately operated commercial schools.

Assisted schools have courses of study similar to those in schools operated by the government, and their autonomy is limited both by their dependence on the government for recurrent and most capital expenditures and by statutory provisions concerning such matters as student enrollment and teacher appointments. Tuition-charging private schools are registered with the government and are subject to supervision only in such areas as school health and safety standards.

Education in government and assisted schools at the primary and secondary levels is free and is funded by the central government. Total educational expenditures increased from TT$23.3 million (for value of the Trinidad and Tobago dollar—see Glossary) in 1960 to TT$62.1 million in 1970. Capital expenditures increased from TT$4.4 million to TT$8.8 million, and public expenditure on education as a proportion of the gross domestic produce (GDP—see Glossary), increased from 2.7 to 3.6 percent. In 1974 the minister of finance estimated that the cost of education for that year would reach TT$121.6 million, more than the total central government budget of 1957 of TT$103 million, and that in 1975 the country's contribution to the University of the West Indies would be TT$16.2 million, about twice the amount contributed in 1970.

In 1970 about 81.8 percent of educational costs were met by the

Table 5. *Trinidad and Tobago, Enrollment in Primary and Intermediate Schools by Kind of School and Sex, 1963 and 1971*

Kind of School	1963			1971		
	Male	Female	Total	Male	Female	Total
Government	24,427	23,192	47,619	29,607	28,596	58,203
Roman Catholic	30,009	30,757	60,766	32,563	33,541	66,104
Anglican	15,227	15,296	30,523	15,273	15,076	30,349
Presbyterian	17,122	15,950	33,072	18,456	18,102	36,558
Methodist	2,005	1,746	3,751	2,155	1,955	4,110
Moravian	318	228	546	337	283	620
Seventh-Day Adventist .	857	893	1,750	1,001	915	1,926
Hindu	9,430	9,364	18,794	11,413	10,833	22,246
Muslim	2,896	2,606	5,502	3,378	3,291	6,669
Other	757	676	1,433	793	741	1,534
TOTAL	103,048	100,708	203,756	114,986	113,333	228,319

Source: Based on information from Trinidad and Tobago, Central Statistical Office, *A Digest of Statistics on Education 1970–71*, Port-of-Spain, 1974, pp. 40–41.

Ministry of Education, Culture, and Community Development. The remainder was shared by the Office of the Prime Minister, the Ministry of Tobago Affairs and the Ministry of Agriculture, Lands, and Fisheries. Nearly 49 percent of all public expenditure on schools was devoted to primary education and nearly 24 percent to general secondary schools. In the 1970 school year 38 percent of all general secondary students were enrolled in private schools, and the funds expended amounted to TT$2.96 million, or about 25 percent of all expenditures at that level.

As the schools opened for the 1975–76 academic year, protests and boycotts were common over unsanitary conditions and failure of the government to complete construction of new buildings. Another bone of contention was the amount of money (TT$16 per student) granted by the government to the assisted schools. The amount had not been changed since 1961, and financial pressures were causing many to raise substantial funds on their own.

During the late 1960s and early 1970s Trinidad and Tobago received a substantial amount of financial and technical assistance from abroad for the expanded educational program, the bulk of it in direct connection with the educational development plan. The International Bank for Reconstruction and Development (IBRD, also known as the World Bank) approved loans of US$9.4 million in 1969 and US$9.3 million in 1973. A third loan to assist in the third and final phase of the development plan was to be negotiated at a later date. The Inter-American Development Bank (IDB) approved two loans in 1972, a US$3.7 million credit toward establishment of a student revolving loan fund and a US$9.4 million credit for new vocational schools. In addition teachers and teachers training assistance were furnished by Canada and the Organization of American States, and fellowships for university study abroad were furnished by the United States, Canada, and the United Kingdom.

THE SCHOOL SYSTEM

The school system in the late 1960s and early 1970s consisted of overlapping elements made up a large primary sector that included both preprimary and postprimary cycles, a small general secondary sector that included a postsecondary cycle for university aspirants, and a still smaller sector of schools providing vocational, technical, agricultural, and teacher training studies in which students were enrolled at both the secondary and the postsecondary levels. The multinational university was not considered part of the school system. Independent Trinidad and Tobago has found this unbalanced and overlapping arrangement unsatisfactory for a variety of reasons. Pursuant to changes recommended by a 1964 planning mission of the United Nations Educational, Scientific and Cultural Organization (UNESCO), the Draft Plan for Educational Development (1968–83) was prepared and approved by the government in 1967. The resulting educational development plan was to provide guidelines for the course of progress in the educational system.

For the 1971 school year, which commenced in September 1970 and concluded in July 1971, the total enrollment was about 280,000. Nearly 230,000 students (more than 81 percent of the total) were engaged in primary and intermediate studies, nearly 45,000 (16 percent) were at the general secondary level, and fewer than 7,500 (less than 3 percent) were enrolled in vocational, technical, agricultural, and teacher training programs (see table 6). It was largely to correct the imbalance between the excessive number of primary and general secondary students and the relatively few engaged in practical studies that the development plan was designed.

Primary and Secondary Schools

Primary school commenced with two optional but well-attended years of kindergarten, or infant school, followed by five years of junior primary school. Attendance was compulsory for students between the ages of six and twelve years, and in the late 1960s virtually all children of primary school age were enrolled in schools.

Upon completing the five junior primary grades, known as standards, students were selected for admission to secondary school by means of the Common Entrance Examination. Secondary places were few in relation to the number of students competing for them; during the 1970 school year only about 16 percent of those completing standard five could be admitted to the secondary program. A majority of the students who were not admitted enrolled in standards six and seven, which made up a two-year senior primary cycle in which the curriculum was largely a repetition of material taught in the junior primary years. A small number

Level of School	1961			1971		
	Male	Female	Total	Male	Female	Total
Primary and Intermediate[1]:						
Infant	29,127	28,110	57,237	30,486	29,095	59,581
Junior primary	56,914	55,287	112,201	67,801	67,677	135,478
Senior primary	9,264	8,743	18,007	16,160	14,470	30,630
Intermediate	1,115	2,017	3,132	539	2,091	2,630
Total	96,420	94,157	190,577	114,986	113,333	228,319[2]
General Secondary:						
Government and assisted	6,840	6,351	13,191	14,541	13,289	27,830
Registered private......	5,291	5,033	10,324	7,105	9,478	16,583
Total	12,131	11,384	23,515	21,646	22,767	44,413
Vocational and Technical	n.a.	n.a.	n.a.	4,586	1,987	6,573
Agricultural...............	n.a.	n.a.	n.a.	128[3]	...	128[3]
Teacher Training	220	238	458	311	399	710
TOTAL	n.a.	n.a.	n.a.	141,657	138,486	280,143

n.a.—not available.
[1] Government and assisted.
[2] Does not include estimated 9,000 (4 percent of primary and intermediate total) in private schools.
[3] Capacity; enrollment figures not available.

Source: Based on information from Trinidad and Tobago, Central Statistical Office, *A Digest of Statistics on Education 1970–71*, Port-of-Spain, 1974, pp. 33, 42–43, 81, 112, 141–43.

also enrolled in five-year intermediate schools. Although the intermediate grades paralleled those of secondary schools and were also known as forms, the curriculum did not take students very far above the primary level. The intermediate schools were listed with the primary units in statistical reporting, and completion of the intermediate course of study brought students little reward other than the right to compete with students completing secondary school in examinations that they had almost no chance of passing.

Secondary education consisted of five forms plus a postsecondary two-year sixth form for students preparing for university admission. The units in this program are sometimes called general secondary schools to distinguish them from vocational and technical institutions at the secondary level.

Only in general secondary schools was a substantial portion of the enrollment private. Private enrollment increased from 10,324 students in twenty-one school units in 1961 to a high of 20,302 in seventy-four units in 1967. Several private schools were closed in succeeding years, and in 1971 there were 16,583 students in sixty units. In 1971 about 37 percent of the general secondary enrollment was private. The substantial increase registered in the early and middle 1960s was a consequence of the inability of secondary schools in the public sector to accommodate the increasing number of students seeking a general secondary education. The private schools have been poorly equipped and financed, their teaching staffs have not been as well trained as those in the public sector, and their students have not performed as well in examinations as those in either government or assisted schools.

In the 1960s and early 1970s students in forms one through five followed a predominantly academic curriculum consisting of a group of ten required courses and one or two electives, principally fine arts subjects. Upon completion of form five they became eligible to take General Certificate of Education "O" level examinations, prepared and graded by boards in the United Kingdom. Students receiving a sufficient number of passing grades were admitted to form six, a two-year program designed specifically as preparation for university matriculation. On completing this form they took General Certification of Education "A" level examinations. A combination of "O" level and "A" level passes was required for university admission.

The "O" level passes served also for admission to postsecondary technical school programs and to the teacher training colleges, which prepared primary-school teachers. For many students leaving school after completing the fifth form, "O" level passes were credentials often demanded by prospective employers. Because university faculties, postsecondary schools, and employers all sometimes required as many as five passes, students took as many examinations as possible to maximize their chances of obtaining the requisite number of passes. Higher schools and prospective employers, when requiring passes in specific subjects, asked most frequently for English and secondly for mathematics. In Trinidad and Tobago proof of a thorough command of standard English was regarded as of primary importance.

Promotion from standard to standard in junior primary school during the 1960s and early 1970s was largely automatic, few students dropped out, and accelerated promotion was common. The retention rate was slightly higher among girls than among boys. Repetition of the fifth and final standard, however, was so common that its enrollment was consistently higher than that in the next lower standard. Girls in particular chose to repeat this year and to make a second attempt at the Common Entrance Examination for secondary school admission. In the two-year senior primary cycle, attrition was heavy between the first and second years; between 1961 and 1971 a yearly average of more than one-third of the first-year students did not continue in the second year. In primary schools in general the attendance rate was fairly high. In 1971 the average daily attendance was a little over 81 percent of enrollment; some primary school systems elsewhere in the Commonwealth Caribbean recorded attendance rates of less than 70 percent.

Dropouts were correspondingly few in secondary schools, although there were more grade repetitions, particularly in the higher forms; in the years from 1961 through 1971 enrollments in form five consistently exceeded those in form four as students repeated the year. During this same period an average of about one student in six who completed form five in government and assisted schools went on to form six. Few private secondary schools included form six in their curricula, and in 1971 less than 2 percent of the private students completing form five entered the sixth form.

The reforms of primary education initiated in the late 1960s were concerned principally with improvement of the quality of primary teaching, curriculum reform, and increasing the number of places in the schools. In 1971 the number of students enrolled in primary and intermediate schools exceeded the number of places in them by 28,000, or about 12 percent.

At the secondary level only a small minority of the school-age population was enrolled, and there was general dissatisfaction with the existing structure of general secondary education. The first phase of the educational development plan was concerned particularly with the reform of general secondary schooling through the establishment of junior secondary schools for forms one through three and senior secondary schools for forms four and five. The two-year form-six cycle was to be continued, but the senior primary and intermediate schools were to be phased out during the 1970s. For the time being, the secondary units offering forms one through five were to continue to function, but by 1983 all children completing the fifth standard of the primary cycle would be able to enter junior secondary school. Thus a general education would be provided to all children through the age of fourteen, and the education of many would be extended by three years. By 1983 some 25 percent of those who had completed the junior secondary cycle would continue their general education in senior secondary schools, and 50 percent would enter an expanded program of vocational and agricultural training.

The plan called for construction of new schools under a formula in which three junior secondary units in an area would feed into one senior unit. In rural areas with populations insufficiently dense to justify separate junior and senior units, combined junior and senior schools consisting of forms one through five would be established; no form six would be offered. The new units were to be so located that they would correct the existing overconcentration of secondary schools on the heavily populated west coast of Trinidad. Ultimately the existing government and assisted secondary units would be converted into junior or senior secondary schools of the new system, but the initial thrust was to establish new junior secondary units and thus increase the number of students in the twelve- to fourteen-year age-group receiving general schooling. To achieve this end the new schools were to be operated on a two-shift basis.

Until junior secondary school places were sufficient to accommodate the entire output of the primary system, selection of students by the Common Entrance Examination would continue. Ultimately this examination would be replaced by one designed for educational guidance and standardization only. Admittance to the senior secondary cycle would be determined by a new examination to be known as the fourteen plus. The educational development plan did not include replacement of the General Certificate of Education "O" level and "A" level examinations.

In the General Certificate of Education series, administered throughout the Commonwealth Caribbean, Trinidadian students have fared somewhat better than those in school systems elsewhere in the area. During the years 1967 through 1972, however, less than 13 percent of all Trinidadian students taking Cambridge "O" level examinations (a smaller number took the London "O" level tests) received the five passes required for full certification.

In addition to being extremely difficult, the examinations are of a generally academic character, and a secondary school system designed largely to prepare students for such tests limits the extent to which the curriculum can be changed to meet local needs. In 1972 Trinidad and Tobago joined the other Commonwealth Caribbean members in forming the Caribbean Examinations Council, through which it was proposed eventually to replace the traditional "O" and "A" level examination with some more responsive to the needs of the area. As of mid-1975 little progress toward this goal had apparently been made.

Under the educational development plan, practical studies were to receive increased emphasis in the junior secondary schools. Agriculture, arts and crafts, industrial arts, and home economics were to be studied, as well as social studies, science, mathematics, English, and Spanish. Forms four and five in the proposed senior secondary schools would offer a broad curriculum; 35 percent of the time would be allocated to such practical options as technology, agriculture, commerce, and home economics. Form six would have a common core of two subjects and three additional elective subjects in either arts or sciences.

Vocational, Technical, and Agricultural Institutions

The government draws a distinction between vocational education in the manual crafts and trades and education for technicians at the subuniversity and university levels. In the early 1970s vocational schooling was furnished at the Point Fortin Vocational Center, and both vocational and technical schooling were available in separate sections of John S. Donaldson Technical Institute in Port-of-Spain, established in 1962, and at the smaller San Fernando Technical Institute, which had opened its doors two years later.

Combined vocational and technical enrollment for 1971 was reported by the Central Statistical Office at nearly 6,600 including part-time students, who made up somewhat over one-half of the total. Other sources, however, indicated that the total enrollment at the three schools had risen from fewer than 1,500 in 1966 to fewer than 3,500 in 1970 and that their output in the late 1960s and early 1970s averaged fifty to sixty technicians and 200 to 220 craftsmen annually. Neither set of data included an estimated 2,500 students in about forty small, poorly equipped private commercial schools or those enrolled in vocational training programs at community centers, trade centers, youth camps, and factory schools (see Literacy and Adult Education, this ch.).

The vocational training program in the early 1970s drew most of its recruits from students who had completed the senior primary school cycle. The technical program was open to students who held "O" level passes in English and one other subject or who passed an entrance examination. Completion of technical studies did not lead to university admission. Both vocational and technical programs were two or three years in duration. At the vocational level dropouts averaged about 40 percent of enrollment, and grade repetitions averaged 10 percent in the late 1960s and early 1970s; figures were similarly high at the technical level.

Vocational and technical schools had difficulty finding qualified teachers to fill vacancies. Both suffered from the poor preparation of entering students and from the high proportion of part-time students, which contributed to the high dropout and grade repetition levels. During the early 1970s employers complained that course material in the vocational program was poorly geared to the needs of the economy. New curricula for the technical program, however, had been developed by committees made up of representatives of industry and government. Graduates experienced no difficulty in finding employment, and even dropouts were often able to obtain work as technicians.

Agricultural training at the postsecondary level was provided by the Eastern Caribbean Institute of Agriculture and Forestry in a two-year program open to holders of General Certificate of Education "O" level passes in at least five subjects. Founded in 1954 on Trinidad as a joint undertaking of several British West Indian dependencies, the institute's administration was taken over by the government in 1964. It has received continuing assistance from the United Nations Food and Agriculture Organization, which in 1971 supplied five of the fifteen teachers on its staff. Enrollment increased from forty-seven in 1964 to over 100 in the early 1970s. The institute, which could accommodate a maximum of 100 students in agriculture and twenty-eight in forestry, annually had forty to forty-five graduates, a majority finding employment in the Ministry of Agriculture, Lands, and Fisheries. In the early 1970s the curriculum was being revised to make it less academically biased and more oriented toward production.

Reform of the vocational and technical training programs was seen as a vitally important element in the educational development plan. After a 1969 study the National Training Board was established as a first step, drawing from the public sector, labor, and management. The board is mandated to advise the government on matters related to vocational and technical schooling and to coordinate training carried out in institutions and industrial enterprises. The board's first meeting was held early in 1972.

Extensive reform of the vocational schooling program was to be part of the second phase of the educational development plan and was to be financed largely by one of the 1972 IDB loans. Closely geared to reform of the secondary school system, the plan called for vocational enrollments to be drawn from graduates of the new junior secondary schools rather than from the old senior primary schools. Accordingly the students would be somewhat older and much better prepared.

The vocational school reform, originally scheduled for completion by 1976, entailed expansion of the Point Fortin school and establishment of seven industrial schools, six on Trinidad and one at Scarborough on Tobago. The curriculum, of varying duration and for both full-time and part-time students, was to include courses in masonry, plumbing, fitting, auto mechanics, and related subjects. The schools were to produce 2,800 craftsmen annually, including 2,100 workers completing work-study apprenticeship programs.

Agricultural schools, also financed by the IDB loan, were to be constructed at Valencia and Palo Seco on Trinidad and at Kendall on Tobago. They were to provide a two-year curriculum emphasizing farm practice, stockraising, use of farm machinery, and rural administration. About 220 students were to be graduated annually.

After the establishment of the new vocational institutions and as a part of the third and final phase of the educational development plan, the two technical institutes were to be expanded and upgraded for the training of more highly skilled technicians. Relocation and expansion of the San Fernando Technical Institute was to be financed through a future credit from the IBRD. Both institutes were to offer courses in electrical and mechanical engineering, laboratory technology, and business management. Course contents were to be revised on the basis of an analysis of technician occupations to be carried out by the National Training Board. The two institutions were to have a total enrollment of approximately 3,500 and an annual output of about 1,000 technicians. The technical institute program was to include establishment of a one-year graduate course at the John S. Donaldson Technical Institute for the training of instructors for the new vocational schools.

Teachers Training Colleges

Training for primary-school teachers during the early 1970s was provided in a two-year course at three government and two small assisted teachers training colleges. The course of study, open to students holding a minimum of five "O" level passes, led to a teaching diploma awarded after a final examination.

All colleges used a revised syllabus introduced in 1970 requiring that 50 percent of class time be devoted to professional studies including practice teaching, 40 percent to general and pedagogical fields, and the remaining

10 percent to elective studies. The syllabus was prepared with the help of specialists provided under the Canadian External Aid Program.

The largest government school, Mausica Teachers Training College, offered preservice training. Modern and well equipped, it was opened in 1962. The remaining schools, all small and poorly equipped, provided in-service schooling to untrained teachers. Total enrollment increased from 458 in 1961 to 710 in 1971. A large majority of students during this period successfully completed their study programs.

The educational development plan called for the establishment of two new teachers colleges, one to be built at Corinth in San Fernando under the first IBRD loan and one to be built later at Valsayn near Port-of-Spain under the second loan. These colleges were to prepare junior secondary as well as primary-level teachers. The enrollment at Mausica was to be increased to 440, the Teachers Training College South was to have an enrollment of 440, and the Valsayn college was to enroll 550. The remaining small colleges were ultimately to be phased out. After 1978 about 550 new teachers were to be graduated annually. In mid-1975 the new Corinth Teachers Training College had been completed, and the number of young people selected for admission to all teacher training colleges in the coming year was announced as 660. Five years earlier it had been less than 400.

By the middle of the 1980s, after the anticipated progressive decline in the population growth rate had caused a leveling off in primary and junior secondary enrollments, the course of study for junior secondary teaching personnel was to be extended to three years. The syllabus for junior secondary teachers would include studies in such fields as industrial arts, general science, home economics, and agriculture, which could not be offered in the colleges that were to be replaced.

Progress of Educational Development Plan

In his 1974 budget speech the minister of finance announced that construction of new school units scheduled under the first phase of the educational development plan was nearing completion. The new units to be ready for use during the 1975 school year included sixteen junior secondary schools having places for 30,200 students and six senior secondary schools having places for 6,800. As a consequence of these new units, a 1975 enrollment of 60,000 students in public secondary schools was anticipated, and 15,300 new students would be admitted to them as compared with 3,900 admitted in the fall of 1964. In addition the new Teachers Training College South would be ready for operation, and construction had commenced on new primary schools, additional junior secondary units, the relocated San Fernando Technical Institute, a teacher training unit at the John S. Donaldson Technical Institute, one of the three planned farm schools, and three of the seven planned vocational training centers.

The progress reported at the beginning of 1974 appeared to be satisfactory, although the minister warned of slowness encountered in the provision of new places. A series of complaints during the early months of 1975 by the School Teachers Association of Trinidad and Tobago, the National Parents' Action Committee, parent-teacher associations, and newspaper editorial writers, however, indicated that the educational development plan was in trouble.

The problem at issue was the disposition to be made of students completing studies in the new junior secondary schools. Some thirteen new primary schools that had commenced operation since 1968 were adding their graduates to the flow of students entering the new junior secondary cycle. The first classes had entered the junior secondary schools in 1972 on a two-shift basis, and the first class of more than 7,000 students was to graduate in July 1975. Only two new senior secondary schools were reported operating, however, although a third was nearing completion, and none of the planned vocational schools were ready for students. One parent-teacher spokesman asked, "Where are the senior secondary schools, vocational schools, and agricultural schools which were to be constructed to accommodate the graduates of the junior secondary schools?"

Suggested solutions to the problem included placing the new graduates in the already crowded assisted secondary units and establishing temporary senior secondary units in existing junior secondary classrooms as a third shift during the hours of 5:30 P.M. to 9:00 P.M. The Ministry of Education, Culture, and Community Development responded to the complaints by announcing that places had been found for nearly all of the upcoming junior secondary graduates. Those not entering the new senior secondary units would be accommodated by conversion of some existing general secondary schools on a crash basis and by fitting additional students into three vocational and technical institutions. Some 6,383 students were later placed in the various schools, about 37 percent of the number envisioned in the goal of the draft educational plan. The ministry also announced that only 15,000 of the planned 28,000 junior secondary school places had been provided and that for the present the Common Entrance Examination would continue to be used for selection of students. It added that discussions should be held at once with the boards of various assisted denominational schools with respect to their schools' conversion into either junior or senior secondary units, a process that would commence in September 1975.

The educational development problem that reached such a critical point in 1975 was the result of both deficient planning and construction delays; one senior secondary school, for example, was less than half built twenty-nine months after the contracted completion date. The minister of finance stated that stringent prequalification rules imposed by international lending agencies, such as IDB and IBRD, had also contributed to the delays.

Government authorities concerned with the educational development

154

plan freely acknowledged that the most significant factors underlying current difficulties had been failures to determine how much the emphasis on vocational schooling should be increased and to implement promptly vocational school construction plans. Developed soon after independence, the Second Five-Year Plan (1964–68) had included provision for ten vocational and three farm schools, but these schools were not built, and the first phase of the educational development plan was devoted almost entirely to general schools. In late 1975 plans for the immediate future called for expansion of the John S. Donaldson Technical Institute rather than for construction of new vocational units.

The draft plan for educational development remained the cornerstone of educational policy, but most vocational training was to be offered not in vocational schools but in integrated upper secondary schools with common facilities and management for pupils pursuing academic, technical, commercial, general industrial, and limited specialized craft training. In 1975 this kind of school was foreseen as the national model for education of junior secondary graduates.

In his 1975 budget speech the minister of finance reaffirmed that the government was committed to an overall restructuring of schools and curricula in order to emphasize practical schooling. Continued emphasis would be placed on establishing junior secondary schools, but senior secondary school construction would be curtailed. Instead construction of the vocational and farm schools for which IDB financing had been obtained would be accelerated and technical institutes expanded. He added that the restructuring would take time and that it would be necessary for parents to accept the relevance of the shift. The kind of academic education parents still seemed to demand would bring only frustration to their children who after years of study could not find jobs because they lacked skills needed by the economy.

TEACHERS

The number of teachers in the public and private school systems increased from fewer than 8,000 in 1963 to nearly 9,000 in 1971. The moderate overall rate of increase no more than kept pace with enrollment growth, but the student-teacher ratios in schools of all kinds compared favorably with those in other Commonwealth Caribbean states and dependencies.

The 1971 student-teacher ratio in government and assisted primary and intermediate schools was about 34.9 to one as compared to 33.4 to one in 1963. The ratio did not differ significantly by geographical location, between government and assisted schools, or between the assisted institutions of different denominations.

In government and assisted secondary institutions the student-teacher ratio declined slightly from 21.9 to one in 1963 to 20.9 to one in 1971. In registered private schools the ratio in 1971 was a substantially higher 29.5 to one. In government vocational and technical institutions in 1971 the ratio was more than sixty-five to one. Part-time teachers were not included in the official statistics, however, and over one-half of the students attended classes on a part-time basis. Data from another source indicated that in 1970 the real student-teacher ratio in government technical and vocational schools was about twenty-five to one. No data were available on ratios in teachers training colleges or private commercial schools.

Women teachers were in the majority at the primary school level, particularly in urban localities. In government and assisted primary and imtermediate institutions the proportion of women teachers rose from 53.8 percent in 1963 to 56.9 percent in 1971, and in 1971 women made up nearly 70 percent of the enrollment in schools of Port-of-Spain and San Fernando. More than 44 percent of the enrollment in teachers training colleges was male, however, and in schools of other kinds men outnumbered women. Women made up 46.4 percent of the teaching staffs in public and assisted secondary schools, 44.2 percent in private secondary schools, and 18.6 percent of the full-time personnel in vocational and technical institutions.

In the 1960s and early 1970s there was a general lack of personnel with pedagogical training. In government and assisted primary and intermediate schools the proportion of trained teachers who had completed teachers training college courses or the equivalent increased from 45 percent of the total in 1963 to 50 percent in 1971. During the same period, however, the proportion with secondary educations declined from 77 to 68 percent, probably a reflection of the considerable number of untrained teachers without secondary schooling who were given in-service instruction at teachers training colleges.

In 1971 a little more than 50 percent of the teachers in government and assisted secondary schools held university degrees, but less than half of these had received pedagogical training. Another 13 percent of the total had specialist diplomas or other specialist qualifications, and the remainder had only general secondary educations. In registered private secondary schools four teachers in five had only secondary school backgrounds without pedagogical training. Qualifications of women teachers were somewhat higher than those of men in both public and private institutions. About one-third of the full-time technical and vocational teachers had a university education or the equivalent, but fewer than one-half of these had received pedagogical training. Most of the remainder had either teacher training or special technical qualifications.

Most of the older teachers with university backgrounds had attended institutions in the United Kingdom. Many of the younger ones had attended North American universities, however, and some had attended the University of the West Indies.

As originally scheduled in the educational development plan, the expansion of the teacher training college program would satisfy the requirements for new and upgraded teachers in primary and junior secondary schools by 1978. Progress achieved during the early 1970s indicated that this goal might come close to attainment (see The School System, this ch.).

During the 1960s and early 1970s the country had no institution for the preparation of secondary teachers. In the early 1970s, however, local intensive training programs were offered on a pilot basis in Trinidad and Tobago with the help of the Organization of American States and UNESCO. By 1975 a diploma program for secondary teachers had been inaugurated in the School of Education at the St. Augustine campus of the University of the West Indies. There were no specific plans for training technical teachers, but the government had undertaken to offer conditions of service sufficiently desirable to attract qualified applicants and to compensate for the relative lack of promotional opportunities available.

HIGHER EDUCATION

Higher education is available in Trinidad and Tobago only at the St. Augustine campus of the University of the West Indies, located on the outskirts of Port-of-Spain. The university is a multinational entity sponsored jointly by all Commonwealth Caribbean states and dependencies; there is only limited participation by Guyana, which maintains its own university. The University of the West Indies was inaugurated in 1948 as the University College of the West Indies, located in the Mona section of Kingston, Jamaica, and received its present name and degree-granting status by royal charter in 1962. The St. Augustine campus was established in 1962 by conversion of the former Imperial College of Tropical Agriculture, and a third campus was added at Cave Hill, Barbados, in 1963.

Courses of study at the three campuses range from one- and two-year certificate and diploma programs to three- to six-year programs leading to first (bachelor) degrees. At the St. Augustine campus undergraduate courses last three years. Graduate programs are available at the university in all studies for which undergraduate degrees are offered. St. Augustine gives special emphasis to the development of research capabilities. Campus publications include *Tropical Agriculture, Cocoa Research Report, Journal of Engineering, U.W.I. Citrus Research Bulletin,* and *U.W.I. Seismic Research Bulletin.*

The chancellorship of the combined university is an honorary position. A vice chancellor serves as administrative head of the three campuses from an office at Mona, and pro-vice-chancellors direct each of the campuses. Much of the operating authority, however, lies with a series of permanent committees.

Because the university is funded by various governments and is accordingly subject to a variety of directive influences, questions have been raised concerning its academic freedom and durability. In the mid-1970s the status of the university faced no serious questions, however, and the Fifth Heads of Government Conference in 1969 had determined that it would continue to function as a multinational institution at least until 1981.

Trinidadian students may enroll at Mona and Cave Hill as well as at St. Augustine, and during the early 1970s a substantial portion of the St. Augustine enrollment came from outside Trinidad and Tobago. Consequently the St. Augustine academic program can be tailored specifically to the country's needs only to a limited extent, and the student body lacks the sense of national identity conducive to producing the undergraduate political activists frequently found on campuses elsewhere in the Americas. Student unrest is sometimes encountered, however, and in 1970 the governor general of Canada was barred from the campus, classes were boycotted, and students supported a bus drivers' strike. A government commission was named to investigate staff appointments, which had been one of the causes of the unrest (see ch. 7; ch. 9).

All university administrators and department heads at St. Augustine must travel frequently to Mona. Papers are marked in Jamaica, and students sometimes complain that as a consequence they are not given proper credit.

The original teaching unit of the St. Augustine campus, the Faculty of Agriculture, was established in 1961 and was followed by the Faculty of Engineering in 1963. In the mid-1970s these two faculties remained the central university units for teaching agriculture and engineering. The Jamaica campus was the site of the central faculties of arts and general studies, education, medicine, natural sciences, and social sciences. The central Faculty of Law was located in Barbados. In the mid-1970s, however, vice deans at St. Augustine headed branches of the faculties of arts and general studies, natural sciences, social sciences, and the school of education.

In the mid-1970s the number of students per teacher was low, many faculty members held advanced degrees, and acceptance of paid employment outside the university was generally prohibited. A professor could receive TT$35,000, a senior lecturer TT$25,000, and a lecturer more than TT$20,000 annually in base pay plus a housing allowance and pension rights. Teaching personnel were recruited elsewhere in the Commonwealth Caribbean as well as at home, and advertisements for teachers appeared in North America and British newspapers.

The number of Trinidadian students enrolled at the St. Augustine campus increased from 632 in 1966 to 1,237 in 1971. During this period enrollment of women increased from 28 to 33 percent of the total. In 1971 some 31.3 percent of the students were studying engineering, and 6.7 percent were studying agriculture in the two central faculties. The remaining 62 percent were enrolled in the branch faculties of arts and general studies, natural sciences, and social sciences.

Overall data concerning enrollments on all three campuses were not available, and published data purporting to show total enrollments on each campus appear usually to include those of nationals only. In the early 1970s, however, the enrollment at Mona was by far the largest, St. Augustine was second in size, and Cave Hill was by far the smallest. According to one estimate in 1971, about one-fourth of the total university enrollment was at St. Augustine.

Official data for 1971 indicate that 1,828 Trinidadian students including 261 women were studying at foreign universities. The data did not show any to be studying at other campuses of the University of the West Indies, and a notation indicated that some women and part-time students may have been omitted. Some 59.6 percent of all Trinidadian university students and 33.7 percent of all women students were studying abroad. Both proportions had declined substantially since 1966, when 71.9 percent of all students and 49.4 percent of all women students had been abroad. In 1971 some 89 percent of those studying outside the West Indies were studying in North America, and 10 percent were studying in the United Kingdom, as compared with 75 percent in North America and 22 percent in the United Kingdom in 1966.

LITERACY AND ADULT EDUCATION

The literacy rate of adults (persons aged fifteen and over) increased from about 74 percent in 1946 to 88 percent in 1960 and to 95 percent in 1970. The rate reported in 1970 was among the highest in the Americas. No data were available concerning the extent to which functional literacy corresponded with the reported rate. The quality as well as the level of literacy is believed to have improved progressively since 1946, however, and the functional rate during the early 1970s to have been extremely high. Newspapers and some other reading material were available even in the smallest villages, farmers in the most remote rural locality sometimes visited urban centers where literacy skills were useful, and in general the conditions under which Trinidadians lived were such that the skills attained in a few years of schooling were seldom eroded through lack of use.

Literacy in 1970 was not significantly lower in the countryside than in urban locaities, and nearly all of the remaining illiterates were either elderly or physically or mentally unable to learn to read and write. The rate by sex for the whole population was not available, but in 1970 some 95 percent of the male members and 85 percent of the female members of the labor force were literate. The rate of about 90 percent for the labor force as a whole was lower than that of the total adult population because of the large number of literate young adults over the age of fifteen who were not yet counted as labor force members.

Adult education was aimed originally at the eradication of illiteracy, but the rise in literacy redirected the emphasis toward other fields of adult study. During the late 1960s and early 1970s a scanty 0.3 to 0.4 percent of the public education budget was allocated annually to adult education, but in 1971 more than 57,000 adults were enrolled in various educational programs excluding literacy, for which no figures were available. Nearly three-fifths were in the counties of St. George and Victoria, which included the cities of Port-of-Spain and San Fernando. Some 40.4 percent of the total were enrolled in vocational studies, 38.2 percent in handicrafts, 12.3 percent in cultural studies, 5.7 percent in the study of nutrition, 0.7 percent in general education, 0.6 percent in academic education, and 2.0 percent in other fields. The enrollment of nearly four out of five adult students in vocational and handicraft studies was a direct consequence of the nature of the work force and the particular demand for labor. On the one hand the high level of unemployment among young adults encouraged enrollment in adult education courses as a way to occupy their time. On the other the shortage of skills and the high demand for skilled labor of all kinds encouraged enrollment in practical studies.

During the early 1970s courses were offered in a variety of public and private programs, not all of them included in the 1971 statistics. Some adult students were enrolled in schools of the regular educational system, including private commercial schools; untrained in-service teachers made up a particularly large proportion of the enrollment at teachers training colleges. The extramural studies program at the university's St. Augustine campus also offered adult courses. Four residential youth camps accommodating 700 youths and young adults offered two-year trade courses, and ten nonresidential youth centers offered part-time training in a variety of simple crafts. A trade center, the first of four planned units, offered a one-year course for welders. Short courses in many community centers, catering mainly to young women, were devoted to such interests as dressmaking, handicrafts, nutrition, home economics, and money management.

A government survey conducted in 1971 found that about ninety business firms were offering in-plant training to more than 3,000 workers in courses lasting from a few days to several years and ranging from management training to the training of semiskilled machine operators. There were about 450 apprentices in industry, over half of the total in government and the petroleum industry.

No adult education programs for farmers were available in the early 1970s. The second phase of the educational development plan, however, called for the establishment of a farmer training center located near the Eastern Caribbean Institute of Agriculture and Forestry. Having a capacity for thirty students, it was to train about 900 farmers annually in one-week courses and sixty extension officers in courses of two weeks' duration. In addition three mobile training units were to carry out demonstrations on selected farms in cooperation with local organizations.

CULTURE

Literature

Despite Spanish, French, and English colonial influences, Trinidad and

Tobago's writing tradition was affected significantly only by the English. In the last years of Spanish rule in the late eighteenth century the printing press was a vehicle for political and religious expression rather than for literary effort. No work by Trinidadian authors in either Spanish or French has been preserved. Only vestiges of these two languages remain, enlivening the English-based Creole and producing a multilingual effect not found elsewhere in the West Indies (see ch. 4). This characteristic has been preserved in literature through the use of written dialect, in both conversation and direct narration.

Literary effort remained at a low ebb for well over a century after the English arrived in 1797, and the few works of descriptive and historical importance were by English writers. The lack of interest in literature was owed in part to the nature of the population and in part to cultural ties with England. Most of the people were either illiterate or semiliterate blacks, coloreds and, by the mid-nineteenth century, East Indians. The small minority that could read—mostly planters and government officials—were more interested in economic than cultural endeavors. Moreover many of them considered Trinidad a temporary stopover on the road to riches that would enable them to return to England, which they considered the seat of education and culture. Consequently those interested in writing moved to England or the United States, where the audiences were larger and opportunities greater.

Although the dearth of literary achievement in Trinidad and Tobago continued into the twentieth century, a cultural and political movement swept throughout the British West Indies in the 1920s and 1930s that greatly influenced the thinking of nascent intellectuals and writers. As a result of this awakening, an impressive literary movement rapidly emerged in Trinidad. This movement was so formidable that literary critic Kenneth Ramchand claimed that in Trinidad and Tobago in the late 1920s and early 1930s "there was a concentration of literary and artistic talent such as had never happened anywhere in the islands before."

Many disciplines were represented in this concentration of creative individuals, which was nationalistic in political outlook and realistic in approach to social problems. Generally known as the Beacon group— after the literary magazine by the same name that flourished between 1931 and 1933—it produced the first wave of West Indian self-awareness, which soon spread from Trinidad to the other islands. The two leading figures of this group were Alfred H. Mendes (1897–) and C.L.R. James (1901–). Mendes and James published the first tangible evidence of the growing awareness in the magazine *Trinidad*, a short-lived precursor of the *Beacon*. Only two issues of *Trinidad* were ever published: one at Easter in 1929 and the other at Christmas in 1930. Nevertheless, they set the tone and pattern for the *Beacon*, which under Albert Gomes was to become the major organ of opinion in Trinidad.

Mendes, a Portuguese Creole like Gomes, published several short stories in the 1930s and 1940s, although his major works were two novels, *Pitch Lake* (1934) and *Black Fauns* (1935). These novels are important for their use of social realism and their ability to portray the misery stemming from poverty and racism. The Trinidadian bourgeoisie, conservative and complacent in its secure social position, was frequently shocked and offended by the frankness of Mendes' work. In speaking of the Beacon group and its position as social gadfly, Mendes has said, "We had three rip-roaring years of tearing into every sanctity and pharisaism of the respectable folk. How hurt they were—but how much they secretly enjoyed it!"

James is considered one of the greatest writers and critics ever produced in the Caribbean region. At various times he has been a teacher, journalist, novelist, and sportswriter. He is strongly committed to socialist philosophy and the pan-African movement, as shown in his prolific and lucid writing. He spent his early life in Trinidad and, after completing his education at Queen's Royal College, he spent the next dozen years teaching, playing cricket, and writing for newspapers. This period was formative for James, who experienced firsthand the disadvantages of having dark skin in Trinidad and the oppressed conditions of the poor.

Although he intended to become a novelist, James produced only one—very powerful—novel, *Minty Alley* (1936). It described the alienation of the educated class of West Indians from the masses. His major work, a definitive contribution to scholarship on Haiti, was *The Black Jacobins: Toussaint L'Ouverture and the San Domingo Revolution* (1938). This work established James as an internationally respected political theorist and historian.

Under the influence of men like Mendes and James, the Beacon group came closer to establishing a permanent artistic and intellectual community in Trinidad—thus stemming the flow of talent to England—than any other West Indian group. In spite of their cohesion and the intensity of their commitment, however, the obstacles to success were too great. Printing facilities and the potential domestic audience were insignificant compared to the facilities and interest to be generated abroad. More important was the seeming inability of these writers to communicate with their own countrymen, who were frequently hostile or unresponsive to their efforts. The abrasive, crusading nature of the group's messages alienated bourgeois sectors of its audience while the masses—who might have found such messages pertinent—were unable to understand them. The dual task of encouraging their countrymen to read while teaching them how to interpret what they read has continued to be one of the most difficult tasks faced by Trinidadian writers.

The hostility and ignorance at home was counterbalanced by the enthusiasm and sophistication of English audiences and critics. As early as 1927 stories by James and Mendes began to appear in English magazines. Their stories and the editorship of *Trinidad* were lauded by Aldous Huxley, who also wrote an introduction to Mendes' first novel. Given such circumstances, Mendes emigrated to New York and James to

London in the early 1930s. Their interest in Trinidadian affairs did not die with their emigration, however; later James returned to the island to become involved in politics.

The dissolution of the Beacon group and the emigration of Mendes and James did not mean the end of creative efforts. Other literary periodicals begun in the islands were anxious to incorporate Trinidadian authors and audience in the movement. The only one to survive the tumultuous years of the 1940s, however was *Bim*, begun in 1942 in Barbados. The purpose of *Bim* has been to foster and encourage creative writing throughout the West Indies, regardless of the author's political affiliation or literary style. More than any other publication, *Bim* has been able to bring together West Indian authors of consistently high quality.

Bim accepted materials from West Indians at home and abroad, serving as a literary channel for the growing number of writers resident in England. This group of expatriates continued to publish the majority of their work in England, however, and received further incentive and funding from the British Broadcasting Corporation (BBC), which broadcast an overseas program, "Caribbean Voices." Between 1943 and 1959 this program broadcast the work of over 200 West Indian writers, including the most prominent Trinidadian authors and poets. Despite their success abroad, publications like *Bim* and the writers themselves have been criticized for not taking a more active part in campaigning against illiteracy among the West Indian public.

During the 1930s and 1940s political activity and public sentiment began to catch up to literary currents, and the surge in Trinidadian writing since 1950 is directly related to the growth of national feeling. Ethnic, national, and personal self-discovery became the most vital issues in both literature and society and gave rise to a variety of themes and techniques. Despite the newness of the literature, it has shown an impressive grasp of traditional literary techniques that, according to some critics, has made it among the best contemporary English literature available. Many writers have not been satisfied with traditional forms, however, and the search for a medium of expression that is uniquely West Indian and specifically Trinidadian has made this literature among the most varied English literature to emerge since World War II.

The theme of self-discovery has created the need for a new voice and a new language, and dialect has come to play an important part in the search for identity, serving to embarrass some and unify others in its West Indian audience. Dialect paints a clearer picture of the subtleties of Trinidadian life than does standard English, for it expresses a way of thinking and feeling. Superfluous words are removed, streamlining phrases and making them apparently simple. This process does not remove or mar the poetic qualities of the language and sometimes enhances its musical quality.

Exploration of the environment—past and present, physical and social—has been a key theme. More specifically this theme has been explored through concern over nature, the pull of the past, discovery of the uniqueness of Creole culture, and the social inequalities found in the islands. Nature is invariably regarded as sensual, and there is none of the sense of fatalism or tragic oppression by the natural world found elsewhere in the Southern Hemisphere. The tranquillity and beneficence of nature frequently is depicted as being in marked contrast to the pathos and chaos of the social and political environment, which is portrayed realistically and often ironically. Stories and novels frequently revolve around the lives of the poor.

The past has a very strong attraction for Trinidadian writers, and in much of their work there is a sense of heritage that extends beyond the Caribbean to England, Africa, and India. In trying to understand their varied and complex ethnic history, writers have exhibited three motifs: embarrassment, ambivalence, and hope, or a sense of the possible. The African heritage has proved irresistible for some authors. James feels that the West Indian need to uncover roots is based upon a desire to come to terms with a social past contained in slavery. Other authors, such as Samuel Selvon (1924–) and Vidiadhar Surajprasad Naipaul (1932–), explore their East Indian past.

The sensitivity toward time and locale has left a special mark on the West Indian personality. It has imparted a sense of living in a transitional society, one in which ambivalence toward the past and its origin in another land dominates. This sentiment and the conflict between the writer and his environment have produced in the Trinidadian imagination a special awareness of exile, which is combined with restlessness and detachment. These feelings manifest themselves in a love-hate relationship with the islands.

Coming to grips with their own Creole culture is another dominant theme. The problem of defining their society for themselves and outsiders is both exhilarating and discouraging. Authors have found themselves interpreting their society for an alternately hostile and receptive audience. They are accused by the middle and upper class of complicity with the radicals and by the radicals of complicity with the bourgeoisie: they are reproached for losing perpective by being too close to the scene for an objective view. The many who live abroad come under special attack for their self-imposed exile. Most authors, however, understand and accept the ambivalence with which they are treated.

All these themes and motifs are found in the work of Trinidad's outstanding novelists, Selvon and Naipaul. Both are East Indians, live outside the Caribbean, and are widely acclaimed in Great Britain for their numerous, well-written novels. Naipaul is also recognized in the United States.

Selvon was born in Trinidad and educated there. Before beginning his literary career, he worked as a telegraph operator and on the staff of the *Trinidad Guardian*, known as the *Guardian*, Trinidad's leading newspaper. While on the staff he began writing poetry and short stories. He

164

was so successful that he went to England in 1950 in pursuit of a literary career. Since then he has published nine novels and traveled extensively.

Selvon's first novel, *A Brighter Sun* (1952), was the first West Indian literary work using Creole as the medium of narration. It thus paved the way for further exploration of the creative possibilities of written dialect. Selvon's work most frequently deals with the poor people of Trinidad at home and abroad, and his style is both humorous and sympathetic. In *Lonely Londoners* (1956) Selvon deals with a group of West Indians living in London and their problems in relating to British society. As in much of Selvon's work, there is little attempt at psychological or emotional depth, and the book is primarily a series of anecdotes and incidents. Nevertheless the reader gains a picture of West Indians as a peripheral element in British society, living in it but never a part of it.

Naipaul has been called one of the greatest living novelists writing in English and is certainly the most respected West Indian writer, although he refuses to be categorized as West Indian. Born in Trinidad, he was educated at University College of Oxford University and has lived in England ever since. His novels include *The Mystic Masseur* (1957), *A House for Mr. Biswas* (1961), and *The Mimic Men* (1967). *A House for Mr. Biswas*, which many consider Naipaul's best novel, describes life in a West Indian Hindu household and the intergenerational conflicts that arises as members of the family try to balance their Indian heritage with their immediate lives in Trinidad. As in much of Naipaul's work, the characters and situations in the book are largely East Indian and poor, and Naipaul treats them with subtlety, humor, and irony.

Naipaul has also published three volumes of short stories and three nonfiction books about the West Indies. All of Naipaul's work shows a deep sensitivity toward the racial and cultural complexity of Trinidadian society and an understanding of its tensions and prejudices. A foreigner might get a better view of Trinidadian society by reading one of Naipaul's works than by reading five scholarly works on ethnic makeup.

Daniel Joseph Samaroo (1927–) and Ismith Khan (1925–) are also of East Indian descent. Samaroo has published only a few short stories, but they are popular for their wit and effective use of dialect. His stories are most effective when read aloud. Khan was educated in Trinidad and the United States and in 1974 was director of third world studies at the University of California at San Diego. He has published two novels, the *Jumbie Bird* (1961) and *The Obeah Man* (1964). *The Jumbie Bird* draws extensively on the author's own life and his struggle between his Indian past and his Western upbringing. *The Obeah Man* is set during Carnival festivities and is considered a significant fictional treatment of folk religious practices and witchcraft (see ch. 4).

One West Indian writer who has not adopted the dominant patterns of social realism and protest is Michael Anthony (1932–). Anthony has become a master storyteller, slowly polishing his style to suit his own sensibility. He was born and educated in a small village in Trinidad and then went to Pointe-à-Pierre to work as a foundryman. He began publishing stories and verse in local newspapers and *Bim*. While still in his early twenties he went to England, worked at various odd jobs, and was eventually employed as a teleprinter operator at Reuters news agency. He continued to publish stories, poems, and novels, and rose to an editorship at Reuters. His three novels are *The Games Were Coming* (1936), *The Year in San Fernando* (1965), and *Green Days by the River* (1967). Like James, Anthony is concerned with sports and their symbolic importance in the small community in the West Indies. *The Games Were Coming*, his first novel, concerns an upcoming bicycle race and its impact upon the characters in the novel.

Ernest Carr has written short stories, poetry, and critical reviews, most of which have been published in Caribbean literary journals. Nearly half of his almost fifty stories have been broadcast in England. He is a highly sensitive writer, and his topics include interethnic relations and the racial snobbery of the colored Creole classes.

Although most of the contemporary Trinidadian poets have been born since 1940, two outstanding poets, Erich Roach (1915–74) and Cecil Gray (1923–), predate this group. Roach was born and educated in Tobago and then moved to Trinidad where he worked as a journalist, reviewer, and feature writer for the *Guardian*. He turned to poetry relatively late in life but has become one of the most gifted lyricists in the West Indies. In the mid-1970s he was the leading poet of his country. Although no book of his poetry has appeared, he is a regular contributor to *Bim* and other literary journals. Throughout much of his poetry Roach uses the concept of Africa as a positive source of spiritual and cultural identity. Nevertheless he is aware of the feelings of rootlessness, marginality, and shame that West Indians manifest toward their ethnic heritage. He mixes this awareness with descriptions of the local setting, and his poetry emerges as a universal view of man's conflicts with life and his search for identity and dignity.

Gray has been involved with education in the islands for many years and in the mid-1970s was senior lecturer in English education at the Jamaica campus of the University of the West Indies. His work has been published in *Bim* and other magazines, and he has edited two anthologies for school-age children: *Response* (1969) and *Bite In* (1972). Much of his poetry is gentle but possesses a background of social consciousness and a sense of justice.

In the mid-1970s there were at least four outstanding young poets in Trinidad. Wayne Brown (1944–), an English honors graduate in 1968, served as a critic of the *Guardian*. His first collection of poems, *On the Coast* (1973), is promising in its rhythm and imagery as well as its dramatic quality. Faustin Charles (1944–) studied in England, where he published his first book of poems, *The Expatriate* (1969). Victor D. Questel and Anson Gonzalez have jointly published a small volume, *Score* (1972). Questel's poetry is sometimes ironic and satirical and frequently protests the exploitation of Trinidadians by the tourist trade. Gonzalez' poetry is in a similar vein and is often political in tone.

Scholarship

From its earliest colonial days well into the mid-1950s, Trinidad and Tobago experienced a far less active intellectual history than other islands in the British West Indies. Whereas books on the history of Jamaica and Barbados were many and of high quality—appearing as early as 1707—books on Trinidad were few. Two major nineteenth-century historians of Spanish Trinidad were E. L. Joseph and Pierre Borde. Joseph, an English Jew, was an adventurer who came to the island in 1820. His *History of Trinidad* (1838) was devoted largely to the charms of the tropical environment. Borde, a Frenchman, spent nineteen years of research for *L'Histoire d'ile de la Trinité sous le gouvernement espagnole* (The History of the Island of Trinidad under the Spanish Government), which appeared in two volumes in 1876. Another two-volume work, *History of Trinidad* by Lionel Fraser, appeared in Port-of-Spain in 1896; it dealt with the period after the English invasion.

No comprehensive histories emerged until the early 1960s when Gertrude Carmichael's *History of the West Indian Islands of Trinidad and Tobago, 1498–1900* (1961) and Eric Williams' *History of the People of Trinidad and Tobago* (1962) appeared. The historian Gordon K. Lewis has argued that Trinidad was ignored by English scholars because of its polyglot ethnic heritage and un-English quality, which made it less attractive to English historians than Barbados or Jamaica.

Not only was there a lack of scholarly interest on the part of British and Trinidadian intellectuals, but a strident anti-intellectualism was present among Trinidadians. This characteristic postponed a coalition between intellectuals and nationalistic elements—such as occurred in Jamaica in the late 1930s—until the mid-1950s, when Williams and his People's National Movement (PNM) ushered in the "revolution of intelligence."

Despite the apparent lack of scholarly endeavor by trained social scientists, many novelists and political activists have made significant scholarly contributions. James, for example, became involved in pan-Africanism, and this interest led to his major work about the Haitian revolution, *The Black Jacobins: Toussaint L'Ouverture and the San Domingo Revolution* (1938). Both a theoretical and historical study, it justified James' intent to present "a book of general historical interest written especially with a view to the elucidation of the African Revolution." James also contributed many works that proved invaluable to an appreciation of the ideology of the independence movement; these include *The Case for West Indian Self Government, World Revolution: Rise and Fall of the Communist International, The History of Negro Revolt*, and *Party Politics in the West Indies*.

Another novelist who has made scholarly contributions is V. S. Naipaul. Although less theoretical and political than James' studies,

Naipaul's nonfiction work is scholarly and well written—and frequently controversial—as is the case with *The Middle Passage* (1962), a nonfiction account of the West Indies. In *An Area of Darkness* (1964) Naipaul recounts a visit to India. Another work of scholarly importance is *The Loss of El Dorado* (1969), a brilliant history of Trinidad.

Many of the scholars emerging from the intellectual furor of the 1950s have become involved with the University of the West Indies, either in Trinidad or in Jamaica. Historian James Millette, for example, headed the Department of History on the St. Augustine campus in Trinidad. He is the author of one book, *The Genesis of Crown Colony Government*, and numerous articles and pamphlets. Millette has also been interested in politics, serving as the general secretary of the United National Independence Party and acting as a seminal influence in the establishment of *Moko*, a radical newspaper.

Another scholar involved with the West Indian university system is Merle Hodge. She was born in Calcutta settlement in Trinidad in 1944 and, after completing her primary and secondary education in Trinidad, she left to study French at the university of London. After traveling extensively in Europe and living in Senegal and Gambia, she published her first novel, *Crick Crack, Monkey* in 1970. She returned to Trinidad the same year and for two years taught in a government secondary school before becoming a lecturer in French Caribbean and French African literature on the Mona campus. She has written several articles, including one on male-female relations in the Caribbean.

Although a native of Guyana, Gordon Rohlehr has contributed to scholarship and literary criticism throughout the Caribbean. He was educated at the Mona campus and Birmingham University in England and in 1968 returned to the West Indies to lecture in English literature on the St. Augustine campus. Rohlehr has written copiously on the literature and culture of the West Indies, and his work has appeared in *New World Quarterly*, *Bim*, *Caribbean Quarterly*, *Moko*, and *Savacou*. Under the auspices of the Government Broadcasting Unit of Trinidad he has also originated a series of half-hour radio programs on calypso music, past and present.

John Stewart was born in Trinidad and, unlike the others mentioned, did his undergraduate and graduate work on the west coast of the United States, receiving his doctorate in 1973. He has taught at various universities in the United States and in 1974 was a visiting lecturer in the English department of the California State University at Fresno. The Royal Society of Literature in London awarded him first prize for his 1971 novel, *Last Cool Days*. He has also written a collection of short stories and some articles, including one on the history of the indigenous black church in the Caribbean.

Several Trinidadian scholars combined disciplines of history, political science, and economics in order to better their understanding of Trinidad in the 1960s and 1970s. They have produced numerous books and articles—many of which have a liberal or socialistic slant—and have participated actively in the political process. A.N.R. Robinson, for example, was educated at Oxford and went on to become deputy leader of the PNM, minister of external affairs, and minister of finance. His book *The Mechanics of Independence*, published in 1971, is considered outstanding.

Selwyn D. Ryan, Ivar Oxaal, and Lloyd Best have also written about restructuring of the Trinidadian economy, black power, and the independence period. Their work is insightful and has been well received by scholars at home and abroad. Ryan's major work, *Race and Nationalism in Trinidad and Tobago: A Study of Decolonization in a Multiracial Society* (1972), and Oxaal's book *Black Intellectuals Come to Power* (1968) are integrated works combining basic information from a wide range of social sciences. Yogendra Malik and John Gaffar La Guerre have been concerned with the East Indians. Malik's book *East Indians in Trinidad* deals specifically with the political role of this segment of the population, whereas *Calcutta to Caroni: The East Indians of Trinidad*, edited by La Guerre, combines a number of articles on history, economics, politics, and sociology. La Guerre, like Best and others, has also been a lecturer on the St. Augustine campus.

Williams is probably Trinidad's outstanding intellectual; some consider him the epitome of the West Indian scholar-politician. As a young man Williams won a scholarship to study at Oxford, where he took honors. He then taught at Howard University in Washington and later became the senior research secretary of the Caribbean Commission, a coordinating body composed mainly of expatriates. His long scholarly training and intellectual discipline led him to study the Caribbean economy closely and to translate his academic knowledge into social action. He resigned from the commission in 1956 to found and head the PNM, which has dominated Trinidadian politics ever since (see ch. 3; ch. 7). His books on the West Indies are considered classics; they include *Capitalism and Slavery*, *British Historians and the West Indies*, *History of the People of Trinidad and Tobago*, and *From Columbus to Castro*.

Music and Dance

The Folkloric Tradition

The music and dance of Trinidad and Tobago and the festivals that inspire and preserve them reflect the country's kaleidoscopic colonial heritage and its multicultural population. Each element of the social mosaic—the Spanish and English colonizers, the French immigrants, the African slaves, and the East Indian indentured laborers—has contributed to a national folkloric tradition considered by many to be the richest of the West Indies. It has been the Afro-West Indian population, however, that has assimilated and synthesized the many minority cultures, has provided the rhythmic common denominator and experiential content of the country's folk music, and has been the source of original musical forms.

The missing element in the country's folkloric tradition is the Amerindian. Very little is known about the music of the indigenous population. Nevertheless, there is a small group that proudly celebrates its Carib and Arawak heritage at the annual feast of Santa Rosa in the town of Arima.

The folk music that is believed to have undergone the least alteration over the centuries is that derived from African rituals. The cult of Shango, for example, was transplanted to Trinidad by the Yoruba of Nigeria. Songs to Shango, the thunder god, are sung in the original African dialect, which is no longer understood by the singers. At Shango ceremonies dances are performed to the beat of drums, and dancers sometimes become "possessed."

The designation big drum dance has been applied to a category of ritual songs and dances invoking the ancestors of various African groups, such as the Ibo, the Congo, and the Yoruba. They were brought to Trinidad by slaves who emigrated from the Grenadines. The bongo songs, also of the big drum dance group, are symbolic of regeneration and were originally sung at wakes; in the West Indies they have developed secularized forms as well.

The Spanish colonizers introduced such instruments as the banjo, mandolin, guitar, and maraca. A number of songs in quick three-four tempo that evolved from the Spanish tradition have retained their popularity as a consequence of the islands' continuous contact with Venezuela. The French settlers, who immigrated in large numbers during the period of the French and Haitian revolutions and came to outnumber the Spanish, contributed their own songs and dances. Some of the Christmas songs that remain popular in Trinidad have been traced back to provinces in France. The so-called *crèches* and *cantiques de Noël*, which evolved from the old noëls of France have taken on livelier Afro-West Indian rhythms, such as the beguine.

The dances known as *bele* and *kalenda* are predominantly of African inspiration but were brought to Trinidad and Tobago during the French revolutionary wars by French African slaves from Martinique and Guadeloupe. They were danced for pleasure rather than used in ritual. Although English and Spanish words are occasionally used, the lyrics are basically a French patois. The *kalenda* is believed to have come to the New World from the coast of Guinea. *Kalenda* songs, which may be on any subject, are composed inpromptu by the singer. The audience accompanies him by handclapping and joins in the refrain. In the ceremony of Canboulay (see Glossary), celebrating the emancipation of the slaves, *kalenda* songs are followed by stick-fighting.

The European songs and dances preserved most nearly in their original forms are the reels, quadrilles, jigs, polkas, and mazurkas introduced by the Scots and English who settled in Trinidad and Tobago. The original

English lyrics have been corrupted by the addition of Spanish, Dutch, French, and African words. Some 200 of these songs were collected by researchers in the early 1950s. Other musical forms that blend European and African words and rhythms are work songs, song games, and religious hymns and chants, somewhat akin to the Negro spirituals that emerged from the mingling of Christian and African religious traditions in the United States.

Although East Indian musical forms have not been assimilated by the Afro-West Indian population, Hindu and Muslim musical cultures in Trinidad and Tobago contain many similarities to, and adaptations of, the older Afro-West Indian forms. The Hosein festival of the Muslims, for example, is a colorful spectacle accompanied by drumbeating and ceremonial stick-fighting.

The Popular Ballad and Modern Musical Expression

The calypso, the musical genre that has drawn international attention to Trinidad, evolved from the folk culture but is considered a popular ballad rather than folk music, as the songs are attributed to specific composers and are used as modern dance music. Although the origin of the term *calypso* has been disputed, one critic firmly believes that it derives from the Ibo word *kaisco* (encore). Elderly Trinidadians listening to calypso often shout *kaisco* when they are particularly pleased with a verse.

Some ethnomusicologists maintain that the calypso emerged as a variant of the *kalenda*. Others use the term *kalenda* to refer only to the stick dances and regard the improvised songs that accompanied them centuries ago as precursors of calypso. Satirical lyrics and contests of wit among singers were noted as early as the 1790s, and Cedric le Blanc reportedly gave command performances of calypso at Government House in the 1860s. The oldest surviving calypso, "Juvé Mamicoa," a traditional Carnival song, is said to have been composed in 1876.

West Indian critics tend to see in the evolution of the calypso and of the instruments that beat out its rhythms the story of the struggle of an oppressed majority to assert itself, politically as well as culturally, and of the gradual retreat of the ruling elite. The African songs, dances, chants, and ceremonies that constituted an aesthetic tie among Afro-West Indians were held in contempt by the European elite throughout some 400 years of colonial rule. As long as the masses appeared to accept their condition of servitude or deprivation, however, their music was seen by their masters as an emotional safety value and, as such, a necessary evil.

As social unrest became apparent, however, this collective form of expression came to be feared as a call to action, a subversive force sounding the death knell not only of Europe's "respectable" cultural transplantations but of its political supremacy as well. Thus colonial authorities, supported by the middle classes who sought to absorb European culture, periodically suppressed the African-inspired sounds and drove them underground. Trinidadian nationalists take pride not only in the uniqueness of their mass-based musical culture but also in its survival and ascendancy under the most adverse circumstances.

Trinidad's spectacular pre-Lenten Carnival, which fosters and sustains much of the country's folk and popular musical expression, originally represented an accommodation by the Roman Catholic Church to the needs of the landlords for an increasing slave population. The taboos attached to sexual license throughout the year were lifted for the duration of Carnival, and the slaves were encouraged to participate in the merrymaking. For the event the Afro-West Indians fashioned their own drums and other instruments from castaway materials and improvised their own songs, reviving their past, recording current events, and expressing their feelings. Confident that the whites did not understand the nuances of their patois, the slaves used their songs to poke fun at the alleged sexual inadequacies of their masters. They also performed satirical dances caricaturing the mannerisms of the Europeans, and gradually socioeconomic and political frustrations crept into their improvised songs.

During Carnival the rural workers flocked from the hills into the cities, dancing the *kalenda* with great fervor. In the 1930s, as the movement toward self-rule gained momentum, the authorities became frightened by the spectacle of the masses stirred to a frenzy by the drums and the drama of the stick dances and banned the use of drums in the cities. The drums were withdrawn to the hills, and the urban poor cast about for another means of producing their rhythms. The material they seized upon was hollow bamboo which, cut in varying lengths, produced a pleasing range of pitches. Thus emerged the so-called tamboo-bamboo bands, and the changers and *kalenda* dancers returned to the streets for Carnival. But this exciting new sound was also found offensive and threatening by the authorities and, like the drums before them, the tamboo-bamboo bands were banned.

Once again the Negro urban youths began to beat out their rhythms on whatever they could find, including the steel rims of car wheels and discarded tin ash cans. But it was the United States Army, stationed on bases in Trinidad during World War II, that provided the Negro musicians with their ultimate weapon. The empty steel drums that had contained oil for the use of the army—discarded by the hundreds, littering the island—were used to reproduce first the rhythms and ultimately the range of tone that gave a new lease on life to the *kalenda* and its offspring the calypso.

Despite their lack of training, the Negro musicians were highly sensitive to differentiation of sound. They soon learned to tune their steel drums, or pans, with great precision, using only hammers and chisels. Ellie Manette of the Invaders Band has been given credit for first marking off notes on his drum and padding the beating sticks with rubber for better resonance. Since then the pans have become so refined that even complicated classical music can be played on them in various keys. Trinidad's steel bands may have as many as 120 players and 150 pans. The bands typically have bass, guitar, and cello pans in the rhythm section, and first and second pans play the melody. Rhythm sections may also include conga drums, tuned car hubs, cowbells, and tambourines, and some bands have introduced electrical amplification and other acoustical innovations.

As before, colonial authorites attempted to ban the new instruments, but it was too late. The North American servicemen had become enthusiastic patrons of the steel bands, as had a great many of the children of the elite. Meanwhile the calypso had become a vehicle of social protest, its lyrics sometimes becoming quite militant. By the late 1940s a cultural revolution was under way; political and social changes were soon to follow.

Today's calypso, in two-four or four-four time and almost entirely in English, has been described as "witty, smutty, topical, and full of double entendre." The minor keys and on-the-spot improvisation of earlier decades have been largely discarded, and the influence of Latin American popular music and North American jazz may be distinguished in some calypso songs. Stimulated by the commercialization of the genre and hotly contested annual competition for calypso monarch of the Carnival, composers turn out some forty or fifty "hit" songs each year. New songs are generally based on some fifty traditional melodies, which are rearranged to accommodate new lyrics. Calypsos generally have four eight-line verses, separated by a four-line chorus. They employ the lower class Creole vocabulary and a simple rhyme scheme. Love and the wiles of women remain the most popular themes, but government leaders ignore the social and political content of these songs at their peril.

Another musical form that evolved from the country's folk culture to become an important element of modern popular music is the limbo. Like the calypso and the steel band, the dance, alleged to have its origins in an ancient African ritual of manhood, has spread throughout the West Indies and has been much in demand by foreign audiences. The most highly skilled limbo dancers are said to be able to slip under a flaming bar just ten inches from the ground without being singed.

The achievement of national independence in 1962 was followed immediately by government initiatives to draw the great mass of the population into the process of cultural liberation and the reconstuction and redefinition of national culture in folk and popular, as opposed to European, terms. The main thrust of this effort has been the Best Village Trophy Competition; it was estimated in the early 1970s that more than half of the national population had participated directly in these lavish community folkloric presentations. Nationwide music festivals and art festivals are also held in alternate years.

A number of small folk ballet and folk dance groups have performed abroad. The limbo company headed by Julia Edwards and Beryl

MacBurnie's Little Carib Company of Dancers are particularly well known. Geoffrey Holder, who spends most of his time in the United States, has also gained an international reputation as an actor, dancer, and choreographer.

The Graphic Arts

In contrast to the folk tradition and vitality of Trinidad's music, the development of the graphic arts is still a nebulous movement; its practitioners have yet to define a national tradition and to achieve popular acceptance. Before 1930 there was little record of painting as anything other than a casual pastime, and serious pursuit of sculpture was not apparent until after independence was achieved.

The initial impetus to the graphic arts was the establishment in 1930 of the Society of Trinidad Independents. Its founders were Alice Pashley, an Englishwoman whose interests included the oriental form of fabric painting known as batik; Amy Leong Pang, a Trinidadian of Chinese descent who had studied painting in China; the art critic Ivy Achoy; and Hugh Stollmeyer, a young painter who had studied in New York. Despite the variety in their backgrounds and interests, all had been influenced to some extent by developments in Paris and particularly by the work of Henri Matisse and Paul Gauguin.

The most prolific painter among the independents was Stollmeyer, who presented fifty-five paintings at a single exhibit. He experimented with sculpture but eventually became absorbed with painting. His themes were drawn from native folklore and local belief; he made generous use, for example, of the goat as a symbol in his drawings and paintings.

The society exhibited regularly for several years, but its defense in 1933 of a Russian artist whose paintings of nudes had been confiscated by Trinidad's customs officials resulted in rebuke by the public, and the demoralized movement was almost dead by the end of the decade. A number of new painters began to exhibit in 1939—among them Sybil Atteck, Boscoe Holder, and Carlisle Chang—but aside from some of the personnel of the Censorship Department few in Trinidad patronized the arts during the war years. Not until 1945, when under the inspiration of Atteck the Trinidad Art Society was formed, was substantial support for the graphic arts forthcoming.

Boscoe Holder, who trained himself in figure drawing by copying photographs from *Esquire*, soon became infamous for his paintings of nudes. Public opinion forced him to clothe his figures; demoralized, he turned from painting to dancing, and in 1949 he moved to the United Kingdom. He nevertheless continues to be regarded by critics as one of the country's most outstanding painters. Boscoe's younger brother, Geoffrey, followed his lead—first into painting, then into dance—and also emigrated. Before leaving the country, however, Geoffrey established himself as a figure painter, featuring figures with long necks in the manner of Amadeo Modigliani.

Abstract painting was introduced in Trinidad in the late 1940s and 1950s by a number of artists, including Nina Lamming Squires, who had studied in London. At the same time two architects, Colin Laird and Oswald Chase, turned to painting and introduced the nonobjective style that had evolved in Paris. Although the abstract and nonobjective trends received little public support, Squires opened a gallery exhibiting these styles in 1960, and a new group of young painters pursued these trends.

Another development of the 1950s was the search for styles and subjects that would be truly representative of Trinidad. The works of M. P. Alladin, Noel Vaucrosson, and Joseph Cromwell are illustrative of this grend. Alladin, who was the director of culture in the Ministry of Education and Culture in the 1970s, depicted the people of the countryside, in particular the poor, the drunk, and the destitute. Cromwell, influenced by the modern school in London, imbued his figures with monumental qualities. Other painters, including Leo Basso and Dominic Isaac, adopted the naive primitive style.

Until the 1960s Trinidadian painters tended to concentrate on the figure. The trend toward landscape painting (as seen in the works of Dermot Louison and Edwin Hing Wan) that has since developed is viewed by one artist and critic as indicative of the inability of younger painters to draw the figure. Shortcomings in drawing and painting techniques have been seen as consequences of inadequate training and apprenticeship programs and the inability or unwillingness of the painter to pursue his art as a profession rather than an avocation.

Theater

Trinidad has no lack of talented and dedicated playwrights. Errol John, for example, internationally acclaimed as an actor as well as a playwright, won the *London Observer* prize from a field of some 2,000 entries from the Commonwealth of Nations for his *Moon on a Rainbow Shawl*. The play, which received enthusiastic reviews in the United States when it opened off Broadway in the mid-1960s, presents a steaming, crowded backyard in Port-of-Spain with humor and pathos.

Errol Hill, playwright, actor, producer, and drama teacher of international repute, excels at satire and comedy and makes full poetic use of the popular speech of his native land. His best known work, *Man Better Man*, a musical folk play, was chosen as the Trinidadian entry in the British Commonwealth Arts Festival in London in 1965. Hill, who compiled a catalogue of West Indian plays in the 1960s, maintained that there were at least nine practicing playwrights in Trinidad, the best of whom exhibited a willingness to grapple with timely, profound local themes. He lamented that they were, nevertheless, having no notable impact on West Indian society because of the dearth of trained actors and directors, the lack of financial backing for dramatic productions, and the limited audience.

In the mid-1970s the University of the West Indies had only two full-time instructors specializing in drama, and only one full-time drama tutor was attached to the Ministry of Education, Culture, and Community Development. Few scholarships were available for theatrical training abroad, and those aspirant actors, directors, composers or designers fortunate enough to receive one of the two or three scholarships awarded annually by the British Council, foreign governments, or private foundations have often been reluctant to return to Trinidad and Tobago. Consequently local playwrights have often been obliged to assemble their own companies and direct their own plays. Another of Trinidad's leading playwrights, Jack Archibald, noted that the audience for live performances in Port-of-Spain did not exceed 1,200.

Although the growth of the theater as a professional medium has been stunted by these mutually reinforcing handicaps, folk theater has received great impetus from the Best Village Trophy Competition, initiated in 1962. Hundreds of amateur groups have performed one-act plays for the biennial festivals of the Trinidad and Tobago Arts Festival Association. Presentations for the village competition have given rise to experimentation in choreography and to a merger of musical and dramatic expression. One critic claims that the foundations have been laid for the creation of a national folk opera.

MASS COMMUNICATION

The Government and the Media

Until independence in 1962 the communications media in Trinidad and Tobago were allowed to develop without much interference from the government, except for sporadic attempts at censorship when opposition to British control became too vocal. After independence two patterns of ownership emerged that had their origins in colonial times: ownership by foreign enterprise and ownership by local government or political party. Gradually the government sought to own or control as many of the media as possible, and by the mid-1970s the government owned one of the two radio stations and the only television station. All but one of the newspapers, however, were privately owned. Not surprisingly the press has generally been more critical of government than has the radio or television.

The government has tended to maintain a close watch over the mass media in order to control opposition and promote national development. The desire for control stems partially from the government's belief that in such a small country even an insignificant rumor could be magnified out of proportion and bring on political disorder. The vituperative comments occasionally made about government officials have also caused the government to protect itself by extending its control. Freedom of the press is guaranteed by the constitution and has generally been observed. Occasionally, however, it has been limited by the sporadic application of certain press censorship laws or during a state of emergency.

The most frequent form of governmental pressure on the press has occurred through its use of libel and sedition laws. It is not uncommon for top government officials to bring a libel suit against a newspaper, as Prime Minister Williams has done. Protection of internal security has also been cited as a reason for the government to justify limiting press freedom. For example, after the black power revolt in April 1970 the Emergency Powers Regulation Act went into effect for seven months to limit publicity given to the leaders of the revolt (see ch. 9). Pictures of the revolt's leaders as well as newspaper publication of their testimony were banned, and only the most cursory information about them could be printed. The government was empowered to control and censor media content and even to ban publication but, despite the critical stance of the press, the government did not make use of these powers. In 1971 a new sedition law was enacted that some journalists find objectionable (see ch. 9).

In addition to direct political pressure the government has the power to apply certain economic pressures. Most of these restrictions are imposed by controlling the issuance of printing and advertising contracts and by licensing. This has not been as stringent a control device in Trinidad and Tobago as it has been in some of the smaller islands, mainly because newspapers have other, sufficient sources of revenue. For example, in 1959 during a heated debate between Williams and the *Guardian*, Williams announced that the newspapers were subsidized by government advertising. In an editorial a few days later the *Guardian* replied that the prime minister's statement had no basis in fact.

John A. Lent, who has written much about the mass media in the Commonwealth Caribbean, has stated that it is both common and acceptable for government officials to denounce the mass media publicly—particularly during election time. He notes that, despite the serious tone ot these threats, little effort has actually been made to carry them out. In Lent's opinion the most active opponent of the media in the entire area has been Williams. Throughout his career Williams has castigated both the print and the broadcast media, although his attacks on the latter have eased since the government's takeover of a radio station and the only television station in 1969.

In the past Williams' favorite target was the *Guardian*, which was controlled by British investor Roy Thomson. Upon occasion Williams accused the *Guardian* of concealing his speeches, intimidating potential foreign investors, and promoting United States and British propaganda. Through a variety of dramatic acts—such as cleaning his shoes with a copy of the newspaper and publicly burning it—the prime minister showed his disfavor. The *Guardian* and its sister newspaper, the *Evening News*, periodically ran editorials claiming solidarity with the community and service to it despite the expatriate status of the owner. In late 1974 the *Guardian* and the *Evening News* passed out of Thomson's hands into those of local investors. There was also some government interest in the holdings.

Some observers, such as the Inter-American Press Association

(IAPA), felt that the constant tension between Williams and the *Guardian* had an effect upon the public and the media. In 1959 when journalists were harassed by political radicals, the *Guardian* openly attributed the trouble to Williams. A decade later, however, the IAPA stated that public sentiment in favor of Williams had affected the media directly: "There is known self-censorship carried out by all media because of fear of reprisals from both government and business interests." The degree of self-censorship is unknown, however, although it is not suspected of being as inhibiting a factor as elsewhere in the Western Hemisphere.

The most important document defining the official relationship between the media and the government has been the Third Five-Year Plan, promulgated in 1969. The stated purpose of this plan was to aid the people in developing a positive national identity. The plan recognized the unique set of historical circumstances that led to a lack of self-confidence on a national scale and the consequent need for a nationally oriented and high-quality mass media system. To this end the principles that were to guide the government's policy toward the mass media were that no transfer of ownership could be made without government permission, that foreign enterprise could neither establish new facilities nor buy existing locally owned ones, and that the government would acquire ownership of radio and control of television stations. Certain provisions were also made for the quality of advertising and the educational goals to be met by the broadcast media.

The plan recognized that both opportunities and problems would develop with government takeover of the broadcast media. On the one hand new opportunities would arise for the creation of national values and styles that could build cultural unity and encourage racial and religious tolerance, and there would be demands for talented local people. On the other hand two sets of problems—one financial and the other political— were predicted. The financial problem is a consequence of the cost of locally produced programs, which are more expensive than imported ones. Such financial constraints have precluded the rapid introduction of high-quality programs produced in Trinidad.

The political problem derived from possible criticism that government ownership of the media indicated a trend toward totalitarianism. The plan recognized that organization and administration could be a problem and stated that no political party should interfere in media management. No political criteria could be applied in selecting staff, and the companies would continue to operate on a commercial basis with a broadly based board of directors.

Finally the plan acknowledged that the public should be informed about the government's activities. According to Lent, access to government information has been hampered by laws restricting reporting, reluctance of government officials to release worthy news items, and government officials' use of the media as a personal political forum. For example, for over five years before the black power revolt of April 1970,

178

Prime Minister Williams had not held a news conference, but between April and August of 1970 he held four such conferences. These meetings, as well as those called by Williams in the late 1950s and early 1960s, have been termed propaganda conferences by some of the press. In the attempt to broaden public access to government information, the plan proposed the publication of an annual handbook and a magazine and the production of an annual film for exhibition at all cinemas.

By mid-1975 much of the five-year plan had been successfuly completed. Local ownership and control of certain media had been secured. Thomson, who during the mid-1960s owned both daily newspapers, half of the radio stations, and shares in the television station, had seen most of his monopolistic holdings phased out. The public had become more aware of such issues as content and quality, and local productions were increasing. A weekly government gazette had been established, and documentary and educational short films were produced at a rate of four or five per year by the Public Relations Division unit under the Office of the Prime Minister.

The major change was the government's purchase of the television station and a radio station. Until 1969 a consortium of investors controlled the only television station. Under this consortium the government and the Columbia Broadcasting System (CBS) each controlled 10 percent, and Thomson and the British company Rediffusion each controlled 40 percent. But in 1969 the Thomson and Rediffusion shares were purchased by the government, leaving CBS with a minority holding. The Trinidad and Tobago Television Company (TTT) operates under the same board of directors as the Trinidad and Tobago National Broadcasting Service (TTNBS) radio station which was established under private ownership in 1957 and bought by the government in 1969. Both stations are still financed through advertising revenue.

Another major shift has occurred in program content. Except for TTT, all stations in the West Indies rely on foreign sources for 60 to 80 percent of their content. Trinidad's locally produced programs included not only news, sports, and government information but also programs that are used by other Commonwealth Caribbean stations. Moreover citizen concern is solicited through newspaper articles. One journalist for the *Guardian* urged the public, "Please write, television is too important a medium to accept blindly."

Government radio has also shifted to more local content. Whereas Radio Trinidad—owned by a subsidiary of Rediffusion—broadcast only 30 percent local fare, TTNBS has increased its local programs to 40 percent after its takeover by the government.

Newspapers and Periodicals

Newspapers play a vital role in the political process. Not only are they a vocal and generally uncensored source of public opinion and information, but the 95-percent literacy rate makes them key disseminators of that information. Compared to newspaper circulations throughout the world, that of the *Sunday Guardian*, which is bought by one-tenth of the population, would rank near the top.

One of the most active newspapers since its inception in 1917 has been the *Trinidad Guardian*, usually called the *Guardian*. For most of its history it was owned by a group of white or near-white businessmen who had a vested interest in maintaining the status quo. Throughout the political turmoil of the 1930s and 1940s—until the rise of Williams as a national political figure in the mid-1950s—the *Guardian* was the major influence molding public opinion and slowing down mass politicization. Small newspapers owned by political parties or political leaders, such as Uriah Butler, chipped away unsuccessfully at the control of mass opinion by the *Guardian*.

Williams realized that if he were to rally mass support successfully behind the PNM he would have to discredit the *Guardian* as a source of opinion on domestic issues. His main weapons in this effort were open ridicule and the *Weekly*, a lively PNM newspaper. Over the next twenty years the conservative *Guardian* continued to clash with Williams' liberal and intensely democratic ideas. During election years the *Guardian* encouraged its readers to value experience in office over party labels, thus putting itself in direct conflict with the growing party movement in the islands. Moreover, although the British Creole interests controlling the *Guardian* were willing to accept constitutional change, they fought the sweeping social changes proposed by Williams.

A similarly conservative stance was taken by the defunct *Trinidad Chronicle*, formerly the *Port-of-Spain Gazette*. Although also forwarding an elitist position, the owners of the *Trinidad Chronicle* were of French and Portuguese descent and represented a distinctly Roman Catholic bias in reporting. The newspaper showed its opposition to the PNM by placing a great many letters from anti-PNM Roman Catholics on the editorial page.

Although Williams' opposition began to loosen the *Guardian's* monopolistic hold on public opinion, the establishment in 1967 of another daily, the *Trinidad and Tobago Express* (known as the *Express*), and several radical weeklies accelerated the trend. Since the mid-1950s the press has grown from a single opinion, elitist medium to a broad-based one representing the full spectrum of political views. The *Express*, such radical weeklies as *People*, *Vanguard* (the organ of the powerful Oilfield Workers Trade Union), the *Bomb*, and *Moko* and intellectual weeklies such as *Tapia*, and the *New World Quarterly*, have all raised the level of public awareness and debate. Although by 1975 both *Vanguard* and *Moko* had ceased publication, the *Bomb* was widely read and controversial. Its editor seldom hesitated to publish anything that would expose problems in the society, and several stories from the *Bomb* were picked up by other newspapers. In the early 1970s many of these newspapers, such as *Vanguard*, depicted the PNM as conservative—just as Williams and the PNM had presented the *Guardian* and its supporters twenty years earlier (see ch. 7).

In the mid-1970s the *Guardian* still claimed the largest daily circulation (over 55,000), followed by the *Evening News* (38,000); the circulation of the *Express* was unknown. Both the *Guardian* and the *Express* also had Sunday editions. There are four privately owned weeklies and a government gazette. One of the newspapers is in Chinese; the others are in English.

About twenty-four periodicals are published—most monthly or quarterly. They deal with social, religious, legal, commercial, and cultural subjects as well as sports, medicine, and agriculture.

Radio, Television, and Films

Radio service has been present in Trinidad and Tobago since the late 1940s. An estimated 293,000 receivers were in use in the mid-1970s—more than three times the number of a decade earlier. Radio Trinidad was established as the island's first broadcasting service in 1947. In the mid-1970s it was still owned and operated by the Trinidad Broadcasting Company, a subsidiary of Rediffusion. Its twenty-kilowatt, mediumwave transmitter covered both Trinidad and Tobago as well as the Windward and Leeward islands, and its one-kilowatt frequency modulation (FM) transmitter served the Port-of-Spain area. Radio Trinidad broadcast a total of 130 hours a week, and its weekly program format included frequent news bulletins, ten and one-half hours of programs produced by the government's Public Relations Division, six fifteen-minute sessions of school broadcasts, and entertainment or cultural programs.

The TTNBS commercial station, Radio 610, also has a mediumwave transmitter, broadcasting at ten kilowatts, and a very-high-frequency (VHF) transmitter in Port-of-Spain, broadcasting at 0.25 kilowatts. In the mid-1970s it broadcast 119 hours weekly, ten and one-half of which were Public Relations Division programs, and relayed seven BBC world service news bulletins daily. Although Radio Trinidad and Radio 610 are owned and operated differently, both derive their income from advertising revenue.

The television station broadcast seventy-three hours of weekly programs, including thirty-seven hours of feature films, thirteen and one-half hours of community interest programs designed to contribute to the government's adult education program, nine and one-half hours of news and information, five hours of programs for special audiences, three and one-half hours of light entertainment, and three hours devoted to literature and the arts. The remainder was used for commercials and sponsored programs. Imported programs still constituted at least 50 percent of the broadcast time, considerably less than the percentage of foreign programs transmitted in the other islands. The bulk of these programs came from the United States, Canada, Australia, and the Federal Republic of Germany (West Germany).

The government and the more educated Trinidadians are sensitive to television's potential role in nation-building. Concern over the content, quality, and origin of programs is frequently expressed in the *Guardian*. One article by a syndicated columnist stated that the quantity of local programs was unimportant if the quality was poor. He recommended better wages for those already employed and to entice people away from other more lucrative areas, such as advertising and teaching. He also suggested a cutback in the work load and an increase in the number of specialists employed. He pointed out that improving equipment was not a guarantee of better programming. Color television, for example, would only accentuate the weaknesses and mistakes in local television. Thus although color might be a diversion, it was not an answer to programming problems.

The *Guardian* has also published an interview with the general manager of TTT in which he stated that the roles of television were to entertain, educate, and inform, although various sectors of the population disagreed over what constituted each role and which was most important. He admitted that foreign programs were the most popular, with both sponsors and audiences, and that they largely sustained the cost of making local productions. When asked why no Indian films appeared on television, he responded that they were not made for sixteen-millimeter projection—the only kind suitable for television—and that they would require the added expense of dubbing or subtitles.

In the mid-1970s there were a total of seventy-seven motion picture houses and four drive-in theaters with a total seating capacity of over 42,100. The average total annual attendance was about 8.5 million—about eight visits per person per year. All feature films were imported, as were the majority of documentary and instructional films shown noncommercially by the thirteen mobile projection units owned and operated by the government. Most films came from the United States, India, Great Britain, and Italy.

Trinidad has had a ground receiver for satellite communication located at Matura Point since 1971. It is owned jointly by the government and private enterprise.

CHAPTER 7

GOVERNMENT AND POLITICAL DYNAMICS

With more than a decade of experience as an independent nation-state, Trinidad and Tobago in 1975 still bears the stamp of the British experience. No indigenous system of central government existed from which a national pattern could be extrapolated, so that its present constitutional apparatus, drafted at independence, is a reflection of centuries-old British constitutional arrangements. Many have questioned the suitability of the Westminster political model for the needs of Trinidadian society.

The framework of government is that of a parliamentary democracy with competing political parties, interest groups, a public service, an independent judiciary, and a free press. As in most systems of government based on the Westminster model, the executive controls parliament. This is true of Trinidad, and the executive has had its hand strengthened by a disorganized and ineffectual parliamentary opposition with no clearly discernible program.

Two major political parties, the People's National Movement (PNM) and the Democratic Labour Party (DLP), have dominated Trinidadian politics since the late 1950s. The PNM, with a highly bureaucratic party structure, spearheaded the independence movement and articulated the need for economic and social reform. The DLP, self-described as advocating "democratic socialism," has not been able to reach a consensus on specific alternatives to the PNM's effort.

New political groups have emerged since 1970 in the wake of violent political disturbances, articulating the need for greater domestic control of national resources, "black" dignity and economic power, and a greater distribution of the society's wealth. These new groups include the Action Committee of Dedicated Citizens (ACDC), the United National Independence Party (UNIP), the National Joint Action Committee (NJAC), the Tapia House Group, and the United Revolutionary Organization (URO). These groups oppose the PNM but have neither developed comprehensive programs with grass-roots support nor run candidates for political office.

Criticism from these new groups and from within the PNM has resulted in a search for new solutions to the pressing social, economic, and political problems. Constitutional reform has been proposed. The Wooding Commission, a constitution commission, was empowered by Parliament to examine the present Constitution and to make recommendations for its revision. A similar exercise has been conducted by a committee of the cabinet. Recommendations from these groups include the adoption of a republican form of government with a president and prime minister; lowering the voting age to eighteen and substituting the ballot box for voting machines; establishing an integrity commission for declaration of personal wealth and holdings by members of Parliament; and the appointment of an ombudsman.

In foreign relations Trinidad and Tobago has assumed its responsibilities as an independent state. It is a member of the United Nations and over thirty regional, Commonwealth of Nations, or world organizations. The country is firmly committed to the Western world but seeks to establish creative relationships with countries under the communist system of government. The maintenance of those existing economic arrangements deemed to be advantageous and the diversification of the economy are important objectives of foreign policy. The causes of Caribbean and Latin American regional integration are also emphasized in the foreign policy of the government. Recognizing the important role that small states can play in world affairs, Trinidad and Tobago has asserted the rights of small countries to full representation at the highest echelons of international organizations.

THE CONSTITUTION AND FORMAL STRUCTURE OF GOVERNMENT

After more than a century of British rule, Trinidad and Tobago celebrated independence from Great Britain under the provisions of the Trinidad and Tobago (Constitution) Order in Council of 1962, effective August 31, 1962. During the years of British tutelage both islands evolved politically through the stages of crown colony government and internal self-government to their present status as components of a unitary state and an independent member of the Commonwealth of Nations with dominion status.

Political Constitutional Development

In 1797 Trinidad became a British crown colony. Under this system of government executive authority was exercised by a governor who served at the pleasure of the secretary of state for the colonies. A legislative council was added in 1831, but no representatives were officially elected. In contrast, Tobago in its early years had experienced briefly a form of representative government with a bicameral legislature. This system, however, was abolished and replaced with crown colony government when the island was annexed to Trinidad in 1889. Elections were first held in Trinidad on February 7, 1925, and universal adult suffrage was introduced in 1945. With universal adult suffrage the qualifications for membership of the legislature were reduced, and thousands of citizens were added to the electoral rolls.

A new constitution was introduced in 1950, which marked a major advance toward responsible government. Besides further increasing the number of elected members in the legislature, the new constitution provided that the executive council should cease to be advisory and should become the principal instrument of policy with a ministerial system in which elected members of the executive were responsible for the administration of government departments. An even greater degree of responsible government and a larger majority of the elected element were provided by the 1956 Constitution, under which the governor continued to preside over an executive council comprising two official and eight elected members, one of whom was the chief minister. After the general elections held in September 1956, Eric Williams became the first chief minister of Trinidad, and for the first time members of a single party had the majority in the executive.

Cabinet government was introduced in 1959 with the following changes: the governor no longer presided over the executive council; the offices of executive council and chief minister were renamed cabinet and premier respectively; and the new premier was empowered to appoint and dismiss ministers and parliamentary secretaries. In 1961 Trinidad and Tobago received full internal self-government within the Federation of the West Indies, of which it was a member. The Constitution of 1961 provided for a bicameral legislative council consisting of a nominated upper house, the Senate, and an elected lower house, the House of Representatives.

The final preindependence constitutional debate was conducted publicly in the Queen's Hall Constitution Conference held in Port-of-Spain during 1962. Members of the loyal opposition in the house pressed for the appointment of a joint select committee of Parliament to consider the draft constitution prepared by the government, to be amended in accordance with the discussions at the Queen's Hall conference.

After this historic conference a delegation from Trinidad and Tobago, including members of government, the opposition, and others, participated in the Independence Conference at Marlborough House in London. The present Constitution and independence for Trinidad and Tobago were the result of that conference.

The 1962 Constitution is divided into nine chapters with 105 sections. According to Section 38, the Constitution may be amended. The principal provisions of the Constitution are described as "entrenched." The most important of these are further described as "specially entrenched." A partial listing of the ordinarily entrenched provisions includes those relating to human rights and fundamental freedoms; prorogation of Parliament; appointment, dismissal, and disciplinary control of judicial officers, public officers, and police officers; removal of diplomatic officials from foreign posts; and protection of pension rights. These may be amended by an affirmative vote of not less than two-thirds of all the members of each house.

The specially entrenched provisions may be amended by an affirmative vote of not less than three-fourths of all the members of the House of Representatives and not less than two-thirds of all the members of the Senate. The specially entrenched provisions deal with the office of governor general, the establishment, composition, annual meetings, and dissolution of Parliament; general elections and appointment of senators; and appointment of commissions dealing with such matters as boundaries, judicial and legal services, elections, and amendment of the Constitution.

In June 1971 the government of Trinidad and Tobago appointed a commission under the Commissions of Enquiry Ordinance to make recommendations for a new document to replace the 1962 Constitution. The commission solicited opinions from all sectors, and Parliament has received its recommendations. After debate and modification, the constitution is expected to be in force by 1976.

Persons born in Trinidad or in Tobago "before or after" August 31, 1962, are described by the Constitution as citizens. Citizenship rights are also extended to persons born of Trinidadian parents abroad and to women who marry residents of the country. Persons with dual citizenship are required to make citizenship declarations at age twenty-two. Failure to renounce citizenship rights to another country automatically terminates Trinidad and Tobago citizenship. Constitutional amendments in 1965 and 1968 pertaining to citizenship have recognized that dual citizenship should be permitted in some instances where serious difficulties could result from insistence on the principle that a citizen of Trinidad and Tobago should be a citizen of no other country.

All citizens are guaranteed the recognition and protection of human rights and fundamental freedoms according to chapter 1 of the Constitution. These rights include the right to life, liberty, and security of person and property; the right of the individual to equality before the law and the protection of the law; respect for private and family life; equality of treatment from any public authority in the exercise of any function; the right to join political parties; freedom of the press; and protection from arbitrary arrest or detention. Discrimination based on race, color, religion, sex, or national origin is forbidden by the Constitution. The Constitution also empowers the governor general to declare a period of public emergency. One such emergency in 1970 and subsequent sporadic acts of political violence have resulted in public unease over emergency powers legislation and concern for the safeguards of civil liberties. Other civil rights issues are handled by the courts, with provisions for prompt hearings.

The Legislature

The national government of Trinidad and Tobago is organized as a parliamentary democracy. As in other independent Commonwealth countries, Queen Elizabeth II serves as queen of Trinidad and Tobago. In consultation with the prime minister, who is head of government, the queen appoints a governor general to serve as her representative and commander in chief.

The Trinidad and Tobago Parliament therefore consists of the queen, the Senate appointed by the governor general in consultation with the prime minister, and the elected House of Representatives. Members of the cabinet are the prime minister, who is head of government, fourteen ministers and an attorney general chosen by the head of government and appointed by the governor general.

The Senate consists of twenty-four members, of whom thirteen are appointed by the governor general on the advice of the prime minister, four on the advice of the leader of the opposition, and seven by the governor general on the advice of the prime minister after consultation with religious, economic, or social bodies or associations from which the prime minister considers that such senators should be selected.

Persons are qualified for appointment to the Senate if they are citizens and at least thirty years of age. The Senate elects a president, deputy president, and its officers from its own ranks.

In 1975 the House of Representatives consisted of thirty-six members. The membership corresponds with the existing number of constituencies. An increase in constituencies and the numbers of representatives in the house occurred in 1966 when new constitutencies were created by order of the governor general on the advice of the house. The Boundaries Commission also provided advice to the House of Representatives. Members of the house must be twenty-one years of age, citizens of Trinidad, and resident in Trinidad for two years preceding the day of nomination for election.

The House chooses its own officers. The speaker and deputy speaker are chosen from members who are not already serving as ministers or parliamentary secretaries or from among persons who are not members of either house. A speaker elected from the house membership will have a casting vote only. One elected from outside the house will have neither an original nor a casting vote. If on any matter the votes of members are equally divided, the motion is lost.

The house initiates money bills, whereas other bills may be initiated in either house. For the conduct of business, quorums are required. The Senate quorum consists of eight senators, and the House of Representatives quorum consists of ten members. Members of Parliament enjoy immunity from all civil or criminal action while speaking during proceedings, but members may be disqualified for undischarged bankruptcy, allegiance to another state, insanity, being under sentence of death, and conviction for offenses relating to elections.

The Executive

The executive authority of Trinidad and Tobago is nominally vested in the queen and is nominally exercised by the governor general, subject to the provisions of the Constitution. The governor general performs ceremonial functions. He is kept informed concerning matters of government, makes appointments to public offices with the prime minister's advice, appoints the leader of the opposition, and has the power of judicial pardon. After independence Trinidad and Tobago's first governor general was Sir Solomon Hochoy, a Trinidadian. He was succeeded by Sir Ellis Clark, a distinguished legal scholar with considerable diplomatic experience.

The focal point of policymaking is the cabinet, which is collectively responsible to Parliament. The cabinet includes the prime minister and the attorney general, appointed by the governor general on the advice of the prime minister. The ministries are: agriculture, lands, and fisheries; education and culture; external affairs; finance; health; home affairs; housing; industry and commerce; labor, social security, and cooperatives; local government; national security; petroleum and mines-public utilities; Tobago affairs; and works.

The leader of the cabinet is the prime minister. He is formally appointed by the governor general, who must select the leader of the party that "commands the support of the majority of members of the House of Representatives." Trinidad has had only one prime minister since its independence—Eric Williams, whose party, the PNM, is in the majority. His cabinet responsibilities and special interests include constitutional matters, community development, public relations, information (press, radio, and films), archives, youth affairs, national awards, public holidays, better village programs, external affairs, finance, and development of the North-West Peninsula.

The prime minister is empowered to choose his ministers and to decide which departments they should administer. He retains the right to a substantial area of patronage and has the right to veto ministry appointments to the offices of permanent secretary, deputy permanent secretary, chief technical officer, deputy chief technical officer, chief parliamentary counsel, director of personnel administration, solicitor general, commissioner of police, and deputy commissioner of police. The prime minister also controls the appointment of the government's principal representatives abroad.

Trinidad and Tobago has long had a two-party system with the existence of an opposition group in Parliament. The leader of the opposition is chosen by the governor general. He is the leader of the party in the House of Representatives that commands the support of the largest number of members of the house in opposition to the government.

Since the 1961 elections the opposition has not been very vigorous in Parliament. The leader of the opposition lived in London and rarely attended sessions during the five-year term from 1961 to 1966. There was little opposition during the 1966–71 sessions of Parliament as members of the opposition continued to protest the use of voting machines in the elections of 1966. In 1971 the opposition boycotted the election, and the PNM won every seat in Parliament. Since 1972 the leader of the

188

opposition has been one of the two PNM members of Parliament who defected from the party.

Administration

A key element in the administration of the multifaceted governmental machinery of Trinidad and Tobago is the vast army of career civil servants. These public officers collect and organize much of the information required for the formulation of policy; theirs is also the task of implementation.

Before independence civil servants, as in Great Britain, were expected to be responsive to the policy demands of whatever government was in power; equal skill and dedication were to be shown in policy implementation. Political administrators had the capacity to influence policy, which was interpreted sometimes as either victimizing or favoring. Therefore the framers of the Trinidad and Tobago Constitution created independent service commissions empowered to appoint, promote, transfer, and discipline personnel in the public career. The intent of the policy was the insulation of career officers from direct political influence. With this protection public servants were to be free to serve with dedication any political administration. Framers of the Constitution also recognized that the political authorities needed powers to ensure efficiency and responsiveness from the bureaucracy—hence the prime minister's power of veto over certain executive appointments. The service commissions deal with public school teachers, judicial and legal service, police, and public service. The procedures for recruitment of officers for these commissions are delineated in the Constitution.

Public service workers are categorized as administrative, professional, executive, technical, clerical, and manual, as in the British civil service. In 1965 Parliament passed a new civil service act in response to widespread dissatisfaction with salaries and other matters as expressed by the Civil Service Association (CSA)—in late 1975 the Public Services Association —to the government. With the improvement of government salary scales and other compensation, the exodus of senior civil servants abated.

The Constitution of 1962 does not provide for appeals from disciplinary action taken by any of the service commissions. A review board was established in October 1966 to receive appeals in disciplinary matters, but it can only act in an advisory capacity since the commission itself was vested with constitutional authority to invoke discipline. Service commissions provide guidelines concerning political activity of public officials, who are able to join political parties, participate in party group activities, and serve as delegates at national conventions. Unlike their counterparts in Jamaica, however, they are unable to run for office.

Local Government

The earliest form of local government was the cabildo, or town council, an institution established by the Spanish government. The cabildo was a corporate body serving an administrative area as a parish vestry, municipal corporation, and ecclesiastical council. The cabildo was empowered to collect taxes in Port-of-Spain, including the harbor, and to supervise the repair and cleaning of streets and markets. It was also responsible for the police, prisons, health and sanitation, and the issue of licenses. In its next phase this council was known as the Port-of-Spain Town Council and finally as the Port-of-Spain City Council.

In the mid-1970s local government was administered by three municipal councils and seven county councils. The three municipalities—Port-of-Spain (1840), San Fernando (1846), and Arima (1888)—are financed through government grants and the levy of rates and taxes. Elected mayors, aldermen, and councillors are responsible for conducting local government affairs. Councillors and aldermen serve for three years, and mayors and their deputies are elected annually. Local government elections have not been held since 1971, however.

At the county level, local government administration derived from a system of wardenship, which was a replica of the French prefect system. The warden coordinated all services and was responsible to the central government for revenue collection, security, allocation of crown lands, roads, and health.

The system of county councils in effect in 1975 had been established in 1946. These county councils were established as advisory bodies to provide administrative assistance to the warden. By 1952 they were invested with executive powers. Their functions were to maintain local roads, cemeteries, recreation grounds, and markets.

The seven councils, including one in Tobago, are: Caroni, St. David and St. Andrew, St. George, Nariva and Mayaro, St. Patrick, Victoria, and Tobago. Representatives to county councils, like their counterparts in municipal councils, are elected officials. Councillors and aldermen serve three-year terms, and chairmen and vice chairmen are elected annually. In each council, one councillor and two aldermen represent each electoral district. Of the two aldermen, one is elected from among members of village councils (in the electoral district), and the second is elected at large from all residents in the constituency.

The Judiciary

The legal and judicial system is based on English common law and practice. The judiciary consists of the High Court and the Court of Appeal, which together constitute the Supreme Court of Judicature. These courts exercise jurisdiction and powers conferred upon them by the Constitution and the Supreme Court of Judicature Act No. 12 of 1962. There are also courts of summary jurisdiction and petty civil courts.

The Court of Appeal consists of four members—a president, who is the chief justice, and three justices of appeal. The Constitution provides for a fourth justice of appeal. The court hears appeals in civil and criminal matters from the High Court, the summary and petty civil courts, and any other inferior court.

In exercising jurisdiction an uneven number of justices—usually three—presides. When hearing an appeal from a judge in chambers or from an inferior court, however, two judges usually preside. Decisions of the Court of Appeal can be taken on appeal to the judicial committee of the Privy Council in England in grave civil or criminal cases. These appeals may be made "as of right" or with the permission of the Court of Appeal.

The High Court consists of ten puisne judges and the chief justice, who is an ex officio member of the High Court. There is vested in the High Court the same original jurisdiction as is vested in or exercised by the High Court of Justice in England under the provisions of the Supreme Court of Judicature (Consolidation) Act of 1925 (U.K.).

Puisne judges are required to retire at age sixty-two. They may be removed from office for misbehavior or inability to perform the functions of office as described by the Constitution. The Judicial and Legal Service Commission makes recommendations to the governor general for appointment or dismissal from public office of persons who are required to possess legal qualifications as described by Parliament.

Most lawyers in Trinidad and Tobago have received their training in the United Kingdom. Barristers are qualified to argue cases in court, whereas solicitors prepare briefs and give legal advice. With the establishment of the Faculty of Law at the University of the West Indies and the professional School of Law by the Council of Legal Education, however, the trend of seeking legal education outside the Caribbean area is expected to diminish, and the distinction between barristers and solicitors will soon be eliminated.

POLITICAL DYNAMICS

In 1975, thirteen years after the achievement of formal independence, Trinidad and Tobago was described as having a democratic political system replete with competing political parties, interest groups, a professional civil service, an independent judiciary, and a free press. Despite all this apparatus the process of democratization is incomplete and, according to Gordon K. Lewis, there is still little "conception of Government in the national sense. Government for most people is something from which to extract special privileges denied to others. Authority is . . . laughed at . . . there is little understanding of the idea of creative partnership between citizen and state."

The search for this creative partnership between citizen and state has been the professed goal of government in Trinidad and Tobago in its social, political, and economic dimensions. As elsewhere the record of experience illustrates the difficulties involved in reconciling general democratic and egalitarian ideals with competing and oftentimes conflicting goals and interests.

The Working of Parliamentary Democracy: Political Parties

The post-World War II period was highly significant in the political development of Trinidad and Tobago. Universal adult suffrage was exercised in the elections of 1946; the fledgling trade union movement reached maturity; a greater degree of responsible government was granted in 1950, together with a move toward a West Indies federation and political autonomy; and, finally, in 1956 the first successful popular nationalist movement emerged.

The elections of 1956 ushered in a two-party system and signaled the temporary eclipse of the multiparty structure. Six political parties and numerous candidates had sought election to the Legislative Council in these elections. The PNM achieved the distinction of being the first single party to have a majority in the executive. The DLP, which did not exist in 1956, later emerged as the minority party to form the opposition in the legislature until 1971. It was a coalition of Hindu and European elements opposed to the Negro-based PNM.

The People's National Movement

The People's National Movement (PNM) had its roots in the work of the Teachers Economic and Cultural Association, whose aims were to fight discrimination against its members in the country's white-dominated school system and to move generally to "uplift the masses." This second aspect of its work was entrusted to a subcommittee of the organization, the People's Education Movement, later renamed the People's Education Group. High-caliber professionals, mainly Negroes and a few Indians, met informally to discuss critical issues relating to the economic, social, and cultural life of the country. The idea of seeking wider currency for their ideas emerged. An affiliation with some existing political group was considered and then abandoned for the establishment of a separate party in order to guarantee the integrity of the new ideas.

Eric Williams, who had outstanding credentials and a research position with the Anglo-American Caribbean Commission, was chosen as spokesman for the new party. His Woodford Square and public library meetings had already earned him a popular following. The refusal of the Caribbean Commission to promote him to the position of secretary general and its policy of requiring advance knowledge of his speeches and written statements on the Caribbean led him to sever relations with the organization.

Freed from his obligations to the commission, Williams proceeded to orient the new political program to the needs of the entire country. A campaign for constitutional reform, calling for a nominated upper house and an elected lower house, was undertaken. Almost 28,000 signatures were collected throughout the country from religious, cultural, and other groups to petition the secretary of state for the colonies. These contacts became the core of the volunteer network that boosted the PNM to victory in the elections of 1956.

The party was organized by the formation of small groups all over the country with lines of communication from constituency groups to a general council and an annual convention, the first of which was held in January 1956. The party was mass based, had heavy support from middle-class Negro elements, and was financed by payment of dues by all members. This was intended to prevent domination of the party by any wealthy interest groups. Broad participation was encouraged in the party's selection of candidates for public office.

The early goals of the PNM were the political education of the people, nationhood, morality in public affairs, and educational reforms. In its first years of power preceding independence the party was instrumental in abolishing crown colony government (1956) and introducing the cabinet system (1959) and internal self-government (1961). It also introduced the techniques of planning in the national economy and reformed the income tax system. Relations between church and state in the field of education were improved by the signing of a concordat with religious denominations to ensure the denominational character of schools and to include them in the government's system of free secondary schools.

The party also changed electoral procedures to include the use of voting machines and a system of permanent voter registration. These electoral reforms have been viewed with suspicion by the opposition as facilitating electoral fraud and the self-perpetuation of the PNM in power.

The Democratic Labour Party

The Democratic Labour Party (DLP) emerged from a coalition of the three political parties that had presented candidates in the 1956 elections: the party of Political Progressive Groups (POPPG), the People's Democratic Party (PDP), and the Trinidad Labour Party (TLP). The POPPG was established in 1947 and was an amalgam of businessmen, professionals, and members of the managerial and executive elite. Its membership was fair skinned and identified with the Chamber of Commerce, the Roman Catholic hierarchy, and the French Creole groups in the society. In its manifesto the POPPG opposed ideas of "class struggle, class oligarchy, dictatorship of the masses, and racial or religious intolerance." These were the evils of the PNM. The standard-bearer of the POPPG was Albert Gomes.

The PDP was the political expression of the Hindu community and was the expression of Indian nationalist aspiration. The TLP claimed to be the true representative of urban workers, following in the tradition of Andrew Arthur Cipriani, an early hero of the labor movement.

The DLP therefore consisted of European and Hindu elements in opposition to the Negro-dominated PNM. From 1956 to independence the DLP systematically opposed the PNM. The DLP criticisms were that the government planned to subject the public service to political control and partisanship; that the PNM was corrupt and was excessively generous in conditions under which it admitted foreign capital to Trinidad and Tobago; that it mishandled the bases agreement of 1941 with the United States; and, finally, that it misused parliamentary institutions.

Since its inception the DLP has been plagued with leadership problems. Rudranath Capildeo, the absentee leader of the opposition, resided in London, where he was a professor of mathematics, and attended sessions of Parliament only a few times each year. This situation was intolerable to party regulars as they witnessed the decline of the DLP in popularity at the polls. At the time of the federal elections of 1958, its first showing as a party, the DLP received 47.4 percent of the votes cast. In 1966 the DLP received only 34 percent of the votes in the general elections, a substantial decline.

Vernon Jamandar succeeded Capildeo as party leader in 1969, and internal strife characterized the party's life. The DLP formed a coalition with another opposition group, the Action Committee of Dedicated Citizens (ACDC). This coalition seemed to augur a breakthrough in race relations as Negroes and Indians found themselves working together in the ACDC-DLP. The party's platform was not very different from that of the PNM, and the short-lived coalition between Negroes and Indians dissolved before the elections of 1971.

The Electoral Process

The PNM and its leadership have been criticized by the traditional DLP sources, from within its own ranks and, in the period beginning in 1970, from new groups in the political arena who have not found the PNM solutions to the country's needs to be sufficiently far reaching. By the 1961 elections the PNM and the DLP were in conflict. The issues that precipitated the confrontation were PNM advocacy of a system of permanent registration of voters through the use of identification cards and the use of voting machines.

The DLP objected to the registration system and suggested that such a mechanism could be exploited by the government because of the personal data compiled in the process. It was also the feeling of the DLP that the government was exploiting the racial situation. Concerning the use of voting machines, the opposition felt that the machines could be adjusted to the advantage of the PNM and that this mechanism would intimidate unsophisticated voters, keeping them away from the polls.

In this way the issues of the conduct of elections and electoral reform were introduced into the political process. These have been live issues in recent political agitation among opposition groups. Their alternatives to the present system consist of replacing voting machines with ballot boxes, lowering the voting age to eighteen, properly delineating constituencies, and (or) replacing the "first-past-the-post" system with some form of proportional representation. Under the existing electoral system, the country is divided into constituencies each of which has a single representative in Parliament. Several candidates may be nominated for

194

each vacant seat, but the candidate with the most votes is the winner. In this system, if there are more than two candidates, the winner may poll fewer votes than the other candidates combined.

Under the present Constitution an elections commission, comprising a chairman and from two to four other members, is responsible for the conduct of elections. The members of this commission are also members of the Boundaries Commission, which has as its responsibility the demarcation and creation of new constituencies. This dual membership role has prompted opposition groups to say that there may be a conflict of interest and to ask for separation of functions.

New Groups, Issues, and Reform of the Political Process

In the 1971 elections the PNM won all thirty-six seats in Parliament. A few weeks before election day the liaison between the DLP and the ACDC was dissolved. Both the PNM and the ACDC presented their platforms to the public in the preceding months of campaigning. Their respective statements, *Perspectives for a New Society* and *Road to Freedom*, reflected the popular pressures for change and reform of the political process.

The PNM in *Perspectives for a New Society* listed the following areas of needed reform: mitigation of racial politics; land reform; a more effective party system; greater economic power for disfranchised groups; increased popular participation in decisions affecting the community; further reconstruction of the educational system emphasizing vocational and technical education; and, finally, far-reaching social change by rational means.

The ACDC–DLP position as expressed in *Road to Freedom* was not very different. This program urged educational reform, opening up the political system, and making the foreign economic sector more responsive to domestic needs. The ACDC later became the Democratic Action Congress, a very active opposition force.

According to the Trinidadian sociologist Selwyn D. Ryan, most people did not believe that it would have made much difference whether the PNM or the ACDC won the elections. Conditions had deteriorated, and there were several groups in the society demanding more thoroughgoing solutions. The most dramatic manifestation of these sentiments had been seen in the previous year, 1970, when the so-called black power movement emerged.

The movement itself in broadest terms was about black dignity, a manifestation of black consciousness, and the demand for black economic power. The movement received publicity on the occasion of the Canadian governor general's visit to Trinidad, when students protested the treatment of Trinidadian students at Sir George Williams University in Canada. The focus of protest was widened to include an examination of such Canadian involvement in Caribbean economies as ownership of banks, insurance companies, and industrial firms. A street march in

February 1970, which began as a demonstration against "Canadian racism and economic exploitation," gradually grew to incorporate a protest against the broader social and economic ills of Trinidadian society, affecting East Indians as well as Negroes.

As a result of the February Revolution, there was a confrontation between the "pragmatism" of the PNM and the radicalism of an assortment of ideological groups. Three groups could be clearly distinguished within this movement: the United National Independence Party (UNIP) founded by James Millette, the National Joint Action Committee (NJAC) lead by Geddes Granger, and the Tapia House Group spearheaded by Lloyd Best. The Tapia House Group is the only one of the groups that continues to have significance in the mid-1970s.

These groups advocated different degrees of and strategies for change. The issues were national control of Trinidad's resources and the redrawing of electoral boundaries that separated the Afro-Trinidadian and East Indian populations.

The United National Independence Party

The United National Independence Party (UNIP), organized by Millette, a lecturer at the University of the West Indies, called for a "deliberate insulation of Trinidad's environment from metropolitan influences . . . which had exacerbated economic and social problems"; bringing the sugar industry under local control and management; and control and ownership of the petroleum industry. Millette stressed the need for academicians to become involved in politics and, by so doing, take political responsibility for their ideas.

The executive council of the UNIP included Negro and East Indian Trinidadians. The party had no great electoral potential and later joined forces with another association, the United Revolutionary Organization (URO).

The National Joint Action Committee

The National Joint Action Committee (NJAC), organized in 1967, consisted of student and youth groups, trade unions, and cultural and sporting organizations. Among their concerns were the revitalization of public opinion in politics and the diminishing of foreign, particularly Canadian, influence in the economy. Granger's eloquence drew a cross section of Trinidadians to hear him, including slum dwellers and unemployed youth. Mass arrests followed the demonstrations led by Granger and the NJAC. The party did not contest the elections of 1971.

The Tapia House Group

The Tapia House Group, founded in 1969 by Best, called for fundamental political reorganization carried out through constitutional reform. As adumbrated in *Constitutional Reform, Tapia's Proposals, June 1971*, the group called for the establishment of a republic; an islandwide system of local councils with authority for governing; a powerful local authority in Tobago; an increase in the size of the Senate and a new basis for selecting its members; a larger national congress with greater influence on appointments and legislation; establishment of a West Indian court and abandonment of appeals to the Privy Council in England; relocation of the capital outside Port-of-Spain; and the establishment of national service to enhance community spirit.

Tapia supported the black power manifestation of February 1970. It also dismissed the programs of the PNM and the ACDC–DLP as ineffectual and accused the prime minister of operating in the manner of a "Caribbean caudillo." The group did not organize itself into a party, however, to contest elections until 1975. Three members of Tapia became appointed members of the Senate in 1975, where they invigorated policy debate for the first time in Parliament since the 1971 election.

Pressures for Reforms

All three groups—NJAC, UNIP, and Tapia—joined forces with the ACDC, the Transport and Industrial Workers Union, the National Freedom Organization, and other small groups to form the URO. This group wanted electoral reform before the upcoming elections in 1971. They advocated a lowering of the voting age to eighteen, a referendum on the use of voting machines, registration of all eligible voters, and the establishment of an independent election and boundaries commission.

In addition to specific proposals for electoral and constitutional reform, these new groups felt that Trinidad and Tobago was becoming a police state. As evidence of this trend they pointed to the passage of the Industrial Stabilization Act of 1965, which limits the freedom to strike; the house arrest of C. L. R. James in 1965; the appointment of a commission of enquiry to investigate subversive activities; and the declared state of emergency in 1970.

The PNM has countered that these groups have not been able to propose any viable alternative to the dominant party's program. Coalitions among them have tended to be short-lived and, although they have decried the overemphasis on charismatic leadership in the Trinidadian political system, they have not been able to provide a cohesive program with appeal to a broad political base.

Pressure from the political left and from within the PNM had resulted in a move toward constitutional reform. After the general elections in May 1971, the government appointed a commission, under the Commissions of Enquiry Ordinance, with terms of reference "to make recommendations for the revision . . . of the constitution."

According to the report of the constitution commission, the Wooding Commission, reform had become necessary because of challenges to constitutional parliamentary politics and the belief that the institutionalized channels of constitutional politics no longer responded unless confronted extralegally, that the political system could not survive in the midst of unrestrained violence, and that constitutionalism would not work in Trinidad and Tobago unless a fundamental reorientation of the economic priorities of the country were undertaken.

The Wooding Commission also underscored the race factor as a significant determinant of political behavior and the decline of Parliament as a vigorous institution. Concerning race, the commission noted that voting patterns tended to follow racial lines, Trinidadians of African origins supporting the PNM and those of Indian descent supporting the DLP.

Various reasons were given for the decline of Parliament. Foremost has been the lack of a viable opposition in the house. The introduction of voting machines and the delimitation of constituency boundaries brought protests from the opposition, expressed by an initial refusal to participate in the proceedings of Parliament. The opposition also lacked leadership.

The Wooding Commission presented its recommendations, including a revised constitution, to the Parliament. Another set of recommendations was prepared by the cabinet. Both documents have been the subject of protracted discussion. A new constitution is expected to emerge from the various proposals presented to the house.

Beyond the issues of revitalizing Parliament, revising the Constitution, decreasing government control of the media, and domesticating the foreign economic sector, there remains the issue of a future leader for the PNM. Since the party's founding in the 1950s Williams has been its leader; he has also been the country's only prime minister since independence. In 1971 he intimated that he might retire. There was speculation concerning a successor because A. N. R. Robinson, before his withdrawal from the PNM, had been seen as the next in line. In 1973, however, Williams actually announced his retirement as political leader of the PNM. At that time he probably would have been succeeded by the attorney general, Karl Hudson-Phillips. Williams, however, was called back from retirement to resume his duties. Three deputies to Williams as political leader of the PNM have been appointed: Kamaluddin Mohammed, legislative affairs; Errol Mahabir, party affairs; and George Chambers, policy.

The multiparty phenomenon characterized politics in the 1950s. A party with grass-roots support and strong leadership brought cohesiveness to the party system. In the 1970s there was some evidence that the multiparty trend could return, and there was much conjecture as to what kind of leadership and political organization could lend coherence to systemic reform and incorporate the demands of the new generation.

FOREIGN RELATIONS

Under British rule responsibility for the conduct of external affairs lay with the Colonial Office. With the attainment of independence Trinidad and Tobago sought to maximize its role in the international arena despite its small size and limited resources.

Before independence the country's external relations consisted largely of bilateral relations with various metropolitan powers, chiefly the United Kingdom. These relations represented varieties of economic arrangements that could not be relied upon indefinitely and did not prove adequate for the needs of an independent Trinidad and Tobago. Consequently Trinidad, like other Caribbean states, sought to diversify its patterns of international contacts to compensate for the changed status of its relationship to the United Kingdom and other metropolitan powers.

In the year of its independence Trinidad and Tobago was admitted to the United Nations and became a member of the Commonwealth of Nations. Five years later, in 1967, it was the first Commonwealth Caribbean (see Glossary) country to seek membership in the Organization of American States (OAS) and the Inter-American Development Bank (IDB). Trinidad and Tobago was a founding member of the Caribbean Free Trade Association (CARIFTA) and also participates in its successor organization, the Caribbean Community (CARICOM), established in 1973.

Foreign Policy Objectives

In its broadest terms the foreign policy of Trinidad and Tobago is concerned with the search for ways and means of strengthening and maintaining the social, economic, cultural, and political interests of Trinidad and Tobago at the international level. These general goals find more concrete expression through the objectives and policies of expanding and diversifying trade and obtaining assistance, ensuring security, and opposing racism and colonialism throughout the world.

Trinidad and Tobago's objectives include safeguarding its access to markets for the traditional agricultural crops—sugar, cacao, coffee, and bananas—and obtaining access for new manufacturing industries. With the expansion of the postindependence economic structure, the government has secured financial, technological, educational, and managerial assistance from public and private sector sources of other countries for the diversification of agriculture, the expansion of the petroleum industry, and the furtherance of industrial production.

After oil and sugar, tourism is Trinidad and Tobago's third largest industry. The government has therefore made the improvement of this sector a priority and promotes its interests abroad.

Trinidad and Tobago, therefore, has adopted a dual strategy of preserving existing economic advantages and diversifying foreign economic relations. In the interests of diversification, Trinidad and Tobago has endeavored to expand its North American trade; has supported the efforts of other developing countries in the United Nations Conference on Trade and Development (UNCTAD) and signed the Lomé Convention guaranteeing to a group of African, Caribbean, and Pacific nations access for agricultural commodities to the European market; has actively supported regional integration efforts among Commonwealth Caribbean countries; has made commitments to participate in the establishment of a Latin American common market; and has joined the OAS, gaining access to additional resources for development.

Like other small countries in world affairs, Trinidad and Tobago recognizes strategic vulnerabilities. Trinidad and Tobago, as a signatory of the Inter-American Treaty of Reciprocal Assistance, known as the Rio Treaty, is a member of the Western Hemisphere security system. The country has firm ties with the United States and its allies and limited relations with communist countries. This Western posture in matters of external security, however, has not precluded its seeking advantageous relations with Cuba and more recently with the People's Republic of China (PRC) and the Soviet Union. More important, pro-Western commitment has not resulted in submissive attitudes to the United States or the United Kingdom in the United Nations where Trinidad and Tobago is heavily aligned with the third world nations.

The country's opposition to racism and colonialism derives from its colonial experience and its legacy. This position finds expression in its support for the United Nations, where Trinidad and Tobago identifies strongly with Afro-Asian nations, although belonging to the Latin American group.

Overseas Representation

In the mid-1970s Trinidad and Tobago maintained diplomatic relations with more than sixty countries. Three kinds of missions represent Trinidad and Tobago interests overseas: bilateral diplomatic missions, missions to international organizations, and consular missions.

Bilateral diplomatic missions are located in political capitals and are designated either embassies or high commissions, which are of equal diplomatic rank. The difference is merely one of terminology, since high commissions are traditionally established in Commonwealth countries and embassies in others.

Permanent missions have been accredited to the United Nations in New York, to its branches in Europe, and to the OAS, headquartered in Washington. Consular missions deal with trade and commercial matters and the welfare of nationals. There are offices in Canada and within the United States.

Domestically matters related to the conduct of external affairs are handled by the Ministry of External Affairs. The prime minister takes a special interest in the operations of this ministry and has frequently held the portfolio of the minister of external affairs.

In keeping with its desire to play a significant role in world affairs, Trinidad and Tobago has diversified its foreign contacts. It has placed highest priority on its relations with Caribbean states; has moved toward closer association with Latin America through membership in the OAS and its related agencies; has made contacts with Afro-Asian states; has made overtures to communist countries; and has maintained good

200

relations with the United Kingdom, Europe, Canada, and the United States.

Relations with Caribbean States

A principal tenet of the foreign policy of Trinidad and Tobago has been the integration of West Indian societies. Since the demise of the Federation of the West Indies, of which Trinidad and Tobago was a charter member, the country has continued its quest for Caribbean unity. In the early years efforts consisted of an offer of unitary statehood with Trinidad and Tobago to all the islands of the eastern Caribbean. Grenada pursued this possibility, but the plan was stillborn for lack of British financial support. A second effort was a call for the establishment of a Caribbean economic community that would embrace the entire English-speaking Caribbean, the states of the Guiana region, the Netherlands Antilles, Martinique, Guadeloupe, Haiti, the Dominican Republic, Puerto Rico, and Cuba. By 1971 all the countries of the former Federation of the West Indies as well as Guyana and British Honduras were participating in CARIFTA. CARICOM emerged in 1973 to replace CARIFTA. The third effort was a summit conference; at the invitation and initiative of Prime Minister Williams, the Commonwealth Caribbean Heads of Government Conference—the first of an ongoing series—was organized in 1963. Such matters as relations between Trinidad and Tobago and Venezuela, cooperation in tourist promotion, support of the University of the West Indies, policy toward Cuba, joint statements concerning the inter-American system, and basic decisions concerning regional cooperation have been agenda items.

Beginning in 1968 Trinidad and Tobago participated in a variety of functional cooperative arrangements, such as the Council of Legal Education and a Caribbean ministers of health conference, as well as the better known efforts in the areas of trade and integration. With both English-speaking and non-English-speaking Caribbean countries, Trinidad and Tobago has sought cooperation concerning the law of the sea and the regime of the ocean bed. During his visit to Cuba in June 1975 Prime Minister Williams received tentative support from Premier Fidel Castro for the establishment of a special regime of the sea for the Caribbean. The Williams proposal calls for a modification of the 200-mile exclusive zone in the region to bring about a mutual sharing among Caribbean states of the resources of the otherwise nationally fragmented 200-mile economic resource zone. Based on a sharing of rights under negotiation as part of the proposed international law of the sea, Williams' proposal would not affect rights of international navigation.

Relations with Latin American States

By becoming the first Commonwealth Caribbean state to seek membership in the OAS, Trinidad and Tobago terminated years of isolation from neighboring states imposed by colonial rule. By the Act of Washington (1964), rules were agreed upon for admission of new members to the OAS. Venezuela, Argentina, and Guatemala initially opposed the entrance of Trinidad and Tobago because of their long-standing claims and boundary disputes with the United Kingdom concerning Guyana, the Falkland Islands, and British Honduras respectively.

OAS membership was advantageous to Trinidad and Tobago primarily for economic reasons. Without membership in the organization, countries could not be members of IDB, whose generous terms of lending attracted all countries in the hemisphere. Since its entrance it has campaigned successfully with other Commonwealth Caribbean members of the IDB to change rules of membership, allowing independent (non-OAS member) countries to accede to bank membership. A further proposal spearheaded by Trinidad and Tobago has been for the creation of a separate Caribbean group with its own executive director within IDB. Trinidad and Tobago has also indicated interest in participating in Latin American integration schemes.

Concerning relations with individual countries, Trinidad's most intense contact has been with its neighbor Venezuela. One of the aims of the PNM in 1956 was the liquidation of a number of disputes between the United Kingdom and Venezuela, which in turn involved Trinidad and Tobago. The disputes were related to the delimitation of territorial waters, illegal immigration, contraband, fishing, and discriminatory trade practices. Most of these differences were resolved satisfactorily shortly after independence. Disputes over fishing rights in the Gulf of Paria and along the Venezuelan coast, however, are continuing problems between the two governments. In 1965 the 30-percent surtax imposed by Venezuela on British-manufactured goods transshipped from Trinidad and Tobago to Venezuela was abolished. A mixed commission was established in 1967 between Trinidad and Tobago and Venezuela to explore Trinidad's participation in trade expansion, education, technical cooperation, migration, and harmonization for policies regarding mineral and petroleum resources.

In early 1975 Prime Minister Williams expressed concern over Venezuela's territorial claims to several offshore islands in the Caribbean and, more important, over the effect on the fragile economic integration and policy coordination efforts of CARICOM of Venezuela's projection of its wealth and influence into the Caribbean matrix. In the light of the alleged ambitions of Venezuela in the Caribbean, Williams had campaigned for the support of the superpowers and of the nonaligned nations for a special regime for the Caribbean Sea.

In 1970 at a special meeting of the Economic and Social Council of the OAS, held in Caracas, the prime minister called for the readmission of Cuba to the inter-American community. After the Caracas meeting Trinidad and Tobago exchanged technical missions with Cuba and in various OAS forums asserted its position on the Cuban question. In the meetings of July 1975 in Costa Rica, Trinidad and Tobago voted with fourteen other OAS members to remove the sanctions that had been imposed on Cuba by that organization in 1964.

Trinidad and Tobago has also shown great interest in Brazil. Increased economic and cultural exchanges between the two countries have been promised. A fisheries agreement reflects the significant dependence on Trinidadian fisherman and shrimpers on the fish stocks off the northeast coast of Brazil.

Relations with Afro-Asian States

Shortly after independence Trinidad and Tobago established diplomatic ties with a few African countries and with India. Trinidad's ties with Africa are mainly cultural and spiritual, although with Nigeria it shares an interest in petroleum technology. With other Commonwealth Caribbean governments Trinidad and Tobago strongly condemns apartheid in South Africa and supports the aspirations of the people of Zimbabwe and the rapid achievement of independence in Namibia. The country has two missions in Africa—one in Addis Ababa with its high commissioner accredited to Kenya, Tanzania, and Zambia, and the other in Nigeria with its commissioner also accredited to Algeria. The prime minister and Trinidadians generally have called for closer cultural and educational ties with Africa. Williams and other top-ranking officials have also visited African countries.

The prime minister has made official visits to India, the homeland of many Trinidadians, and to Japan. Trinidad has received aid and some technical assistance from India. The high commissioner to India is also accredited to Singapore and serves as ambassador to Japan and Sri Lanka.

Relations with Communist States

At the time of independence Trinidad and Tobago invited representatives of the Soviet Union and Yugoslavia to attend independence ceremonies. Diplomatic relations were established with Cuba (1962), Romania (1972), the PRC (1974), the Soviet Union (1974), and Hungary (1975).

The Soviet Union in October 1962 offered economic assistance to Trinidad and Tobago. In 1965 the prime minister accepted an invitation from Moscow to visit the Soviet Union at a future date; he made an official visit from June 30 to July 7, 1975. Views were exchanged on a variety of world issues and on prospects for the development of cooperation in the fields of education, science and technology, maritime shipping, fishing, and air communications. The working out of agreements on these matters was planned for August 1975 in Port-of-Spain. At the same time negotiations on developing trade between Trinidad and Tobago and the Soviet Union would be conducted.

In July 1975 Prime Minister Williams also visited Romania, where prospects for economic cooperation in ore, petrochemicals, engineering, building materials, and agriculture were discussed. Romania has a well-established domestic oil-drilling and refining industry, which has been of interest to Trinidad and Tobago in the expansion of its petroleum industry.

In both 1974 and 1975 Prime Minister Williams paid official visits to the PRC. As a result of the representations made by the 1975 Trinidad and Tobago Economic Mission to the Far East, the PRC began trade relations with Trinidad. The commodities initially exported were cocoa, coffee, and asphalt, on an experimental basis. The PRC has established a small embassy and a nonresident ambassador in Port-of-Spain. The government of Trinidad and Tobago has in turn announced that it will establish a similar mission in Peking.

Relations with the United Kingdom, Canada, and the United States

Since independence Trinidad and Tobago has pursued a policy of maintaining relations with her preindependence metropolitan trading partners while diversifying her foreign economic and political relations.

The United Kingdom, Canada, and the United States accounted for most of Trinidad and Tobago's external trade. It was therefore important that relations be maintained. At independence Trinidad was no longer eligible to receive funds from the Colonial Development and Welfare Fund. In its place Britain offered a small aid package with rather limited terms. Trinidad refused the aid package and was for a while the only former British colony not receiving aid from Great Britain. The United States has provided some aid and technical assistance, and Canada has been somewhat more generous.

After independence Trinidad sought to maintain the system of preferential agreements on agricultural products in British and Canadian markets but was keenly aware of the indefinite future of these arrangements. Consequently Trinidad looked toward its own economic diversification and a search for new trading partners.

In 1962, however, Trinidad explored associated status with the European Economic Community (EEC). In the event Great Britain entered the EEC, it was believed Trinidad would have a continued market for agricultural commodities. By 1967 the idea of associated status was dropped in favor of diversifying foreign relations in other directions. Commonwealth preferences are being phased out and are being replaced with the generalized preferences offered under the Lomé Convention (1975) and the United States Trade Act.

In the 1960s Trinidad made great efforts to expand trade with the United States and Canada through legislation and promotional efforts to increase private investment from these sources. By the mid-1970s this trend had ceased, and efforts were being directed at diversifying sources of outside investment and an assertion of greater national control over foreign business enterprises in Trinidad. Trinidad and Tobago shared the concern of other Commonwealth Caribbean countries about the limits placed on immigration to the United Kingdom, Canada, and the United States. In the 1960s Trinidad explored such opportunities in Africa. Kenya and Tanzania expressed a willingness to receive Trinidadian immigrants.

Trinidad and Tobago has not had many disagreements in its postindependence period with the United Kingdom, the United States, or Canada. The most serious confrontation concerned the return of the Chaguaramas naval base, which was a part of the Anglo-American wartime lend-lease arrangements. Trinidad and Tobago insisted that the United States renegotiate the agreements. This claim was an assertion of Trinidad's territorial sovereignty. Years of debate, protest, and negotiation finally led to the beginning of a three-stage negotiation between the United States, United Kingdom, and Trinidad. The Tobago negotiating conference resulted in recognition by the United States of Trinidad's right to negotiate the issue. The settlement included American aid for Trinidad and also rights to Chaguaramas until 1977. In 1967, however, the base was abandoned. It was Trinidad's first diplomatic victory.

CHAPTER 8

ECONOMY

Petroleum production and refining lead the growth of the economy and account for the major share of exports and government revenues. The gross domestic product (GDP) growth rate fluctuates in accordance with the growth rate of the petroleum industry. The 1955–62 period experienced a high level of economic growth because of a petroleum boom, but the growth rate slowed during the rest of the 1960s as petroleum expansion ceased. In the early 1970s, however, new petroleum and natural gas discoveries and higher international prices brought a rapid increase in exports and revenues. The increased revenues earned by the government caused some international lending agencies to cease ranking Trinidad and Tobago as either an underdeveloped or a developing country.

Although oil revenues have made the country financially secure, twin problems of high inflation and unemployment still remained in 1975. The government hoped to use some of the increased revenues to create new jobs and to subsidize some consumer products in order to lower the unemployment rate, estimated at 14 percent in 1974, and to combat inflation. Until 1972 Trinidad and Tobago had the reputation of being a country with fairly stable prices. Inflation had exerted only moderate pressures, and the consumer price index had average annual increases of only 2.2 percent during the 1961–65 period, 3.9 percent from 1966 to 1970, and 3.5 percent in 1971. Prices rose by 9.3 percent in 1972, however, and soared by 23 percent in 1973 and by 25 percent in 1974. Much of the inflation was imported—caused by increased prices of imported foods, consumer durables, and component parts for assembly plants. During 1973 imported goods contributed 75 percent to the annual price increase. The government has been tightening consumer credit and the supply of money and granting subsidies to producers of certain foods and items, and it has imposed price controls on many other products and on services as part of its campaign to fight inflation.

The country has a strong tradition of trade unionism, and more and more labor contracts are being tied to the consumer price index, thereby defeating the government's inflationary fight. Any union representing at least 51 percent of the work force must be recognized by an employer as the bargaining agent for all employees. Most collective bargaining agreements are on a company rather than an industry-wide basis. About 60 percent of all employees in the country, including agricultural workers, are covered by collective bargaining agreements. Where trade union representation is absent, terms of employment are worked out by wage councils established by the government for specific trades and industries.

In 1973 there were over 150 registered trade unions, including fifteen employer associations, which are given trade union status, and about twenty-five miscellaneous organizations that had decided to register as trade unions. The total number of workers belonging to trade unions was about 95,000, but ten unions accounted for three-fourths of the total membership. About fifty unions have formed the Trinidad and Tobago Labor Congress, recognized by the government as the sole spokesman for organized labor. Some major unions have not joined the labor congress, and a few of the more militant, politically oriented unions have formed the Council of Progressive Trade Unions.

Until 1965 there were many work stoppages, often over recognition rights (a strike between rival unions over bargaining rights in the sugar industry hurt that industry in 1974 and 1975). The Industrial Stabilization Act of 1965 provided for compulsory recognition by management and for the settlement of disputes by means of the Industrial Court, which also hears complaints about excessive prices. On July 30, 1972, the new Industrial Relations Act replaced the 1965 law; it permitted strikes under certain conditions except for strikes that might harm essential services. The new law also brought previous labor legislation up to date and incorporated some new principles, such as the right of recognized unions to receive dues from all employees whether or not the employees are members of the union. In order to hold a legal strike, unions must obtain a certificate from the Ministry of Labor, Social Security, and Cooperatives, that an unresolved dispute exists. If a strike is deemed illegal, the union may lose its bargaining rights. Government employees are represented by one of several associations that have been accorded union status for bargaining purposes. The Civil Service Special Tribunal of the Industrial Court handles disputes concerning public service employees. Decisions of the tribunal are binding upon the civil servants for a period of five years. Civil servants may not strike; if they do, they are subject to fines and imprisonment.

NATIONAL ACCOUNTS

No official national account data had been published since 1968, and all data available in 1975 were based upon estimates or approximations made by the government or by international agencies. Only the Central Bank, the Price Commission, and the Central Statistical Office (CSO) compiled reliable data. Other agencies collected and published data that were subject to error because of inexperienced staff and therefore were not reliable. According to the best estimates, the gross national product (GNP) grew by about 5.5 percent in 1971, by 3 percent in 1972, by 3.5 percent in 1973, and by an estimated 5 percent in 1974. The growth rate for 1975 was forecast at between 5 and 6 percent. Growth rates in earlier years had been much higher, and the average annual rate for the 1954–72 period was 5.4 percent.

The current price GNP was estimated at the equivalent of US$1,180 million in 1973 and per capita income at US$1,110. The per capita income was the fourth highest in the Western Hemisphere, and the country ranked thirty-fifth in the world, a fairly high ranking for a small population. There are extremes in the distribution of income: large numbers of persons were unemployed and had no income while workers in the petroleum sector had per capita income of US$5,000 in the early 1970s. In the same period workers outside the petroleum sector earned about US$750 annually and agricultural employees about US$325. A mid-1960s study of income based upon 1,000 households indicated that the upper 20 percent received about 50 percent of all income of the survey group, whereas the bottom 20 percent received under 4 percent of the total income. Despite the uneven distribution of income, the vast extremes of high and low income characteristic of other developing countries are not present in Trinidad and Tobago, and the distribution pattern resembles that in industrialized nations, including the United States. The majority of workers earned the equivalent of between US$50 and US$250 per month; 21 percent earned less than US$50, and another 21 percent earned more than US$250.

A 1974 tax amendment provided for additional income to wage earners in the form of profit sharing to begin that year. Employees can opt either to receive an annual cash bonus or to have all or part of the bonus placed into a fund that would be used to purchase shares of the firm's stock. Shares left in the fund until retirement are transferred to the worker tax free. If they are transferred before retirement, the worker pays an income tax ranging from 5 to 20 percent, depending upon the market value of the stock.

The distribution of GDP indicates that trade and petroleum have alternated as the leading sector (see table 7). The relative share of all other major sectors except agriculture has also fluctuated; a revision of the official 1968 national accounts based on newer data indicated that the contributions of agriculture and manufacturing had been set too high and trade and transportation had been underestimated.

ROLE OF GOVERNMENT

Trinidad and Tobago has gone further in the control of the economy than any other Caribbean country except Cuba. At the time of independence the government believed that unemployment, the major problem then facing the country, could not be substantially reduced unless decisionmaking was in government hands. Further, many decisions affecting the economy, particularly in the petroleum and sugar sectors, were made outside the country. Thus since independence the government has been seeking a greater role in the economy, and government participation in the development of new industries is becoming common policy. In 1975 the government directly owned all or part of thirty-two companies.

The government became the major investor in the sugar industry in 1970. It owned one of seven petroleum-producing companies outright and had equity positions in two others. In 1974 it took over the retailing operations conducted by gasoline stations throughout the country by purchasing all of them and turning them over to the National Petroleum Marketing Company. The government owns the only flour mill and has investments in hotels, meatpacking, and several other industries. It owns a few of the banks and most of the utilities and telecommunications systems. Some companies are acquired in order to prevent backruptcy of a labor-intensive industry, and from time to time the government resells the stock. All acquisitions of companies, foreign and domestic, have been by purchase at mutually agreed upon prices; there have been no instances of expropriation.

Economic planning is carried out by the Ministry of Planning and Development, created in 1968 to replace the former Planning Office. The ministry sets overall developmental policy and general goals. It draws up annual, medium-term, long-term, and regional plans. Detailed studies and the evaluation of projects are hampered, however, by the lack of qualified staff. Four major development plans have been drafted, and three have been implemented. The First Five-Year Plan (1958–62) concentrated on improving infrastructure to support industrialization of the country. Priority was placed on improving harbors, roads, water supplies, and electricity, although land reclamation, housing, and education were also stressed. The year 1963 was used to plan for the Second Five-Year Plan (1964–68) and to complete projects undertaken under the first plan. The second plan emphasized agricultural diversification, industrialization, telecommunications, and tourism. The Third Five-Year Plan (1969–73) placed emphasis on diversification in the belief that the petroleum industry was entering a period of decline and could not be relied on as the prime stimulant. New oil discoveries were not foreseen at that time.

The Fourth Five-Year Plan (1974–78), although drafted, was not adopted when it became apparent in 1973 that the flow of revenue from petroleum would be increasing rapidly. The targets of the fourth plan had been predicated upon smaller revenues. Instead the government decided to maximize the revenue from petroleum to develop new industries, particularly those that are energy related. The Petroleum Development Fund, which was forecast to earn about TT$7 billion between 1974 and 1978, was created in 1974, and the total cost of the new projects under discussion was estimated at TT$6 billion (for value of the Trinidad and Tobago dollar—see Glossary).

A number of long-range regional plans were used as guidelines within each five-year development plan. The Tobago Regional Development

Table 7. *Trinidad and Tobago, Distribution of Gross Domestic Product,*
1960 and 1970–72
(in percent)

Sector	1960	1970	1971	1972
Trade	19.6	15.0	14.9	15.6
Petroleum, refining, mining....................	18.4	17.7	15.3	14.5
Government	...[1]	11.2	14.0	14.0
Transportation and communication	4.6	15.5	14.2	13.6
Manufacturing	15.5	11.7	11.6	12.3
Construction	14.2	5.6	7.7	7.3
Other services	13.0	4.7	6.3	6.7
Finance	...[2]	5.4	5.7	5.9
Agriculture, forestry, fishing[3].................	14.7	7.2	4.6	4.6
Rental.......................................	...[1]	3.7	3.6	3.5
Utilities	...[4]	2.3	2.1	2.0
TOTAL	100.0	100.0	100.0	100.0

[1] Included in other services.
[2] Included in trade.
[3] Sugarcane production accounted for nearly 2 percent annually from 1970 to 1972.
[4] Included in construction.

Plan, prepared originally in 1965, is continually modified and is used as a prototype for other areas. These include the Port-of-Spain Capital Regional Plan, designed to redevelop the central business district and the port area; the Northwest Peninsula Plan (also called the Chaguaramas Action Plan) to develop tourism, agriculture, and government housing; the West Coast Region Plan to diversify the central sugar area by encouraging new industry at the Point Lisas port and industrial park; and the South-Western Region Plan for the development and diversification of the oil field area. Some special agencies have been created to implement the regional plans, such as the Point Lisas Industrial Development Corporation and the Chaguaramas Development Authority.

The Industrial Development Corporation (IDC) began operations in 1959 as a centralized agency to carry out functions pertaining to development previously performed by other agencies. The IDC was also given land to develop into industrial parks, including water, power, and sewerage facilities. Firms producing products not previously made in the country can be awarded pioneer status, under which a number of fiscal benefits are available. Through 1972 over 860 different activities had been granted some form of fiscal incentive, although more than 200 were not taken up by the producer, were not yet in production, or had been revoked. In 1973 the government adopted the common fiscal incentives approved by the Caribbean Free Trade Association (CARIFTA) (see Regional Economic Cooperation, this ch.). The formula used to determine the kind and length of fiscal benefits to be granted was made more

211

complicated, and by 1975 it was not certain what effect the changes might have had on potential industries seeking fiscal incentives.

PUBLIC FINANCE

Budget

The fiscal year (FY) is the calendar year, January 1 to December 31. The budget is listed by ministries and other government agencies, and within each ministry and agency the breakdown is detailed by subunits. There are separate line items for salaries, other charges (mainly travel and housekeeping supplies), extraordinary expenses (equipment), subventions (transfers and subsidies), and development (capital expenses). A functional breakdown of the budget is available only for current expenses and in a summary form without any detail. Expenditures pertaining solely to Tobago are listed separately by some ministries; otherwise most expenditures for Tobago fall under the Ministry of Tobago Affairs.

Budgets are often increased beyond the approved figures by means of supplemental appropriations. Generally the current account is in surplus, but the capital account is not, and overall deficits frequently occur. The deficits are easily financed, mainly by domestic borrowing plus some foreign financing. Budgets have risen fairly rapidly. The actual budgetary expenditures for 1969 were TT$325 million. In 1970 the budget was originally approved for TT$375 million but was later revised to TT$409 million. By 1974 the final approved budget was TT$974 million (the original 1974 budget had been set at only TT$633, but larger oil revenues permitted an increase), and the projected budget for 1975 was TT$1.3 billion. In the budgets of the early 1970s about 34 percent went for the category of other charges, 30 percent for salaries, 24 percent for capital expenses, 9 percent for subventions, and 3 percent for extraordinary expenses. About 38 percent of current expenditures went for social services, education accounting for about 18 percent and health services for about 10 percent; 27 percent was for general services of the government, including defense and police; which accounted for nearly 10 percent; 11 percent was designated for all economic services; 6 percent for community services; and the balance for all other functions.

On the local level the municipalities have some limited revenue-raising powers, but the counties do not. Both receive annual transfers from the central government to carry out their operations. Most local expenditures are for public services, such as the maintenance of streets and bridges, sanitation, street lighting, parks, markets, and cemeteries. Some expenses are for public housing, salaries, and the interest on local public debt (all local administrations have borrowed funds from financial institutions). In addition to grants from the central government, municipalities receive some revenue from property taxes and the issuance of licenses and permits. Local budgets have fluctuated from surplus to deficit and back again with more years of surpluses than of deficits. Budgets are not large; for example, the budget in 1972 for Port-of-Spain was only TT$9.3 million; for the borough of San Fernando, TT$3.8 million; and for the small borough of Arima, only TT$781,000.

The composition of government revenue should be altered remarkably from 1975 on as a result of new petroleum taxes negotiated with the oil companies in 1974. Because of the increased revenue from petroleum, all other taxes were lowered in 1975. These other taxes include income, excise, customs, inheritance, property, motor vehicles, sales, entertainment, and miscellaneous licenses and taxes. Nontax revenue is also important; it includes royalties, interest on government accounts, post office receipts, earnings of government entities, pension contributions, repayment of loans made by government financial institutions, and miscellaneous fees. Capital receipts, another source of revenue, include loans, concession fees, lotteries, and grants.

Since January 1, 1974, oil companies have paid several kinds of taxes. A petroleum production levy is paid monthly to offset a subsidy enacted by the government to keep retail prices of gasoline, kerosene, and diesel fuel low. Royalties are also assessed but are based on market prices. The royalty rate was 12.5 percent for existing concessions and 15 percent for new concessions. Most importantly oil companies pay an income tax called the petroleum profit tax, based on net profits of production and marketing as determined from tax reference prices—rather than actual sales prices; the rate of 47.5 percent for 1974 and 50 percent thereafter. In lieu of income taxes the refineries pay a processing tax based on the number of barrels processed. The tax was initially set at the equivalent of US$0.10 per barrel for one refinery and US$0.15 for others.

Individuals and corporations are subject to an income tax, which before 1974 accounted for between 40 and 43 percent of total revenue. The upper tax rate for most corporations was 45 percent, and that for individuals was 50 percent. Because of numerous allowances and deductions for individuals, however, many persons do not have any tax obligations. The higher allowances granted in FY 1975, for example, were estimated to release about TT$50 million into the economy as persons earning under the equivalent of US$250 monthly would no longer pay income tax.

Customs duties are relatively low, but some rates are moderate to high. The highest rate in the customs schedule was 70 percent of value. Items originating in the Commonwealth of Nations are accorded preferential rates—generally 10 percentage points less than the general rate, but this was to be phased out on January 1, 1976. Export duties are levied on asphalt and sugar. Since January 1, 1975, the tax on sugar exports has been graduated and depends on sales price, and the funds are earmarked to provide subsidies to sugarcane farmers if future sales decline.

Excise taxes are levied on certain domestically produced items. The rates are specific and are paid by the manufacturer. Some of the items on which excise duties are levied are rum, beer, fuels and oils, matches, and copra. A sales tax, called the purchase tax, is imposed upon the first marketing stage of a selected group of imported and domestically produced items. The tax may be paid by wholesalers or by importers, the rates varying with the kind of merchandise. In FY 1975 the purchase tax on manufactured goods was either lowered or abolished. Before then it had provided as much as 8 percent of total revenue.

Other taxes include property taxes, which are levied against all real estate; stamp taxes (required on all receipts for money over TT$5), all real estate transactions, all checks, and on certain other business documents; alcoholic beverage taxes, of which there were more than three dozen categories; twenty-four different motor vehicle taxes; estate and inheritance taxes, levied on all estates over TT$20,000, the rates varying with the degree of relationship of the recipient; dozens of miscellaneous licenses; and an unemployment levy. The unemployment tax, paid by corporations and some individuals, was under judicial review in 1975 regarding its constitutionality. The rate was 5 percent of net profits of corporations and 5 percent of the taxable income in excess of TT$10,000 for individuals.

Public Debt

The country has a relatively low level of public debt, although the debt has been growing, and its international credit rating is considered very high. At the end of 1974 total domestic debt was TT$381 million and total foreign debt TT$239 million. Some of the debt was short-term high interest, but repayment entailed no difficulty. The largest share of the domestic debt—about one-third—was in treasury bills. They are usually of ninety-one days' duration, and most of them are purchased by the commercial banks. The balance of the domestic debt consists of miscellaneous long-term securities; at the end of 1974 there were fifty-nine different issuances, the oldest outstanding dating from 1959. Maturity dates ranged from five to thirty years, and interest paid was between 6.5 and 8.5 percent.

About two-thirds of the external debt was contracted directly by the central government and the balance by other government agencies with central government guarantees. Most of the foreign debt was medium term, maturities ranging between six and ten years. The largest percentage of the external debt—about 40 percent—was held by private financial institutions, reflecting the Central Bank's borrowing in Europe on what is called the Eurodollar market. About one-fourth of the foreign debt was accounted for by loans from the International Bank for Reconstruction and Development (IBRD, also known as the World Bank), 14 percent by bonds sold in the United Kingdom, 6 percent by loans from the Export-Import Bank of the United States, 5 percent by loans contracted in Canada, and the balance by miscellaneous bonds and loans from the Inter-American Development Bank (IDB).

214

	1969	1970	1971	1972	1973
Goods and Services:					
Merchandise	35.4	−77.0	−264.4	−323.8	−122.5
Freight	1.7	1.7	2.2	3.3	4.6
Transportation................	28.7	46.8	86.2	90.5	123.1
Travel	21.2	2.0	21.9	45.6	69.6
Investment income	−137.0	−122.0	−123.1	−132.8	−170.7
Other government services	11.4	12.7	12.0	15.3	0.5
Other services	−10.0	−19.0	−0.3	−1.0	61.3
Transfers:					
Private	4.2	4.2	4.5	4.3	−4.3
Government	−6.3	−8.8	−13.7	−11.7	−13.7
Total Current Account	−50.7	−159.4	−274.7	−310.3	−52.1
Capital Account:					
Direct investment	114.4	166.4	205.9	166.6	128.4
Other private	12.9	6.6	16.8	−1.7	−66.3
Government borrowing	12.1	−7.9	3.9	38.8	56.4
Subscriptions	−1.9	−2.6	−2.7	−2.7	−0.8
Other government assets	−5.5	3.0	27.9	−1.4	8.9
Special drawing rights	...	14.8	13.3	13.3	...
Total Capital Account	132.0	179.8	265.1	212.9	126.6
Errors and Omissions	−87.7	−36.1	52.5	51.8	−107.3
Overall Balance of Payments	−6.4	−15.7	42.9	−45.6	−32.8

... means none.

* For value of the Trinidad and Tobago dollar—see Glossary.

Source: Based on information from Trinidad and Tobago, Central Statistical Office, *The Balance of Payments of Trinidad and Tobago 1973*, Port-of-Spain, October 1974, pp. 1–12.

Balance of Payments

Balance-of-payments data before 1973 are not comparable to 1973 and afterward because of a change of methodology adopted in 1973 and the use of different sources for the raw statistics. Large amounts have had to be listed in the category of errors and omissions because of a lack of information regarding the proper account to classify certain transactions (see table 8). During the 1969–73 period there were overall deficits annually except for 1971, when a surplus occurred. Favorable balances were also forecast for 1974 and 1975. International reserves, which had been as low as US$35 million at the end of 1973, slowly recovered and stood at US$370 million by February 1975.

The merchandise account reflects the difference between exports and imports and is usually negative. Freight, which is generally positive, includes only receipts from airfreight carried by the national carrier,

British West Indies Airways (BWIA), whereas transportation, also positive, includes air fares, sea cargo receipts and expenditures, and sales of bunker fuel and supplies to visiting vessels. The travel account, also always positive, is mainly the earnings from tourism less the expenditures of residents traveling abroad. Investment income, another large deficit account, is the difference between the interest earned by residents, banks, and the government on overseas investments and the remittance abroad of dividends, interest, and profits earned by nonresidents in the country. The account entitled other government services constitutes receipts from international institutions and foreign diplomats operating in the country minus governmental payments to international institutions and the cost of operating Trinidadian diplomatic establishments overseas. Other services include such items as advertising, management fees, royalties, and insurance. The large credit in this category for 1973 reflects the income earned from the processing of crude oil in the domestic refineries for a fee. Transfers are mainly the remittance by individuals and private institutions to and from abroad plus governmental contributions abroad. In the capital account, government borrowing reflects loans received minus repayments for previous loans, subscriptions are quotas for international organizations, other government assets are changes in external investments, and special drawing rights are allocations by the International Monetary Fund to the country when international reserves started to fall.

Foreign Assistance

Foreign assistance has become a two-way street for Trinidad and Tobago. By the end of 1974 the country had received the equivalent of nearly US$200 million in loans and grants from international lending agencies and foreign governments. The largest source has been the IBRD, which had committed nearly US$100 million from 1962 to the end of 1974. The loans had been made for such purposes as electric power, telecommunications, agriculture, education, highways, and family planning. The country joined the IDB in 1967 and by the end of 1974 had received over US$25 million for sanitation, education, transportation, agriculture, housing, and technical cooperation.

Because of its increased revenues from petroleum, Trinidad and Tobago found itself in the position of assisting other countries, mainly those in the Caribbean Community (CARICOM). By mid–1975 it had supplied those countries with more than TT$104 million in various forms of assistance. The largest sum, TT$50 million, was lent to Jamaica to help its balance-of-payments difficulties. It also lent funds to Guyana for the same purpose, purchased government securities from Grenada, and established a trust fund in the Caribbean Development Bank for the exclusive use of the less developed members. In late 1974 the government purchased US$10 million worth of IDB bonds and lent the IBRD US$5 million for general operations.

Foreign investment is generally welcomed but under certain conditions. Government policy states that there will be little or no foreign investment in utilities. Joint state or private Trinidadian participation is required in gas and oil production, in new industries using gas and oil as raw materials, and in the exploration and exploitation of natural resources. Certain activities are restricted to domestic ownership; in 1975 these included wholesale and retail trade, mass media, land development, small tourist facilities, fishing, and furniture construction. Foreign firms are encouraged to reinvest a certain percentage of their profits in the country but only in such a manner as not to dominate the industry. In an effort to afford greater opportunity for domestic participation, the government has prohibited the ownership of new investment by foreigners except in special cases. If a foreign firm is accorded majority ownership, there must be a timetable leading to the divestiture of control through the selling of shares either to the public or to the government. An association with domestic firms is also welcomed and, as an inducement for such association, no public contracts are awarded to foreign firms unless they are so associated.

The actual number of foreign firms operating in the country may be smaller than had been believed. A 1973 survey conducted by the government indicated that there were fewer than 100 enterprises that could be defined as being under foreign investment: any company in which more than 25 percent of the stock was held by nonresidents. The survey noted, however, that there may have been "quite a significant coverage deficiency," since newly established firms were omitted and a number of others not included on the statistical register. A later survey, conducted in 1975 by the leading newspaper, indicated there were about 180 companies with some foreign ownership then operating in the country. The newspaper pointed out that those firms employed a total of about 25,000 Trinidadians and thus were very important to the economy. The government put the total book value of the foreign firms at the equivalent of only US$750 million in 1973, but later estimates placed the book value at about US$1 billion at the beginning of 1975. The largest share, about 71 percent, was invested in petroleum, 6 percent in food processing, 4 percent in miscellaneous assembly operations, 3 percent each in chemicals, marketing, and services, and the balance in all other sectors. About US$500 million was held by United States firms, mainly in petroleum and petrochemicals. Other major investors are from the United Kingdom and Canada, and Japanese investment was starting to grow.

FINANCIAL SYSTEM

In 1964 two important laws regarding the fiancial system were enacted: the Central Bank Act and the Commercial Banking Act. The Central Bank Act established the Central Bank of Trinidad and Tobago, granting it all customary powers and duties of a central bank. The bank is sole issuer of bank notes and coins, regulates credit and foreign exchange, and can buy and sell securities, discount commercial paper and notes for other banks, and underwrite government loans. It may lend up to 15 percent of estimated central government annual revenue to the government. If the advance is not repaid before the end of the fiscal year, it is deducted from the following year's advance. The Central Bank does not engage in commercial banking. Although it has extensive authority under the law, it uses its powers sparingly, except for the enforcement of credit regulations.

There are a number of specialized financial institutions owned by the government. The IDC, in addition to promoting new projects and administering the fiscal incentives available to new industry, also provides financing to small businesses through its Small Business Division (see Role of Government, this ch.). The Trinidad and Tobago Development Finance Company, established in 1970, helps create and expand productive enterprises including agriculture and tourism. It is the only financial institution offering long-term loans of over TT$50,000; it will also take an equity position by purchasing stock of the new company. During its first three years of operation over 11 percent of its disbursements were in the form of equity purchases.

The Agricultural Development Bank, which replaced the former Agricultural Credit Bank that had been in existence since 1917, lends funds to individual farmers, cooperatives, and credit societies. The government owns 94 percent of the bank's stock, and about 1,100 private farmers own the balance. It also may accept deposits from the public and may sell its own securities in order to raise operating capital. Most of its loans have gone to the livestock sector, and vegetable farmers, citrus growers, and food processers have received smaller amounts. The Trinidad and Tobago Mortgage Finance Company, partially owned by the government, helps to finance official housing programs. The Post Office Savings Bank, created in 1936, accepts deposits but makes no loans, and withdrawals require a three-day waiting period. For these reasons it was not a very popular financial institution. The Trinidad and Tobago Credit Union Bank restricts membership to credit unions, which make deposits and borrow for relending to individual members. There were about 300 credit unions in the country with a total membership over 27,000.

In 1975 there were eight commercial banks in the country with over eighty-five branches. Most of the commercial banks originally were foreign owned, but under an amendment to the banking act they have been encouraged to reincorporate as local companies, and some have started to sell shares to the public. One, the former Bank of London and Montreal, was sold to the government in 1970 and renamed the National Commercial Bank. Those that incorporate locally have also been re-named; for example, the Royal Bank of Canada became the Royal Bank of

218

Trinidad and Tobago in 1972. A commercial bank called the Workers Bank was created in 1971 under government stimulation. Most of its stock is held by trade unions, cooperatives, credit unions, and individuals, the government owning only 15 percent. To help facilitate its growth, the Workers Bank was made exempt from payment of income taxes and stamp duties for a period of five years, and any dividends that it pays out during the same five-year period are also exempt from taxation.

Among the miscellaneous financial institutions are the building and friendly societies, savings banks, finance companies, trust companies, pension funds, insurance companies, and the securities exchange. Building societies receive deposits and make mortgage loans to the public. Friendly societies are mutual insurance associations that make loans to cover financial setbacks and also to finance burials of their beneficiaries. Finance companies provide installment credit to consumers making large purchases, such as vehicles and appliances, but they also lend funds to businesses for the purchase of machinery and equipment. Most of their capital is raised by deposits from the public. Trust companies are affiliated with the commercial banks but operate independently from them. They also provide long-term credit and accept deposits from the public.

The insurance companies constitute a significant source of funds. Each company must maintain a fund equivalent to the total amount of its liabilities and reserves. A percentage of that fund—70 percent in 1975—must be invested within the country, and another percentage—10 percent in 1975—has to be invested in another member country of CARICOM. Insurance companies, like commercial banks, must become local companies and spin off part of their equity (25 percent) to local shareholders; the deadline for compliance with this requirement is January 1, 1978. Companies not complying with the law presumably would leave the country because the loss of certain tax benefits would make it no longer profitable to operate. In 1975 the government proposed to create a joint government and privately owned insurance company to insure all government property in the country and to engage in ordinary insurance business.

More than 150 private pension funds exist in addition to the National Insurance Board. Most pension funds are administered by insurance companies and like them are subject to the terms of the insurance act, although some are self-administered or managed by the trust companies. A certain percentage of their funds must be invested in the country, and most of the investment has been in government securities. The National Insurance Board also purchases government securities and invests in mortgages and long-term certificates of deposit (see ch. 5).

A tiny stock exchange, the Trinidad Call Exchange, is operated by a group of financial institutions that includes the Central Bank, the Ministry of Finance, commercial banks, and two stockbrokerage firms. Both governmental and private securities are traded, but the exchange has not been very successful in raising new capital for business firms. Very few companies have issued equity shares that are traded publicly; thus only several dozen private stocks and bonds are listed. More trading on the exchange is in government securities than in securities of private firms. Most companies raise capital by means of bank loans because they are reluctant to publish the financial statements required in order to sell stock. Well-established firms with a good public image have no difficulty in selling stock. Employees usually are given first option for the stock offer, and sometimes the firm arranges for banks to lend the employees money for the purchase.

As part of the fight against inflation, the government followed a tight credit policy in 1974 and 1975 and also urged the commercial banks to alter their credit portfolios by directing more loans to productive sectors and fewer loans to consumer spending. Despite the government's desire, at the end of 1974 total outstanding loans in the banking system had risen to over TT$675 million; consumer nonbusiness loans accounted for 35 percent of the total, slightly more than the share a year before. About 33 percent of the consumer loans were for the purchase of motor vehicles, and 15 percent each went for home furnishings and home improvements. About 20 percent of total credit was for manufacturing in both 1973 and 1974, commerce absorbed 16 percent of the total in 1974 (down from 18 percent in 1973), loans to the government accounted for 14 percent in 1973 but only 11 percent in 1974, agriculture received 3 percent of the total in both years, and all other economic sectors shared the balance.

Credit, if available, is not as costly as in many developing countries. The average weighted interest rate charged on all loans in 1974, including real estate purchases, was between 10 and 11 percent, only two percentage points higher than in 1969. The average interest paid on deposits ranged between 5 and 6 percent. Low- and middle-income persons who are not able to obtain credit from formal financial institutions often enter into an informal rotating mutual savings arrangement called a *sous-sous*. The arrangement permits the accumulation of a large amount of money at little cost. A group of persons form a temporary association; one member is designated the banker or captain of the *sous-sous*. All members contribute an identical sum of money regularly, usually weekly, and each member in turn receives the total amount less a small commission for the banker. The *sous-sous* continues until all members have received a draw, called a hand. The process may then be repeated, or the group may dissolve. The use of a *sous-sous* arrangement is declining as more and more persons have access to formal credit and also partly because of the legal requirement that the banker must register with the banking authorities as a trustee of funds.

The unit of currency, adopted on December 14, 1964, is the Trinidad and Tobago dollar, whose symbol is TT$. Before that time the British West Indian dollar was the unit of currency. Some official publications occasionally drop the symbol TT and only use the symbol $, thereby creating potential confusion with the United States dollar for end users of statistical data. The TT$ is divided into 100 cents; banknotes come in denominations of one, five, ten, and twenty dollars and coins in one-, five-, ten-, and twenty-five-, and fifty-cent pieces. In addition a small quantity of TT$ one and TT$ five coins have been circulating since 1972. The Barbados dollar, the Jamaica dollar, the Guyana dollar, and the East Caribbean dollar also are seen in Trinidad and Tobago, but they are not legal tender, and the Central Bank has reciprocal arrangements with those countries to purchase all bank notes presented to monetary authorities for repatriation.

From its adoption and until December 1971 the exchange rate was TT$ equal to US$0.50. Between December 1971 and July 3, 1972, the rate of exchange was TT$1 equal to US$0.54. Since July 3, 1972, the Trinidad and Tobago dollar has been tied to the British pound, and all transactions in currencies linked to the pound take place at the official rate—TT$4.80 equals one British pound. All other currencies are exchanged at freely fluctuating rates that depend on the strength of the pound in world money markets. The Central Bank issues daily official rates for the United States dollar, Canadian dollar, deutsche mark, French franc, Japanese yen, Swiss franc, Guyanan dollar, Jamaican dollar, and East Caribbean dollar. Only authorized dealers as designated by the Central Bank may deal in foreign currency, traveler's checks, and gold. The link to the pound has some drawbacks for, despite its backing by sufficient reserves, the Trinidad and Tobago dollar falls when the British pound falls. Its freely fluctuating rate has ranged from TT$1.84 to TT$2.33 equal to US$1, although it is considered a relatively strong currency. Periodically the financial community calls upon the government to reconsider the pros and cons of maintaining the link to the pound.

INDUSTRY

Petroleum and Mining

The petroleum industry consists of three elements: exploration and production of oil, refining and desulfurization, and natural gas. The first successful oil well in the world was drilled in Trinidad in 1857, but production was sporadic until 1910, when exploration was stimulated by the British government's decision to substitute oil for coal as a fuel for its navy. About twelve oil fields were discovered in the southwest and two in the southeast of Trinidad; a total of over 1.2 billion barrels had been extracted by 1970. In 1968, however, production started to decline as the oil fields—particularly those on land—began to peter out. Fortunately offshore explorations were successful, and production once again started to increase after 1972. In 1975 production was running at the rate of 200,000 barrels per day, 75 percent coming from offshore oil fields.

Proven reserves in that year were estimated at 612 million barrels, enough to last until 1995 at the current extraction rates. All oil companies, however, were optimistic about discovering additional reserves; two companies were actively exploring off the northern and eastern coasts in 1975, and many others obtained concessions the terms of which required prompt initiation of exploratory activities.

Seven companies were successfully producing petroleum in 1975; Amoco Trinidad Oil Company, the largest producer, accounted for over half of total production. Amoco's oil fields are off the east coast and produce a high-grade, low-sulfur oil. The government owns one company, the Trinidad and Tobago Oil Company, formerly Shell Trinidad, purchased in 1974. The government also had a share in the Trinidad-Tesoro Petroleum Company and was negotiating in 1975 to purchase the Texaco-Trinidad Oil Company including its refinery. During the early 1970s all new exploration contracts negotiated with oil companies have contained production-sharing clauses. Under the terms of contracts companies are responsible for all costs of exploration and exploitation. A minimum number of wells must be drilled, and there must be a guaranteed level of expenditure. If petroleum is discovered, production is shared with the government on a prearranged basis. Contracts are terminated if oil is not discovered within six years.

There are two large and two small refineries in the country with a total capacity over 460,000 barrels per day, and there is a 100,000-barrels-per-day desulfurization plant at the Texaco refinery. Since Trinidad's domestic crude production was never expected to reach high levels, both of the large refineries built were designed to process imported crude oil, which has been imported since 1939 for processing and refining for a fee and then reexported. All of the oil imports are for the refineries, and some foreign trade sources do not include data for oil imported and exported under processing agreements.

Natural gas, previously flared off, is being utilized for industrial purposes. It generates most of the electricity and is used as a fuel for the oil refineries and a number of manufacturing plants. Gasfields have been discovered off the east coast with proven reserves for about twenty years as of 1975. Pipelines were under construction in that year to bring the natural gas across the island to the Point Lisas Industrial Estate, where major projects were being planned. Long-range plans include construction of an offshore collector network to bring gas to the mainland from fields as distant as forty-five miles. All gas must be sold to the government at these offshore collection points for resale and distribution.

Mining activities are not very extensive, asphalt being the major product produced. Natural asphalt has been dug from the famous pitch lake at La Brea for centuries. It is refined, packaged, and exported. There are also measurable quantities of quarry products—gravel and sand, clays, limestone, gypsum, and porcellanite, a construction rock

Table 9. Trinidad and Tobago, Industrial and Mineral Production, Selected Products, 1970–74

Industry	Unit	1970	1971	1972	1973	1974
Asphalt........	long tons	128,219	121,903	113,627	107,800	81,574
Beer	thousands of gallons	3,299	3,728	4,010	4,559	3,709
Cement........	thousands of metric tons	271.2	255.6	286.8	256.6	241.2
Crude oil	millions of barrels	51.0	47.1	51.2	60.7	68.1
Fertilizers	thousands of short tons	611.4	568.6	629.5	459.0	411.0
Limestone	thousands of cubic yards	259.9	120.3	656.3	n.a.	n.a.
Motor vehicles .	thousands	6.3	7.0	10.9	8.9	6.1
Natural gas	millions of cubic feet	121,060	109,814	104,338	119,353	127,704*
Radios and television sets	thousands	19.5	17.5	29.8	33.5	25.2
Refined petro-leum products	thousands of barrels	150,258.6	141,503.4	138,895.0	135,812.2	130,800.0
Refrigerators ..	thousands	8.5	15.6	20.4	20.7	n.a.
Rum	thousands of gallons	1,726.5	1,886.6	2,473.6	2,443.7	4,332.3
Soaps	millions of pounds	14.3	12.1	11.9	13.1	11.7*
Stoves.........	thousands	11.6	21.8	23.9	15.4	n.a.

n.a.—not available.
* Estimate.

used to build roads but with a potential for cementmaking and low-cost housing construction.

Manufacturing and Construction

Before 1950 there was very little manufacturing in the country. The existing industries were engaged in food processing—mainly sugar, rum, fats, and oil—textiles and clothing, and petroleum products associated with the refineries. In 1950 the government passed the Aid to Pioneer Industries Ordinance, which granted certain tax benefits in order to attract new industry. Over the years other benefits were added, such as the provision for industrial estates, including factories built to specific needs and leased for a long term. By 1975 there were over 600 factories making, processing, or assembling more than 400 categories of goods (see table 9).

Most of the new items are substitutes for light manufactures previously imported. A number of the plants import components and assemble the items for which only a few parts are made domestically. These are mainly electrical equipment, such as television sets, refrigerators, radios, and air conditioners. Some of the other items being produced are adhesives, beverages, building materials, paper products, ceramic articles, cosmetics, detergents, household appliances, furniture, industrial chemicals, paints, pharmaceuticals, plastic articles, and rubber products. There are also a number of heavy industries: cement, vehicle assembly, metalworking, and ship repairs. Three motor vehicle assembly plants produce a dozen makes. There is a large demand for vehicles, partly stimulated by low-interest government loans to civil service employees for the purchase of vehicles. Dry dock facilities at Chaguaramas Bay can handle vessels of up to 20,000 tons. At least three petrochemical complexes were being planned in 1975. If they come to fruition, the country could become a major petrochemical producer.

Many of the industries are high cost because of the small domestic market protected by import restrictions. Excluding sugar and petroleum, 90 percent of all industrial items are for the domestic market. Only 10 percent of manufactures are exported, and four-fifths of that goes to CARICOM countries (see Regional Economic Cooperation, this ch.). In order to provide more employment the government would prefer to see more labor-intensive industries develop, particularly textiles and garments, which have shown rapid growth. More than sixty-five companies were making clothes in the 1970s, an increase from only nine in 1962. They employed over 6,000 people and stimulated other industries, such as buttonmaking and accessories. Other labor-intensive industries are cottage industries and handicrafts. There are many shops and individuals producing such small items as musical instruments, handbags, shoes, and furniture. Many persons work at home and receive their raw materials from central clearinghouses that also purchase the finished goods.

Another growth industry has been the processing of foods, usually a traditional industry. In Trinidad and Tobago, however, a surge of interest occurred during the 1960s in processing locally grown foods, and by 1972 there were more than seventy firms in operation, up considerably from fourteen small plants ten years previously. Beverages, soft and hard, are also popular. One product manufactured only in Trinidad and Tobago is angostura bitters, used as a flavoring in drinks, juices, and soups. The rums of the country also have a good reputation.

The construction industry is stimulated by government housing projects, tax incentives for private residential construction, higher mortgage limits than in the past, and new factories for industrial development. Only a few domestic construction firms, however, have the technical, financial, and managerial ability to carry out major projects. Local companies usually associate with foreign firms for major contracts. Many of the domestic suppliers of building materials fail to live up to specifications or fall behind delivery schedules. One new inexpensive product for the construction industry produced since 1973 is particle board made from bagasse, the residue from sugarcane milling.

The Trinidad and Tobago Productivity Centre, partly financed by the United Nations Special Fund, attempts to improve productivity and management techniques. It provides consulting services and training programs and conducts research in a company's specific problems. The Caribbean Industrial Research Institute was established in 1970, also with United Nations assistance to prepare industrial standards and conduct feasibility studies for government and private companies. Other Caribbean countries use the institute's facilities on a fee basis. The Trinidad Manufacturers Association, a voluntary organization, provides its members with certain services, including market trends and a listing of business opportunities.

Electricity

Trinidad and Tobago is one of three countries in the Western Hemisphere with no hydroelectricity and no identifiable hydropotential. Yet both the per capita installed capacity and the per capita output are the highest in all of Latin America. Almost all of the electricity is generated by natural gas, and rates are low because of the ready availability of the fuel. The government-owned Trinidad and Tobago Electricity Commission, with more than 2,000 employees and installed capacity of 359,000 kilowatts in 1975, supplied all the electricity except for a few private plants owned by large industries generating electricity for their own use. Those plants had a total capacity of 50,000 kilowatts and sometimes sold part of the production to the Trinidad and Tobago Electricity Commission.

All communities in Tobago and about 85 percent of Trinidad had access to electricity in 1974, and the government had plans to extend the grid to the rest of the island. The main power station located in Port-of-Spain generates about 75 percent of the total supply. Two others, at the town of Penal and at Point Lisas, supply most of the balance. A small plant fueled by diesel oil is located on Tobago but is used only for standby service; Tobago usually receives its electricity by means of underseas cables from Trinidad. The standby plant is placed into service when outages occur on the transmission lines, as happened in 1975.

AGRICULTURE

Agricultural production has been falling and not keeping up with population growth. Using 100 as the base figure for the 1961–65 period, for example, total agricultural production in 1973 was estimated at only eighty-four and per capita production at an even lower seventy-five. Historically agriculture has been characterized by a dichotomy between small, low-yielding peasant farms and larger, modern, highly productive estates. The estates produced export cash crops, such as sugar, cacao, and citrus, while the smaller farms grew food crops, such as rice, peas, beans, yams, corn, and miscellaneous vegetables and fruits.

Food imports, particularly of meat, wheat, rice, and fish, have been rising rapidly and reached such proportions that in 1974 the government decided to promote the increased production of food crops for domestic use. The Food Development Fund was set up with part of the increased petroleum revenues, the Agricultural Development Bank increased its loan program, more subsidies were to be given to farmers, and the marketing and distribution system was to be modernized.

Beginning in 1975 some of the subsidies, however, were being replaced by a system of guaranteed prices with assured marketing outlets. The Food Development Fund is to be used to help bring into production large and small projects, particularly on idle land, and to conduct marketing and research operations.

Land Use and Tenure

The most recent agricultural census was the agricultural census of Trinidad and Tobago of 1963, although the data for Tobago were for 1964 because a hurricane struck the island during the census period and data collecting was postponed. Generally a plot under one acre was not recorded as a farm unless one-eighth of it was already planted in a crop or it contained one head of livestock or twelve of poultry. Some landless farms were recorded—those where a person raised at least ten pigs or 200 chickens on property that was not otherwise used for farming. Before the 1963 census a partial census had been taken in 1956 and a complete census in 1946.

The 1963 census indicated a total of 35,800 farms in the country; they occupied about 42 percent of the total land area, or over 531,000 acres. Over 60 percent of the farmland was in crops, 25 percent was wooded or mountainous, about 4 percent was in pasture, and the balance was either idle or used for other purposes. The average farm size was over 14.8 acres, but the majority, 25,800 farms, were between one and nine acres and totaled only 94,700 acres. There were 7,500 farms between ten and twenty-four acres, and the rest were over twenty-five acres; forty-two were over 1,000 acres each and totaled over 131,000 acres. Of the 35,800 total farms 4,000 were on Tobago and added up to 45,800 acres. Only 800 of the farms on Tobago were over ten acres yet they accounted for 33,300 acres. Many of the landholders in the country did not reside on their farms but lived elsewhere and commuted to their plots. A large number stated that their primary occupation was not in agriculture and that farming was only a secondary source of income.

The numerous small landholdings developed out of several historical sources. After emancipation the estate provision grounds formerly used by the slaves were given to many of them as inducements to remain and work on the estates. In the 1880s most of the major sugar plantations on

Tobago were broken up after bankruptcy, and plots were sold to peasants who had saved some money. Over the years landless farmers who saved their wages have been able to acquire property of their own. When the indenture system was introduced during the 1890s, many sugar estates on Trinidad started to least back or sell five-acre plots of land on the periphery of the estates to workers whose terms of indentureship were over. Some small farms were created under land settlement programs, and squatters operate small plots of state land. The position of former squatters is being legalized, but new squatters are evicted.

Many of the small farms raise vegetables; this is profitable and returns an adequate income when the land is intensively utilized and improvements are made in cultivation methods. Fragmentation is widespread; some sugarcane farms are known to consist of five to eight noncontiguous plots. The large number of plots is conducive to predial larceny as the farmer cannot continually watch all his holdings.

The 1963 census reported that over 18,000 farms, or more than 50 percent of the total, were operated by the owner; over 10,600 farms, or about 30 percent of the total, were operated by renters, and the balance were operated under various tenure arrangements. The farms operated by the owners totaled 67 percent of total farmland; rented farmland totaled only 9 percent. Many properties have been handed down by succession within families without legal transfer of title. A certificate of ownership can be obtained if evidence can be shown that the land has been in the family for at least forty years. In 1975 legislation was introduced to shorten this time to thirty years. Many farmers who own their own land also rent supplemental property. This is particularly true of farmers having medium-sized sugarcane crops, who rent land from the large sugar estates. Rents charged by estates are generally low, especially for tenants who are descendants of the original indentured workers. Rents charged by small- and medium-scale farmers who are no longer working their own land, however, tend to be fairly high. Rights to tenancy are also sold among tenants.

Trinidad and Tobago has not been faced with agrarian reform problems of the dimensions encountered in other countries. Fairly large areas are owned by the government and are available for distribution. The state owns as estimated 588,000 acres on Trinidad and nearly 13,000 acres on Tobago. Although much of the state land is in forest reserves, there is enough arable land. Additionally some large estates have been sold to the government for redistribution.

Land settlement programs were started as far back as 1934. The early programs were of two kinds: sale of two-acre plots and rental of one-acre plots with a purchase option. Not enough infrastructure was provided to the early settlements, however, and many of the original plots were later abandoned. From 1934 through 1964 about 2,240 farmers received a total of 5,000 acres under the first land settlement program. Over the ensuing years the government realized that, rather than appropriating land for redistribution for subsistence farms, it should encourage the establishment of medium-sized family farms and could increase food production and generate sufficient income for the family. Thus a new program, the Crown Lands Development Project, which is viewed as more nearly agrotechnical than agrarian, was begun in 1965.

Under the new program the size of the farms to be distributed is determined by the amount of land required to provide a family with a net income of TT$125 per month at 1966 prices. The sizes range from five acres for vegetables, tree crops, and pig breeding, to ten acres for tobacco and between fifteen and twenty acres for dairy farms. Farmers receive a twenty-five-year lease, renewable for similar periods. The leases are transferable to heirs. Applicants for land under the new program must be between the ages of twenty-one and thirty-one and have had some farming experience, but all land recipients receive extensive training in modern methods for several weeks before being permitted to occupy their new farms.

All farms are turned over to the recipient in a basic, partially developed, or fully developed stage. Under basic development some infrastructure is provided—buildings, roads, water, and electricity. Under partial development the land is cleared, but no buildings are provided. Fully developed farms contain housing, trees, and animals, and the land is cleared. All inputs, such as fertilizer and seeds for all kinds of farms, are provided at cost or on credit. The Crown Lands Development Project was deemed partially successful during its first ten years of operation. Some 1,200 new farms were created, and milk, pork, poultry, and tobacco production, as well as production of some other crops, increased markedly. Some farmers, however, reverted to growing subsistence crops with which they were more familiar and abandoned the more profitable vegetable growing.

Cultivation methods vary by geographical region. Some mechanization is found in level areas, but traditional cultivation techniques predominate, and much hand labor is utilized. Many farmers clear their ground by burning; the technique is illegal without a license, but the prohibition is not enforced. Although many farmers, particularly those who have more than one plot, raise various crops, a large number practice monoculture. For example, an estimated 40 percent of sugarcane farmers grow nothing else on their farms.

The fact that almost all agricultural machinery and equipment must be imported adds to their cost. Between 200 and 300 tractors are imported annually, and about 14 percent of the farms in the sugarcane industry have tractors. Ploughs, however, are found on only about 8 percent of the sugar farms, and about 40 percent have carts. The use and production of fertilizers remained steady for a number of years, between 25,000 and 27,000 tons being used annually. In 1973 one of the three fertilizer plants in the country was converted into a hydrogen factory because of unused capacity. By 1975 a regional need for fertilizer in the Caribbean led to the

Crop	1970	1971	1972	1973	1974
Bananas	9.0	8.0	8.0	8.0	n.a.
Cacao	5.6	4.1	5.0	3.0	4.0*
Citrus	40.0	32.0	23.0	8.0	60.0*
Coffee	4.1	2.9	3.0	1.8	2.2
Copra	11.0	13.0	13.0	11.0	12.0
Molasses	91.0	85.0	94.0	92.0	89.0
Rice	19.0	10.0	10.0	110.0*	n.a.
Sugarcane	2,718.0	2,610.0	2,349.0	2,428.0	n.a.
Sugar, refined	224.0	221.0	232.0	188.0	186.0
Sweet potatoes	3.0	3.0	3.0	4.0	n.a.
Tobacco	0.2	0.2	0.2	0.3	0.3
Tomatoes	5.0	3.0	4.0	4.0	n.a.

n.a.—not available.
* Estimate.

planning of a new plant with a capacity of 400,000 tons, mainly for export. Agricultural research is conducted at four institutions: the Faculty of Agriculture of the University of the West Indies (with concentration on root crops); the Central Experimental Station of the Ministry of Agriculture, Lands, and Fisheries; the Sugar Research Station; and the Coconut Growers Association.

Crops

Many crops are grown, but few are raised in significant quantities (see table 10). Sugarcane is the major crop; almost all of it is raised in Caroni and Victoria counties. It can grow in other parts of the country, but because of the climate the sugar content of the cane is lower elsewhere. The total acres planted usually vary between 90,000 and 112,000; around 105,000 acres were under cultivation in 1975. Not all of the sugarcane is harvested. Heavy rains in some years, as in 1972, cause large quantities to be left in the fields, and in other years, as in 1975, labor disputes cause losses of the crop. Fires, some deliberately set, are another problem for the industry.

Historically sugarcane was produced by a large number of private estates; in the 1890s there were more than 300 estates, each with its own sugar mill. By 1975 there were only three companies in operation, plus thousands of small-scale sugarcane farmers. The three companies owned a total of six mills and ground the cane of the small farmers on a contract basis. The largest company and also the largest single landowner in the country is the Caroni Sugar Company, owned mainly by the government together with about 3,500 minority stockholders. Caroni owns over 72,000 acres including land it rents to small-scale farms. It employs directly more than 22,000 people, and its four mills grind about 90 percent of all sugarcane produced annually. The other two plantations are the Orange Grove National Company, 100 percent government owned, and Forres Park, 100 percent privately owned. Each operates one small sugar mill.

The number of small-scale sugarcane farmers has been progressively declining. Most of them are descendants of the East Indians brought over to work as indentured laborers for the estates. When their term of indenture was over, many remained in the country and obtained plots of land on which they raised sugarcane. There were as many as 20,000 independent sugarcane farmers in the 1920s, but the number had dropped to about 10,000 by 1975. Few young men were interested in becoming sugarcane farmers, and the average age of these farmers was high; 71 percent of the total were over forty in 1970. The small sugarcane farms account for about 40 percent of annual production although production on many of them was very low. Each of some 60 percent of the farms produced less than fifty tons of sugarcane annually, and only 800 of the independent farmers cultivated plots of more than ten acres. The small-scale farmers deliver their sugarcane to specified points where it is weighed and loaded on vehicles belonging to the sugar mills.

More land is planted in cacao trees than in sugarcane. Cacao used to be an important crop for many small-scale farmers and is the leading crop on Tobago. Cacao, the bean from which chocolate and cocoa are derived, has been grown since 1525, and during the latter half of the nineteenth century it replaced sugar as the most valuable crop. Trinidad was once the world's second leading cacao producer, but disease and competition from other countries caused the crop to drop in importance during this century. The variety grown in Trinidad has a flavor that is much in demand for blending, and premium prices are usually received.

Between 8,000 and 9,000 farmers, most of whom have small groves, grow cacao. Over 80 percent of total production comes from about 1,600 of the larger farms. Yields depend upon the kind of soil and the amount of rainfall and vary considerably, from a low of 200 pounds of beans per acre to a high of 1,500 pounds. High-yielding varieties are available from the government at no cost, but many farmers are reluctant to replace their older trees because the newer varieties produce beans of uneven size that cause processing difficulties. The Cocoa Board of Trinidad and Tobago operates a subsidy scheme, provides the new seedlings, and lends some financial assistance. A separate government agency, the Cocoa and Coffee Industry Board, sets regulations and grading standards and purchases cacao from the small-scale farmer for export. The larger producers market their crops through a cooperative exporting agency, the Cocoa Planters Association.

Another important cash crop for farmers is citrus, mainly grapefruit and oranges. When disease started to affect the cacao trees, many farmers turned to citrus fruit as an alternative crop. Citrus is exported as whole fruit, juices, and preserves. Between 85 and 90 percent of all citrus production comes from farmers who are members of the Cooperative Citrus Growers Association, which operates its own processing plants and does its own exporting. One processing plant, handling limes only, is owned by the government, which also was negotiating with the Cooperative Citrus Growers Association in 1975 for government participation in the enterprise in order to qualify it for guaranteed loans needed to modernize the processing facilities.

The second most important cash crop on Tobago is coconuts, which are also grown along the coasts of Trinidad. Much of the coconut crop is grown on estates, although many small farmers are involved. The entire crop is used domestically in copra, soap, oils, and fats. The Coconut Growers Association operates several processing plants and also manufactures and markets coconut products. Coffee is raised almost exclusively by cacao farmers as a subsidiary crop, and there are very few coffee farms in the country. Although production is limited, the quality of coffee is high because processing standards are closely followed. All unsold stocks are purchased from growers and stored by the government until they can be sold for export.

Rice is an important food crop, but not enough is grown domestically to meet demand. Many farmers raise rice as a subsistence crop and do not market their surpluses. The existence of consumer price controls is cited as the main reason that farmers do not market more of the crop. The government is attempting to rehabilitate idle land on which rice had previously been grown in order to increase production, bring new ricelands into production, and build modern rice mills to minimize processing losses.

Tobacco is grown in small but steadily increasing quantities. Tobacco farmers are under contract to the West Indian Tobacco Company, which provides technical advice and maintains crop standards. The best grade tobacco is grown on Tobago, where it provides an important source of income. Numerous vegetables are grown in the country, but nearly one-third of production comes from one small farming town, Aranjuez, near Port-of-Spain. Most of the Aranjuez farmers use very modern cultivation techniques and constantly improved seeds. A small but profitable industry is honey. The Cooperative Beekeeper Society handles all sales for the more than 300 apiaries in the country.

Livestock, Fishing, and Forestry

There is not much large livestock in the country, although the government has been stimulating the growth of this sector, particularly beef and dairy cattle. The 1963 agricultural census indicated that only about 7,500 farmers reported having some dairy cattle, 2,100 farmers had some beef cattle, 1,700 had some draft animals, and another 1,700 had water buffalo. By the early 1970s there were only 67,000 head of all kinds of cattle in the country in addition to about 55,000 pigs, 38,000 goats, and

7,000 sheep. Goats, pigs, and donkeys are found almost exclusively on the very small farms and water buffalo almost exclusively on the large farms. Horses and cattle are raised on farms of all sizes. Farmers with work animals often hire them out to transport produce for other farmers.

Beef production does not meet demand. Milk production has been increasing steadily, but domestic production provided only about 11 percent of consumption in 1974. Most of the increase has come from the 260 dairy farms established under the Crown Lands Development Project and the dozen very large commercial dairy farms. Some of the dairy farms have well-managed pastures of pangola grass, but the percentage of farmland in pastures is the smallest in all of Latin America. Pork production was also increasing in response to governmental stimulation, but the industry was hit very hard by hog cholera in 1973, and the original level of stock was not rebuilt until 1975. Meanwhile substantial quantities of frozen pork were imported to meet demand.

More success has been achieved in the poultry industry. The country has become self-sufficient in poultry meat and eggs to such a point that occasional gluts occur and the government has to store the surplus. There were more than 14 million chickens in 1975, for example, produced on about 5,000 farms. The main reasons for the rapid growth of the poultry industry were fiscal incentives granted to producers and breeders and quotas placed on the importation of poultry meat. Further growth beyond 1975, however, was expected to be hindered by retail price controls, which cut into producers' profits.

The government has also turned its attention to stimulating the fishing industry. An estimated 3,000 full-time and 2,200 part-time fishermen, mostly using small craft, catch about 13,000 tons annually. Less than half that total, however, is marketed domestically because most of the tuna, shrimp, and other crustaceans are exported. A wide variety of fish are caught, the most prevalent being kingfish, grouper, redfish, and snapper. There are more than sixty-three fishing beaches on Trinidad and several on Tobago, but only a few have handling, storage, and preserving facilities. Most of the crafts, called pirogues, are under thirty feet long, and many are powered by outboard motors. They usually have a captain and a two- or three-man crew. Some captains rent their boats and gear from suppliers on a share-the-catch basis. There are about 100 fairly large tuna and shrimp trawlers operating out of Trinidad ports; many of them are foreign owned and have Trinidadian crews. A number of disputes have arisen between Trinidad and Tobago and Venezuela and Brazil over the trawlers' fishing in territorial waters claimed by those countries. The disputes surface periodically and are settled temporarily.

Since fish has become an important part of the diet, particularly in Tobago, the goverment has been attempting to reduce the need for imports of fish by increasing the domestic supply. The National Fisheries Company operates its own trawlers and processing plants and supplies gas and diesel fuel to fishermen at subsidized prices. The government also operates a fish farm, where fish are raised for sale to the public. In 1974 the Fisheries Development Fund was established to finance modern fishing methods and facilities. In 1975 the United Nations-sponsored Caribbean Fisheries Training Institute opened at Chaguaramas to train fishermen from Trinidad and Tobago and other Caribbean countries.

There is an official hunting season from October through March. Such animals as the agouti, deer, and wild hog are caught, as well as wild turkeys, ducks, and alligators. Turtles are also hunted, but legislation was pending in 1975 to make turtle hunting illegal.

Forestry is a small industry despite the fact that about 43 percent of the country is forested. The forests have been protected from excessive exploitation since 1765, and many of them are owned by the government, which intends to maintain them as a permanent supply of timber and to prevent soil erosion and flooding. About 4.9 million cubic feet of wood were produced annually in the early 1970s, mostly for industrial use but partly for firewood and charcoal. Production has been declining from the level of the 1960s, and the number of sawmills has decreased; there were only sixty still in operation in 1972. More than sixty different species of trees are exploited, but 60 percent of production comes from ten species, particularly mora, carapa, mahoe, cedar, and teak. Teak was introduced into the country in 1913, and by 1975 there was 20,000 acres of teak plantations. Tree plantations of other managed species covered about 17,000 acres. Some of the exotic woods are exported, but much more timber is imported than is produced annually.

TRADE AND TRANSPORTATION

The country's importance in world trade is larger than its size indicates—it ranks forty-fourth among importing nations. A business elite exists; data from several studies indicate that they are mainly Trinidadian and foreign whites and some Chinese. There are very few Negroes and East Indians in decisionmaking positions. Business activities are generally relaxed and not sophisticated. There is little delegation of authority, especially in family-run firms (see ch. 4).

Foreign Trade

Foreign trade data tend to be distorted because of the petroleum refining industry. Large quantities of crude oil are imported for processing and then exported as refined petroleum products. In some published trade and balance-of-payments data these figures may not be listed or may be listed as valuation adjustments or as a processing fee. From 1969 through 1973 imports exceeded exports annually (see table 11). Preliminary reports for 1974, however, indicated a favorable balance of trade, solely because of the petroleum trade.

The leading export by far is petroleum and derivative products. The level grew steadily after the first petroleum export was made in 1910 until by the 1970s it accounted for between 80 and 83 percent of all annual exports. The second leading export has been sugar, which accounted for 4 to 5 percent of annual exports during the early 1970s. The Commonwealth Sugar Agreement under which Trinidad and Tobago sold part of its sugar to the United Kingdom at a fixed guaranteed price expired at the end of 1974, and all subsequent sugar sales were made at world market prices. Apart from petroleum and sugar very few items are exported in large quantities. Other products exported include chemicals, fertilizers, cosmetics, clothing, footwear, paper products, coffee, citrus, and cacao.

Some export promotion is carried out in order to diversify exports. The Export Promotion Office of the Ministry of Commerce and Industry explores the market potential of certain commodities in selected countries and supports exporters initially penetrating such markets. In 1975 trade missions were sent to the Far East, including the People's Republic of China (PRC), and some trade ties resulted. Commercial relations have also been increasing with the Soviet Union, Cuba, and Romania. The Productivity Centre of the IDC maintains an export advisory service for new exporters, and the Export Credit Insurance Company was created by the government in 1974 to help stimulate export sales. One private bank, the Royal Bank of Trinidad and Tobago, began its own export promotion service in 1973, under which it will make feasibility studies of the market potential of any product for any exporter at no charge. If a market is found to exist, the bank for a fee will attend to all warehousing, shipping, and documentation.

Although crude petroleum accounts for about half of all imports by value, a wider range of products is imported than exported. Agricultural products, mainly such foods as cereals and dairy and meat products, accounted for between 11 and 12 percent of total imports during the 1960s but rose to 18 percent in 1973 and soared to over 24 percent in 1974. Mining construction and industrial machinery usually account for 5 to 7 percent of total imports, motor vehicles for around 3 percent, electrical machinery for 2 to 3 percent, iron and steel and paper products for about 2 percent, and all others for the balance.

There are some restrictions on foreign trade. Certain products can only be imported by the government; these include rice and other agricultural products listed in the Agricultural Marketing Protocol to CARIFTA. In order to protect domestic industries, an import negative list is maintained. Items on the list, which numbered nearly 500 by 1975, are quantitatively restricted, and import licenses are required to import any of them. Licenses are also required to import any goods from a number of countries: Albania, Bulgaria, the PRC, Czechoslovakia, the German Democratic Republic (East Germany), Hungary, the Democratic People's Republic of Korea (North Korea), Poland, Romania, Yugoslavia, and the Soviet Union. No trade is permitted with Southern Rhodesia or South Africa. Exports of about forty items require a license to any destination; these include animals, firearms, and gold.

Table 11. Trinidad and Tobago, Exports and Imports, 1969–74
(in millions of United States dollars)

Year	Exports	Imports
1969	474	483
1970	481	542
1971	519	663
1972	557	763
1973	692	777
1974	2,030*	1,842*

* Preliminary estimates.

The United States has become the most important market for the country's exports. During the 1958–60 period the United States took only 18 percent of total exports. By 1968 this has risen to over 42 percent and in 1973 it had jumped to over 54 percent. The United States has become the leading market mainly because of the large quantities of petroleum products being exported. The United Kingdom, once the leading market with 30 percent of total exports from 1958 to 1960, fell to third place by 1973 with only 5 percent. The exports to the United Kingdom consist mainly of sugar and citrus. Sweden moved into second position in 1973 as a leading market with almost 7 percent of the total. Guyana, Jamaica, and Canada followed in that order with between 2 and 4 percent each. Other countries took smaller percentages, petroleum being the prime export except to the Netherlands, which is the leading market for exports of asphalt. Manufactured goods constitute a very small percentage of total exports, and most of them go to members of the Caribbean Common Market. For example, nearly 80 percent of all clothing exports, 50 percent of all refrigerator production, 15 percent of all radios, and 10 percent of all television sets assembled were exported to CARICOM members in 1972.

The origin of imports changed during the early 1970s. Saudi Arabia moved into first place in 1973, contributing more than 24 percent of total imports, all in the form of crude petroleum. Previously Saudi Arabia had supplied no more than 15 percent of the total. The United States was the second leading supplier of imports in 1973 with 16 percent of the total. It had been the principal supplier during 1971 and 1972 with about 18 percent. Principal imports from the United States are machinery, wheat, textiles, paper, chemicals, corn, telecommunications equipment, and plastics. The United Kingdom, once the prime source of imports (31 percent from 1958 to 1960), was in third place in 1973 with 11 percent, mainly vehicles, machinery parts, iron and steel, medicinal products, chemicals, and printed matter. Indonesia moved up from supplying less than 2 percent of imports to over 9 percent during 1972 and 1973, all petroleum. Venezuela supplied over 5 percent in 1973 (down from over 10 percent in previous years), Canada was supplying a steady annual 4 percent, and Japan was steady with 3 percent of the total. Other suppliers with statistically important amounts were Ecuador, Nigeria, the Federal Republic of Germany (West Germany), New Zealand, Guyana, and the Netherlands. Canada supplies paper, vegetables, textiles, flour, and fresh meat; Ecuador and Nigeria, petroleum; New Zealand, meat, milk, and cheese; the Netherlands, vegetables, milk, and plastics; Guyana, rice, clothing, small fishing boats, and medicinal products; and West Germany, machinery parts, vehicles, plastics, and textiles.

Domestic Trade

Business organizations are either sole proprietorships (which are the most numerous), partnerships (which may include up to twenty people), cooperatives, or corporations. Corporations are governed by the Companies Ordinance (1939), which makes a distinction between private and public companies. In this sense a public company is not one that is owned by the government but rather one that sells stock to the public. A private company does not sell its stock to the public, limits its stockholders to between seven and fifty people, and restricts the transfer of shares between them. Private companies do not have to hold statutory meetings or file annual reports. They are the more popular form of incorporation, particularly for family-owned businesses; in 1972 there over 2,700 of them and only fifty public corporations. About twenty-six consumer cooperatives selling groceries and general merchandise have affiliated into the Federation of Consumer Co-operative Societies in order to make wholesale purchases of goods, supplies, and equipment for the members' retail operations. In addition some agricultural marketing cooperatives exist.

Retail operations range from modern department stores to street vendors. New contemporary shopping centers with several levels of malls can be found in Port-of-Spain and San Fernando. There are chain department, drug, and grocery stores, discount outlets, and the familiar five-and-ten store. The first supermarket opened in 1950 and quickly became a common part of the marketing system. The largest supermarket chain, domestically owned, operated sixteen stores in the country in 1975 plus two stores in Jamaica and was envisaging branches in other Caribbean islands. Smaller grocery stores specialize in home delivery in order to compete with the supermarkets, and some sell on credit. In rural areas multipurpose or general stores operated by East Indians and Chinese can be found, but they seldom carry many perishables. They usually carry small quantities of many articles and will even break open packages to sell less than a unit size. There are a fairly large number of specialty stores, such as appliance or furniture stores. Street vendors abound and even sell at night by candlelight but are prohibited within a one-mile radius of the central market of Port-of-Spain. The law was being strictly enforced in 1975. There are both urban rural markets where wholesale and retail operations are carried on. The largest market is the central market outside Port-of-Spain. An important farmers' market is held every Saturday at Scarborough on Tobago.

Most agricultural products move through one of about eighteen markets, which are operated by a city or county with the exception of the central market, which is managed by the Central Marketing Agency (CMA). The CMA was established in 1966, replacing a marketing board that had been in existence since 1949, in order to regulate most of the wholesale trade. The CMA will purchase from farmers all products that receive price supports. It has its own storage facilities, although the storage and transportation facilities were considered insufficient to handle all the produce offered by farmers. Its early years of operation were also hampered by a lack of qualified staff. In the 1970s the CMA was improving its facilities and procedures and was guaranteeing to purchase all produce contracted for. In 1975 it started to issue daily wholesale and retail price ranges for most products. Some farmers sell directly to consumers, and others sell to wholesalers and retailers. Most farmers have to deliver their produce to the buyer, but some are transporting it collectively in order to cut costs. Livestock is sold by farmers by the head rather than by weight, which is not conducive to improving husbandry practices. Poultry moves directly from producers to supermarkets, to retailers in public markets, or to consumers from producer-owned outlet stores.

English weights and measures had been the standard (with the use of some metric measures) until 1968, when the CARIFTA members decided to establish national metrification committees to study a possible shift to the metric system. The Trinidad and Tobago Metrification Board decided that the country should eventually adopt the metric system, and in 1970 the government accepted the recommendation. In 1975 the metrification board was educating the public about the metric system, and the first changeover was the reporting of weather data in the metric system effective July 1, 1975.

Transportation and Telecommunication

A long-range transportation study is slowly being implemented, although much of the transportation system is not being maintained and costs of distribution are high. There are inadequate parking facilities in cities, and heavy vehicles must load and unload in the streets, causing urban congestion. Because of poor road conditions the country has a high accident rate, and in many areas older bridges are too narrow for wide buses and trucks.

A railroad network begun in 1876 and finished in 1913 emanated from Port-of-Spain, stretching eastward and southward; railroad stations served as areas of urbanization. By 1965, however, rising annual deficits forced a government decision to phase out railroads in favor of other means of transportation, and the last government railroad line was closed in 1968. Sugar companies, however, continued to operate several lines to transport sugarcane from the fields to the mills, although plans also existed to phase out part of that network.

There were about 4,500 miles of roads in 1975, about 1,750 being classified as main roads maintained by the Works Department. Over 2,600 miles of roads are local roads maintained by the Ministry of Local Government, and the balance are maintained by local authorities. More than 4,000 miles of roads are considered all-weather roads, and about 2,500 miles are paved. The government has been surfacing the remainder at a slow pace—100 miles annually in 1974 and 1975. Delays and detours caused by work improvements add to congestion and driver frustration.

There were about 113,000 vehicles registered in mid-1974. Bus service is poor and sporadic although cheap, but taxi transportation is widely available and relatively inexpensive. Bus service throughout both islands is provided by a government entity, the Public Transport Service Corporation, established in 1965 to take over all operations of private concessionaires. Buses reach most towns and villages, and hourly express service is maintained between Port-of-Spain and San Fernando. Free bus transportation is provided for schoolchildren. More than 8,000 taxis operate throughout the country, and in addition numerous private vehicle owners may carry paying passengers in areas not served by taxis. Most taxis are route taxis, which drive along fixed routes like buses, picking up passengers along the way; their fares depend on the distance traveled.

There are two airports in the country, one on each island. Piarco International Airport, located seventeen miles east of Port-of-Spain, operates around the clock and can accommodate aircraft of all sizes. It was being expanded, and remodeling was scheduled for completion by 1978. Piarco is a busy airport as it is a connecting point for air traffic between Europe and the Americas, between North and South America, and between the various Caribbean islands. Crown Point Airport is located at the tip of Tobago; it can also accommodate night flights.

BWIA, founded in the 1940s as a subsidiary of the British Overseas Airways Corporation, was purchased by the government of Trinidad and Tobago in 1962 and has been rapidly expanding its operations. The airline's losses are subsidized by the government, enabling it to compete with major world airlines. Its assets were valued at TT$100 million in 1975. Until 1972 BWIA also owned and operated the Leeward Islands Air Transport (LIAT), a feeder airline connecting the smaller islands. LIAT was sold because of lower revenues than anticipated and was in financial difficulties by 1975. Another government-owned airline, Trinidad and Tobago Air Services, provides scheduled service between the two islands. Its aircraft, however, were frequently out of service for repairs during 1975, often leaving passengers stranded.

The country has nine seaports, a fairly large number for a small area, eight of which are on Trinidad and one on Tobago. Most are special-use seaports. Port-of-Spain is the principal port for general cargo and refrigerated goods and also operates as a bunkering port for vessels traveling between North and South America. Although its channel is deep, very large ships cannot berth; they must anchor far out and use lighters for unloading. The warehouse space had become inadequate by 1975, and the costs of operation were increasing. The Port Authority, which operates the seaport, was attempting to mechanize cargo handling, including the use of a special container terminal.

Pointe-à-Pierre and Point Fortin are almost exclusively petroleum importing and exporting seaports. In fact half of all foreign trade tonnage is handled by Pointe-à-Pierre. Brighton is the export point for asphalt. Chaguaramas and Tembladora are used mainly as transshipment ports; bauxite brought in by small vessels from Surinam and Guyana is stored until there is enough to warrant export by large vessels. Both of those seaports are also used by coastal shipping, and Chaguaramas receives some petroleum imports. Sugar is exported from Goodrich Bay and from Point Lisas, and some sugar goes out from Port-of-Spain. Scarborough is the only seaport on Tobago. No wharfage is available for large vessels at Scarborough, and few call there. Most goods and passengers are taken to Port-of-Spain by coastal steamers for transshipment. The coastal steamers are operated by the Government Shipping Service, a subsidiary of the Port Authority.

Telecommunications are provided by the government and by private companies. The Trinidad and Tobago Telephone Company (TELCO), owned by the government, is responsible for domestic telephone and telex service (telegraph exchange service for subscribers). There were 66,000 telephones in operation in 1974, almost all of which had direct dialing to anywhere in the country. Demand for telephones exceeded the facilities, and an expansion program was begun in 1974 to add about 25,000 lines to the system. The Trinidad and Tobago External Telecommunications Company (TEXTEL), owned jointly by the government and the United Kingdom firm of Cable and Wireless, provides all international services including maritime communications and is also responsible for the domestic telegraph service. International service is considered good. It uses satellites to connect with Europe and North America, a microwave system to reach the Caribbean islands and some neighboring mainland countries, and very high frequency radio to some other areas. There are only three telegraph offices in the country, in Port-of-Spain, San Fernando, and Scarborough, and telegrams are delivered by hand from those localities to the rest of the country.

Tourism

For years tourism was not as important to the economy of Trinidad and Tobago as it was to that of other Caribbean islands. The Trinidad and Tobago government did not pursue tourist promotion as avidly as others did. The official policy toward tourism was guided by three social principles: to preserve national dignity there must be free access to all beaches (that is, no beaches may be reserved for hotel guests only); casinos are not permitted; and no land can be sold to foreigners—it can only be leased on long terms. This principle was designed to prevent speculation.

Yet tourism has shown some increase—total visitors rose from 315,000 in 1972 to 371,000 in 1973—and it does bring in foreign exchange—TT$117 million in 1973, which was more than sugar exports brought in that year. Its contribution to GDP rose from 2 percent in 1960 to about 4 percent by 1970. Mindful of these facts the government has altered its previous policy of not encouraging tourism and has been providing fiscal incentives for private hotel construction. It also owns two hotels outright and has a share in another. The government-owned Hotel Management Company provides services to smaller hotels, and the Trinidad and Tobago Hotel and Catering School, established in 1960, helps to improve service standards and train personnel. The school provides students with practical experience by catering parties and festivities for charitable organizations. Upon completion of the course students are placed in temporary jobs for a probationary period before they can receive their diplomas. Conversational French and Spanish are also taught, and workers who have received overseas jobs are trained before leaving the country.

Tourists come either for the beaches or for the country's cultural attractions, which include the annual Carnival—considered the major attraction—the steel bands, calypso music, limbo dances, and village folklore contests. The best village cultural group receives an overseas trip at the expense of the government as a tourism promotion. Tourists who prefer beaches and the idyllic life usually go to Tobago. Little Tobago Island off the coast of Tobago is a wild bird sanctuary and is occasionally visited by tourists.

The largest percentage of tourists are what are called temporary halt visitors, such as cruise ship passengers. Their stay tends to be short and their expenditure small. Of the tourists who are not classified as temporary halt visitors and who remain for some length of time, the largest percentage, about one-third, usually comes from the United States. A large number of them, however, are Trinidadians residing in the United States who return to visit friends and relatives. They are classified as private home tourists because they seldom stay at hotels.

REGIONAL ECONOMIC COOPERATION

Trinidad and Tobago is a member of several Caribbean regional organizations, of which the most important are the Caribbean Community (CARICOM) and the Caribbean Common Market. Trinidad and Tobago is more committed than other members of the organizations to economic integration and is usually one of the first to implement new measures. The origins of CARICOM go back to 1965, when Guyana,

Barbados, and Antigua signed an agreement calling for a free trade area, a customs union, and an economic community. In 1966 it was amplified to permit the membership of other Commonwealth Caribbean (see Glossary) countries. A supplementary agreement in 1968 turned that original agreement into the Caribbean Free Trade Association (CARIFTA), and the CARIFTA treaty came into force on May 1, 1968; about 90 percent of all imports between members were duty free by 1971.

Original signatories to CARIFTA were Trinidad and Tobago, Antigua, Barbados, St. Kitts-Nevis-Anguilla, Dominica, Grenada, St. Lucia, and St. Vincent. Jamaica and Montserrat joined in August 1968, and Belize became a member in May 1971. The Bahamas did not join CARIFTA but participated in some of its ancillary organizations. The seven territories of Antigua, Dominica, Grenada, St. Kitts-Nevis-Anguilla, St. Lucia, St. Vincent, and Montserrat formed a subregional grouping called the Eastern Caribbean Common Market (ECCM) that entered into force on July 15, 1968, to take advantage of special concessions accorded them by the other members. CARIFTA drew upon the European Free Trade Association treaty as a model and, although it was mainly a customs union, it was envisaged as a first step to greater regional economic integration. Some items, however, were placed on reserve or restricted lists, which meant that they were accorded no tariff reductions or that the reductions were to be made at a slower rate. The Agricultural Marketing Protocol to the CARIFTA agreement stipulates twenty-two products that must be imported from member countries unless supplies in the entire region do not meet demand.

CARIFTA's governing body had little power to resolve the growing number of differences between members, and the initial thrust of the organization was starting to lose momentum. Trinidad and Tobago, Guyana, Barbados, and Jamaica therefore signed a treaty on July 4, 1973, setting up the framework for CARICOM and the ancillary Caribbean Common Market. The CARICOM treaty provides for a common external tariff that becomes effective on a different date for each member, common fiscal incentives, common income tax systems, common company laws, common exchange rates, the joint promotion of tourism, the coordination of economic policy, and the free movement of citizens within the common market. CARICOM accorded special privileges and benefits to the other members of CARIFTA when they joined the new organization. The treaty permitted countries to join either CARICOM or the Common Market or both, and non-Commonwealth countries are permitted to apply for associate membership (CARIFTA had permitted non-Commonwealth countries to establish a special relationship called liaison status).

Belize, Dominica, Grenada, St. Lucia, St. Vincent, and Montserrat joined CARICOM on May 1, 1974; Antigua joined on July 4, 1974; and St. Kitts-Nevis-Anguilla joined on July 26, 1974. The Bahamas, Haiti, and Surinam indicated that they would like to join the new organization eventually, and Mexico signed an agreement creating a joint commission to promote business, science, and culture between itself and CARICOM. Since CARIFTA arrangements were being superseded by CARICOM, a number of the members officially withdrew from CARIFTA and, although no formal declaration was ever made, CARIFTA effectively ceased to exist when all its members joined CARICOM. During the existence of CARIFTA Trinidad and Tobago had benefited; every year it had had a favorable balance of trade with every other member.

CARIFTA's secretariat, located in Guyana, became the Caribbean Community Secretariat on August 1, 1973. It has a number of permanent committees. The governing body, however, is called the Heads of Caribbean Governments Conferences and meets periodically to set policy guidelines. All previously existing regional organizations became associate institutions of CARICOM, including the Caribbean Development Bank, the Caribbean Investment Corporation, the Caribbean Meteorological Council, and the Regional Shipping Council. The Caribbean Development Bank was formed in 1970 by members and nonmembers of CARIFTA. In 1975 bank members included CARICOM members plus the Bahamas, Canada, Colombia, the British Virgin Islands, the Turks and Caicos Islands, Venezuela, and the United Kingdom. When Colombia and Venezuela joined in 1972, they agreed to contribute funds but not to request any loans for a period of five years. The bank adopted rather conservative lending policies and did not live up to its original expectations. The policy was expected to be altered in the mid-1970s after a change in top management occurred in 1973. The Caribbean Investment Corporation was created on June 1, 1973, to channel funds to the less developed members; funds come from the more developed members, but policymaking is in the hands of the less developed. The Caribbean Integration Fund, to be administered by the Caribbean Development Bank, was being set up in 1975 by Trinidad and Tobago with excess earnings from petroleum operations. Further, the formation of a regional agricultural corporation that would be jointly owned by the member governments was being studied. The new entity would be permitted to invest in any member's territory in order to increase agricultural production, process food, and engage in marketing operations. Trinidad and Tobago was expected to be the prime contributor, providing fertilizer from its proposed new fertilizer plant would be its contribution to the new company (see Industry, this ch.).

CHAPTER 9

NATIONAL SECURITY

In 1975 the national security forces of Trinidad and Tobago consisted of the Defense Force and the Police Service. The Defense Force included a small army generally called the Regiment, having an authorized strength of 750, and a coast guard unit having an authorized strength of 350. There was no air force. The Police Service numbered about 3,800 men and was augmented by the Prison Service possessing a staff of about 650. The projected strength of the police force for the end of 1976 is 5,000.

Although generally capable of maintaining law and order throughout the country, the police force was confronted with a rising crime rate and numerous acts of violence generated by widespread industrial unrest. Police were used extensively to break up strike demonstrations. Small-scale guerrilla activities caused some disturbances but were not of sufficient magnitude to hamper police operations significantly. The increasing number of traffic fatalities was occasionally attributed to insufficient highway patrols, but informed opinion placed the major emphasis on the oversaturation of the inadequate system.

There was some evidence of popular mistrust and suspicion of the Police Service. This was prevalent in the East Indian community, caused in part by the small percentage of East Indians in the police force. An important source of irritation in 1975 was the ban on marching, instituted by the government and enforced by the police, the commissioner of police having the authority for restricting or denying marching permits. Modeled on the British system, the police traditionally were unarmed, but their arming has increased steadily since 1970.

The first significant threat to the government since the attainment of independence in 1962 was the series of disturbances in 1970, sometimes called the revolution, which were initiated by a black power movement led by students and supported by other dissident elements. The student movement was modeled on black power activities on American and Canadian campuses. Dissidents included unemployed youth, of which there was a great number, and political leaders who had opposed Prime Minister Eric Williams throughout his leadership in both the colonial and independent periods (see ch. 7; ch. 8). During the disturbances a small group within the army became involved in activities against the government. Order was restored in a few days, but arrests and trials continued for several months.

Participation of elements of the army on the side of the dissidents was attributed by at least one source to low morale caused by the lack of a purposeful mission. The small size and limited resources of the country precluded the establishment of an armed force capable of taking any significant action against foreign aggression. Internal security was primarily the responsibility of the police. The Defense Act of 1962, which established the Defense Force, made no provision for community service activities. Consequently the army had a limited role in national life and in fact had very few contacts with the population prior to the 1970 disturbances. Some community service projects were introduced in the 1970s. In addition the army was used in 1975 to deliver fuel oil, gasoline, and sugar during major strikes in the oil and sugar industries. The coast guard had a more challenging mission, including patrolling coastal areas and providing aid to ships in distress.

As a result of the disturbances, the government took several steps to increase controls over dissident elements in the population. An unsuccessful attempt was made to pass the National Security Act (Public Order Bill) of 1970, which would have severely limited existing civil rights. The Sedition (Amendment) Act of 1971 and the Summary Offences (Amendment) Act of 1972, which did become law, placed some restrictions on freedom of speech and the right to demonstrate. The declaration of a state of emergency by the prime minister appeared imminent during the industrial strikes of 1975, and numerous arrests were made; nevertheless, in the latter part of that year, a substantial degree of freedom remained. Criticisms of the government were expressed openly, the press was uncensored, and marches and demonstrations were carried out within the limits established by law. The report of the Constitution Commission of Trinidad and Tobago, issued in January, 22, 1974, placed great stress on guaranteeing human rights and freedom.

PUBLIC ORDER

The Ministry of National Security

Prior to the disturbances of 1970, public order and national security were the responsibility of the Ministry of Home Affairs. After the declaration of a state of emergency on April 21, 1970, immediate steps were taken to restore order; the Ministry of Home Affairs was abolished and was reorganized as the Ministry of National Security. The responsibilities of the new ministry included the Immigration Service, the Fire Service, the Prison Service, the Police Service, the army, the coast guard, and the National Emergency Relief Organization (NERO). In 1974 the total personnel, military and civilian, of the ministry and its constituent parts numbered about 6,800, and its budget was estimated at TT$50.6 million (for value of the Trinidad and Tobago dollar—see Glossary). The estimates for 1975 envisioned increasing personnel to 7,400 and the budget to TT$61 million.

The Police Service

The Police Service has existed from colonial times to the present and developed the main features of its current organization under British rule. Consequently organization, regulations, procedures, and uniforms reflect British models adapted to a tropical setting. Organized as the Trinidad Constabulary Force in the early decades of the twentieth century. it became the Trinidad and Tobago Police Force in 1938 and the Police Service in 1965. The Police Service Act of 1965 provided the legal basis for the mission of the service, staffing, pay and allowances, retirement system, and related matters.

The act established two schedules of police officers: commissioned officers, which include the commissioner of police, deputy commissioners, assistant commissioners, senior superintendents, superintendents, and assistant superintendents; and noncommissioned ranks, which consist of inspectors, sergeants, corporals, and constables. In 1974 the total police service professional and administrative staff of 3,800 included about 2,400 holding the rank of constable.

The Police Service was charged with the maintenance of public order and internal security, the prevention and detection of crime, the apprehension of offenders, and the control of traffic. Ceremonial duties related to the governor general's office, formerly a police function, had been assigned to the Regiment in 1962. After 1970 the police once again were charged with those duties.

The Police Service is centralized at the national level with headquarters at Port-of-Spain. The service is headed by the commissioner of police, assisted by three deputy commissioners. The commissioner and deputy commissioners are appointed by the governor general with the advice of the prime minister. The deputy commissioner for administration supervises finance, personnel, training, the highway patrol in the northern part of the country, transport, telecommunications, and the mounted branch. The deputy commissioner for operations is responsible for police units throughout the country and prevention and detection of crime. He is assisted by an assistant commissioner for crime who supervises the criminal records office and the criminal investigations department. The third deputy commissioner is in charge of the Special Branch, which is concerned with intelligence, subversion, and similar matters.

In 1962 the country was divided into six police divisions: northwestern, northern, central, southern, southwestern, and Tobago. A total of sixty police stations were located in towns and villages throughout the country. By 1975 the number of divisions had been increased to nine, and the Police Service was organized into a north unit, operated from the central headquarters in Port-of-Spain, and a south unit, headquartered in San Fernando. Locations of individual stations have been changed from time to time to meet changing local needs. Government quarters are provided for married commissioned and noncommissioned personnel at major stations. A traffic branch is located in Port-of-Spain and a training school in St. James Barracks, St. James, the former headquarters of British troops in Trinidad. In 1975 special units included a predial larceny mobile patrol charged with the control of theft from landed estates, an estate police unit called the antisquatting brigade assigned to prevent illegal settling on private lands, and the police band.

A volunteer reserve police force, called the special reserve police, was organized in 1939 to assist the regular police. In 1975 its strength was about 660, and its members, located throughout Trinidad and Tobago, were attached to the division of the regular police. The special reserve police were under the jurisdiction of the commissioner of police and were commanded by a senior superintendent.

In addition to the national Police Service, Port-of-Spain maintains a municipal police force of about forty men. They are charged primarily with the protection of buildings, parks, and other installations under municipal jurisdiction.

In spite of the large East Indian population, the Police Service consists predominantly of Negroes. At the time of independence East Indian membership in the service was estimated at 2.5 percent, and the figure has changed very slowly since that time. One source placed it at 4.7 percent in 1965, and in 1975 the force was still reported to be overwhelmingly Negro. Various explanations have been given for this imbalance. Until recently the East Indian population was predominantly rural, more interested in keeping its children to labor on the plantations than in striving to provide them with the education needed to qualify for government service. Both qualifications and selection procedures favored the Negro population. Minimum requirements for height and chest measurements excluded many East Indians because of their smaller stature. Screening of applicants was generally done by authorities, most of whom were Negro. With the rise of an educated professional and business class in the East Indian population and the elimination of the differences in educational opportunities, the continuing low representation of East Indians in the Police Service was attributed by at least one observer to ethnic discrimination.

The Trinidad and Tobago (Constitution) Order in Council of 1962 established a Public Service Commission to appoint persons to public positions and to exercise disciplinary control over them, and a Police Service Commission to carry out the corresponding responsibilities in the police force. The chairman or deputy chairman of the Public Service Commission serves as chairman of the Police Service Commission. The other four members are appointed by the governor general with the advice of the prime minister. In its 1974 report the constitution commission recommended that the Police Service Commission be renamed the Protective Services Commission and that the prison and fire

246

services, which were under the jurisdiction of the Public Service Commission, be transferred to protective services. Action on the recommendation was still pending in 1975.

Police recruits were assigned to St. James Barracks for an initial training program of several months duration. Training programs at the advanced level were also provided, and some experienced officers were sent abroad for specialized training. For example, from 1971 to 1975 nine officers were sent to the United States. The International Police Academy, the United States Border Patrol Academy, the United States Naval Training Center in Illinois, and the United States Bureau of Narcotics and Dangerous Drugs participated in the training programs.

The Police Service Act authorized the formation of a police association empowered to represent the police in discussions with the government about pay, allowances, grievances, and other matters of concern to the service. Members of the Police Service are forbidden to make public statements on controversial matters except within narrowly defined limits and with the prior approval of the commissioner of police.

Incidence of Crime

A summary of crime statistics for the 1962–72 period appeared in the Trinidad and Tobago *Annual Statistical Digest 1971–72*. Crimes were classified in three categories: serious crimes, minor crimes, and minor offenses. Serious crimes included murder, manslaughter, felonious wounding, other crimes against the person, housebreaking and burglary, grand larceny (more than TT$96), forgery, perjury, unlawful assembly, riot, treason, sedition, and violations of current laws. Minor crimes were defined as indecent assault and assault on police, embezzlement, false pretenses, petty larceny, unlawful possession and entrance, possession of housebreaking instruments, and wounding and assault causing bodily harm. Minor offenses included simple assault, breaches of the peace, gambling, offenses under shop hours ordinances, and numerous others not separately classified.

During the 1962–72 period reports to the police on serious crimes showed an increase of almost 175 percent (see table 12). The increase in prosecutions and convictions was much smaller, 77 percent and 30 percent respectively. The convictions secured in 1972 for serious crimes were about 10 percent of the number of serious crimes reported to the police in the same year. Minor crimes and offenses fluctuated during the period, and the convictions in both categories decreased.

The statistical digest showed that an increase of almost 200 percent in serious crime was attributable primarily to crimes against property. Prosecutions for murder and manslaughter showed relatively little change, averaging about sixty-eight cases per year.

The Narcotics Control Ordinance of January 1, 1965, included marijuana as a scheduled narcotic; penalties ranged up to eighteen months on summary conviction for possession and up to seven years for conviction for trafficking. The number of convictions had risen sharply since 1968, reaching 610 in 1973 in contrast to well under 100 cases per year from 1965 to 1968.

Prosecuted traffic cases decreased from 26,000 in 1963 to 23,000 in 1972. Newspaper reports in 1975, however, indicated a growing concern with the traffic problem; deaths resulting from traffic accidents showed an increase over the previous year.

Criminal Procedure

The legal and judicial systems of Trinidad and Tobago are based on British models. Spanish law was followed until 1845 when the Spanish system was repealed and replaced by the British. All common law, doctrines of equity, and general statutes that were in force in England on March 1, 1848, became applicable to Trinidad. English common law and doctrines of equity originating between 1848 and 1962 were generally accepted by the Trinidad and Tobago courts but were not necessarily binding. English statutes of that period were applicable to Trinidad and Tobago if they so stated.

Lawyers admitted to practice in the United Kingdom were entitled to practice in Trinidad and Tobago, and graduates of certain listed universities were exempt from taking examinations before the Trinidad and Tobago Law Society. Legal training is conducted by the Council of Legal Education (CLE) of the University of the West Indies. The director of the CLE is located at the Mona campus in Jamaica, and a deputy director is in charge of the CLE at the St. Augustine campus in Trinidad.

The Constitution of 1962 gave comprehensive authority over criminal cases to the attorney general. Specifically the attorney general was empowered to institute criminal proceedings according to the laws of Trinidad and Tobago, take over proceedings instituted by any other authority, or discontinue, at any stage before judgment was delivered, and proceedings instituted by himself or another authority. In exercising these powers he was not subject to direction or control by any other authority.

A court system was established to deal with civil and criminal cases at all levels: justices of the peace at the lowest level, magistrates' courts, and the Supreme Court of the Judicature. The latter consists of the High Court, which has original jurisdiction, and the Court of Appeal (see ch. 7). A number of problems, however, are inherent in the system. All police officers having the rank of inspector or higher are ex officio justices of the peace, but they do not "in any way act judicially as a Justice, either in any court or in any other manner, except when especially appointed so to act." The lower level of judicial administration is performed by the magistrates, who also serve as petty civil judges. They exercise a wide summary jurisdiction in criminal cases. On the civil side they are limited to cases involving petty claims. Consequently a large number of relatively minor cases overcrowd the High Court, which is the next level

Table 12. Trinidad and Tobago, Incidence of Crime by Category, 1962 and 1972*

	1962	1972	Percent Change
Total Crimes Reported			
Serious crimes	2,619	7,143	+173
Minor crimes	10,189	10,323	+1
Minor offenses	36,008	31,405	−13
Prosecutions Instituted			
Serious crimes	1,179	2,092	+77
Minor crimes	3,039	2,937	−3
Minor offenses	12,780	8,973	−30
Trials Pending at End of Year			
Serious crimes	711	1,355	+91
Minor crimes	1,621	1,451	−10
Minor offenses	7,062	3,411	−52
Convictions			
Serious crimes	567	737	+30
Minor crimes	1,599	1,486	−7
Minor offenses	6,462	5,562	−14

* Does not include traffic violations.

Source: Based on information from Trinidad and Tobago, Central Statistical Office, *Annual Statistical Digest 1971/72*, Port-of-Spain, November 1973, p. 59.

of jurisdiction. The Court of Appeal must hear appeals that originate in the magistrates' courts, the High Court, the Industrial Court (which rules on industry and labor disputes), and the Income Tax Appeals Board. Decisions of the Court of Appeal, especially in cases involving capital punishment, may be appealed to the judical committee of the Privy Council in London. As early as 1966 Sir Hugh Wooding, the chief justice, pointed out that the entire legal and judicial system should be overhauled to reflect the needs of the social order of Trinidad and Tobago rather than to reflect a general model designed for the "Empire."

Penalties for crime included fines, imprisonment, corporal punishment, and death. Corporal punishment was rarely used, and opposition to it was strong. Nevertheless a case of assault against a woman in 1975 resulted in a sentence of twelve years in prison and "15 strokes with the birch." The sentence in a rape case was seven years' imprisonment and ten strokes. Among juvenile offenders corporal punishment was used only a few times per year. In the eleven years from 1962 to 1972 the death sentence was carried out eighty-six times. Prison sentences tended to be short: of 1,277 persons committed to prison in 1972, only 139 were committed for eighteen months or more.

The judicial process is characterized by lengthy delays. For example, an execution was carried out in May 1975 for a murder committed in February 1972. In the intervening years the case had moved through the High Court, the Court of Appeal, and a final appeal to the judicial committee Privy Council. Of the twenty men in death row at the Royal

Gaol on June 1, 1975, five had been committed in 1973, three in 1974, and twelve in 1975. The major source of delays was the appeals procedure. Almost all persons sentenced to death appealed to the Court of Appeal and if that failed to the judicial committee of the Privy Council. The workload of the Court of Appeal was too heavy for the small number of judges to master effectively. Furthermore, the Court of Appeal could not proceed until it had received the necessary documentation from the High Court; and the High Court was staffed inadequately to provide the records expeditiously.

A law reform commission was established in 1970 to make recommendations for improving and expediting legal procedures. The commission anticipated slow but substantial legal reforms, including reform of criminal law.

A study carried out in an East Indian village found that the village pandit, a local religious leader, played an important extralegal role in the settlement of small disputes. The pandit had no specific authority to arbitrate disputes. Several considerations, however, justified his extralegal activity. As a religious leader, he was interested in helping to maintain peace in the community, and success in arbitration enhanced his general standing in the community, which in turn added to his effectiveness in his purely religious function.

The police and the local courts were effective instruments of social control despite the mistrust of many villagers. The courts had the power to enforce their decisions, whereas the extralegal procedures of the pandit were based on persuasion. Nevertheless, numerous minor disputes between individuals or families were settled through the intervention of the pandit, thereby evading court costs and frequently reducing local animosities. Serious crime was practically never involved in these proceedings.

The Prison Service

The Prison Service Act of 1965 provided the legal basis for the establishment, mission, staffing, pay and allowances, retirement system, and related matters of the Prison Service. The total strength of the Prison Service in 1974 was 644, of whom 531 were classified as prison officers and the others as clerical and other administrative personnel. The estimated budget for 1975 envisioned an increase in staff to 1,079, of whom 1,011 were to be prison officers. The service was headed by the commissioner of prisons and staffed, in order of rank, by a deputy commissioner, senior superintendents of prisons, prison superintendents, prison assistant superintendents, prison supervisors, prison welfare officers, and two classes of prison officers, supported by clerical and administrative staff.

In 1975 the country had three prisons: the Royal Gaol in Port-of-Spain, the island prison on Carrera Island in the Chaguaramas area, and Golden Grove prison near Arouca. The Royal Gaol and Carrera Island were miximum security prisons. Golden Grove was an open prison, designed for first offenders of minor crimes and others well on the way to rehabilitation. From 1962 to 1972 the end-of-year prison population increased from 924 to 1,021. The prison population in 1975 was about 1,100. The female prison population was small, usually less than 5 percent of the total. Offenders under the age of sixteen were classified as juveniles and were not processed through the prison system. They could be committed to an orphanage or to an industrial school. The cost of operating the prisons approached TT$4 million in 1972.

Internal Security

Extensive strikes in the oil and sugar industries in 1975 were accompanied by a number of acts of violence. An unexploded bomb was found under a stage during the 1975 Carnival. The houses of several Texaco Company officials were bombed with considerable damage to property but no loss of life. Fires were set in the canefields. In March sugar and petroleum workers organized a massive march, estimated to involve 10,000 persons, which was to proceed from San Fernando to Port-of-Spain in spite of a state of emergency declared by the prime minister that forbade such marches. Police broke up the demonstrations using sticks and tear gas and arrested union leaders and other prominent participants, all of whom were released on bail within a few hours. Some were subsequently convicted on minor charges and received modest fines.

It was estimated that a total of 45,000 people were on strike in the oil, sugar, electricity, and transportation industries in the spring of 1975, and tension was high. Restrictions on marches were a constant source of irritation between the police and the union. Union leaders argued that restrictions would lead to more strikes. The commissioner of police, who had the authority to issue or restrict march permits, stated that he would maintain law and order without fear or favor.

Major strikes were settled in the late spring and early summer of 1975 relieving a situation that had reached dangerous proportions. The commissioner of police, however, continued to rule unfavorably on actions for marching permits. For example, in response to an application by the United Labour Force for an eleven-mile march on Labour Day (June 19), he authorized the last mile only and added stipulations for control of the meeting that was scheduled to follow it.

Politically motivated guerrilla activities were reported in the 1972–75 period but they were of minor proportions. A small Marxist-oriented group calling itself the National United Freedom Fighters (NUFF) staged raids on police stations, banks, and communication centers. The leader was killed by the police in late 1973, and the group's activities diminished. The alleged southern leader of the freedom fighters, who was sought for questioning in connection with a murder and several robberies, was killed by the police in May 1975. Since that time NUFF for all practical purposes has ceased to exist. At no time did guerrilla activity pose a serious threat to the government.

The greatest threat to the administration of Prime Minister Williams occurred in the spring of 1970 when a black power movement, organized by students of the University of the West Indies (St. Augustine campus) and supported by various dissident groups, initiated a series of major disturbances that led to a declaration of a state of emergency and included an uprising by a portion of the Defense Force (see ch. 7).

The black power movement reflected the widespread unrest at American and some Canadian universities during the 1960s. In 1967 Geddes Granger and some other student activists at the Trinidad campus of the University of the West Indies organized a loose federation of radical students, unemployed persons, and older radicals who had been in the forefront of the opposition to Williams' leadership of both the late colonial and independence periods. The federation, known as the National Joint Action Committee (NJAC), established contacts with other opposition organizations such as the Tapia House Group, headed by Lloyd Best, lecturer at the University of the West Indies and outspoken critic of the Williams administration.

In February 1970 West Indies students enrolled at Sir George Williams University in Montreal participated in wrecking the computer center at the university and were brought to trial. On February 26, 1970, students in Trinidad led a protest march to the Canadian High Commission and the Royal Bank of Canada in Port-of-Spain, terminating in a temporary takeover of the Roman Catholic cathedral. Several student leaders were arrested.

A black power march through the streets of Port-of-Spain on March 4 attracted about 10,000 persons. On March 12 a march proceeded from Port-of-Spain to the sugar belt, terminating at Couva, under the slogan, "Indians and Africans Unite Now." Thousands joined the march en route. On April 6 the police shot a young follower of the NJAC. His funeral drew one of the largest crowds ever assembled in Port-of-Spain, estimated by one source at 65,000. Tensions increased sharply. By April 20 plans had been made for a general strike and massive demonstrations.

On April 21 Prime Minister Williams declared a state of emergency. Black power leaders, as well as prominent labor leaders and members of the opposition, were arrested. A curfew was imposed. Skirmishes with the police, fires, and alarms occurred in downtown Port-of-Spain. Part of the Defense Force, stationed at Teteron Bay, mutinied and tried to organize a march on Port-of-Spain, which was prevented by the intervention of the coast guard stationed nearby.

The exact order of events on April 21 and 22 is not clear. After the declaration of a state of emergency, the commander of the army, who was not at his headquarters at Teteron Bay, telephoned his deputy to warn him about two lieutenants suspected of being sympathetic to the black power movement. The deputy confined the lieutenants to the guardhouse that night, causing substantial resentment among the enlisted men. The next morning another lieutenant, perhaps under duress, accompanied some soldiers on a rescue mission to release the imprisoned lieutenants. Shots were fired, and in the resulting confusion the lieutenants were freed. With the support of some troops, the mutineers seized the headquarters and captured the deputy commander. Attempts were made to organize a march to Port-of-Spain, but the coast guard stationed nearby fired on the exit road and munitions area, thereby preventing the march. The former commander of the Regiment, who had retired in 1968, was recalled to duty, promoted to brigadier, and placed in command of the Defense Force. He took charge of negotiations with the mutineers and, after several days of discussions, the mutiny was terminated, and the principals were placed under arrest.

The ensuing trials failed to establish unequivocally whether the lieutenants were simply trying to improve conditions in the Regiment, as they claimed in their defense, or whether they intended to take over the government. According to one study, many independent observers believed that the lieutenants had treasonable objectives and had established links with radical elements in the city. One of the student leaders who had been arrested after the February 26 march stated in a court hearing, "You policemen should be on our side. The army is on our side. All we need now is your help to seize power."

In the following months the movement was suppressed. Between April and November eighty-seven soldiers and fifty-four civilian militants were arrested and charged with treason, sedition, or mutiny. The lieutenants who had led the mutiny were tried and sentenced, but their sentences were later set aside by the Court of Appeal. One of them appeared in the strikes of 1975 as the head of the islandwide Canefarmers' Trade Union.

Leaders of the opposition argued that the uprisings resulted in moving the government to the right and in constricting the fundamental liberties of the people. In articles written in June and July 1970 James Millette, a professor at the University of the West Indies and leader of the United National Independence Party, stated that the ultimate purpose of the present-day government was to rob the people of their fundamental rights. He maintained that even the conservative business community agreed with his viewpoint. Lloyd Best, speaking in December 1970, argued that Williams could maintain his position only by ruling through terror and that he could no longer tolerate opposition of any kind. Selwyn D. Ryan, a professor in Great Britain and student of Trinidadian affairs, saw in the sequence of recent events—the black power demonstrations, the army mutiny, the imposition of a state of emergency, the reintroduction of flogging, and the arrest of radical black leaders—the end of the Williams era. He pointed out that the young and the alienated were demanding that Williams "move on into history." Prime Minister Williams in an article appearing in a volume commemorating ten years of independence admitted "We have had to strengthen our legislation against subversive tendencies, and to take the necessary steps under the Constitution to declare, more than once, a state of Emergency, where public order was threatened."

On August 7, 1970, the government introduced the draft National Security Act of 1970, which was widely interpreted as a direct attack on the constitutional rights of the people. The bill proposed to regulate public meetings and marches; penalize persons for inciting others to racial hatred or violence or for making unlawful statements; prohibit quasi-military organizations; give power of entry to the police to search for, and seize, firearms; and empower the minister of national security to issue detention orders, restrict the movement of suspected persons, and restrict the right of citizens to leave the country. The reaction to the bill was so universally violent that the government was forced to withdraw it in September.

Failure to pass the act was followed by the successful passage of the Sedition (Amendment) Act of 1971 and the Summary Offences (Amendment) Act of 1972. The constitution commission, appointed by the governor general in 1971 and chaired by Chief Justice Wooding, stated in its report that the chapter of the constitution on fundamental rights and freedoms was a matter of "most anxious concern" to people who submitted memoranda to the commission or attended its meetings and national convention. The commission cited the sedition and the summary offenses acts as arousing fears that such abridgements would continue.

As a result of the strikes of 1975 the government attempted to pass a Criminal Law (Amendment) Bill, generally called the antisabotage bill. There was general opposition to the bill on the grounds that it was unnecessary since existing laws were adequate to prosecute sabotage cases. Action on the bill was postponed several times, and it had not been resolved by June 1975.

The constitution commission submitted its draft constitution in January 1974. A cabinet committee prepared an alternative version in 1975. Both were under discussion by the cabinet and Parliament in the summer of 1975. Both drafts contained significant safeguards for fundamental rights.

NATIONAL DEFENSE

In March 1962 Lord Louis Mountbatten, chief of the United Kingdom Defense Staff, visited Trinidad and Tobago to discuss defense needs with Williams. Agreement was reached that a small defense force, consisting of land and sea units, should be established. The Defense Act of 1962 was passed and took effect on June 1, 1962. The act remained in effect after independence except for some changes in terminology.

Mission, Organization, and Control of the Defense Force

The Defense Force of Trinidad and Tobago consists of an army unit, generally called the Regiment, and the coast guard. There is no air force. The Defense Force was placed under the Ministry of Home Affairs, reorganized in 1970 as the Ministry of National Security.

The mission of the force as stated in the 1962 act was the defense of the country and such other duties as might from time to time be defined by the minister of home affairs. In 1964 the prime minister stated that the purpose of the Regiment was to resist external aggression until friendly help could intervene and to assist the civil power in maintaining law and order and in protecting internal security. In addition he looked upon the Regiment as the symbol of independence.

The authorized strength of the Regiment in 1975 was 750 men, organized as an infantry battalion composed of four companies commanded by a colonel. Logistical and administrative services were organized into one section of battalion headquarters. A loosely organized reserve force was maintained by assigning officers and men to the reserve upon completion of their active duty. Members of the reserve could be called up for duty or training for periods not to exceed twenty-eight days in a year. In case of emergency they could be recalled to active service. In addition to the reserve the Defense Act provided for a volunteer defense force consisting of volunteer officers commissioned directly for the force and volunteer enlistees. The volunteer force could be attached to regular units of the Defense Force. It was projected to be a second infantry battalion but has never exceeded company strength.

The coast guard was formed from the Police Marine Branch in 1962 by transfer of the personnel and launches of the former to the new unit. The authorized strength of the coast guard in 1975 was 350 men. It was headed by a coast guard officer having the rank of commander although the authorized rank for the position, according to the Defense Act, was captain. The equipment of the coast guard consisted of four Vosper Thornycraft fast patrol boats, each composed of a complement of twenty-six men and equipped with light armaments; a fixed-wing aircraft—Cessna model 402B; and two Gazelle light helicopters.

The Defense Force as a whole was commanded in 1975 by a brigadier. Both the army and the coast guard were headquartered at Chaguaramas, the former at Teteron Barracks on Teteron Bay and the latter at nearby Staubles Bay. The Defense Force Headquarters was at Carenage Bay (Williams Bay), Chaguaramas, about four miles east of the other two.

The Chaguaramas Bay area was developed as a United States naval base during World War II. As part of a lend-lease agreement between the United States and Great Britain in 1941, the United States had obtained a ninety-nine-year lease for the establishment of the naval base at the Chaguaramas site in exchange for some ships delivered to Great Britain. The United States continued to occupy the base after the war, using it as a tracking station in connection with activities in the Caribbean area.

Williams, in his role as premier in the late colonial period, placed great emphasis on renegotiating the United States lease as a key requirement in the preparations for complete independence. Chaguaramas had also been proposed as the site of the capital for the Federation of the West Indies. Successful negotiations were completed in 1960, and the United States Naval Base was closed in 1967. The last United States installation will be relinquished in 1977. When the Defense Force was established in 1962, unused and overgrown facilities at Teteron Bay provided a readily available site for the headquarters of the army, while the coast guard took control of Staubles Bay, the headquarters of its predecessor unit.

The Defense Force and the National Economy

Military expenditures totaled about TT$10 million in 1972, which was about 0.50 percent of the gross national product (GNP), one of the lowest figures in the Caribbean and Latin America. Neither the manpower requirements nor the total expenditures are sufficient to exert a significant influence on the economy.

Manpower and Training

Officers for the Defense Force had to be recommended by a board established for that purpose by the governor general. The power of appointment to a commission was exercised by the governor general, acting on behalf of the queen. Enlisted men were recruited officers appointed by the minister of national security. Although the Defense Act authorized enlistment for varying periods, the usual term was six years. A twelve-year enlistment could include color (active) service and a term of service in the reserve. Enlistments could be repeated to a maximum of twenty-two years.

Because of the small size of the Defense Force, military academies could not be maintained. Training was conducted directly through the headquarters of the two units and through subordinate units. In addition to garrison training, the Regiment undertook extensive field training, especially after 1970. Young officers have been trained at Sandhurst and at the United States Army Jungle Warfare School in Panama. Members of the army participated regularly in pan-American games and frequently took prizes in marksmanship.

The coast guard obtained valuable training and experience in connection with the acquisition of the four Vosper Thornycraft fast patrol boats, designed and built in Portsmouth, England. Two were obtained in 1965 and the other two in 1972. The Vosper Thornycraft was originally a ninety-five-foot craft, but some modifications in the newer models changed the length to 103 feet. In each case, prospective commanders and crews were sent to England to participate in shakedown cruises, after which the boats were taken to Trinidad under their own power via Lisbon, the Canary Islands, the Cape Verde Islands, and Barbados. The vessels were equipped with temporary upper deck fuel tanks for the voyage to ensure an adequate margin in the event of bad weather. The coast guard participates when possible in joint training exercises with visiting naval units. Such exercises have been held with visiting British, United States, and Venezuelan ships.

In a statement in 1964 the prime minister emphasized that in addition to military training, soldiers should learn a trade and have the opportunity to pursue other educational aspirations. Thus all the specialized personnel needs of the Regiment, such as barbers, bakers, cooks, carpenters, and plumbers, could be provided internally. Furthermore, upon completion of their military duty soldiers could more readily take their place in civilian life. The evidence indicated, however, that the army did not present an adequate challenge to its men. One observer characterized the army in 1970 as a "well-trained and bored infantry outfit with some NATO equipment, nothing to do but drill, and with no promotion prospects."

Ranks, Uniforms, and Awards

Ranks in the Defense Force generally corresponded to those of the British military forces. The highest ranks authorized by the Defense Act of 1962 were colonel in the army and captain in the coast guard. The Defense Act authorized the governor general to appoint an officer as commander of all units of the force. The commander designated in 1970, who had retired from the army with the rank of colonel in 1968, was promoted to brigadier upon his recall to active duty (a rank not specified in the Defense Act), perhaps to give him a higher rank than the commander of the coast guard, who at that time held the rank of captain. The brigadier was still on active duty in 1975.

Uniforms were originally supplied by the British and in mid-1975 continued to be modeled on the British pattern. Field uniforms consisted of long fatigue trousers and jackets, combat boots, web belts, and visored caps or tropical helmets. Garrison uniforms were open necked, short-sleeved shirts, usually worn with shorts. Dress and parade uniforms for officers and men were utilized as the occasion demanded. Insignia followed British patterns, appropriately modified to display Trinidad and Tobago national symbols.

The government of Trinidad and Tobago has established a series of national awards for distinguished service to the country. In order of precedence they are: Trinity Cross; Chaconia Medal, Gold; Chaconia Medal, Silver; Chaconia Medal, Bronze; Humming Bird Medal, Gold; Humming Bird Medal, Silver; Humming Bird Medal, Bronze; Public Service Medal of Merit, Bronze. The Public Service Medal of Merit, Gold, has been awarded to the commander of the Defense Force, the incumbent commander of the Regiment and his immediate predecessor who was in command at the time of the uprisings in April 1970, and the incumbent commander of the coast guard and his immediate predecessor.

Logistics

Logistical requirements are processed through the administrative and logistical section of battalion headquarters or its counterpart in the coast guard. All hardware—vessels, vehicles, and weapons—is procured from Great Britain. Uniforms and field equipment were originally procured from Great Britain, but in 1975 local production was being promoted. General supplies and equipment and barracks furniture and equipment were produced locally. Financial control, medical services, barracks construction and maintenance, servicing of vehicles, and rationing arrangements were worked out in conjunction with other government agencies. In 1972 Trinidad and Tobago received US$2 million in military aid from Great Britain, the only substantial amount since independence.

Military Justice

In accordance with the Defense Act of 1962 officers and enlisted men on active duty in the mid-1970s were subject to military law until discharged or transferred to the reserve. Members of the reserve or the volunteer forces were subject to military law whenever they were called to active duty for training or other purposes.

Punishments for offenses defined by the act varied from death, at one extreme, to payments of damage or extra field duty at the other, depending on the severity of the offense. Trial procedures could be either summary (carried out by the commanding officer of the accused and subject to review by higher authority) or by court-martial. An ordinary court-martial usually consisted of an officer designated as president of the court and two other officers. If an officer was being tried or if the death penalty was a possible verdict, a court-martial required five members. Sentences by a court-martial could be appealed to the supreme court and, if the latter considered the decision to involve a point of law of exceptional public importance, it could authorize a further appeal to the judicial committee of the Privy Council.

Morale Factors

The trials following the disturbances of 1970 produced strong evidence that morale in the Regiment was extremely poor. The defense lawyer for one of the lieutenants argued that discipline in the army had disappeared, and all kinds of corruption and profiteering were common. He further asserted that gambling and drinking were not only prevalent but were actually encouraged by senior officers.

Beginning in 1970 definite steps were taken to improve the situation in the army and to regain the confidence of the government and of the people. The most important change in policy and procedures was the introduction of community service projects. Activities were concentrated in less populated areas and included help to farmers to bring out their produce from remote and inaccessible parts of the country, reconstruction of bridges that had been washed out by heavy rains, and assistance in building community centers.

In 1970 a catholic priest called upon the Defense Force for assistance in improving conditions in a poverty-stricken village. The commander of the force released seven members of the Regiment and five of the coast guard for full-time work on the project, which later expanded its service to numerous parts of the country. Members of the Defense Force supervised projects including a welding shop, a plumbing institute, a medical clinic, two farms, and a bakery. Training courses were organized for the participants, and some were sent to the university for specialized training.

Conditions of service were generally favorable compared to conditions in civilian life. In times of high unemployment the Defense Force provided at least a limited number of positions at reasonable pay. Although troops in the field endured some hardships, food and quarters were adequate. Officers could retire with a pension after twenty-two to twenty-six years of service, depending on rank. Enlisted men could retire after twenty-two years.

In July 1974 the twelfth anniversary of the Regiment was celebrated in a ceremony at Teteron Barracks, attended by the governor general and other dignitaries. At that time the commanding officer of the Regiment expressed satisfaction at the progress made toward regaining the confidence of the government and the people in the four years since 1970 and assured the government of the Regiment's "uncommitted loyalty and devotion to the country."

BIBLIOGRAPHY

Chapters 1–6 (Social)

Abrahams, Roger D. "British West Indian Folk Drama and the Life Cycle Problem," *Folklore* [London], LXXXI, Winter 1970, 241–265.

————. "Pull Out Your Purse and Pay: A Saint George Mumming from the British West Indies," *Folklore* [London], LXXIX, 1968, 102–201.

Ahiram, E. "Distribution of Income in Trinidad-Tobago and Comparison with Distribution of Income in Jamaica," *Social and Economic Studies* [Kingston], XV, No. 2, June 1966, 103–120.

Akong, Roy. "Pan." Page 89 in Roy Boyki (ed.), *Patterns of Progress: Trinidad and Tobago, Ten Years of Independence.* Port-of-Spain: Key Caribbean Publications, 1972.

Alleyne, Michael. "Educational Planning in Trinidad and Tobago," *Caribbean Studies* [Rio Piedras, Puerto Rico], XI, No. 4, January 1972, 73–81.

Argyle, Barry. "A West Indian Epic," *Caribbean Quarterly* [Kingston], XIV, No. 4, December 1970, 61–69.

Augier, Roy, and Shirley Gordon. *Sources of West Indian History, 1942–1958.* London: Longmans, Green, 1962.

Ayearst, Morley. *The British West Indies: The Search for Self-Government.* New York: New York University Press, 1960.

Baum, Daniel Jay. *The Banks of Canada in the Commonwealth Caribbean: Economic Nationalism and Multinational Enterprises of a Medium Power.* New York: Praeger, 1974.

Bell, Robert R. "Marriage and family differences among lower-class Negro and East Indian women in Trinidad," *Race* [London], XII, No. 1, 1970, 59–73.

Bentley, Gerald, and Frances Henry. "Some Preliminary Observation on the Chinese in Trinidad." Pages 19–33 in Frances Henry (ed.), *McGill Studies in Caribbean Anthropology.* (Occasional Paper, Series No. 5.) Montreal: Center for Developing Area Studies, McGill University Press, 1969.

Bonaparte, Tony H. "The Influence of Culture on Business in Pluralistic Society: A Study of Trinidad, West Indies," *The American Journal of Economics and Sociology,* XXVIII, No. 3, July 1969, 285–300.

Boodhoo, Ken I. "Sugar and East Indian Indentureship in Trinidad," *Caribbean Review* [Hato Rey, Puerto Rico], V, No. 2, April–June 1973, 17–20.

Borde, Percival. "The Sounds of Trinidad; The Development of the Steel

Drum Bands," *The Black Perspective in Music*, I, No. 1, Spring 1973, 45–49.

Borde, Pierre-Gustave Louise. *Histoire de l'Ile de la Trindad, I, 1498–1622 et II, 1622–1797*. Paris: Masonneuve, 1882.

Boyki, Roy (ed.). *Patterns of Progress: Trinidad and Tobago, Ten Years of Independence*. Port-of-Spain: Key Caribbean Publications, 1972.

Braithwaite, Edward. "Jazz and the West Indian Novel," *Bim* [St. Michael, Barbados], XI, No. 44, January–June 1967, 275–284.

Braithwaite, Lloyd. "Social Stratification in Trinidad," *Social and Economic Studies* [Mona, Jamaica], II, Nos. 2 and 3, October 1953, 5–175.

Brereton, Bridget. "The Experience of Indentureship: 1845–1917." Pages 25–38 in John G. La Guerre (ed.), *Calcutta to Caroni: The East Indians of Trinidad*. Port-of-Spain: Longmans Caribbean, 1974.

Briddenbaugh, Carl, and Roberta Briddenbaugh. *No Peace Beyond the Line: The English in the Caribbean, 1626–1690*. New York: Oxford University Press, 1972.

Bryans, Robin. *Trinidad and Tobago*. London: Faber and Faber, 1967.

Bullbrook, J. A. "The Ierian Race." Pages 3–47 in Historical Society of Trinidad and Tobago (ed.), *Public Lectures*. Port-of-Spain: Government Printers, 1940.

Burns, Sir Alan. *History of the British West Indies*. New York: Barnes and Noble, 1965.

Butland, Gilbert J. *Latin America: A Regional Geography*. (3d ed.) New York: John Wiley and Sons, 1972.

Camejo, Acton. "Racial Discrimination in Employment in the Private Sector in Trinidad and Tobago: A Study of the Business Elite and the Social Structure," *Social and Economic Studies* [Mona, Jamaica], XX, No. 3, September 1971, 294–318.

Carmichael, Gertrude. *The History of the West Indian Islands of Trinidad and Tobago, 1498–1900*. London: Alvin Redman, 1961.

Carr, W. I. "The West Indian Novelist: Prelude and Context," *Caribbean Quarterly* [Kingston], XI, Nos. 1 and 2, March-June 1965, 71–84.

Carrington, Edwin. "Industrialization by Invitation in Trinidad since 1950." Pages 143–153 in Norman Girvan and Owen Jefferson (eds.), *Political Readings in the Economy of the Caribbean*. Kingston: New World Group, 1971.

———. "Trinidad's Post-War Economy, 1945–1950." Pages 121–143 in Norman Girvan and Owen Jefferson (eds.), *Readings in the Political Economy of the Caribbean*. Kingston: New World Group, 1971.

Chang, Carlisle. "Painting in Trinidad." Pages 25–37 in Errol Hill (ed.), *The Artist in West Indian Society: A Symposium*. Mona, Jamaica: Department of Extra-Mural Studies, University of the West Indies, n.d.

Clarke, Colin G. "Residential Segregation and Intermarriage in San

Fernando, Trinidad," *Geographical Review*, LXI, 1971, 198–218.

Collens, J. H. *Handbook of Trinidad and Tobago.* Port-of-Spain: Government Printery, 1912.

Comitas, Lambros, and David Lowenthal. *Slaves, Free Men, and Citizens: West Indian Perspectives.* Garden City, New York: Doubleday, Anchor Books, 1973.

————. *Work and Family Life: West Indian Perspectives.* Garden City, New York: Doubleday, Anchor Books, 1973.

Cook, Robert, "Islands of Contrast in the Caribbean," *World Health* [Geneva], February–March, 1974, 16–21.

Coombs, Orde (ed.). *Is Massa Day Dead? Black Moods in the Caribbean.* Garden City, New York: Doubleday, Anchor Books, 1974.

Coulthard, G. R. *Race and Colour in Caribbean Literature.* London: Oxford University Press, 1962.

Coulthard, G. R. (ed.) *Caribbean Literature: An Anthology.* London: University of London Press, 1966.

Cracknell, Basil E. *The West Indians: How They Live and Work.* New York: Praeger, 1974.

Craig, Hewan. *The Legislative Council of Trinidad and Tobago.* London: Faber and Faber, 1951.

Crassweller, Robert D. *The Caribbean Community: Changing Societies and U.S. Policy.* New York: Praeger, 1972.

Craton, Michael. "The Role of the Caribbean Vice Admiralty Courts in British Imperialism," *Caribbean Studies* [Rio Piedras, Puerto Rico], XII, No. 2, July 1971, 5–21.

Crowley, Daniel J. "Toward a Definition of Calypso," Pt. I, *Ethnomusicology*, III, No. 2, May 1959, 57–66.

————. "Toward a Definition of Calypso," Pt. II, *Ethnomusicology*, III, No. 3, September 1959, 117–123.

Crowley, D. S. "Plural and Differential Acculturation in Trinidad," *American Anthropologist*, LIX, No. 5, October 1957, 817–824.

Crusol, Jean. "Trinidad and Tobago." Pages 377–402 in Émile Desormeaux (ed.), *Economie Antillaise.* Pointe-à-Pitre, Guadeloupe: Encyclopédie Antillaise, 1973.

Dauxion-Lavaysse, Jean François. *Venezuela, Trinidad, Margarita-Tobago* (1st ed., 1820.) Westport, Connecticut: Negro Universities Press, 1960.

Davy, John. *The West Indies before and since Slave Emancipation* (1st ed., 1854.) (Reprint, West Indies Studies Series, No. 22.) London: Frank Cass, 1971.

Demographic Yearbook, 1954. New York: Statistical Office, Department of Economic and Social Affairs, United Nations, 1955.

Demographic Yearbook, 1964. New York: Statistical Office, Department of Economic and Social Affairs, United Nations, 1965.

Demographic Yearbook, 1973. New York: Statistical Office, Department of Economic and Social Affairs, United Nations, 1974.

Desormeaux, Émile (ed.). *Économie Antillaise*. Pointe-à- Pitre, Guadeloupe: Encyclopédie Antillaise: 1973.

Dookeran, Winston. "East Indians in the Economy of Trinidad and
Tobago." Pages 69–83 in John G. La Guerre (ed.), *Calcutta to Caroni:
The East Indians of Trinidad*. Port-of-Spain: Longmans Caribbean,
1974.

Durbin, M. A. "Formal Changes in Trinidad Hindi as a Result of
Language Adaptation," *American Anthropologist*, LXXV, No. 5,
1973, 1670–1681.

Ehrlich, A. S. "History, Ecology, and Demography in the British
Caribbean: An Analysis of East Indian Ethnicity," *Southwestern
Journal of Anthropology*, XXVII, No. 2, 1971, 166–180.

Elder, J. D. *From Congo Drum to Steelband: A Socio-Historical
Account of the Emergence and Evolution of the Trinidad Steel
Orchestra*. St. Augustine, Trinidad: University of the West Indies,
1969.

———. "The Future of Music in the West Indies: Folk Music." Pages
38–45 in Errol Hill (ed.), *The Artist in West Indian Society: A
Symposium*. Mona, Jamaica: Department of Extra-Mural Studies,
University of the West Indies, n.d.

———. "The People and Their Culture." Pages 80–84 in Roy Boyki (ed.),
*Patterns of Progress: Trinidad and Tobago, Ten Years of Indepen-
dence*. Port-of-Spain: Key Caribbean Publications, 1972.

Evans, F. C. A. *A First Geography of Trinidad and Tobago*. Cambridge:
Cambridge University Press, 1968.

Evans, Vernon. "The Future of Music in the West Indies: Art Music."
Pages 46–54 in Errol Hill (ed.), *The Artist in West Indian Society: A
Symposium*. Mona, Jamaica: Department of Extra-Mural Studies,
University of the West Indies, n.d.

Farrell, Joseph P. "Education and Pluralism in Selected Caribbean
Societies." Pages 341–361 in Joseph La Belle (ed.), *Education and
Development: Latin America and the Caribbean*. Los Angeles: Latin
American Center, University of California 1972.

Freilich, Morris, and Coser A. Lewis. "Structural Imbalances of
Gratification: The Case of the Caribbean Mating System," *British
Journal of Sociology* [London], XXIII, No. 1, March 1972, 1–19.

Gomez, Albert. *Autobiography*. Port-of-Spain: Key Caribbean Publications, 1975.

Gordon, Shirley C. "Documents Which Have Guided Education and
Policy in the West Indies: Education Comm. Report. Trinidad, 1916,"
Caribbean Quarterly [Kingston], X, No. 2, June 1969, 19–39.

Goslinga, Cornelis C. *The Dutch in the Caribbean, 1580–1680*. Gainsville:
University of Florida Press, 1971.

Goveia, Elsa. "The University of the West Indies and the Teaching of
West Indian History," *Caribbean Quarterly* [Kingston], XV, Nos. 2
and 3, June–September 1969, 6–63.

Green, Helen Bagenstose. "Caribbean Blacks and West African Blacks: A Study in Attitude Similarity and Change," *Interamerican Journal of Psychology*, IV, Nos. 3 and 4, 1970 189–201.

Grimes, John. "Caribbean Music and Dance," *Freedomways*, IV, No. 3, Summer 1964, 426–434.

Gutierrez, Horacio F. *Overview of the Medical and Clinical Activities Performed by the Family Planning Associations of the Western Hemisphere, January 1–December 31, 1972*. New York: Medical Division, Western Hemisphere Region, International Planned Parenthood Federation, 1973.

Hamshere, Cyril. *The British in the Caribbean*. Cambridge: Harvard University Press, 1972.

Harewood, Jack. "Changes in the Use of Birth Control Methods," *Population Studies* [London], XXVII, No. 1, March 1973, 33–56.

———. "Racial Discrimination in Employment in Trinidad and Tobago Based on Data from the 1960 Census," *Social and Economic Studies* [Mona, Jamaica], XX, No. 3, September 1971, 267–293.

Harman, Jeanne, and Harry E. Harman. *Fielding's Guide to the Caribbean, Plus the Bahamas 1974* (5th ed.) New York: Fielding Publications, 1973.

Harris, Wilson. "History, Fable, and Myth in the Caribbean and Guianas," *Caribbean Quarterly* [Kingston], XVI, No. 2, June 1970, 1–32.

Henry, Frances (ed.). *McGill Studies in Caribbean Anthropology*. (Occasional Paper, Series No. 5.) Montreal: Center for Developing Area Studies, McGill University, 1969.

Henry, Frances, and Saberwal Satish. *Stress and Strategy in Three Field Situations*. New York: Holt, Reinhart, and Winston, 1969.

Herskovits, Melville Sear, and Frances Herskovits. *Trinidad Village*. New York: Octagon Books, 1964.

Hicks, Fredrick. "Making a Living During the Dead Season in Sugar-Producing Regions of the Caribbean," *Human Organization*, XXXI, No. 1, Spring 1972, 73–81.

Higman, B. W. "The Chinese in Trinidad, 1806–1838," *Caribbean Studies* [Rio Piedras, Puerto Rico], XII, No. 3, October 1972, 21–44.

Hill, Errol. "West Indian Drama." Pages 7–15 in Errol Hill (ed.), *The Artist in West Indian Society: A Symposium*. Mona, Jamaica: Department of Extra-Mural Studies, University of the West Indies, n.d.

Hill, Errol (ed.). *The Artist in West Indian Society: A Symposium*. Mona, Jamaica: Department of Extra-Mural Studies, University of the West Indies, n.d.

Historical Society of Trinidad and Tobago. *Publications (800–1043) of Colonial State Papers from the Sixteenth to the Nineteenth Century*. London: HMSO, n.d.

Hoetink, H. *Caribbean Race Relations: A Study of Two Variants*.

London: Oxford University Press, 1967.

Horowitz, Michael. *Peoples and Cultures of the Caribbean.* Garden City, New York: Natural History Press, 1971.

Hunte, George. *The West Indian Islands.* New York: Viking Press, 1972.

Hymes, Dell (ed.). *Pidgin and Creole Languages.* London: Cambridge University Press, 1971.

Ifill, Barbara. "The Richest Trade Center of the Indies: A Vision of Trinidad's Future," *Caribbean Quarterly* [Kingston], X, No. 4, December 1964.

Inter-American Development Bank. *Economic and Social Progress in Latin America: Annual Report, 1972. Washington: 1972.*

————. *Economic and Social Progress in Latin America: Annual Report, 1973.* Washington: 1973.

————. "An International Project for the Financing of Education." (Latin American Workshop sponsored by the Center for Education and Development Studies of Harvard University from January 29 to February 1, 1973 at Cartagena, Colombia.) Washington (mimeo.).

————. *Socio-Economic Progress in Latin America: Annual Report, 1971.* Washington: n.d.

————. *Socio-Economic Progress in Latin America: Social Progress Trust Fund Tenth Annual Report, 1970.* Washington: 1971.

————. *Statistical Data on the Latin American and Caribbean Countries, 1972.* Washington: n.d.

International Bank for Reconstruction and Development. *Report on Employment in Trinidad and Tobago.* Washington: 1973.

International Labour Office. *Bulletin of Labour Statistics, First Quarter 1975.* Geneva: 1975.

International Labour Organization. International Research and Documentation Centre on Vocational Training. CINTERFOR. (Seminar on vocational training in the Caribbean Countries. Kingston, July 24–26, 1972. Project 115, Montevideo.) 1973.

James, C. L. R. *East Indians of West Indian Descent.* Port-of-Spain: Ibis Publications, 1969.

————. *The Life of Captain Cipriani: An Account of British Government in the West Indies.* London: Nelson Lares Coulton, 1932.

————. "The Mighty Sparrow." Pages 373–381 in David Lowenthal and Lambros Comitas (eds.), *The Aftermath of Sovereignty: West Indian Perspectives.* Garden City, New York: Doubleday, Anchor Books, 1973.

Jha, J. C. "Indian Heritage in Trinidad (West Indies)," *Eastern Anthropologist* [Lucknow, India], XXVII, No. 3, 1974, 211–234.

John, Janheinz. *Neo-African Literature: A History of Black Writing.* New York: Grove Press, 1970.

Johnson, David Meritt. "Cultural Homogeneity and Occupational Multiplicity among Trinidadian Fishermen." Unpublished Ph.D. dissertation. Chapel Hill: University of North Carolina, 1972.

Joseph, E. L. *History of Trinidad* (1st ed., 1830.) (Reprint for the Cass Library of West Indian Studies.) London: Frank Cass, 1970.

Klass, Morton. *East Indians in Trinidad: A Study of Cultural Persistence.* New York: Columbia University Press, 1961.

La Guerre, John G. (ed.) *Calcutta to Caroni: The East Indians of Trinidad.* Port-of-Spain: Longmans Caribbean, 1974.

Laird, Colin. "The Meaning of Art." Pages 69–78 in Errol Hill (ed.), *The Artist in West Indian Society: A Symposium.* Mona, Jamaica: Department of Extra-Mural Studies, University of the West Indies, n.d.

Lamming, George. "Caribbean Literature: the Black Rock of Africa," *African Forum,* I, No. 4, 1966, 32–56.

Lamont, Norman. *Problems of the Antilles.* Glasgow: John Smith and Sons, 1912.

Laurence, K. O. "The Settlement of Free Negroes in Trinidad Before Emancipation," *Caribbean Quarterly* [Kingston], IX, Nos. 1 and 2, 1963, 26–52.

Lengermann, Patricia Madoo. "The Debate on the Structure and Content of West Indian Values: Some Relevant Data from Trinidad and Tobago," *British Journal of Sociology* [London], XXIII, No. 3, 1972, 298–311.

———. "Working-class Values in Trinidad and Tobago," *Social and Economic Studies* [Mona, Jamaica], XX, No. 2, June 1971, 151–163.

Lent, John A. "Commonwealth Caribbean Mass Media: History and Development," *Gazette* [Deventer, the Netherlands], XIX, No. 2, 1973, 91–106.

———. "Press Freedom in the Commonwealth Caribbean, " *Index* [London], II, No. 3, Autumn 1973, 55–70.

———. "The Price of Modernity," *Journal of Communication,* XXV, No. 2, Spring 1975, 128–135.

———. "Small Caribbean Media Avoid Foreign Ownership," *Journalism Quarterly,* LII, No. 1 Spring 1975, 114–117.

Lewis, Gordon K. *The Growth of the Modern West Indies.* New York: Monthly Review Press, 1968.

Livingston, James T. *Caribbean Rhythms: The Emerging English Literature of the West Indies.* New York: Washington Square Press, 1974.

Lloyd, Anthony J., and Elaine Robertson. *Social Welfare in Trinidad and Tobago.* Port-of-Spain: Antilles Research Associates, 1971.

Louis, James (ed.). *The Islands in Between: Essays on West Indian Literature.* London: Oxford University Press, 1968.

Lowenthal, David. *West Indian Societies.* New York: Oxford University Press, 1972.

Lowenthal, David, and Lambros Comitas. *Consequences of Class and Color.* Garden City, New York: Doubleday, Anchor Books, 1973.

Lowenthal, David, and Lambros Comitas (eds.). *The Aftermath of Sovereignty: West Indian Perspectives*. Garden City, New York: Doubleday, Anchor Books, 1973.

McMurtrie, Douglas. *Notes on the Beginning of Printing on the Island of Trinidad*. Fort Worth: National Association for Printing Education, 1943.

McNamara, Rosalind. "Music in the Caribbean," *The Caribbean* [Hato Rey, Puerto Rico], XIV, No. 3, March 1960, 45–49.

———. "Music in the Caribbean," Pt. 2, *The Caribbean* [Hato Rey, Puerto Rico], XIV, No. 4, April 1960, 69–70, 84–85, 100.

Mahar, John Lindsay. "Trinidad Under British Rule, 1797–1950." Unpublished Ph.D. dissertation. Madison: University of Wisconsin, 1955.

Malik, Yogendra K. "Agencies of Political Socialization and East Indian Ethnic Identification in Trinidad," *Sociological Bulletin* [Bombay], 18, No. 2, September 1969, 101–121.

———. *East Indians in Trinidad: A Study in Minority Politics*. London: Oxford University Press, 1971.

———. "Socio-Political Perceptions and Attitudes of East Indian Elites in Trinidad," *Western Political Quarterly*, XXIII, No. 3, September 1970, 552–563.

Mansingh, Surjit. "Background to West Indies Federation: British Rule in the Caribbean 1920–1947." Unpublished Ph.D. dissertation. Washington: The American University, 1972.

Martin, Tony. "C. L. R. James and the race/class question," *Race* [London], XIV, No. 2, October 1972, 183–193.

Matthews, Thomas G. "The Caribbean: The National Period." Pages 139–150 in Roberto Esquenazi-Mayo and Michael C. Meyer (eds.), *Latin American Scholarship since World War II*. Omaha: University of Nebraska Press, 1971.

Millette, James. *The Genesis of Crown Colony Government: Trinidad, 1783–1810*. Port-of-Spain: Moko Enterprises, 1970.

Mordecai, Sir John. *Federation of the West Indies*. Evanston: Northwestern University Press, 1968.

Morgan Guaranty Trust Company. *Bank and Public Holidays Throughout the World, 1973*. New York: 1972.

Mulchansingh, Vernon C. "A Model Approach to the Understanding of the Transportation Network in Trinidad West Indies," *Caribbean Quarterly* [Mona, Jamaica], XVI, No. 3, September 1970, 23–51.

———. "The Oil Industry in the Economy of Trinidad," *Caribbean Studies* [Rio Piedras, Puerto Rico], XI, No. 1, July 1971, 73–100.

Naipaul, V.S. *An Area of Darkness*. London: André Deutsch, 1964.

———. *The Loss of El Dorado: A History*. London: André Deutsch, 1969.

———. *The Middle Passage*. London: André Deutsch, 1962.

National Academy of Sciences. *In Search of Population Policy: Views from the Developing World*. Washington: 1974.

National Council on Marine Resources and Engineering Development. *Marine Science Activities of the Nations of Latin America*. Washington: GPO, April 1968.

Nettleford, Rex. "Caribbean Perspectives: The Creative Potential and the Quality of Life," *Caribbean Quarterly* [Kingston], XVII, Nos. 3 and 4, December 1971, 114–127.

———. "The Dance as an Art Form: Its Place in the West Indies," *Caribbean Quarterly* [Kingston], XIV, Nos. 1 and 2, 1968, 127–135.

Newton, A. P. *The European Nations in the West Indies, 1493–1688*. (Pioneer Histories.) London: A, and C. Black, 1933.

Nicholls, David G. "East Indians and Black Power in Trinidad, " *Race* [London], XII, No. 4, April 1971.

Niehoff, Arthur, and Juanita Nieoff. *East Indians in the West Indies*. (Publications in Anthropology, No. 6.) Milwaukee: Public Museum, 1960.

Noel, Jesse A. "Spanish Colonial Administration and the Socio-Economic Foundations of Trinidad." Unpublished Ph.D: dissertation. Cambridge: Cambridge University, 1966.

Odle, Maurice. *Pension Funds in Labour Surplus Economies*. Mona, Jamaica: Institute of Social and Economic Research, University of the West Indies, 1974.

Organización de los Estados Americanos. *América en Cifras 1972: Situación Cultural: Educación y Otros Aspector Culturales*. Washington: 1973.

———. *América en Cifras 1972: Situación Fisíca: Territorio y Clima*. Washington: 1972.

———. *América en Cifras 1972. Situación Social: Hogar, Habitación, Mejoramiento Urbano, Prevision Social, Asisténcia Medica y de Salud, y Trabajo*. Washington: 1973.

———. *América en Cifras 1974. Situación Demográfica: Estado y Movimiento de la Población*. Washington: 1974.

———. *América en Cifras 1974. Situación Economica: 5 Precios, Salarios, Consumo y Otros Aspectos Económicos*. Washington: 1974.

Organización de los Estados Americanos. Secretaría General. *Boletín Estadístico*. No. 118. Washington: April 1975.

Organization of American States. General Secretariat. *Image of Trinidad and Tobago*. Washington: February 1974.

———. *Twenty-one Latin American Meals*. Washington: n. d.

Ottley, C. R. *The Story of Tobago*. London: Longman Group, 1973.

Oxaal, Ivar. *Black Intellectuals Come to Power*. Cambridge, Massachusetts: Schenkman Publishing, 1968.

Pan American Health Organization. *Annual Report of the Director 1972*. (Official Document, No. 124.) Washington: August 1973.

———. *Facts on Health Progress 1971*. (Scientific Publication, No. 227.) Washington: September 1971.

————. *Health Conditions in the Americas, 1965–1968.* (Scientific Publication, No. 207.) Washington: 1970.

————. *Reported Cases of Notifiable Diseases in the Americas, 1969.* (Scientific Publication, No. 247.) Washington: 1972.

Parry, J. A., and P. M. Sherlock. *A Short Histoy of the West Indies.* London: Macmillan, 1968.

Pearse, Andrew. "Carnival in Nineteenth Century Trinidad," *Caribbean Quarterly* [Kingston], IV, Nos. 3 and 4, June 1946, 175–193.

Political Account of the Island of Trinidad. London: Cadell and Davies, 1807.

Population Council. *Country Profiles: Trinidad and Tobago.* New York: August 1971.

Price Waterhouse. *Information Guide for Doing Business in Trinidad and Tobago.* Chicago: October, 1970.

Ragatz, Lowell Joseph. *The Fall of the Planter Class in the British Caribbean, 1763–1833.* New York: Century, 1928.

————. *A Guide to the Official Correspondence of the Governors of the British West Indies Colonies with the Secretary of State, 1763–1833.* London: The Bryan Edwards Press, 1930.

Ramchand, Kenneth. *West Indian Narrative: An Introductory Anthology.* London: Thomas Nelson and Sons, 1966.

————. *The West Indian Novel and its Background.* London: Faber and Faber, 1970.

Reynolds, Jack. "Family Planning Dropouts in Trinidad: Report of a Small Study, "*Social and Economic Studies* [Kingston], XX, No. 2, June 1971, 176–187.

Robinson, A. N. R. *The Mechanics of Independence.* Cambridge: MIT Press, 1971.

Robinson, Harry. *Latin America: A Geographic Survey.* New York: Praeger, 1967.

Rodman, Hyman. *Lower-Class Families: The Culture of Poverty in Negro Trinidad.* New York: Oxford University Press, 1971.

Roppa, Guy, and Neville E. Clarke. *The Commonwealth Caribbean: Regional Cooperation in News and Broadcasting Exchanges.* Paris: United Nations Educational, Scientific and Cultural Organization, 1969.

Rubin, Vera, and Marisa Zavalloni. *We Wish to be Looked Upon: A Study of the Aspirations of Youth in a Developing Society.* New York: Teacher's College Press, 1969.

Ruddle, Kenneth, and Donald Odermann (eds.). *Statistical Abstract of Latin America, 1971.* Los Angeles: Latin American Center, University of California, December 1972.

Ryan, Selwyn D. *Race and Nationalism in Trinidad and Tobago: A Study of Decolonization in a Multiracial Society.* Toronto: University of Toronto Press, 1972.

Samroo, Brinsley. "Politics and Afro-Indian Relations in Trinidad."

Pages 84–97 in John G. La Guerre (ed.), *Calcutta to Caroni: The East Indians of Trinidad.* Port-of-Spain: Longmans Caribbean, 1974.

———. "The West Indies and Canada: Maritime Missionary Motives in British Colonies." (Paper Read to North American Seminar.) March 6, 1975 (mimeo.).

Schwartz, Barton M. *Caste in Overseas Indian Communities.* San Francisco: Chandler, 1967.

———. "Patterns of East Indian Family Organization in Trinidad," *Caribbean Studies* [Rio Piedras, Puerto Rico], V. No. 1, April 1965, 23–36.

Schwartzbaum, Allen, and Malcolm Cross. "Secondary School Environment and Development: The Case of Trinidad and Tobago," *Social and Economic Studies* [Kingston], XIX, No. 3, September 1970, 368–388.

Sealy, Clifford. "Art and the Community." Pages 55–68 in Errol Hill (ed.), *The Artist in West Indian Society: A Symposium.* Mona, Jamaica: Department of Extra-Mural Studies, University of the West Indies, n. d.

Sebeok, Thomas Albert. *Current Trends in Linguistics: Ibero-American and Caribbean Linguistics*, IV. The Hague: Mouton, 1969.

Seymore, A. J. "The Novel in the British Caribbean, III," *Bim* [St. Michael, Barbados], XI, No. 44, January–June 1967, 238–242.

Shephard, C. Y. "British West Indian Economic History in Imperial Perspective." Pages 47–67 in Historical Society of Trinidad and Tobago (ed.), *Public Lectures.* Trinidad: Government Printers, 1940.

Simpson, George Eaton. "Afro-American Religions and Religious Behavior," *Caribbean Studies* [Rio Piedras, Puerto Rico], XII, No. 2, July 1972, 5–30.

———. *Religious Cults of the Caribbean: Jamaica, Trinidad and Haiti.* (Monograph Series, No. 7.) Rio Piedras: Institute of Caribbean Studies, University of Puerto Rico, 1970.

Simpson, Joy. *A Demographic Analysis of Internal Migration in Trinidad and Tobago.* Mona, Jamica: Institute of Social and Economic Research, University of the West Indies, 1974.

Singh, Gadraj. "Industrial Relations in Trinidad and Tobago, " Pages 197–201 in International Labour Organization (ed.), *Labour Management Relations Series: Labour Relations in the Caribbean Region.* Geneva: 1974.

Singh, Kelvin. "East Indians and the Larger Society." Pages 39–68 in John G. La Guerre (ed.), *Calcutta to Caroni: The East Indians of Trinidad.* Port-of-Spain: Longmans Caribbean, 1974.

Singh, Paul. "Problems of Institutional Transplantation: The Case of the Commonwealth Caribbean Local Government System," *Caribbean Studies* [Rio Piedras, Puerto Rico], X, No. 1 April 1970, 22–51.

Smith, Bradley. *The Guide to the Caribbean: Escape to the West Indies.* (3d ed.) New York: Alfred Knopf, 1961.

Smith, Michael G. *The Plural Society in the British West Indies.*

Berkeley: University of California Press, 1965.

――――. *West Indian Family Structure.* Seattle: University of Washington Press, 1962.

South American Handbook, 1974. (Golden Jubilee ed.) Bath, England: Trade and Travel Publications, 1974.

Statistical Yearbook, 1973. (25th ed.) New York: Statistical Office, Department of Economic and Social Affairs, United Nations, 1974.

Stewart, William A. "Creole Languages in the Caribbean." Pages 34–54 in Frank A. Rice (ed.), *Study of Role of Second Languages in Asia, Africa, and Latin America.* Washington: Center for Applied Linguistics, 1962.

Stone, Carl. *Stratification and Political Change in Trinidad and Jamaica.* (Sage Professional Papers, No. 01–026.) Beverly Hills: Sage, 1974.

Thomas, Roy Darrow. *The Adjustment of Displaced Workers in a Labour Surplus Economy.* Mona, Jamaica: Institute of Social and Economic Research, University of the West Indies, January 1972.

Tinker, Hugh. *A New System of Slavery.* London: Oxford University Press, 1974.

Trinidad and Tobago. *Draft Plan for Educational Development in Trinidad and Tobago, 1968–83.* Port-of-Spain: Government Printery, 1968.

――――. *Estimates of Expenditures for the Year 1971.* Port-of-Spain: Government Printery, 1971.

――――. *Estimates of Expenditures for the Year 1975.* Port-of-Spain: Government Printery, 1975.

――――. *Second Five-Year Plan 1964–1968 as Approved by Parliament, December 31, 1964.* Port-of-Spain: Government Printery, n.d.

――――. *Third Five-Year Plan 1969–1973 as Approved by Parliament, December 31, 1969.* Port-of-Spain: Government Printery, n.d.

Trinidad and Tobago. Central Statistical Office. *Annual Statistical Digest 1971–1972.* Port-of-Spain: Government Printery, November 1973.

――――. *A Digest of Statistics on Education 1970–71.* Port-of-Spain: Government Printery, 1974.

――――. *Household Budgetary Survey 1971–72* (Continuous Sample Survey of Population, Publication No. 22.) Port-of-Spain: July 1974.

――――. *Labour Force by Sex, Age, Industry, Occupation, Type of Worker.* LF 1–4. (Continuous Sample Survey of Population, Publication No. 5.) Port-of-Spain: May 1966.

――――. *Labour Force by Sex, Age, Industry, Occupation, Type of Worker.* LF 1–12. (Continuous Sample Survey of Population, Publication No. 24.) Port-of-Spain: October 1974.

――――. *Population Abstract, 1960–1970, Including Projection 1970–1985.* Port-of-Spain: Central Statistical Printing Unit, January 1973.

――――. *Quarterly Economic Report, July-September 1974.* January,

1975.

——. *Statistical Pocket Digest*. Port-of-Spain: Central Statistical Office Printing Unit, 1973.

Trinidad and Tobago. House of Representatives. *Budget Speech 1974 by the Honorable G. M. Chambers, Minister of Finance, Delivered January 21, 1974*. Port-of-Spain: Government Printery, 1974.

——. *Budget Speech 1975 by the Honorable G. M. Chambers, Minister of Finance, Delivered December 20, 1974*. Port-of-Spain: Government Printery, 1974.

Trinidad and Tobago Businessmen's Association. *A Businessmen's Guide to Trinidad and Tobago*. n. pl: Carib Publications, 1974.

Trinidad and Tobago Electricity Commission. *Annual Report 1972*. San Fernando: 1973.

Trinidad and Tobago Directory of Commerce, Industry, and Tourism. (1972 ed.) Port-of-Spain: International Publications, December 1971.

Trinidad and Tobago Information in Brief. Arima: Trinidad and Tobago Printing and Packaging, May 1975.

Ullman, James, and Al Dinhofer. *Caribbean Here and Now, 1971–72*. New York: Macmillan, 1970.

United Nations. *Population and Vital Statistics Report: Data Available as of 1 April 1975*. (Statistical Papers, Series A, XXVII, No. 2.) New York: 1975.

United Nations Educational, Scientific and Cultural Organization. *World Survey of Education, III: Secondary Education*. New York: International Documents Service, Columbia University Press, 1961.

——. *World Survey of Education. IV: Higher Education*. New York: UNESCO Publication Center, 1966.

——. *World Survey of Education. V: Educational Policy, Legislation and Administration*. Paris: 1971.

United Nations. United Nations Institute of Training and Research. "The Brain Drain From Five Developing Countries: Cameroon, Colombia, Lebanon, The Philippines, Trinidad and Tobago." New York: 1971 (mimeo.).

U.S. Agency for International Development. *Population Program Assistance*. Washington: October 1970.

——. *Selected Economic Data for the Less Developed Countries*. Washington: July 1974.

U.S. Department of Commerce. "Holiday Calendar Can Aid Business Traveling," *Commerce Today*, V, No. 6, December 12, 1974, 31–36.

U.S. Department of Commerce. Bureau of International Commerce. *Basic Data on the Economy of Trinidad and Tobago*. (Overseas Business Reports, OBR 70–87.) Washington: GPO, December 1970.

U.S. Department of Health, Education, and Welfare. *Social Security Programs Throughout the World, 1973*. Washington: GPO, December 1973.

U.S. Department of Labor, Bureau of Labor Statistics. *Labor Law and*

Practice in Trinidad and Tobago by Norene A. Halvonik. (BLS Report, No. 319.) Washington: GPO, 1967.

Warner, Maureen. "African Feasts in Trinidad," *Bulletin of the African Studies Association of the West Indies* [Kingston], IV, December 1971, 85–94.

———. "Cultural Corporation, Disintegration, and Syncretism in a 'House for the Biswas'," *Caribbean Quarterly* [Kingston], XVI, No. 4, December 1970, 70–79.

———. "Some Yoruba Descendants in Trinidad," *Bulletin of the African Studies Association of the West Indies* [Kingston], III, December 1970, 9–16.

Webb, Kempton E. *Geography of Latin America: A Regional Analysis.* (Foundations of World Regional Geography.) Englewood Cliffs: Prentice-Hall, 1972.

Weisbord, Robert G. "British West Indian Reaction to the Italian-Ethiopian War: An Episode and Pan-Africanism," *Caribbean Studies* [Rio Piedras, Puerto Rico], April 1970, 34–51.

Weller, Judith Ann. *The East Indian Indenture in Trinidad.* (Caribbean Monography Series.) Rio Piedras, Puerto Rico: Institute of Caribbean Studies, 1968.

West Indies and Caribbean Year Book 1974. Croydon, England: Thomas Skinner Directories, 1974.

Williams, Eric. *Capitalism and Slavery.* Chapel Hill: University of North Carolina Press, 1944.

———. *Economics of Nationhood.* Port-of-Spain: Government Printery, September 1959.

———. *History of the People of Trinidad and Tobago.* New York: Praeger, 1962.

———. *Inward Hunger.* Chicago: University of Chicago Press, 1971.

———. "Trinidad and Tobago," *Current History*, LVI, No. 329, January 1969, 47–49 and 54.

Woodcock, Henry Iles. *A History of Tobago* (1st ed., 1871.) (The Cass Library of West Indian Studies.) London: Frank Cass, 1971.

Wooding, H. O. B. "The Constitutional History of Trinidad and Tobago," *Caribbean Quarterly* [Kingston], VI, Nos. 3 and 4, May 1960, 143–176.

World Communications. New York: Unipub, 1975.

Worldmark Encyclopedia of the Nations, III: Americas. (Ed., Louis Barron.) New York: Worldmark Press, Harper and Row, 1967.

World of Learning, 1974–75, II. London: Europa Publications, 1974.

Wrong, Hume. *Government of the West Indies.* Oxford: Clarendon Press, 1923.

(Various issues of the following were also used in the preparation of these chapters: *Financial Times* [London], January–May 1975; *Labour Force by Sex, Age, Industry, Occupation, Type of Worker* [Port-of-Spain], May 1966–November 1974; and *Trinidad Guardian* [Port-of-Spain], January–July 1975.)

Chapter 7 (Political)

Ayearst, Morley. *The British West Indies: The Search for Self-Government.* New York: New York University Press, 1960.

Barrow, Errol, "A Role for Canada in the West Indies," *International Journal* [Toronto], XIX, Spring 1964, 170–187.

Bell, Wendell. *The Democratic Revolution in the West Indies.* Cambridge, Massachusetts: Schenkman Publishing, 1967.

Bland, C. L. "Canada and the Commonwealth Caribbean," *Foreign Trade* [Moscow], CXXVI, October 1966.

Braithwaite, Lloyd. "The Problem of Cultural Integration in Tobago," *Social and Economic Studies* [Mona, Jamaica], June 1954.

Carnegie, A. R. "Judicial Review of Legislation in the West Indies Constitutions," *Public Law* [London], Winter 1971, 276–287.

Davison, R. B. *Black British.* London: Oxford University Press, 1966.

De Kadt, Emanuel (ed.). *Patterns of Foreign Difference in the Caribbean.* London: Royal Institute of Internal Affairs, Oxford University Press, 1972.

Edmondson, Locksley G. "Canada and the West Indies: Trends and Prospects," *International Journal* [Toronto], XIX, Spring 1964, 188–201.

Ferguson, Gale H. (ed.) *Contemporary Inter-American Relations: A Reader in Theory and Issues.* Englewood Cliffs: Prentice-Hall, 1972.

Fraser, Duncan. "The West Indies and Canada: The Present Relationship." Chapter in *The West Indies and the Atlantic Provinces of Canada.* Halifax: Institute of Public Affairs, Dalhousie University, 1966.

Girvan, Norman and Owen Jefferson (eds.). *Readings in the Political Economy of the Caribbean.* Kingston: New World Publications, 1971.

Glassner, Martin Ira. "The Foreign Relations of Jamaica and Trinidad and Tobago 1960–65," *Caribbean Studies* [Rio Piedras, Puerto Rico], X, No. 3, October 1970, 116–150.

Great Britain. British Information Services. *Trinidad and Tobago: The Making of a Nation.* New York: Reference Division, British Information Services, 1962.

James, C. L. R. "Dr. Eric Williams, P.N.M. Political Leader; A Convention Appraisal," *The Nation* [Port-of-Spain], March 18, 1960.

————. *The Life of Captain Cipriani: An Account of British Government in the West Indies.* London: Nelson Larcs Coulton, 1932.

Levitt, Kari, and Alister McIntyre. *Canada-West Indies Economic Relations.* Montreal: Private Planning Association of Canada and the

Center for Developing Area Studies, McGill University, 1967.

Lewis, Gordon K. *The Growth of the Modern West Indies*. New York: Monthly Review Press, 1968.

———. "The Trinidad and Tobago General Election of 1961," *Caribbean Studies* [Rio Piedras, Puerto Rico], II, No. 2, July 1962, 2–30.

Linton, Neville. "Regional Diplomacy of the Commonwealth Caribbean," *International Journal* [Toronto], XXVI, No. 2, Spring 1971. Lowenthal, Abraham. "Toward a New Caribbean Policy," *School of Advanced International Studies (SAIS) Review 1975*, XIX, No. 1, 1975, 5–19.

Lowenthal, David. "Black Power in the Caribbean Context," *Economic Geography*, No. 1, January 1972, 116–134.

———. "Levels of West Indian Government," *Social and Economic Studies* [Mona, Jamaica], XI, December 1962, 363–391.

Malik, Yogendra K. "Agencies of Political Socialization and East Indian Ethnic Identification in Trinidad," *Sociological Bulletin* [Bombay], 18, No. 2, September 1969, 101–121.

———. *East Indians in Trinidad: A Study in Minority Politics*. London: Oxford University Press, 1971.

———. "Socio-Political Perceptions and Attitudes of East Indian Elites in Trinidad," *Western Political Quarterly*, XXIII, No. 3, September 1970, 552–563.

Mau, James A. *Social Change and Images of the Future*. Cambridge, Massachusetts: Schenkman Publishing, 1968.

Millette, James. *The Politics of Succession: A Topical Analysis of the Political Situation in Trinidad and Tobago*. (Three articles published in the *Trinidad Express* June 9 and 16 and in *Moko* July 17, 1970.) Port-of-Spain: Moko Enterprises, 1972.

Mitchell, Sir Harold. *Contemporary Politics and Economics in the Caribbean*. Athens: Ohio University Press, 1968. Nicholls, David G. "East Indians and Black Power in Trinidad," *Race* [London], XII, No. 4, April 1971.

Organization of American States. *First Special Inter-American Conference: Final Act*. (OEA Series C, 1.12.) Washington: Pan American Union. December 1964.

———. *Primera Conferencia Interamericana Extraordinaria: Documentos de la Conferencia*. (OEA Series E, XII.1.) Washington: Pan American Union, December 1964.

Oxaal, Ivar. *Black Intellectuals Come to Power*. Cambridge, Massachusetts: Schenkman Publishing, 1968.

Peach, Ceri. *West Indian Migration to Great Britain*. London: Oxford University Press, 1968.

Phillips, Fred A. "Policies and the Administration of Justice in Newly Independent Countries," *The University of Toronto Law Journal* [Toronto], XVI, Winter 1965–66, 395–405.

Pierre, Lennox, and John La Rose. *For More and Better Democracy, For a Democratic Constitution for Trinidad and Tobago*. Port-of-Spain:

West Indian Independence Party, 1955.

Prieswerk, Roy (ed.). *Documents on International Relations in the Caribbean.* Rio Piedras: University of Puerto Rico Press, 1970.

————. *Regionalism and the Commonwealth Caribbean: Papers Presented at the Seminar on the Foreign Policies of Caribbean States.* (Special Lectures April–June 1968, Series No. 2.) St. Augustine, Trinidad: Institute of International Relations, University of the West Indies, 1969.

————. "The Teaching of International Relations in the Caribbean," *Caribbean Quarterly* [Mona, Jamaica], XVII, No. 1, March 1971, 16–22.

Rao, K.L.K., and G. N. Nagar. *India's Trade Prospects with West Indies with Special Reference to Trinidad and Tobago.* New Delhi: Indian Institute of Foreign Trade, September 1965.

Report of the Trinidad and Tobago Independence Conference. London: HMSO, 1962.

Ryan, Selwyn D. *Race and Nationalism in Trinidad and Tobago: A Study of Decolonization in a Multinational Society.* Toronto: University of Toronto Press, 1972.

Seers, Dudley. "A Step Towards A Political Economy of Development," *Social and Economic Studies* [Mona, Jamaica], XVIII, No. 3, September 1969, 218–253.

Springer, Hugh W. *Reflections on the Failure of the First West Indian Federation.* Cambridge: Center for International Affairs, Harvard University, July 1962.

Trinidad and Tobago. *Constitutional Instruments and Report.* Port-of-Spain: Government Printery, 1970.

————. *Trinidad and Tobago (Constitution) Orders in Council, 1956.* Port-of-Spain: Government Printery, 1956.

————. *Trinidad and Tobago (Constitution) Orders in Council, 1962.* Port-of-Spain: Government Printery, 1962.

Trinidad and Tobago. Constitution of Trinidad and Tobago. *Minority Report.* Port-of-Spain: Trinidad and Tobago Publications, 1974.

Trinidad and Tobago Legislative Council. *Statement by the Honorable Chief Minister, on the U.S. Leased Areas in Trinidad and Tobago.* Port-of-Spain: Government Printery, June 20, 1958.

U.S. Congress. 93d Session. House of Representatives. Committee on Foreign Affairs. Subcommittee on Inter-American Affairs. *United States Caribbean Policy September 1973.* Washington: GPO, 1974.

Vandenbosch, Amry. "The Small States in International Politics and Organization," *The Journal of Politics*, XXVI, No. 2, May 1964, 293–312.

Williams, Eric. *The Case for Party Politics in Trinidad and Tobago.* Port-of-Spain: Teachers Economic and Cultural Association, 1955.

————. *Constitution Reform Speech before the House of Representatives.* Port-of-Spain: Government Printery, December 8, 13, 17, 1974.

————. *Constitution Reform Speech before the House of Representatives December 13 and 17, 1974*. Port-of-Spain: Government Printery, 1975.

————. "Education of a Young Colonial," *PNM Weekly* [Port-of-Spain], I, No. 1, June 18, 1956.

————. "Education of a Young Colonial," *PNM Weekly* [Port-of-Spain], I, No. 13, September 13, 1956.

————. *The History of Chaguaramas*. Port-of-Spain: PNM Publishing, n.d.

————. *History of the People of Trinidad and Tobago*. London: André Deutsch, 1964.

————. *History of the People of Trinidad and Tobago*. Port-of-Spain: PNM Publishing, 1962.

————. *My Relations with the Caribbean Commission, 1943–1955*. Port-of-Spain: Peoples Educational Movement of the Teachers Economic and Cultural Association, 1955.

————. *Politics and Culture*. Port-of-Spain: The Nation, September 1, 1958.

————. *Premier's Tribute to Tagore*. Port-of-Spain: PNM Publishing, 1961.

————. "The Small Nation with a Big Contribution," *New Commonwealth* [London], XLV, March 1967, 107–109.

————. "Trinidad and Tobago: International Perspectives," *Freedomways*, IV, No. 3, Summer 1964, 331–340.

Wooding, H. O. B. "The Constitutional History of Trinidad and Tobago," *Caribbean Quarterly* [Kingston], VI, Nos. 3 and 4, May 1960, 143–159.

————. "Trinidad and Tobago," *International Encyclopedia of Comparative Law*, I, National Reports, May 1973, T27–T30.

(Various issues of the following were also used in the preparation of this chapter: *Daily Mirror* [Port-of-Spain], January 1964; *Embassy of Trinidad and Tobago Newsletter* [Washington], April–August 1975; *The Nation* [Port-of-Spain], 1962–68; *PNM Weekly* [Port-of-Spain], September 1958; and *Trinidad Guardian* [Port-of-Spain], December 1957–July 1975.)

Chapter 8 (Economic)

Ahiram, E. "Distribution of Income in Trinidad-Tobago and Comparison with Distribution of Income in Jamaica," *Social and Economic Studies* [Kingston], XV, No. 2, June 1966, 103–120.

Baum, Daniel Jay. *The Banks of Canada in the Commonwealth Caribbean: Economic Nationalism and Multinational Enterprises of a Medium Power.* New York: Praeger, 1974.

Bonaparte, Tony H. "The Influence of Culture on Business in a Pluralistic Society: A Study of Trinidad, West Indies," *The American Journal of Economics and Sociology,* XXVIII, No. 3, July 1969, 285–300.

Boodhoo, Ken I. "Constitutional Independence and Economic Dependence: Implications of Multinational Corporate Activity in Trinidad." (Paper prepared for delivery at Latin American Studies Association Meeting, November 10–16, 1974 in San Francisco) 1974 (mimeo.)

——. "Sugar and East Indian Indentureship in Trinidad," *Caribbean Review* [Hato Rey, Puerto Rico], V, No. 2, April–June 1973, 17–20.

Boyki, Roy (ed.). *Patterns of Progress: Trinidad and Tobago, Ten Years of Independence.* Port-of-Spain: Key Caribbean Publications, 1972.

Brewster, Havelock. "Caribbean Economic Integration: Problems and Perspectives," *Journal of Common Market Studies* [Oxford], IX, No. 4, June 1971, 282–298.

Camejo, Acton. "Racial Discrimination in Employment in the Private Sector in Trinidad and Tobago: A Study of the Business Elite and the Social Structure," *Social and Economic Studies* [Mona, Jamaica], XX, No. 3, September 1971, 294–318.

Central Bank of Trinidad and Tobago. *Annual Report for Year Ended 31st December 1973.* n. pl., n. pub., n.d.

——. *Statistical Digest* [Port-of-Spain], VIII, No. 2, February 1975.

Commonwealth Caribbean Regional Secretariat. *CARIFTA and the New Caribbean.* Georgetown, Guyana: 1971.

——. *From CARIFTA to Caribbean Community.* Georgetown, Guyana: 1972.

De Castro, Steve, and Monty Dolly. "The Feasibility of Caustic Soda/Chlorine Production in Trinidad and Tobago," *Social and Economic Studies* [Kingston], XXI, No. 4, December 1972, 404–461.

Edwards, O. T. "The Development of Small Scale Farming: Two Cases from the Commonwealth Caribbean," *Caribbean Quarterly* [Mona, Jamaica], XVIII, No. 1, March 1972, 59–71.

Evans, F. C. A. *A First Geography of Trinidad and Tobago.* Cambridge: Cambridge University Press, 1968.

Ferrer, V. O., and D. Toolsie. "Growth Problems in the Broiler Industry in Trinidad." Pages 318–325 in M. N. Alexander (ed.), *Proceedings of the First West Indian Agricultural Economics Conference*. St. Augustine, Trinidad: Department of Agricultural Economics and Farm Management, University of the West Indies, February 1966.

Girvan, Norman and Owen Jefferson (eds.). *Readings in the Political Economy of the Caribbean*. Kingston, Jamaica: New World Publications, 1971.

Hagleberg, G. B. "The Caribbean Sugar Industries: Constraints and Opportunities." (Antilles Research Program, Occasional Paper, No. 3.) New Haven: Yale University Press, 1974.

Harewood, Ainsworth. "Land Settlement in Trinidad and Tobago." Pages 80–105 in M. N. Alexander (ed.), *Proceedings of the First West Indian Agricultural Economics Conference*. St. Augustine, Trinidad: Department of Agricultural Economics and Farm Management, University of the West Indies, February 1966.

Hunte, George. *The West Indian Islands*. New York: Viking Press, 1972.

Inter-American Center of Tax Administration. *Sales Tax in CIAT Member Countries and in the Countries Member of the European Economic Community*. (Studies on Tax Administration, No. 14.) Panama: 1974.

————. *Tax Incentives in the American Countries*. (Fifth General Assembly, Document V–A, No. 1.) Rio De Janeiro: CIAT Executive Secretariat, 1971.

Inter-American Development Bank. *Economic and Social Progress in Latin America: Annual Report, 1972*. Washington: 1972.

————. *Economic and Social Progress in Latin America: Annual Report, 1973*. Washington: 1973.

————. *Fifteen Years of Activities, 1960–1974*. Washington: 1975.

Inter-American Development Bank. Economic and Social Development Department. *Latin America in the World Economy: Recent Developments and Trends*. Washington: 1975.

International Labour Office. *Labour Relations in the Caribbean Region*. (Labour-Management Relations Series, No. 43.) Geneva: 1974.

International Monetary Fund. *International Financial Statistics: April 1975*. Washington: 1974.

International Monetary Fund and International Bank for Reconstruction and Development. *Direction of Trade, March 1975*, Washington: 1975.

Katzin, Margaret Fisher. "Partners: An Informal Savings Institution in Jamaica," *Social and Economic Studies* [Mona, Jamaica], VIII, No. 4, October 1959, 436–440.

Kidd, George P. "The CFTC: Skilled and Expert Mutual Self-help Underdevelopment, and an Expression of a Sense of Community," *Commonwealth* [London], XVII, No. 3, June-July 1974. 9–11.

Le Veness, Frank Paul. *Caribbean Integration: The Formation of*

CARIFTA and the Caribbean Community. (Papers in Government and Politics. Research Series, No. 2) New York: Department of Government and Politics, St. John's University, August 1974.

————. *Development Politics in the Commonwealth Caribbean* (Paper prepared for delivery at the 1973 annual meeting of the American Political Science Association, Jung Hotel, New Orleans, September 4–8 1973) New Orleans: American Political Science Association, 1973.

————. *Regional Integration: The Case of the Commonwealth Caribbean.* (Paper presented at the International Studies Association, Chase-Park Plaza Hotel.) Saint Louis, Missouri: March 20, 1974.

Lovell, Trevor. "Trinidad's Development Project Aids Farmers and Farm Trade," *Foreign Agriculture,* IX, No. 38, September 20, 1971, 10–11.

McDonald, Vincent R. (ed.) *The Caribbean Economies and Perspectives on Social, Political, and Economic Conditions.* New York: MSS

McIntyre, A. and B. Watson. *Studies in Foreign Investment in the Commonwealth Caribbean.* I. Trinidad and Tobago. Mona, Jamaica: University of the West Indies, 1970.

MacMillan, Andrew. "Aranjuez: A Case Study in Rural Development," *Journal of Administration Overseas* [London], IX, No. 2, April 1970, 84–95.

Marahaj, Dayanan D. "The Small Farmer in the Trinidad Sugar Industry." Pages 104–128 in Dayanan Maharaj and John Strauss (eds.), *Proceedings of the Fifth West Indian Agricultural-Economics Conference.* St. Augustine, Trinidad: University of the West Indies, December 1970.

Marczell, Peter. "Personal Savings in Trinidad and Tobago," *Savings Bank International* [Geneva], II, June 1973, 13–15, 17–19, 21–22.

Meijers, H. "CARIFTA and Association." Pages 55–71 in H. Meijers and Ko Swan Sik (eds.), *Netherlands Yearbook of International Law 1970.* Leiden, the Netherlands: A. W. Sijthoff, 1971.

Mulchansingh, Vernon C. "A Model Approach to the Understanding of the Transportation Network in Trinidad, West Indies," *Caribbean Quarterly* [Mona, Jamaica], XVI, No. 3, September 1970, 23–51.

————. "The Oil Industry in the Economy of Trinidad," *Caribbean Studies* [Rio Piedras, Puerto Rico], XI, No. 1, July 1971, 73–100.

Organización de los Estados Américanos. Instituto Interamericano de Estadistíco. *America en Cifras 1974: Situación Económica I, Agricultura, Ganaderia, Silvicultura, Caza y Pesca.* Washington: Secretaría General de la Organización de los Estados Americanos, 1974.

Organization of American States. Department of External Cooperation. International Trade Unit. *The Impact of Trade Policy on Exports in Oil Rich Countries.* Washington: 1975.

Organization of American States. General Secretariat. Department of Information and Public Affairs. *Image of Trinidad and Tobago.* Washington: February 1974.

Organization of American States. Inter-American Conference of Ministers of Labor. Permanent Technical Committee on Labor Matters. *Summary of National Reports on the Labor Situation in the Hemisphere.* Washington: 1968.

Organization of American States. Inter-American Economic and Social Council. *Domestic Efforts and the Needs for External Financing for the Development of Trinidad and Tobago.* (OEA Series II, XIV, CIAP 539.) Washington: General Secretariat of the Organization of American States, 1972.

Pan American Union. *Cacao: The Chocolate Tree.* (Commodity Series.) Washington: 1968.

Price Waterhouse. *Information Guide for Doing Business in Trinidad and Tobago.* Chicago: October 1970.

Rajbansee, Joseph. *Civil Service Associations and Unions in the Commonwealth Caribbean.* (Trade Union Education Institute. Occasional Papers in Industrial Relations, No. 1.) Mona, Jamaica: TUEI, Department of Extra-Mural Studies, University of the West Indies, n.d.

Rampersad, Frank B. *Growth and Structural Change in the Economy of Trinidad and Tobago, 1951–1961.* Mona, Jamaica: University of the West Indies, 1963.

Rampersad, Frank B., and J. A. Alcantara. "Problems of Capital Accumulation in Agriculture." Pages 35–79 in M. N. Alexander (ed.), *Proceedings of the First West Indian Agricultural Economics Conference.* St. Augustine, Trinidad: Department of Agricultural Economics and Farm Management, University of the West Indies, February 1966.

Raulins, Ruth. "Trinidad and Tobago Agricultural Census." Pages 120–133 in M. N. Alexander (ed.), *Proceedings of the First West Indian Agricultural Economics Conference.* St. Augustine, Trinidad: Department of Agricultural Economics and Farm Management, University of the West Indies, February 1966.

Richards, Vincent A. E. "Development Prospects in the Commonwealth Caribbean in the 1970s." Pages 269–286 in David H. Pollock and Arch R. M. Ritter (eds.), *Latin American Prospects for the 1970s.* New York: Praeger, 1973.

Scholz, William L. "Problems Face Trinidad Sugar, Cocoa, Citrus Export Industries," *Foreign Agriculture,* XIII, No. 15, April 14, 1975, 12–13.

Seers, Dudley. "A Step Towards a Political Economy of Development," *Social and Economic Studies* [Mona, Jamaica], XVIII, No. 3, September 1969, 218–253.

Segal, Aaron. *The Politics of Caribbean Economic Integration.* (Special Study, No. 6.) Rio Piedras: Institute of Caribbean Studies, University of Puerto Rico, 1968.

Thomas, Clive Y. *The Structure, Performance, and Prospects of Central*

Banking in the Caribbean. Mona, Jamaica: Institute of Social and Economic Research, University of the West Indies, 1972.

Thomas, Roy Darrow. *The Adjustment of Displaced Workers in a Labour Surplus Economy.* Mona, Jamaica: Institute of Social and Economic Research, University of the West Indies, January 1972.

Trinidad and Tobago. *Estimates of Expenditures for the Year 1975.* Port-of-Spain: Government Printery, 1975.

———. *Estimates of Revenues and Expenditures for the Year 1971.* Port-of-Spain: Government Printery, 1971.

———. *Estimates of Revenues for the Year 1975.* Port-of-Spain: Government Printery, 1975.

———. *Third Five-Year Plan 1969–1973 as Approved by Parliament, December 31, 1969.* Port-of-Spain: Government Printery, n.d.

Trinidad and Tobago. Central Statistical Office. *Annual Statistical Digest 1971–1972.* Port-of-Spain: Government Printery, November 1973.

———. *The Balance of Payments of Trinidad and Tobago, 1973.* Port-of-Spain: October 1974.

———. *Overseas Trade 1973.* Pt. B. Port-of-Spain: December 1974.

———. *Statistical Pocket Digest.* Port-of-Spain: Central Statistical Office Printing Unit, 1973.

Trinidad and Tobago. House of Representatives. *Budget Speech 1974 by the Honorable G. M. Chambers, Minister of Finance. Delivered January 21, 1974.* Port-of-Spain: Government Printery, 1974.

———. *Budget Speech 1975 by the Honorable G. M. Chambers, Minister of Finance, Delivered December 20, 1974.* Port-of-Spain: Government Printery, 1974.

Trinidad and Tobago. Industrial Development Corporation. *The Trinidad and Tobago Industrial Development Corporation, 1959 to 1969.* Port-of-Spain: 1969.

Trinidad and Tobago Businessmen's Association. *A Businessmen's Guide to Trinidad and Tobago.* Carib Publications, 1974.

Trinidad and Tobago Electricity Commission. *Annual Report 1972.* San Fernando: 1973.

Trinidad and Tobago Directory of Commerce, Industry, and Tourism. (1972 ed.) Port-of-Spain: International Publications, December 1971.

Trinidad and Tobago Directory of Industries, 1970–71. Arima: Trinidad and Tobago Industrial Development Corporation, n.d.

Trinidad and Tobago Information in Brief. Arima: Trinidad and Tobago Printing and Packaging, May 1975.

"Trinidad and Tobago Tax and Para-Tax Revenue, 1970–1972," *Boletín Estadístico*, No. 115, January 1975, 22–24.

Trinidad Chamber of Commerce. *The Trinidad and Tobago Building, Construction, and Services 1971 Trade Directory.* Port-of-Spain: 1971.

United Nations. *Monthly Bulletin of Statistics*, XXIX, No. 4, April 1975. December 25, 1972, 89–102.

United Nations. Economic Commission for Latin America. *Economic Survey of Latin America 1972.* New York: ECLA, 1974.

United Nations. United Nations Industrial Development Organization. *Small-Scale Industry in Latin America.* New York: UNIDO, 1969.

U.S. Agency For International Development. Bureau for Program and Management Services. Office of Financial Management. *Latin America: Economic Growth Trends.* Washington: September 1974.

U.S. Department of Agriculture. Economic Research Service. *The Agricultural Situation in the Western Hemisphere: Review of 1972 and Outlook for 1973.* (ERS, Foreign, No. 351.) Washington: April 1973.

————. *Agricultural Trade of the Western Hemisphere.* (ERS, Foreign, No. 328.) Washington: February 1972.

U.S. Department of Commerce. Bureau of International Commerce. *The Caribbean Free Trade Association,* by Raymond S. Yaukey. (Overseas Business Reports, OBR 72–058.) Washington: GPO, November 1972.

————. *Foreign Trade Regulations of Trinidad and Tobago* (Overseas Business Reports, OBR 70–15.) Washington: GPO, February 1970.

U.S. Department of Commerce. Domestic and International Business Administration. *The Caribbean Community and Common Market: Their Implications for United States Business.* (Overseas Business Reports, OBR 75–25.) Washington: GPO, June 1975.

————. *Market Profiles for Latin America and the Caribbean.* (Overseas Business Reports, OBR 74-63.) Washington: GPO, December 1974.

————. *World Trade Outlook for Latin America.* (Overseas Business Reports, OBR 75–14.) Washington: GPO, March 1975.

U.S. Department of Commerce. Domestic and International Business Administration. Bureau of International Commerce. *Trinidad and Tobago.* (Foreign Economic Trends and Their Implications for the United States, ET 74 050.) Washington: GPO, May 1974.

U.S. Department of Labor. Bureau of Labor Statistics. *Labor Law and Practice in Trinidad and Tobago* by Norene A. Halvonik. (BLS Report, No. 319.) Washington: GPO, 1967.

U.S. National Council on Marine Resources and Engineering Development. *Marine Science Activities of the Nations of Latin America.* Washington: GPO, 1968.

West Indies and Caribbean Year Book 1974. Croydon, England: Thomas Skinner Directories, 1974.

"Widening of the Caribbean Integration Process," *Economic Bulletin for Latin America,* XIX, Nos. 1 and 2, 1974, 80–86.

World Bank. *The World Bank Atlas: Population, Growth Rate, and GNP Tables.* Washington: 1974.

"Worldwide Production," *The Oil and Gas Journal,* LXX, No. 52, December 25, 1972, 102–121.

"Worldwide Refining," *The Oil and Gas Journal,* LXX, No. 52,

Zur, Moses. "The Development of Agriculture in Israel and Its Application to Trinidad." Pages 253–272 in M. N. Alexander (ed.), *Proceedings of the First West Indian Agricultural Economics Conference*. St. Augustine, Trinidad: Department of Agricultural Economics and Farm Management, University of the West Indies, 1966.

(Various issues of the following were also used in the preparation of this chapter: *Barclays International Review* [London], August 1973–September 1974; *Business Latin America* [New York], December 1974–July 1975; *Commerce Today* [Washington], July 1974–July 1975; *Financial times* [London], October 1973–July 1975; *Foreign Agriculture* [Washington], March–July 1975; *The Gleaner* [Kingston], February–July 1975; *IMF Survey* [Washington], December 1974–July 1975; *Inter-American Bulletin on Taxation* [Washington], April 1974–June 1975; *Monthly Bulletin of Statistics* [New York], December 1974–June 1975; *New York Times*, February 1974–July 1975; *OAS Chronicle* [Washington], November 1974–June 1975; *Quarterly Economic Report* [Port-of-Spain], January–August 1974; *Trinidad Guardian* [Port-of-Spain], May–July 1975; *U.S. Embassy Miscellaneous Reports* [Port-of-Spain], May 1974–1975; *Wall Street Journal* [New York], July–December 1974, *Washington Post*, July 1971–July 1975; and *World Agricultural Production and Trade* [Washington], March–June 1975.)

Chapter 9 (National Security)

Allum, Desmond. "Legality vs. Morality: A Plea for Lt. Raffique Shah." Pages 330–348 in David Lowenthal and Lambros Comitas (eds.), *The Aftermath of Sovereignty: West Indian Perspectives.* Garden City, New York: Doubleday, Anchor Books, 1973.

Best, Lloyd. "The February Revolution." Pages 306–329 in David Lowenthal and Lambros Comitas (eds.), *The Aftermath of Sovereignty: West Indian Perspectives.* Garden City, New York: Doubleday, Anchor Books, 1973.

Boyki, Roy (ed.). *Patterns of Progress: Trinidad and Tobago, Ten Years of Independence.* Port-of-Spain: Key Caribbean Publications, 1972.

Brash, B. H. M. "The New Fast Patrol Boats," *Trinidad and Tobago Coast Guard* [Port-of-Spain], II, No. 3, August 1971, 14.

Cracknell, Basil E. *The West Indians: How They Live and Work.* New York: Praeger, 1974.

Dishman, Robert B. "Cultural Pluralism and Bureaucratic Neutrality in the British Caribbean." (Paper presented at the American Political Science Association Meeting of August–September 1974 in Chicago.) 1974 (mimeo.).

Dupuy, Trevor N. *The Almanac of World Military Power.* (3d ed.) New York: R. R. Bowker, 1974.

Fraser, H. Aubrey. "The Law and Cannabis in the West Indies, "*Social and Economic Studies* [Mona, Jamica], XXIII, No. 3, September 1974, 361–385.

Hooker, James R. *Anatomy of a Mutiny: Trinidad in a Non-Carnival Mood.* (American Universities Field Staff. Fieldstaff Reports. Mexico and Caribbean Area Series, VII, No. 1.) Hanover, New Hampshire: AUFS, February 1972, 1–7.

Hunte, George. *The West Indian Islands.* New York: Viking Press, 1972.

Lowenthal, David. *West Indian Societies.* New York: Oxford University Press, 1972.

Lowenthal, David, and Lambros Comitas (eds.). *The Aftermath of Sovereignty: West Indian Perspectives.* Garden City, New York: Doubleday Anchor Books, 1973.

Malik, Yogendra K. *East Indians in Trinidad: A Study in Minority Politics.* London: Oxford University Press, 1971.

Marshall, O. R. "West Indian Land Laws: Conspectus and Reform," *Social and Economic Studies* [mona, Jamaica], XX, No. 1, March 1971.

Millette, James. *The Politics of Succession: A Topical Analysis of the Political Situation in Trinidad and Tobago.* (Three articles published in the *Trinidad Express* June 9 and 16 and in *Moko* July 17, 1970.) Port-of-Spain: Moko Enterprises, 1972.

Ottley, Carlton Robert. *A Historical Account of the Trinidad and Tobago Police Force from the Earliest Times.* Glasgow: Robert McLehose, The University Press, 1964.

Oxaal, Ivar. *Race and Revolutionary Consciousness: A Documentary Interpretation of the 1970 Black Power Revolt in Trinidad.* (Schenkman International Studies in Political and Social Change.) Cambridge, Massachusetts: Schenkman Publishing, 1971.

Ryan, Selwyn D. *Race and Nationalism in Trinidad and Tobago*: A Study of Decolonization in a Multinational Society. Toronto University of Toronto Press, 1972.

Schwartz, Barton M. "Extra-Legal Activities of the Village Pandit in Trinidad," *Anthropological Quarterly*, XXXVIII, No. 2, April 1965, 62–71.

Tinidad and Tobago. "Drum Head Ceremony to Celebrate the Twelfth Anniversary of the First Battalion, The Trinidad and Tobago Regiment at Teteron Barracks in July 1974." Trinidad and Tobago Regiment, 1974 (mimeo.).

————. *Estimates of Expenditures for the Year 1975.* Port-of-Spain: Government Printery, 1975.

Trinidad and Tobago. Central Statistical Office. *Annual Statistical Digest 1971/72.* Port-of-Spain: Government Printery, November 1973.

Trinidad and Tobago. Constitution Commission of Trinidad and Tobago. *Report of the Constitution Commission Presented to His Excellency the Governor-General on January 22, 1975.* Port-of-Spain: 1974.

Trinidad and Tobago. Laws, Statutes, etc.

An Act to Make Provisions Respecting the Public Safety, Public Order and Defense of Trinidad and Tobago (Draft Public Order Bill, 1970.) Port-of-Spain: Government Printery, 1970.

Defense Act, No. 7 of 1962. Port-of-Spain: Government Printery, 1962.

"Police Service Act, No. 30 of 1965." Pages 395–427 in *Trinidad and Tobago during the year 1965.* Port-of-Spain: n. d.

"Prison Service Act, No. 32 of 1965." In *Trinidad and Tobago Acts Enacted by the House of Representative and Senate of Trinidad and Tobago during the Year 1965.* Port-of-Spain: n.d.

"Sedition (Amendment) Act, No. 36 of 1971." Pages 235–243 in *Trinidad and Tobago Acts Passed in 1971.* Port-of-Spain: Government Printery, 1971.

"Summary Offences (Amendment) Act, No. 1 of 1972." In *Trinidad and Tobago Acts Enacted by the House of Representatives and Senate of Trinidad and Tobago during the Year 1972.* Port-of-Spain: n.d.

Trinidad and Tobago (Constitution) Order in Council, 1962. Port-of-

Spain: Government Printery, 1962.

Trinidad and Tobago Information in Brief. Arima: Trinidad and Tobago Printing and Packaging, May 1975.

U.S. Arms Control and Disarmament Agency. *World Military Expenditures and Arms Trade, 1963–1973*. (ACDA Publication, No. 74.) Washington: GPO, 1975.

U.S. Embassy in Port-of-Spain. Unpublished letter to Department of State, June 26, 1975, with enclosure. Subject: National Defense and Public Order.

The West Indies and Caribbean Year Book, 1974. (Comp., F. McG. Hislop.) London: Thomas Skinner Directories, 1974.

Wooding, Hugh. "Law Reform Necessary in Trinidad and Tobago," *Canadian Bar Journal* [Ottawa], IX, No. 4, August 1966, 292–298.

(Various issues of the following were also used in the preparation of this chapter: *Financial Times* [London], October–November 1973; *Foreign Broadcast Information Service Daily Reports* [Washington], January–May 1975; *Jamaica Gleaner* [Kingston], March 1975; *Latin America* [London], February 1971–October 1972; *Lawyers of Americas* [Miami], and *Trinidad Express* [Port-of-Spain], July 1974.)

GLOSSARY

calypso—Popular ballad composed annually for Trinidad's Carnival. The genre, dating back at least to the late eighteenth century, is believed to have derived such characteristics as topicality, allusion, and improvisation from African songs.

calypsonians—Those who compose and sing calypsos.

Canboulay—(French: Cannes brûlées; Spanish: kambulé) A ceremonial torch procession in commemoration of emancipation that became a feature of the Carnival festivities.

colored—A commonly used term that refers to descendants of unions between individuals of European and African stock, who may also be referred to as brown or mixed (q.v.).

Commonwealth Caribbean—A term used to designate all present and former dependencies of the United Kingdom located in or adjacent to the Caribbean Sea. Includes Trinidad and Tobago, Jamaica, Barbados, Antigua, the Bahamas, Guyana, Dominica, St. Kitts-Nevis-Anguilla, Belize, St. Vincent, St. Lucia, Grenada, Montserrat, the Cayman Islands, the British Virgin Islands, and the Turks and Caicos Islands. Independent states all hold membership in the Commonwealth of Nations.

county—The principal administrative subdivision. There are eight counties, further subdivided into wards. Island of Tobago is an independent ward, not attached to a county. The city of Port-of-Spain and boroughs of San Fernando and Arima have municipal governments and are not part of the counties in which they are located.

Creole—Historically those born in Trinidad as opposed to those born in Europe or Africa. In current usage a group of people descended from either or both ancestral elements as opposed to descendants of other ethnic groups (East Indian, Chinese, and so forth). Also refers to cultural patterns and language of this group.

Creolization—Refers to process by which individuals or groups are assimilated into Creole culture.

East Indians—Official census classification and a term used to refer to the descendants of indentured laborers from the Indian subcontinent.

fiscal year (FY)—Calendar year January 1–December 31.

gross domestic product (GDP)—The value of output of goods and services produced within Trinidad regardless of ownership, measured in current cost terms.

mixed—Official census classification and a term used to refer to the racial mixture of many Trinidadians. Although this group contains representatives of many ethnic groups, most members contain an appreciable degree of Negro ancestry. Persons of mixed descent who are of Afro-European origin may be referred to as brown or colored (q.v.).

Negro—Official census classification and a term used to refer to the descendants of African slaves. Such persons may also be referred to as black.

non-Creole—A group of people who came to Trinidad after the European and African (Creole) complex was established—about the middle of the nineteenth century. Group includes descendants of East Indians, Chinese, Middle Easterners, and Portuguese. Also refers to the cultural patterns, customs, and institutions of this group, which differ from each other and from those of the Creoles (q.v.).

Trinidad and Tobago dollar—symbol is TT$. Divided into 100 cents. From December 1964 to December 1971 exchange rate was TT$1 equals US$0.50. From December 1971 to July 3, 1972, rate was TT$1 equals US$0.54. From July 3, 1972, to mid-1975 the Trinidad and Tobago dollar was tied to British pound at an official rate of TT$4.80 equals one British pound (£). Rates on other currencies fluctuated daily and ranged from TT$1.84 to TT$2.07 equal US$1 during that period.

INDEX

from, 146, 153, 214, 217; education in, 60, 252; migration to, 21; missionaries from, 59, 106; trade, 66, 204, 205, 235, 236, 242

Canboulay: 50

cancer: 119, 120

Capildeo, Rudranath: 76, 194

Carib Indians: 9, 13, 35, 37, 38, 61, 84

Caribbean Commission. *See* Anglo-American Caribbean Commission

Caribbean Common Market: ix, 5, 235, 240, 241

Caribbean Community (CARICOM): ix, 199, 201, 202, 216, 224; trade, 235, 240, 241, 242

Caribbean Development Bank: ix, 216, 241

Caribbean Free Trade Association (CARIFTA): 199, 201, 211, 234, 241, 242

Carmichael, Gertrude: 167

Carnival 49–50, 110, 111, 114, 129, 134–135, 171, 172, 173, 240

Caroni County: 17, 18, 190, 229; labor force, 29, 118

Caroni Plain: 9, 15

Caroni River: 8, 10, 11, 12

Caroni Sugar Company: 26

Carr Ernest: 166

Carrera Island: 250

Cascade River: 18

cascadura: 13

cassava: 37, 38

caste system: 86, 105

censuses: 3, 17, 19, 20, 25, 36, 43; agriculture, 226, 231; education, 58

censorship: 176, 178

Central Bank: 208, 217, 219, 221

Central Statistical Office: 20, 31, 129, 208

Cerro del Aripo: 9

Chacachacare Island: 10

Chacon, José María: 42, 43, 44, 45

chaconia: 12

Chaguaramas area: 211, 233, 250, 255, 256; industry, 224, 239; naval base, 71, 76, 135, 205

Chambers, George: 198

Chang, Carlisle: 174

Charles, Faustin: 166

Chase, Oswald: 175

chickens: 112, 232, 237

children: 111, 136; child labor, 29, 141; illegitimacy, 20, 97, 102; status, 101, 102

China, People's Republic of: 200, 203, 204, 234

Chinese people: vii, viii, 3, 29, 53, 80, 82, 84, 87, 88, 90, 91; employment, 236; language, 181; religion, 103; social class, 95, 98

Christians (*see also* Anglicans; Protestants; Roman Catholics): viii, 79, 83, 85, 86, 89, 92, 97, 98, 100, 103–104; private schools, 138

church and state relations: 172, 193

Church of England. *See* Anglicans

Cipriani, Andrew Arthur: 58, 65, 66, 67, 68, 72, 193

Citizens Home Rule Party: 69

citizenship: 186

citrus fruit: 229, 230, 234, 235

civil rights and liberties: 103, 176, 185, 186, 244, 251, 254

civil service: 8, 28, 29, 30, 34, 94, 126, 189; unions, 208

Clark, Ellis: 188

Clarkson, Thomas: 47

climate: 14–15

clothing: 109, 114, 133, 235

coast guard: 243, 244, 253, 254, 256

coconuts: 229, 231

cocorico: 12

coffee: 44, 204, 229, 230, 231

Colombia: 242

Columbia Broadcasting System: 179

Columbus, Christopher: 1, 9, 35, 36, 60

Columbus, Diego: 38

Commonwealth Caribbean: viii, ix, 9, 111, 199, 201, 241

Commonwealth of Nations: ix, 1, 199, 213

communications (*see also* newspapers; radio and television; telephone and telegraph services): ix, 27, 211

communist countries (*see also* China, People's Republic of; Soviet Union): 5, 200, 203–204, 234

constitutions: 184–185, 186, 190, 198, 246, 254; elections, 195; rights, 103, 176

construction industry: 13, 224; employment, 27, 28, 31

consumer goods: 130, 131, 133, 207, 224, 236

cookery: 113

coolies: 54, 85

cooperatives: 128, 219, 231, 236

Corinth Teachers Training College. 153

cost of living: 119, 130, 131; price controls, 207

cotton: 38, 44

counties: ix, 8, 190

Courland: 1, 61; River, 9; Valley, 19

courts: ix, 46, 190, 248

Couva: 38

Creole dialect (*see also* French creoles): 139, 161, 163, 165; grammar, 58

Creoles: vii, 83–84, 95; class, 81, 99; culture, 86, 87, 88, 90, 92, 96, 138; employment, 52, 55; religion, viii, 57; social system, 77, 78, 91, 102

crime and punishment: 71, 243, 245, 247–249
Cromwell, Joseph: 175
crops: 112, 226, 229–231
Crown Lands Development Project: 18, 228, 232
CSO. *See* Central Statistical Office
Cuba: 200, 201, 202, 203, 209; trade, 234
Cumano: 49
currency: ix, 220–221

dasheen: 113
de Berrio, Don Antonio: 39
de Berrio, Fernando: 39
de las Casas, Bartolomé: 37, 38, 40
death rate: vii, 20, 21, 120, 122
Defense Force: x, 243, 244, 254, 259; mutiny, 252; uniforms, 114, 257
Democratic Action Congress: 5, 195
Democratic Labour Party (DLP): ix, 4, 75, 76, 183, 192, 193, 194, 195
development plans (*see also* Caribbean Development Bank; Crown Lands Development Project; Draft Plan for Educational Development): 145, 210, 211, 216, 218, 226; Second Five-Year Plan, 23; Third Five-Year Plan, 14, 178
diabetes: 119
Diego Martin River: 18, 117
diet and nutrition (*see also* foods): viii, 3, 111–113, 233
disease: viii, 2, 62, 110, 119–121
domestic trade: 27, 88, 236–237; retailing ownership, 210
Dominica: 48, 241
Dominican Republic: 201
Donaldson Institute. *See* John S. Donaldson Technical Institute
douglas: 88, 93
Draft Plan for Educational Development: 137, 146, 150, 151, 153
Dragons Mouth: 9, 10, 37

East Indians (*see also* Hindus; Muslims): vii, 78, 79, 115, 116, 134, 169, 171, 182, 243; class and status, 93, 94, 95, 96, 97, 108, 246; diet, 111, 112; employment, 29, 92, 98, 230, 236; politics, 67, 71, 72, 73; population, 3, 21, 82; religion, viii, 103, 105, 106; schools, 60, 73, 90, 138, 140, 141, 142; social system, 77, 79, 81, 85–87, 91, 92, 101, 102, 131, 136, 250
Eastern Caribbean Institute of Agriculture and Forestry: 151
economy: ix, 2, 207–209
Ecuador: 236
education (*see also* schools): viii, 30, 58–60,

131, 133, 140–160, 238, 257; budget, 212; means of mobility, 94; unemployment and, 32–33
Edwards, Julia: 173
El Dorado legend: 39
electricity: 110, 117, 222, 225
Elliot, Charles: 57
emergency powers: 186, 244, 251, 252
emigration (*see also* immigration): vii, 2, 7, 21, 25, 30, 34, 118, 123
England. *See* Great Britain
English language: vii, 46, 71, 73, 78, 79, 95, 141, 148; newspapers, 181; Trinidad English, 107; 108, 173
Erin Point: 37
ethnic groups (*see also* Creoles; East Indians; indigenous peoples; Middle Easterners; Negroes; Portuguese people; white population): vii, viii, 3, 4
Export-Import Bank: 214
exports: x, 14, 233, 235; petroleum products, 36, 63, 222; sugar, 36, 43, 213, 234

Falquez, Manuel: 42, 44
family: 78, 87, 100–103
family planning: 20, 23–25, 121, 125
Federation of the West Indies: 1, 22, 36, 75, 76, 185, 201
fertilizers: 223, 228, 242
festivals. *See* Carnival; holidays
fiscal incentives: 211, 218, 240, 241
fiscal year: 212
fish and fishing (*see also* territorial waters): 13, 27, 100, 111, 132, 202, 211; consumption as food, 112, 129, 133; industry, 232–233; seasonal work, 25, 26
Fletcher, Murchisson: 68, 70
folk music and dancing: 135, 136
foods: 129, 131, 133; cultural symbol, 86, 87; imports, 112, 234; meat, 231, 232, 236; processing, 223, 224
Ford Foundation: 31
foreign aid (*see also* International Bank for Reconstruction and Development): given, x, 216; received, 145, 146, 199, 216, 258
foreign debt: 214
foreign oil companies: 68, 217, 222
foreign relations: 5, 184, 198–205, 257
foreign trade (*see also* exports; imports): ix, 199, 203–204, 233–236
forestry: 12, 151, 227, 233
Forster Commission: 69
France: 1, 36, 39, 42, 44, 48, 61; trade, 40, 43
Fraser, Lionel: 167
French Creoles: viii, 95; patois, 9, 79, 107, 108, 170

Vitoria, Francisco de: 38
vocational and technical education: viii, 2, 30, 140, 144, 146, 147, 151, 156; vocational, 145, 148, 150, 152, 153, 155, 160
voting machines: 184, 193, 194, 197

wages and salaries: 28, 129, 130, 189; oil industry, 63–64; sugar plantations, 54
Wan, Edwin Hing: 175
Warner, Charles: 57
water buffalo: 231, 232
water supply: 65, 110, 116–117
water transport: ix, 232, 239
weapons: 243, 258
weights and measures: 237
welfare: 126–128
West Germany: 181, 236
West Indian National Party: 72
white population: vii, 3, 29, 82; social class, 80, 81, 84, 90, 91, 94, 95–96
Wilberforce, William: 47
wildlife: 12–13, 233
Williams, Prime Minister Eric: 5, 74–75, 199;
author and scholar, 74, 76, 139, 167, 169; political role, 64–65, 192, 198; prime minister, 185, 188, 201, 202, 203, 255; quoted, 58, 253; suppression of civil rights, 177, 178, 244, 251, 252; travels, 204
Windward Islands: 22
women (see also marriage): 20, 83, 101, 114, 132, 251; education, viii, 159; employment, 8, 29, 30, 32, 100, 129–130, 156; health, 111; life expectancy, 21
Wood, E. F. L.: 66
wood products and lumber. See forestry
Woodford Square: 74
Wooding Commission: 183, 197, 198, 249, 254
work permits: 29
World Bank. See International Bank for Reconstruction and Development
World War II: 71

yaws: 120
young people: 33–34; juvenile crime, 249, 251

Zimbabwe: 203

PUBLISHED AREA HANDBOOKS

550–65	Afghanistan	550–68	Iran
550–98	Albania	550–31	Iraq
550–44	Algeria	550–25	Israel
550–59	Angola	550–69	Ivory Coast
550–73	Argentina	550–177	Jamaica
550–176	Austria	550–30	Japan
550–169	Australia	550–34	Jordan
550–175	Bangladesh	550–56	Kenya
550–170	Belgium	550–50	Khmer Republic (Cambodia)
550–66	Bolivia	550–81	Korea, North
550–20	Brazil	550–41	Korea, South
550–168	Bulgaria	550–58	Laos
550–61	Burma	550–24	Lebanon
550–83	Burundi	550–38	Liberia
550–166	Cameroon	550–85	Libya
550–96	Ceylon	550–163	Malagasy Republic
550–159	Chad	550–172	Malawi
550–77	Chile	550–45	Malaysia
550–60	China, People's Rep. of	550–161	Mauritania
550–63	China, Rep. of	550–79	Mexico
550–26	Colombia	550–76	Mongolia
550–67	Congo, Democratic Republic of (Zaire)	550–49	Morocco
		550–64	Mozambique
550–91	Congo, People's Republic of	550–35	Nepal, Bhutan and Sikkim
550–90	Costa Rica	550–88	Nicaragua
550–152	Cuba	550–157	Nigeria
550–22	Cyprus	550–94	Oceania
550–158	Czechoslovakia	550–48	Pakistan
550–54	Dominican Republic	550–46	Panama
550–155	East Germany	550–156	Paraguay
550–52	Ecuador	550–92	Peripheral States of the Arabian Peninsula
550–43	Egypt		
550–150	El Salvador	550–42	Peru
550–28	Ethiopia	550–72	Philippines
550–167	Finland	550–162	Poland
550–173	Germany, Federal Republic	550–160	Romania
550–153	Ghana	550–84	Rwanda
550–87	Greece	550–51	Saudi Arabia
550–78	Guatemala	550–70	Senegal
550–174	Guinea	550–86	Somalia
550–82	Guyana	550–93	South Africa, Republic of
550–164	Haiti	550–171	Southern Rhodesia
550–151	Honduras	550–95	Soviet Union
550–165	Hungary	550–27	Sudan, Democratic Republic of
550–21	India	550–47	Syria
550–154	Indian Ocean Territories	550–62	Tanzania
550–39	Indonesia	550–53	Thailand

550–178	Trinidad and Tobago	550–71	Venezuela
550–89	Tunisia	550–57	Vietnam, North
550–80	Turkey	550–55	Vietnam, South
550–74	Uganda	550–99	Yugoslavia
550–97	Uruguay	550–75	Zambia

☆ U.S. GOVERNMENT PRINTING OFFICE : 1976—O-211-451/15